T0210716

Lecture Notes in Computer Science 9625

Commenced Publication in 1973
Founding and Former Series Editors:
Gerhard Goos, Juris Hartmanis, and Jan van Leeuwen

More information about this series at http://www.springer.com/series/7407

Vanderlei Bonato · Christos Bouganis
Marek Gorgon (Eds.)

Applied Reconfigurable Computing

12th International Symposium, ARC 2016
Mangaratiba, RJ, Brazil, March 22–24, 2016
Proceedings

 Springer

Editors
Vanderlei Bonato
University of Sao Paulo
São Carlos
Brazil

Christos Bouganis
Imperial College London
London
UK

Marek Gorgon
AGH University of Science and Technology
Krakow
Poland

ISSN 0302-9743   ISSN 1611-3349   (electronic)
Lecture Notes in Computer Science
ISBN 978-3-319-30480-9   ISBN 978-3-319-30481-6   (eBook)
DOI 10.1007/978-3-319-30481-6

Library of Congress Control Number: 2016932321

LNCS Sublibrary: SL1 – Theoretical Computer Science and General Issues

Printed on acid-free paper

This Springer imprint is published by SpringerNature
The registered company is Springer International Publishing AG Switzerland

Preface

Reconfigurable computing technologies offer the promise of substantial performance gains over traditional architectures via customizing, even at runtime, the topology of the underlying architecture to match the specific needs of a given application. Contemporary configurable architectures allow for the definition of architectures with functional and storage units that match in function, bit-width, and control structures the specific needs of a given computation. The flexibility enabled by reconfiguration is also seen as a basic technique for overcoming transient failures in emerging device structures. The growth of the capacity of reconfigurable devices, such as FPGAs, has created a wealth of new research opportunities and intricate engineering challenges. Within the past decade, reconfigurable architectures have evolved from a uniform sea of programmable logic elements to fully reconfigurable systems-on-chip with integrated multipliers, memory elements, processors, and standard I/O interfaces. One of the foremost challenges facing reconfigurable application developers today is how to best exploit these novel and innovative resources to achieve the highest possible performance and energy efficiency. Recent developments in industry reveal a growing interest in the integration of configurable and reconfigurable technologies with more traditional processing devices. To face the programming challenges that this evolution has exacerbated, we have also witnessed the definition of programming languages and execution models aiming at enabling highly productive design methodologies for these emerging systems.

Over the last 11 years, the International Applied Reconfigurable Computing (ARC) symposium series (www.arc-symposium.org) has provided a forum for dissemination and discussion of this transformative research area. The ARC symposium was first held in 2005 in Algarve, Portugal. The second edition took place in Delft, The Netherlands, in 2006 and was the first edition to have its proceedings published by Springer as a volume of its *Lecture Notes in Computer Science* series. Subsequent ARC yearly editions were held in Rio de Janeiro, Brazil (2007), London, UK (2008), Karlsruhe, Germany (2009), Bangkok, Thailand (2010), Belfast, UK (2011), Hong Kong, SAR China (2012), Los Angeles, USA (2013), Algarve, Portugal (2014), and in 2015 in Bochum, Germany. This year the symposium (ARC 2016) returned to Rio de Janeiro, Brazil, during March 22–24, 2016, and was co-chaired by Prof. Vanderlei Bonato from the The Institute of Mathematical and Computer Sciences (ICMC), University of Sao Paulo (USP), Brazil, and Dr. Aravind Dasu from the Information Sciences Institute, University of Southern California (USC), USA. This year's edition included a series of international invited speakers from the areas of reconfigurable technology and evolutionary computing. They expressed their views on the future of this technology and also its application in evolutionary computing algorithms. The technical program also included mini-courses focusing on tools and applications of FPGA in areas such as high-performance computing, streaming data, and data-flow computation and programming models and languages.

The technical program chairs for ARC 2016 were Dr. Christos Bouganis from Imperial College London, UK, and Dr. Marek Gorgon from AGH University of Science and Technology, Poland. A total of 47 papers were submitted to the symposium from 20 countries: Australia (1), Belgium (1), Brazil (6), China (2), Colombia (3), Ecuador (1), France (1), Germany (6), Hong Kong (1), India (2), Japan (3), Republic of South Korea (1), Mexico (2), Pakistan (1), Poland (1), Portugal (1), Romania (1), Switzerland (2), UK (7), and USA (4). All submissions were evaluated by at least three members of the Program Committee. After careful selection, 20 papers were accepted as full papers (acceptance rate of 42.5 %) and eight as short papers (global acceptance rate of 59.5 %). Those accepted papers formed very interesting symposium program, which we consider to constitute a representative overview of ongoing research efforts in reconfigurable computing, a rapidly evolving and maturing field. In addition the proceedings also included three invited papers as part of a special technical session on funded R&D projects in the area of configurable and embedded computing. Following the ARC's tradition, the Technical Program Committee chairs selected a limited set of regular papers for consideration for a special issue of the Elsevier journal *Microprocessors and Microsystems: Embedded Hardware Design* (MICPRO) devoted to this year's ARC.

Several people contributed to the success of the 2016 edition of the symposium. We would like to acknowledge the support of all the members of this year's Steering and Program Committees in reviewing papers, in helping with the paper selection, and in giving valuable suggestions. Special thanks also to the additional researchers who contributed to the reviewing process, to all the authors who submitted papers to the symposium, and to all the symposium attendees. Last but not least, we are especially indebted to Juergen Becker from the University of Karlsruhe and to Alfred Hoffmann and Anna Kramer from Springer for their support and work in publishing this book as part of the LNCS series.

January 2016

Aravind Dasu
Christos Bouganis
Marek Gorgon
Vanderlei Bonato

Organization

The 2016 International Workshop on Applied Reconfigurable Computing took place in Mangaratiba, Rio de Janeiro, Brazil, during March 22–24, 2016.

General Chairs

Vanderlei Bonato	University of São Paulo, Brazil
Aravind Dasu	University of Southern California, USA

Program Chairs

Christos Bouganis	Imperial College London, UK
Marek Gorgon	AGH University of Science and Technology, Poland

Proceedings Chair

José Nelson Amaral	University of Alberta, Canada

Finance Chair

Eduardo Marques	University of São Paulo, Brazil

Sponsorship Chairs

Edson Borin	University of Campinas, Brazil
Miguel O. Arias Estrada	National Institute for Astrophysics, Optics and Electronics, Mexico

Publicity Chairs

Alba Cristina M.A. de Melo	University of Brasília, Brazil
Kuan-Ching Li	Providence University, Taiwan
Nuno Roma	Instituto de Engenharia de Sistemas de Computadores (INESC), Portugal

Web Chair

Carlos R.P. Almeida Junior	University of São Paulo, Brazil

Local Arrangements

Alexandre Delbem	University of São Paulo, Brazil
Fernanda G.L. Kastensmidt	Federal University of Rio Grande do Sul, Brazil
Marcio Merino Fernandes	Federal University of São Carlos, Brazil
Ricardo dos Santos Ferreira	Federal University of Viçosa, Brazil
Rodolfo Azevedo	University of Campinas, Brazil

Steering Committee

Hideharu Amano	Keio University, Japan
Jürgen Becker	Universität Karlsruhe, Germany
Mladen Berekovic	Braunschweig University of Technology, Germany
Koen Bertels	Delft University of Technology, The Netherlands
João M.P. Cardoso	University of Porto, Portugal
Katherine (Compton) Morrow	University of Wisconsin-Madison, USA
George Constantinides	Imperial College of Science, Technology and Medicine, UK
Pedro C. Diniz	USC Information Sciences Institute, USA
Philip H.W. Leong	University of Sydney, Australia
Walid Najjar	University of California Riverside, USA
Roger Woods	The Queen's University of Belfast, UK

Program Committee

Gabriel Almeida	Leica Biosystems
Rodolfo Azevedo	University of Campinas, Brazil
Zachary Baker	Los Alamos National Laboratory, USA
Juergen Becker	Karlsruhe Institute of Technology, Germany
Koen Bertels	TU Delft, The Netherlands
Matthias Birk	Karlsruhe Institute of Technology, Germany
Joao Bispo	Universidade Técnica de Lisboa, Portugal
Vanderlei Bonato	University of Sao Paulo, Brazil
Christos Bouganis	Imperial College London, UK
Stephen Brown	Altera and University of Toronto, Canada
João Canas Ferreira	Universidade do Porto, Portugal
Joao Cardoso	Universidade do Porto, Portugal
Cyrille Chavet	Université de Bretagne-Sud, France
Ray Cheung	City University of Hong Kong, SAR China
Daniel Chillet	CAIRN - IRISA/ENSSAT, France
Kiyoung Choi	Seoul National University, South Korea
Paul Chow	University of Toronto, Canada

Kentaro Sano	Tohoku University, Japan
Marco Domenico Santambrogio	Politecnico di Milano, Italy
Pete Sedcole	Celoxica
Yuichiro Shibata	Nagasaki University, Japan
Dimitrios Soudris	National Technical University of Athens, Greece
David Thomas	Imperial College, London, UK
Tim Todman	Imperial College, UK
Pedro Trancoso	University of Cyprus, Cyprus
Chao Wang	University of Science and Technology of China, China
Markus Weinhardt	Osnabrück University of Applied Sciences, Germany
Theerayod Wiangtong	Mahanakorn University of Technology, Thailand
Yoshiki Yamaguchi	University of Tsukuba, Japan
Wenwei Zha	Virginia Tech Configuration Computing Lab, USA

Additional Reviewers

Cho, Jae Min
de La Chevallerie, David
Deniz, Pedro
Gottschling, Philip
Harbaum, Tanja
Haron, Adib
Iorga, Dan
Joseph, Moritz
Kalms, Lester
Kaufmann, Paul
Killian, Cedric
Lee, Jinho
Liu, Junxiu

Maragos, Konstantinos
Martinez, Leandro
Meisner, Sebastian
Pereira, Erinaldo
Reder, Simon
Rettkowski, Jens
Rosa, Leandro
Ruschke, Tajas
Sidiropoulos, Harry
Song, Hyunjik
Wehner, Philipp
Wolf, Dennis
Yu, Jintao

Contents

Multicore Systems

Invited Paper on Funded RD Running and Completed Projects Posters

Invited Talks

The VINEYARD Approach: Versatile, Integrated, Accelerator-Based, Heterogeneous Data Centres

Christoforos Kachris[1]([✉]), Dimitrios Soudris[1], Georgi Gaydadjiev[2],
Huy-Nam Nguyen[3], Dimitrios S. Nikolopoulos[4], Angelos Bilas[5],
Neil Morgan[6], Christos Strydis[7], Christos Tsalidis[8], John Balafas[9],
Ricardo Jimenez-Peris[10], and Alexandre Almeida[11]

[1] Institute of Computer and Communications Systems (ICCS), Athens, Greece
kachris@microlab.ntua.gr
[2] Maxeler Technologies, London, UK
[3] Bull Systems, Les Clayes-sous-Bois, France
[4] Queen's University of Belfast (QUB), Belfast, UK
[5] Foundation for Research and Technology (FORTH), Heraklion, Greece
[6] The Hartree Centre, Warrington, UK
[7] Neurasmus BV, Rotterdam, The Netherlands
[8] Neurocom Luxembourg, Luxembourg City, Luxembourg
[9] ATHEX, Athens, Greece
[10] LeanXcale, Brunete, Spain
[11] Globaz, Oliveira de Azeméis, Portugal

Abstract. Emerging web applications like cloud computing, Big Data and social networks have created the need for powerful centres hosting hundreds of thousands of servers. Currently, the data centres are based on general purpose processors that provide high flexibility buts lack the energy efficiency of customized accelerators. VINEYARD aims to develop an integrated platform for energy-efficient data centres based on new servers with novel, coarse-grain and fine-grain, programmable hardware accelerators. It will, also, build a high-level programming framework for allowing end-users to seamlessly utilize these accelerators in heterogeneous computing systems by employing typical data-centre programming frameworks (e.g. MapReduce, Storm, Spark, etc.). This programming framework will, further, allow the hardware accelerators to be swapped in and out of the heterogeneous infrastructure so as to offer high flexibility and energy efficiency. VINEYARD will foster the expansion of the soft-IP core industry, currently limited in the embedded systems, to the data-centre market. VINEYARD plans to demonstrate the advantages of its approach in three real use-cases (a) a bio-informatics application for high-accuracy brain modeling, (b) two critical financial applications, and (c) a big-data analysis application.

Keywords: Hardware accelerators · Data centre · Heterogeneous · Big data

© Springer International Publishing Switzerland 2016
V. Bonato et al. (Eds.): ARC 2016, LNCS 9625, pp. 3–13, 2016.
DOI: 10.1007/978-3-319-30481-6_1

1   Introduction

Cloud computing, Big Data and social networks are some of the emerging web applications responsible for the significant increases in data-center workloads during the last years. In 2015, the total network traffic of the data centres was around 4.7 Exabytes and it is estimated that by the end of 2018 it will cross the 8.5-Exabyte mark, following a cumulative annual-growth rate (CAGR) of 23 % [1] (Fig. 1). In response to this scaling in network traffic, data-centre operators have resorted to utilizing more powerful servers. Relying on Moore's law for the extra edge, CPU technologies have scaled in recent years through packing an increasing number of transistors on chip, leading to higher-performance ratings. However, on-chip clock frequencies were unable to follow this upward trend due to strict power-budget constraints. Thus, a few years ago a paradigm shift to multicore processors was adopted as an alternative solution for overcoming the problem. With multicore processors one could increase server performance without increasing their clock frequency. Unfortunately, this solution was soon found to scale poorly in the longer term, as well. The performance gains achieved by adding more cores inside a CPU come at the cost of various, rapidly scaling complexities: inter-core communication, memory coherency and, most importantly, power consumption [2].

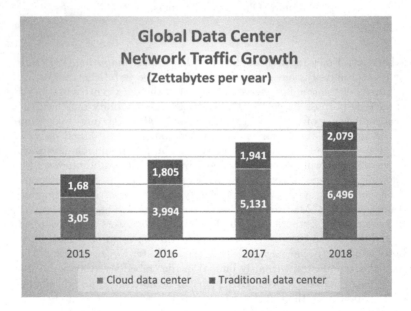

Fig. 1. Network-traffic projections for traditional and cloud-based data centres. By 2018, more than three quarters (78 %) of workloads will be processed by cloud data centers; 22 % will be processed by traditional data centers. [Source: Cisco Global Cloud Index] (Color figure online)

In the early technology nodes, advancing from one node to the next allowed for a near doubling of the transistor frequency, and, by reducing the voltage, power density remained nearly constant. With the end of Dennard scaling, advancing from one node to the next still leads to an increase in transistor density, but their maximum frequency remains roughly the same and the voltage does not decrease accordingly. As a result, the power density increases now with every new technology node. The biggest challenge, therefore, now consists of reducing power consumption and energy dissipation per mm^2 of chip area. The failure of Dennard scaling, to which the shift to multicore chips is partially a response, may soon limit multicore scaling just as single-core scaling has been curtailed. This issue has been identified in the literature as the "dark-silicon" era in which some of the areas in a chip are kept powered down in order to comply with thermal constraints [3].

A solution that can be used to overcome this problem is the use of application-specific accelerators. Specialized multicore processors with application-specific acceleration modules can leverage the underutilized die area to overcome the initial power barrier, delivering significantly higher performance for the same power envelope [4]. The main idea is to use the abundant die area by implementing application-specific accelerators and dynamically powering up only those accelerators suitable for a given workload. This approach can be applied either at fine-grain level (using accelerators inside the chip) or at coarse-grain level (using rack-based accelerators). In the latter case, the accelerators can either be located on the same board with the server processor or in a different blade/rack. The use of highly specialized units designed for specific workloads can greatly enhance server processors and can also increase significantly the performance of data centres subject to a maximum power budget.

This paper presents an overview of the VINEYARD H2020 project towards the development of an integrated platform for the efficient utilization of hardware accelerators in the data centres. VINEYARD aims to develop an integrated platform for energy-efficient data centres based on new servers with novel, coarse-grain and fine-grain, programmable hardware accelerators. It will, also, build a high-level programming framework for allowing end-users to seamlessly utilize these accelerators in heterogeneous computing systems by using typical data-centre programming frameworks (e.g. MapReduce, Storm, Spark, etc.).

2 VINEYARD Objectives

Today's data centres consist of homogeneous processing systems (general-purpose processors) and process high volumes of data by consuming excessive amounts of power. Future heterogeneous data centres consisting of different kinds of accelerators (FPGAs, GPUs, etc.) will be able to provide higher performance under lower power consumption. However, to maintain in such heterogeneous systems the ease of programming of homogeneous ones, an integrated run-time scheduler and manager will be required to hide low-level details and relieve the user from the programming complexities involved (per different accelerator type).

VINEYARD will aim specifically at the automatic utilization of accelerators through developing such an *integrated framework* that will control the hardware accelerators while the user will still be allowed to use typical parallel-programming frameworks.

VINEYARD will develop an *energy-efficient, integrated platform* for data centres that will consist of (1) energy-efficient servers based on customized hardware accelerators (novel programmable dataflow engines and FPGA-based servers), and (2) a software framework that will allow users to seamlessly utilize hardware accelerators in heterogeneous computing systems by using traditional data-centre and multi-core programming frameworks (e.g. MapReduce, Storm, Spark, etc.).

More specifically, the VINEYARD project will develop novel servers based on *programmable dataflow accelerators* that can be customized based on the data-centre's application requirements. These programmable dataflow accelerators will be used not only to increase the performance of servers but also to reduce the energy consumption in data centres. Furthermore, VINEYARD will develop a *programming framework* that will hide the complexity of programming heterogeneous systems while at the same time providing the optimized performance of customized and heterogeneous architectures. The programming framework will leverage workload-specific accelerators based on the application requirements in a seamless fashion. The idea is that the user will work with familiar programming frameworks (e.g. MapReduce, Storm, Spark, etc.) while a *run-time manager* selects appropriate accelerators based on application requirements such as execution time, power consumption, fault tolerance and security (Fig. 2). Finally and as part of the software framework, VINEYARD will provide the necessary *middleware* that binds together servers with accelerators. Along this task, VINEYARD will consider both *physical servers* and *virtual machines (VMs)*. The middleware shall also handle QoS (Quality-of-Service) concerns that arise with the shared use of the accelerators.

Figure 2 depicts the high-level diagram of the VINEYARD framework. Applications that are targeting heterogeneous data centres using traditional servers or micro-servers are programmed using traditional data-centre frameworks, such as MapReduce, and widely used data-management technologies, such as SQL (both OLTP and OLAP for operational databases and data warehouses), NoSQL (a key value data store), and Complex Event Processing (CEP). However, some of the tasks are common across several applications such as data sorting, key/value processing, encryption, compression, pattern matching, and so on, and are extremely computationally intensive. These tasks can be implemented in hardware as customized intellectual-property (IP) accelerators that can achieve much higher performance with lower power consumption. The implementation of the hardware accelerators can be achieved using traditional hardware-description languages (VHDL, Verilog) or other high-level (OpenCL) or domain-specific languages (i.e. OpenSPL). These hardware accelerators can be hosted in a repository that will interface with the run-time scheduler.

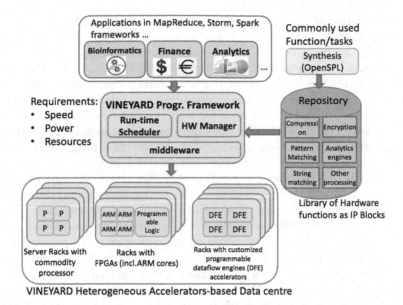

Fig. 2. High-level block diagram of the VINEYARD integrated framework. Different blocks can be seen: VINEYARD programming framework and middleware (red box), traditional servers and accelerator-based servers (purple boxes) and hardware-IP repository (green cylinder) (Color figure online).

The main objectives of the VINEYARD project are:

- **Objective 1:** *Development of novel Programmable Dataflow Engines (DFE) for servers:* One of the main objectives of VINEYARD will be the development of novel programmable dataflow engines (hardware accelerators) based on coarse-grain programmable components that can be coupled to servers' processor in heterogeneous data centres. The integration of the programmable hardware accelerators and traditional processors will produce integrated, high-performance and energy-efficient heterogeneous servers leading to more energy efficient data centres with higher processing power.
- **Objective 2:** *Development of novel FPGA-accelerated servers:* The most recent FPGAs that have been developed in the last years incorporate not only programmable logic but also energy-efficient embedded processors (i.e. ARM). Next generation FPGAs will incorporate four or more of high performance energy-efficient processors. VINEYARD will develop novel server blades that will be based on high performance and energy-efficient FPGAs that incorporate multiple ARM cores.
- **Objective 3:** *Development of an integrated programming framework:* This framrwork will be used for the programming of heterogeneous systems consisting of general-purpose processors (CPUs), and accelerators (programmable dataflow engines and FPGAs) based on traditional data-centre programming frameworks (e.g. Spark, Storm, and MapReduce). The framework will hide

the complexities of controlling the hardware dataflow accelerators from the user while it will also allow the instantiation of IP modules as pluggable components in the same way that software packages are currently used.

– **Objective 4:** *Development of a run-time scheduler/orchestrator:* This scheduler will control the utilization of the accelerators based on the application requirements (execution time, power consumption, available resources, etc.). It will allow the optimum utilization of the available hardware accelerators based on the use-case constraints. The run-time system that will be developed will be integrated to the run-time systems of the data-centre programming frameworks (MapReduce etc.)

– **Objective 5:** *Development of a novel Virtual-Machine (VM) appliance model for provisioning of data to shared accelerators:* Targeting cloud deployments, the VINEYARD VM appliance will bring both tangible and novel results. The enhanced VINEYARD middleware will augment the functionality of the orchestrator by enabling more informed allocation of tasks to accelerators. The VINEYARD framework will allow the virtualized utilization of hardware accelerators in the servers (Server Function Virtualization - SFV) in the same way that Network Function Virtualization is used to virtualize network functions providing higher flexibility, lower cost and optimized resource utilization.

– **Objective 6:** *Ecosystem Establishment and Support:* Effort will be spent on the establishment of an ecosystem for empowering open innovation based on hardware accelerators as data-centre plugins, thereby facilitating innovative enterprises (large industries, SMEs, and creative start-ups) to develop novel solutions using VINEYARDS's leading edge developments. The ecosystem will bring together existing communities from all relevant stakeholders including providers of hardware-IP technologies, data-centre developers, data-centre operators and more. Stakeholder involvement will be realized through the consortium partners, the representation of communities within the consortium, as well as through the involvement of third-parties based on open calls. This ecosystem will allow the promotion of open, pluggable, custom hardware accelerators that can be used in data centres in the same way that software libraries are currently being utilized. Furthermore, the development of this new ecosystem will enable users from different sectors (open-source communities, universities, research centres, start-ups, etc.) to contribute application-specific accelerators in a repository that can be accessed by data-centre operators.

3   The VINEYARD Approach

In this section we will present in more detail the three main building blocks of the project: the programmable dataflow accelerators, the VINEYARD programming framework and the VINEYARD middleware.

3.1   Accelerator-Based Servers

In the last few years, data centres have experienced a significant increase in the network traffic they handle largely due to the wide adoption of many web applications such as cloud computing and big data. To cope with this rise in computational and communication demands, data centers have boosted the performance of their server processors which has led to a drastic increase in the power-consumption profiles. Currently, one of the main challenges for data-centre operators is reducing the power costs of their servers that account for over 45 % of the overall data-centre power consumption.

Modern server processors contain many levels of caching, forwarding and prediction logic to improve the efficiency of the traditional processor architecture; however the model is inherently sequential with performance limited by the speed at which data can move around this loop.

A dataflow computing model explicitly addresses this issue by minimising and optimising the flow of data. Current dataflow-computing solutions utilise FPGA chip technology, which despite inherent inefficiencies has been shown to lead to orders-of-magnitude lower power consumption and lower data-centre space needs. For example, recent journal publications [5,6] report on production-level use of dataflow computing. The delivery of a Maxeler dataflow machine to JP Morgan, as part of an award-winning initiative described in the Wall Street Journal [7], yielded the computational power of 128 Teraflops (equivalent to over 12,000 high-end x86 control flow cores) within the space and power envelope of a single 40U rack.

Current dataflow engines implemented with FPGAs offer considerable advantages in performance and "performance per Watt". However, FPGAs are a general base technology which has significant limitations and is expensive in silicon area. For example, an FPGA is 18–35x less area efficient than an ASIC at implementing circuits, with a 3–4x higher critical path delay (i.e. decrease in clock frequency). Despite this cumulative 54–140x technology disadvantage, dataflow engines incorporating FPGAs have demonstrated high performance and energy efficiency for a broad range of applications due to the efficiency of the dataflow architecture.

Given such encouraging results, we propose in VINEYARD the development of custom dataflow servers optimised for high-performance, power-efficient implementations of data-centre applications. These servers will maintain the capabilities of FPGAs to implement the dataflow computing paradigm while tackling the sources of inefficiency.

3.2 Programming Framework

The current state of the art in programming frameworks lacks a clean solution for integrating the FPGA hardware-software stack with the programming-language runtime system on the host servers. The gap exists from both a semantical and a resource-management perspective. Questions on how accelerator code and state is managed by a high-level functional programming model and runtime system remain largely open. A task abstraction, representing the accelerator as a versioned function to the programming model appears to be the most promising approach [8] but lacks transparency and breaks key desirable properties of functional parallel programming. Furthermore, scheduling, communication and synchronisation in the runtime system are fundamentally influenced by the presence of accelerators. The integration of accelerators with data-management technologies can be more natural due to the declarative nature of queries that can better exploit the data flow model to be implemented in the accelerators.

While bare-metal implementations of MapReduce, OpenCL and other high-level languages for FPGA accelerators have existed for some time [9–11], these implementations are localised and designed to support efficient translation to FPGA hardware rather than integration with the host software stack. The programmability of hardware accelerators (i.e. based on FPGAs) must improve if they are to be part of mainstream computing and data centres.

Combining a host-side programming model with the accelerator programming model in a hybrid solution is a challenging and rather inflexible proposition, both due to semantical conflicts (e.g. differences in memory models) and due to performance implications, notably contention between runtime systems for shared resources [12].

Furthermore, despite efforts to virtualize programmable and hardware accelerators, such as GPUs and FPGAs [13,14], the virtualization methods deployed, notably pass-through and device-drive level, introduce non-trivial performance interference within and between VMs. These are hardly traceable, let alone resolvable by programming models and runtime systems. VINEYARD aspires to address the open challenges in integrating programmable and hardware accelerators to the predominant software stacks used for data analytics in the Cloud:

(a) hide the accelerator from the programmer by presenting it as a pure library function, embeddable in query processing, data processing or aggregation tasks, and by extension to analytical libraries written on top of high-level programming models;
(b) extend the runtime systems of high-level analytics languages to handle efficiently scheduling, communication, and synchronisation with programmable accelerators; and
(c) improve the performance robustness of analytics written in high-level languages against artefacts of virtualization, notably performance interference due to contention on shared resources and hidden noise in hypervisors and hosting VMs.

3.3   Virtualization and Middleware

In principle, the deployment model of accelerators in the data centre can take two basic but different forms: (a) Accelerators can be attached directly to servers and used by local workloads, or (b) accelerators can be shared over the network among many servers and their workloads.

The accelerators – whether GPUs, FPGAs or multicore CPUs – are assigned to tasks which they can perform more efficiently than general-purpose servers. The expected returns in cost, power and execution time are promising, but data movement is a large challenge that underlies the whole proposition. Accelerators take data from the "slow" CPU path, process them in their customized hardware engines, and return the results either for storage in a file or directly to the memory system or for further processing by other accelerators or servers. The dominant programming frameworks in scale-out data centres have been streamlined to minimize the movement of data; thus, at the end of the day, the value of accelerator-based data centres will be weighed against the cost of the extra data copies that they introduce. With VINEYARD, we will speedup data communication through a system fabric that provides efficient communication primitives, to unify the accelerators with the servers and to reconcile them with the current computing frameworks.

Virtualization support is an additional, significant dimension of data-centre infrastructures. Virtual Machines (and other similar types of technologies such as Containers) offer a mechanism for increasing consolidation of workloads on physical servers and achieving better utilization, isolating software versions and domains, and decoupling administrative domains i.e., clients from providers. Therefore, when examining the potential of accelerators in data centres, it is essential to deal with the implications of, and to accrue the benefits from, Virtual Machines. We note that the presence of tenant VMs inside the data centres is orthogonal to accelerator virtualization [15]. VMs typically access the available hardware resources through a hypervisor, complicating the software segments of I/O stacks and increasing overheads. In addition, sharing the I/O paths among multiple VMs endangers isolation and quality-of-service. Clearly, sluggish and unreliable communication between VMs and accelerators impedes their co-existence in cloud data centres.

Overall, in VINEYARD we will introduce a novel VM appliance model for provisioning of data to shared accelerators. Targeting cloud deployments, this VINEYARD effort can bring both tangible and novel results. The enhanced VINEYARD middleware augments the functionality of the orchestrator, by enabling more informed allocation of tasks to accelerators.

4   VINEYARD Use Cases

Within VINEYARD, an integrated data centre will be developed and will be evaluated through three real-life workloads and industrial benchmarks for financial applications, data management, and scientific computing. The first workload that will be evaluated will be in the domain of *financial applications*. For this reason the Greek Stock Exchange Market will be used as an end-user demanding (a) real-time analytics which are necessary for market surveillance and decision management, and (b) rapid computations for risk management, as an additional computation step within the trade process chain.

The second workload that will be evaluated will be in the domain of scientific computing, and more specifically in the domain of *computational neuroscience* which aims at better understanding the working of the human brain through simulating biologically plausible neural models. The particular application is a high-performance, high-accuracy simulation of the Olivocerebellar system of the brain, crucial to the understanding of cerebellar functionality [16]. The Olivo-cerebellar system is critical for facilitating motor function – among other functionality – in humans. Better modeling and understanding of its function can lead to major breakthroughs in the treatment of various cerebellum-related degenerative diseases such as autism, fragile-X syndrome etc. It will also lead to a deeper understanding of motor control resulting in new automation and robotic technologies, and improved brain-computer interfaces (BCI).

The third workload is a data-management case based on TPC-C (on-line transaction processing (OLTP) benchmark) and TPC-H (decision support benchmark). TPC-C is representative of the transactional workloads run at operational databases of enterprises. It will be run on top of the LeanXcale OLTP database to represent the full stack of enterprise OLTP applications. TPC-H is representative of the analytical workloads run at data warehouses of enterprises. It will be run on top of the LeanXcale OLAP database to evaluate the efficiency improvements for analytical queries. Finally, Linear Road will also be used as a representative workload in IoT applications and will be run on top of the LeanXcale CEP engine to evaluate CEP workloads.

5   Conclusions

The main goal of the VINEYARD project is to develop a new framework for the efficient integration of accelerators into commercial data centres. The VINE-YARD project will not only develop novel accelerator-based servers but will also develop all the required systems (hypervisor, middleware, APIs and libraries) that will allow the users to seamlessly utilize the accelerators as an additional cloud resource. The efficient utilization of accelerators in data centres will significantly improve the overall performance of cloud-based applications and will also reduce the energy consumption in the data centres. Finally, VINEYARD aspires to foster the innovation of soft-IP accelerators in the domain of cloud computing by the promotion of a central repository for the hosting of the relevant accelerators.

Acknowledgment. This project has received funding from the European Union's Horizon 2020 research and innovation programme under grant agreement No 687628.

References

1. Cisco Visual Networking Index: Global Mobile Data Traffic Forecast Update, 2014–2019. White Paper, Cisco, Inc
2. Esmaeilzadeh, H., Blem, E., Amant, R.S., Sankaralingam, Karthikeyan, Burger, Doug: Power challenges may end the multicore era. Commun. ACM **56**(2), 93–102 (2013)
3. Esmaeilzadeh, H., Blem, E., St, R., Amant, K.S., Burger, D.: Dark silicon and the end of multicore scaling. In: Proceedings of the 38th Annual International Symposium on Computer Architecture, ISCA 2011, pp. 365–376. ACM, New York (2011)

4. Hardavellas, N., Ferdman, M., Falsafi, B., Ailamaki, A.: Toward dark silicon in servers. IEEE Micro **31**(4), 6–15 (2011)
5. Lindtjorn, O., Clapp, R., Pell, O., Haohuan, F., Flynn, M., Mencer, O.: Beyond traditional microprocessors for geoscience high-performance computing applications. IEEE Micro **31**(2), 41–49 (2011)
6. Weston, S., Spooner, J., Racaniere, S., Mencer, O.: Rapid computation of value and risk for derivatives portfolios. Concurr. Comput. Pract. Exper. **24**(8), 880–894 (2012)
7. Clark, D. Maxeler makes waves with dataflow design. Wall Street J. Blog **13** (2011)
8. Bueno, J., Martorell, X., Badia, R.M., Ayguadé, E., Labarta, J.: Implementing OmpSs support for regions of data in architectures with multiple address spaces. In: Proceedings of the 27th International ACM Conference on International Conference on Supercomputing, ICS 2013, pp. 359–368. ACM, New York (2013)
9. Shan, Y., Wang, B., Jing Yan, Y., Wang, N.X., Yang, H.: FPMR: MapReduce framework on FPGA. In: Proceedings of the 18th Annual ACM/SIGDA International Symposium on Field Programmable Gate Arrays, FPGA 2010, pp. 93–102. ACM, New York (2010)
10. Athanas, P., Kepa, K., Shagrithaya, K.: Enabling development of OpenCL applications on FPGA platforms. In: Proceedings of the IEEE 24th International Conference on Application-Specific Systems, Architectures and Processors (ASAP), ASAP 2013, pp. 26–30. IEEE Computer Society, Washington, DC (2013)
11. Owaida, M., Bellas, N., Daloukas, K., Antonopoulos, C.D.: Synthesis of platform architectures from OpenCL programs. In: Proceedings of the IEEE 19th Annual International Symposium on Field-Programmable Custom Computing Machines, FCCM 2011, pp. 186–193. IEEE Computer Society, Washington, DC (2011)
12. Pan, H., Hindman, B., Asanović, K.: Composing parallel software efficiently with lithe. In: Proceedings of the 31st ACM SIGPLAN Conference on Programming Language Design and Implementation, PLDI 2010, pp. 376–387. ACM, New York (2010)
13. Becchi, M., Sajjapongse, K., Graves, I., Procter, A., Ravi, V., Chakradhar, S.: A virtual memory based runtime to support multi-tenancy in clusters with GPUs. In: Proceedings of the 21st International Symposium on High-Performance Parallel and Distributed Computing, HPDC 2012, pp. 97–108. ACM, New York (2012)
14. Wang, W., Bolic, M., Parri, J.: pvFPGA: accessing an FPGA-based hardware accelerator in a paravirtualized environment. In: Proceedings of the Ninth IEEE/ACM/IFIP International Conference on Hardware/Software Codesign and System Synthesis, CODES+ISSS 2013, pp. 10:1–10:9. IEEE Press, Piscataway (2013)
15. Chen, F., Shan, Y., Zhang, Y., Wang, Y., Franke, H., Chang, X., Wang, K.: Enabling FPGAs in the cloud. In: Proceedings of the 11th ACM Conference on Computing Frontiers, CF 2014, pp. 3:1–3:10. ACM, New York (2014)
16. Smaragdos, G., Isaza, S., van Eijk, M.F., Sourdis, I., Strydis, C.: FPGA-based biophysically-meaningful modeling of Olivocerebellar neurons. In: Proceedings of the ACM/SIGDA International Symposium on Field-programmable Gate Arrays, FPGA 2014, pp. 89–98. ACM, New York (2014)

A Design Methodology for the Next Generation Real-Time Vision Processors

Jones Yudi Mori[1,2]([envelope]), André Werner[1], Arij Shallufa[1],
Florian Fricke[1], and Michael Hübner[1]

[1] ESIT - Embedded Systems for Information Technology,
Ruhr-University Bochum, Bochum, Germany
{Jones.MoriAlvesDaSilva,Andre.Werner-w2m,Arij.Shallufa,
Florian.Fricke,Michael.Huebner}@rub.de
[2] Department of Mechanical Engineering, University of Brasília, Brasília, Brazil

Abstract. In this work we present a methodology to design the next generation of real-time vision processors. These processors are expected to achieve high throughput with complex applications, under real-time embedded constraints (time, fault-tolerance, silicon area and power consumption). To achieve these goals, we propose the fusion of two key concepts: the Focal-Plane Image Processing (FPIP) and the Many-Core architectures. We show the concepts and ideas to build-up a methodology able to offer both design space exploration, and a customized programming toolchain for the final architecture. We present implementation details and results for working parts of the framework, and partial results and general comments about the work-in-progress.

Keywords: ASIP · Image processing · Processor architecture · Real-time

1 Introduction

Smart Cameras are special cameras which do not only acquire, compress and transmit images, but are capable of processing them to extract useful information. Complete IP/CV (Image Processing and Computer Vision) applications should be executable in modern Smart Cameras. With the growing of the Internet of Things (IoT) and the CyberPhysical Systems (CPS), a single device will be expected to run several complex applications simultaneously.

A real-time IP/CV system is composed by two main parts: acquisition and processing. The acquisition part is in general a standard cmos sensor array which provides a pixel stream and some synchronization signals. The main problem in standard acquisition systems is the bottleneck in the pixel stream, since the pixels are transmitted one by one [6]. The hardware architectures commonly used in the processing part (DSP concepts, VLIW, SIMD operations) are not able to achieve the constraints in throughput, fault tolerance, silicon area and power consumption [12].

© Springer International Publishing Switzerland 2016
V. Bonato et al. (Eds.): ARC 2016, LNCS 9625, pp. 14–25, 2016.
DOI: 10.1007/978-3-319-30481-6_2

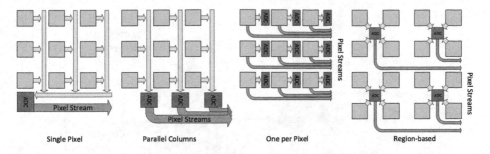

Fig. 1. Readout schemes in a Pixel Array.

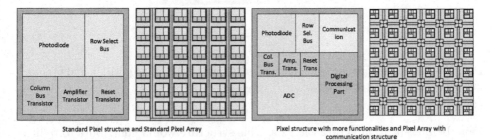

Fig. 2. Fill-factor reduction when adding more functionalities to the image sensor.

To eliminate (or, at least, to minimize) the acquisition bottleneck problem, two main solutions can be found in the literature. The first one is to replicate the amplifier and ADC (analog to digital converter), adding one pair for each row (or for each column). The second solution is to have one pair (amplifier/ADC) per pixel [16]. The last option allows for full acquisition parallelism, however it is too expensive for standard cameras, being used only in scientific/industrial custom applications. To better explore the interface acquisition/processing, we propose a different way to acquire the pixels: to add the pair amplifier/ADC for regions of the sensor array. As will be explained later in the text, the configuration we propose offers several advantages in the envisioned architecture. In Fig. 1 we can see the four types of acquisition systems discussed here.

A different camera concept was created some years ago, with the aim of achieving high throughput: the Focal-Plane Image Processing (FPIP) concept is based on inserting small processing elements (PEs) close to the pixel sensors, minimizing the transmitting paths and allowing also for parallel acquisition [2,11]. In Fig. 2 we can see the structure of single standard pixel. The fill-factor is the percentage of the chip area which is photosensitive. As can be seen in the picture, the addition of an ADC and a PE to the pixel area would reduce considerably the fill-factor, and by consequence, the image quality would be degraded. In addition, due to the limited area available, the PEs found in the literature are mostly analog filters and/or small digital ones, and do not offer too much flexibility. Figure 2 shows issues related to the communication structure which

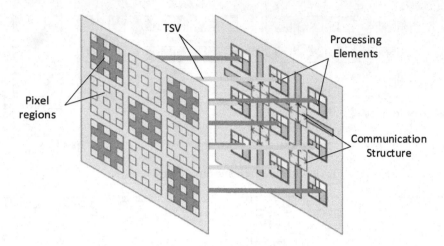

Fig. 3. Envisioned hardware configuration: a 3D integration of acquisition and processing parts using TSV technology.

must be present to integrate the PEs. This structure would contribute to reduce even more the sensor's fill-factor.

We propose a hardware configuration to integrate the acquisition and the processing parts in a more interesting architecture. Figure 3 shows the concept. The sensor array has spatially distributed pairs amplifier/ADC, each pair being responsible for a region of the image. Using the Through Silicon Vias (TSV) technology, the outputs of the ADCs are sent to an underlying processing layer. The processing layer is a manycore architecture composed by distributed pixel registers which receive the pixel stream from the ADCs. A PE is responsible to process each region, and a communication infrastructure allows for data exchange among them. With this configuration, both the acquisition and the processing parts can explore a higher amount of parallelism.

The design of such architecture is not easy, since the PEs and the communication structure must be developed with focus in the application and in the embedded hardware constraints (silicon area, power consumption, thermal distribution and so on). In addition, software related issues must be solved. The programming model must be able to explore the parallelism in the applications, considering the spatial distribution of PEs, the distributed input streams, and the synchronization and data exchange issues.

In this project we show a methodology to help the design of such system, and also to provide an efficient parallel programming model. This work provides a general overview of subprojects (complete and work-in-progress) integrated as a design methodology. Considering this, no exclusive section about literature review is provided. However, before explaining each subproject, we provide specific motivation and state-of-art. In Sect. 2 we show in details how the framework was conceived. Finally, in Sect. 3, we have a discussion about the issues and next steps of the project.

2   Design Methodology

In this section we discuss the concepts and ideas behind the proposed methodology. We start the analysis with a SystemC/TLM2.0 simulator used to analyze communication patterns for different IP/CV algorithms. This analysis is used to determine geometric constraints and a rough structure for the architecture. After that, we analyze the IP/CV application domain, in order to show how the domain-specific characteristics shape and constrain the design space. After that, we show the development of some tools which help in the design decision making. The first tool performs a static analysis over the application's source code, in order to determine the algorithm's structure. Then another tool generates a SystemC/TLM2.0 model which estimates parameters to help the design of the PEs microarchitectures.

2.1   High-Level Analysis of Communication Patterns

To determine a starting point for the architecture design, we developed a simulation tool based on SystemC/TLM2.0 models. This tool should be able to extract communication patterns from IP/CV algorithms simulations. Figure 4 shows the main modules of the developed tool: *Px-Unit, Functions Library*, and *Data-Flow Controller*, described as follows:

– *Px-Unit:* It is a module that represents an unit with the following content: the input pixel value; the pixel position in the image; pixel values in intermediate images; status flags; and the image processing algorithm behavior described using the *Functions Library*. It also has a cycle counter (similar to a Program Counter in processor architectures) responsible for synchronizing the *Px-Unit* with the *Data-Flow Controller*.
– *Functions Library:* It was created to implement all operations needed to compute each output pixel. It covers since simple arithmetic operations until calls for memory access. The algorithm behavior of *Px-Units* is implemented using these functions, as a common programming library.
– *Data-Flow Controller:* It is a module created to instantiate an array of *Px-Units* representing the Pixel Array. It is responsible for writing the input values inside each *Px-Unit*. When a *Px-Unit* needs a pixel value from another one, it calls access functions from the *Data-Flow Controller* which will register this call (the instant it occurs, the caller and the callee, etc.). After registering the call, the controller takes the value from the source unit and gives to the caller unit.

Figure 4 shows how the data exchange among two *Px-Units* is performed. The annotations file is the output obtained after a simulation. In the *Data-Flow Controller* block, several different parameters can be configured. We performed simulations for different topologies to determine the communication needs, bottlenecks and possible solutions. These are only rough topology models, considering the relative position among Pixels and PEs.

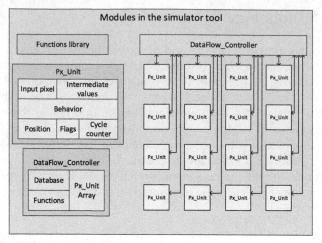

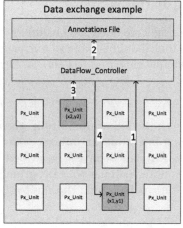

1 – A Px_Unit(x1,y1) calls the Data-Flow Controller asking for data from another Px_Unit(x2,y2).

2 – The Data-Flow Controller register the call data (caller position, source position and caller cycle_counter).

3 – The Data-Flow Controller asks the calle for the requested data.

4 – The Data-Flow Controller sends to the caller the requested data.

Fig. 4. Main modules of the simulation tool, and a sample data exchange among two *Px-Units*.

There are two main features to determine in this part: (a) if the Pixels will be stored internally or externally to the PE; (b) how the communication among PEs will be organized. If we choose the alternative to store Pixels internally to the PEs, all data requests from outside would cause the PE to stop processing the IP/CV algorithm, to deal with the communication tasks. Considering that each is surrounded by at least 4 neighbors, depending on the algorithm, the amount of data requests can lead the system to fail in achieving the desired throughput. From now on, we assume the Pixels in a location external to the PEs (a Register File, a Scratch-Pad Memory, etc.). Also, as the requests can come at the same time from different directions, more than one access should be possible at the same time. Considering the communication among the PEs, the action of accessing a Pixel value should be transparent to the PE. In this work

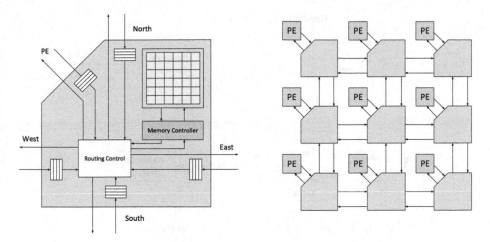

Fig. 5. Selected system's topology: mesh Network-on-Chip with special routers.

we consider Networks-on-Chip (NoCs) as good alternatives to solve our communication needs. NoCs are scalable, and as we have homogeneous communication patterns, their performance will be efficient enough for most applications.

Figure 5 shows the topology which offers the highest throughput. It is similar to a standard Mesh NoC [13], but with special Routers able to store internally the Pixels of an image region. In addition, this topology fits the geometric constraints defined by the Pixel Array with Region-based readout.

2.2   Analysis of the Application Domain

In the parallel processing domain, one of the most important goals is to identify and explore the maximum amount of parallelism possible [9]. Looking to the IP/CV algorithms, and considering the spatial distribution of PEs over the image area, we can identify a coarse-grained parallelism. In the IP/CV domain, the OpenCV library [1] is one of the most used collection of algorithms. It is used for educational, industrial and scientific purposes, and can be considered as a informal standard.

With the increasing number of complex IP/CV commercial applications, the industry identified the need for an IP/CV standard *de facto*. The Chronos Group [8] released in 2014 the first version of the OpenVX standard. OpenVX is a set of rules and design patterns created to describe IP/CV applications. Similar to other standards, like OpenCL and OpenGL, the OpenVX actuates as a *frontend* for application's description. The *backend* should be created by each hardware manufacturer, accordingly to its architecture's characteristics [8].

OpenVX defines a programming model based on graphs, composed by nodes and links. Each node is a complete IP/CV algorithm (filtering, motion detection, arithmetic operations among images, and so on) Fig. 6. In general, both input and output of a node are images. In our approach we consider that each PE is

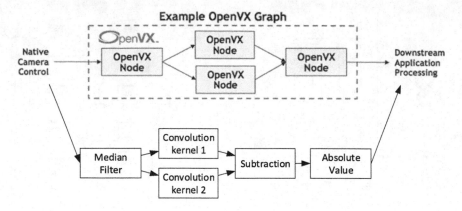

Fig. 6. OpenVX Graph of a simple application.

responsible for computing the output values of a sub-image. This means that the algorithms in each node must be executed by all the PEs simultaneously. We define here the concept of Core-Code: the code necessary to generate a single output pixel. Each OpenVX node can be mapped to a Core-Code. This means that each PE will execute the Core-Code repeatedly for all Pixels in its own region. Each PE operate independently from the other when performing the same node, what means that the only synchronization among PEs occurs when they start/finish a node [12].

2.3   Static Analysis of Aplication's Core-Codes

In the last section we determined the Core-Codes as the codes to be executed in each PE. A complete IP/CV application is composed by several OpenVX nodes, what means several Core-Codes. The PEs must be designed to be able to process the sequence of nodes efficiently. There are several works in the literature regarding the design of Application Specific Instruction-Set Processors (ASIP). An ASIP is a processor architecture specially tuned for an application domain. An ASIP should be able to provide a medium term between the flexibility (programmability) of common General Purpose Processors (GPPs), and the efficiency of direct hardware implementations.

A straightforward approach was used to determine the PE's microarchitecture from the application's Core-Codes. A tool for graph generation from the Core-Codes was created. This tools is based on the Clang compiler from the LLVM project [10]. The starting point of the analysis is the Abstract Syntax Tree (AST), which is sintactically, semantically and type-checked. However, no optimization is performed in this step, what means that our systems depends on code-quality. To avoid issues, a library of nodes is available for OpenVX descriptions.

By the time of this work was written, this tool had some restrictions: pointer variables and arrays not supported; jump operations not supported; the function

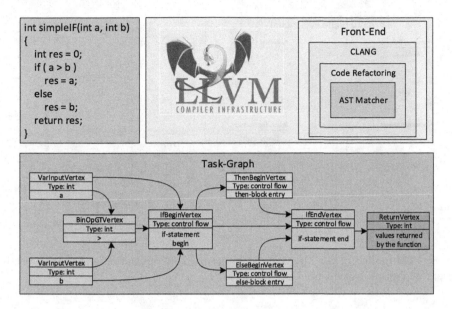

Fig. 7. Graph generator based on LLVM: sample example for a simple function.

may have only one return statement, on its end. The graphs generated have some
properties, like: parameters and literals are inputs; vertices are basic operations
of the C programming language; edges represent dependencies, data and control
flow; function return value is the output. matcher, to extract the algorithm's
structure and create a the graph. At this moment, this tool is able to handle
most of the ANSI C language specification. For each Core-Code in an application,
a new graph is generated. Figure 7 shows the graph generated for a sample
Core-Code.

2.4   Parameterizable SystemC/TLM2.0 Simulator

This tool receives the graphs from the last Section and generates a SystemC/
TLM2.0 representation of the manycore architecture. By using a library of SystemC blocks, the graphs are rebuilt and grouped in high-level models of the PEs.
A *Core wrapper* handles TLM communication between partners, the transaction
object contains information about the dependencies and the target generates
results for the dependencies. Some advantages in the use of TLM are: PE model
is separated into communication and functionality; few functions make the model
easy to understand; sparsely connections for dependencies, because they are only
for external communications needed. Figure 8 shows the TLM models for the PEs
(with the graph inside) and the manycore organization. The simulations allow
to extract in more details informations regarding the communication patterns
among PEs, and also timing and resources needs inside the PEs.

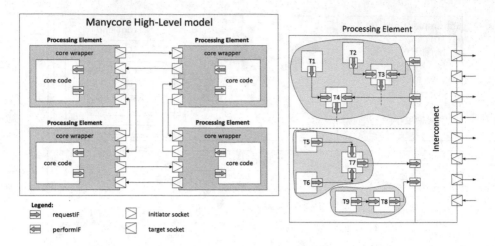

Fig. 8. TLM models of the Manycore architecture: communication and spatial distribution, and graph-based Core-Codes in each PE.

2.5   Processing Element Parameter Estimation

As explained previously, due to the design constraints and restrictions in area, power consumption and speed, the PEs must be specialized for the application domain we are exploring. Flexibility for changes after the chip design is important to allow for new application's implementation over the architecture. However, specialization and flexibility are quite antagonic.

[9] states that one of the key concepts to achieve high efficiency in IP/CV processing is the parallelism exploration. IP/CV applications have different levels of parallelism. In Sect. 2.2 we explored the coarsest level, by dividing the image into regions allocated to each PE. Regarding the PE's microarchitecture, solutions exploring the Instruction Level Parallelism (ILP) are among the most efficient.

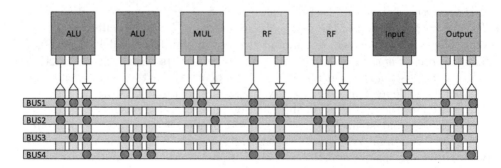

Fig. 9. Sample Transport Triggered Architecture processor.

From the literature we could identify that several different architectures have been tested for IP/CV algorithms, each one with different efficiency, advantages and disadvantages. Architectures such as VLIW (Very Large Instruction Width) are strong candidates to be used in our system, considering that they offer a throughput higher than the common RISC architectures, and are more flexible in comparison with embedded GPUS [7]. Hardware accelerators, like the ones generated by the LegUp framework [3] are also interesting and can be quite fast, however there is a lack of flexibility. Once the accelerators are defined,

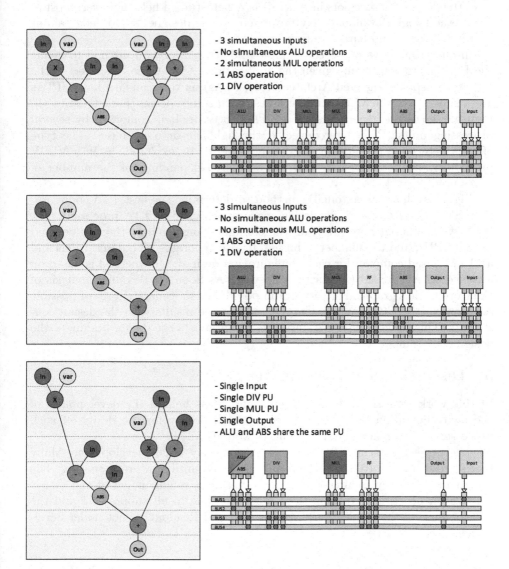

Fig. 10. From the graph to the TTA configuration: same application, different hardware implementations.

new applications maybe would not benefit from these already implemented accelerators, resulting in bad efficiency.

ASIPs (Application Specific Instruction Set Processors) are considered as well-balanced solutions for embedded systems. They offer some advantages from GPPs (e.g. programmability) and from hardware accelerators (e.g. special complex instructions). In [14] the authors suggest a methodology based on graphs to help the design of processor architectures. [5] shows a method based on profiling and microarchitecture's templates to ASIP customization. The design of ASIPs (and the design of processors in general) is a well-studied field, however, most of the methodologies available relay too much on the designer's knowledge about both application and hardware features.

In our project, we proposed a simple and straightforward method to define the PE's microarchitecture given the application's Core-Code. We selected the use of Transport Triggered Architectures (TTAs) as the standard basis. TTAs are a superset of the VLIW architectures, with some special characteristics [4]. Figure 9 shows the general idea of a TTA processor. It is composed by several processing units (PUs) interconnected through one or more buses. The type of PUs determine the amount of ILP possible to be explored (as in a VLIW processor) and deep bypasses can be configured depending on the number of buses used.

Figure 10 shows an automatic method to determine the best TTA configuration. TCE is a framework for design space exploration of TTA processors [15]. It allows the designer to select all the configurations (mainly the number and types of PUs, and the number of buses). It also generates RTL descriptions and a LLVM based compiler for each configuration desired. Our method is based on a mixed ALAP/ASAP (As Last As Possible/As Soon As Possible) analysis of the Core-Code's graphs. For each graph possibility we generate a set of possible solutions in the TCE environment, comparing the results with the design constraints. This cycle is repeated until the design meets the design fits under the design constraints.

3   Discussion and Conclusion

In this work we discussed the concepts and ideas behind the development of the next generation vision processors. A methodology for the design of such processors was explained and some parts were detailed.

The project presented in this work is currently under development. Many issues are still not solved, but the results achieved until now are promising. The design methodology is already able to generate a rough model of the many-core vision processor. Optimizations must be done in all subprojects and the development of the Analog part (Acquisition and Readout) is not under development yet.

Acknowledgment. The authors would like to acknowledge CAPES Foundation/Brazilian Ministry of Education (Science without Borders Program, Grant Process Nr. 9054-13-8) and the support received from the University of Brasilia.

References

1. Opencv: Open source computer vision. Technical report. www.opencv.org
2. El Gamal, A., Fowler, B.A., Yang, D. X.: Pixel-level processing: why, what, and how? In: Proceedings of the SPIE, Sensors, Cameras, and Applications for Digital Photography, vol. 3650 (1999)
3. Canis, A., Choi, J., Aldham, M., Zhang, V., Kammoona, A., Czajkowski, T., Brown, S.D., Anderson, J.H.: LegUp: an open-source high-level synthesis tool for FPGA-based processor/accelerator systems. ACM Trans. Embed. Comput. Syst. (TECS) **13**(2), 24 (2013)
4. Corporaal, H.: Microprocessor architectures: from VLIW to TTA (1997)
5. Eusse, J., Williams, C., Leupers, R.: Coex: a novel profiling-based algorithm/architecture co-exploration for ASIP design. In: 2013 8th International Workshop on Reconfigurable and Communication-Centric Systems-on-Chip (ReCoSoC), pp. 1–8, July 2013
6. Fossum, E.R., Kemeny, S.: Camera on a chip. In: The World and I, pp. 178–185 (1996)
7. Hoozemans, J., Wong, S., Al-Ars, Z.: Using VLIW softcore processors for image processing applications. In: Proceedings of the 15th International Conference on Systems, Architectures, Modeling and Simulation (SAMOS) (2015)
8. Openvx 1.01 specification. Technical report (2015). https://www.khronos.org/openvx/
9. Kehtarnavaz, N., Gamadia, M.: Real-time image and video processing: from research to reality. Synth. Lect. Image Video Multimedia Process. **2**(1), 1–108 (2006)
10. Lattner, C., Adve, V.: LLVM: a compilation framework for lifelong program analysis & transformation. In: 2004 International Symposium on Code Generation and Optimization, CGO 2004, pp. 75–86. IEEE (2004)
11. Mori, J., Huebner, M.: A high-level analysis of a multi-core vision processor using systemC and TLM2.0. In: 2014 International Conference on ReConFigurable Computing and FPGAs (ReConFig), pp. 1–6, December 2014
12. Mori, J.Y., Llanos, C., Huebner, M.: A framework to the design and programming of many-core focal-plane vision processors. In: 2015 International Conference on Embedded and Ubiquitous Computing (2015)
13. Sepulveda, M., Diguet, J.-P., Strum, M., Gogniat, G.: NoC-based protection for SoC time-driven attacks. IEEE Embed. Syst. Lett. **7**(1), 7–10 (2015)
14. Trajkovic, J., Gajski, D.D.: Custom processor core construction from C code. In: 2008 Symposium on Application Specific Processors, SASP 2008, pp. 1–6. IEEE (2008)
15. Viitanen, T., Kultala, H., Jaaskelainen, P., Takala, J.: Heuristics for greedy transport triggered architecture interconnect exploration. In: 2014 International Conference on Compilers, Architecture and Synthesis for Embedded Systems (CASES), pp. 1–7, October 2014
16. Zarandy, Á.: Focal-Plane Sensor-Processor Chips. Springer, New York (2011)

EEG Feature Extraction Accelerator Enabling Long Term Epilepsy Monitoring Based on Ultra Low Power WSNs

Evangelinos Mariatos, Christos P. Antonopoulos,
and Nikolaos S. Voros$^{(\boxtimes)}$

Technological Educational Institute of Western Greece, Patras, Greece
{emariatos, cantonopoulos, voros}@teiwest.gr

Abstract. Wireless sensor networks based on miniaturized ultra low power nodes are increasingly utilized in highly demanding cyberphysical systems required to offer extended time periods of non-intrusive and unattended monitoring of specific biophysical signals. However, although significant performance enhancements are offered by state of the art WSN platforms, still scarce energy availability comprises the Achilles' Hill of respective platforms. A prominent approach to remedy this deficiency is to transfer part of the overall processing applied on raw data into the WSN node, aiming to reduce drastically the amount of data than need to be wirelessly transmitted, thus allowing the radio chip to be turned off most of the time. The proposed approach has been applied in the context of ARMOR project, which focuses on EEG based Epilepsy monitoring and automated seizure detection, considering that seizure detection is based upon specific EEG feature vectors representing just $\sim 5\%$ of the total amount of raw data. In that respect, this paper presents the design, implementation and evaluation of a novel EEG feature vector extraction hardware accelerator module. The validity of the module's functionality is verified against already published Matlab based seizure detection algorithms while performance benefits are also estimated.

1 Introduction

Cyberphsical systems (CPS) are an ubiquitous infrastructure of miniaturized wireless devices, able to offer signal acquisition from physical world, are one of the most attractive yet challenging ICT objectives engaging a wide range of engineering research areas. Towards making CPS a reality, Wireless Sensor Networks appear as a prominent technological infrastructure offering ideal characteristics as well as comprising one of the most active research areas in wireless networking [1, 2].

Critical advancements in Wireless Sensor Network (WSNs) able to drive the effort of CPSs pertain to both the hardware and software aspects. Focusing on the former aspect, very large integration system techniques, new processing architectures offering substantial processing capabilities with ultra low power demands, integration of a wide variety of communication interfaces as well as integration of any kind of sensor pave the way towards widespread and omnipotent utilization [3–7].

© Springer International Publishing Switzerland 2016
V. Bonato et al. (Eds.): ARC 2016, LNCS 9625, pp. 26–37, 2016.
DOI: 10.1007/978-3-319-30481-6_3

However, despite the significant enhancements, WNSs are still characterized by devastating deficiencies prohibiting utilization in general purpose and particularly in demanding applications [8]. In such cases, a more drastic approach increasingly attracting attention advocates the design and development of hardware based algorithms able to process data on the WSN sensor itself, providing that this process significantly reduces the volume of data wirelessly transferred. Such hardware accelerators effectively comprise ultra low power components, in which the energy required to process raw data and wirelessly transmitting the processed data is significantly lower than the energy required by typical radio chips to transmit the raw data.

In order such approaches to be feasible and effective, in-depth understanding and analysis of the application in hand is required. The ARMOR project [15] tackles epilepsy monitoring comprising a critical application of particularly high demands and of high sensitivity. In this context, an objective of paramount importance is the development of algorithms for automatic identification of epileptic seizures [9]. In this quest WSN can be proven invaluable enabling the continuous monitoring of a person in a wide variety of environments such as home, work or even outdoors [10].

However, such monitoring entails the continuous acquisition of a high number of electroencephalogram (EEG) sensors (in the order of a few tens) creating samples at frequency from 500 Hz up to 2500 Hz. As it is easily understood such scenarios result in excessive volumes of data that must be transmitted through WSNs, which leads to WSN node energy depletion in few hours (or even less), as well as network traffic congestion which results in degrading the overall network performance.

Aiming to mitigate such deficiencies, this paper presents a hardware based accelerator able to process EEG data in real time on the WSN node. According to this approach, it is calculated that the node needs to transmit only the feature vectors of the modality (i.e. EEG signals) instead of all the raw data acquired. As shown, such capability yields a 95 % decrease of the data transmission required for Epilepsy seizure automatic identification. The proposed hardware accelerator has been thoroughly validated in comparison with the Matlab based feature vector extraction algorithms [14, 15]. Moreover, the evaluation of the efficiency of the hardware accelerator reveals significant enhancements compared to software based implementations.

The rest of the paper is structured as follows: Sect. 2 offers important background information justifying the proposed approach and indicating potential benefits, while Sect. 3 presents an abstract view of the design and implementation of the proposed accelerator; Sect. 4 presents in detail performance characteristics and evaluation results; finally, Sect. 5 summarizes the main conclusions of this work.

2 Rationale

A wireless sensor system is typically a low-cost, low-complexity, low-power device. Typically, such systems are built around micro-controllers with embedded or external wireless networking hardware, and all data processing is performed by the micro-controller in software. In some cases, however, adding an external hardware accelerator is justified for reasons that include:

- A hardware accelerator can pre-process the signals efficiently without burdening the main processing unit while leading to reduced data rates. Pre-processing that leads to smaller data rates is a good way to minimize the amount of wireless traffic thus boosting the data transferring capabilities of the network.
- The system can save power due to reduced wireless traffic and avoid unnecessary operations. In some cases, the software and the radio part can even be shut-down or in a deep sleep mode, waiting for the hardware to initiate traffic when and only when it is required.
- Running this pre-processing in software is not a practical solution if the algorithms are demanding, since a typical embedded microcontroller does not have sufficient processing power and memory availability.

Regarding the wireless sensor system deployed in ARMOR project, the seizure detection system reads a number of signals from sensors and conveys them via a wireless connection to a decision-making algorithm. Figure 1 provides a quick overview of this concept.

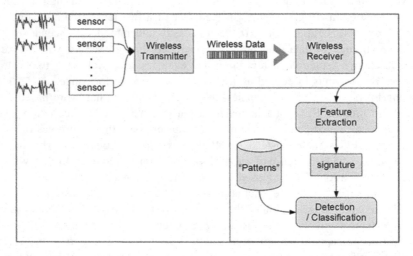

Fig. 1. Wireless sensor data acquisition and transfer to seizure detection system

The two shortcomings of this architecture that we try to address with our approach, both stem from the need to transmit the entire sampled signal all the time. This is not desired because:

- Sending all data means that the RF transmitter has to be active all the time, which consumes a lot of power on the wireless node making its battery last for less time.
- Having to send all channels at the full rate means that the wireless medium is loaded with a lot of constantly streaming data, leaving little if any space for other networks to co-exist and thus compromising the reliability and robustness of the link.

In order to minimize wireless traffic, what we try in this paper is to move parts of the decision-making algorithm on the wireless node. Specifically, we aim to move the feature extraction part into the sensor node. Such an approach can yield significant benefits since this is the part of the algorithm that actually needs all the raw sensor data.

By extracting the features locally, the amount of data that has to be transferred can be drastically reduced. In a typical scenario, each of the signals will have 256 Hz sampling frequency at two bytes per sample and the following extracted features operation will occur every 500 ms:

- Zero Crossing Rate [11]
- Signal Total Energy [12]
- Signal Energy Per Band in 4 Bands [13]

This is illustrated in Fig. 2.

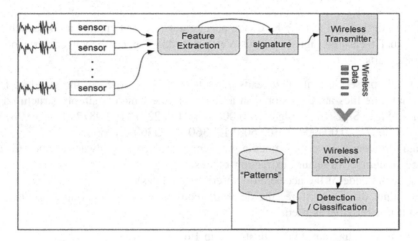

Fig. 2. Feature extraction data processing integrated in the WSN sensor

If we transmit the full signal, the required data for one second will be:

$$DataRate = Number\_of\_Signals \times Samples/second \times Bits/Sample = 64 \times 256 \times 16 = 263\,Kbps$$

If, instead, we only have to transmit the extracted features. The rate is:

$$DataRate = N_s \times f_w \times N_f \times B_f = 64 \times 2 \times 6 \times 16 = 12\,Kbps$$

where:
N_s = Number of sampled signals
f_w = feature detection windows per second
N_f = Number of features per detection window
B_f = number of bits representing each feature
which saves 95 % of wireless data transmission. The benefits of this reduced data transfer are:

(a) Better utilization of the wireless band. At 5 % of the original, there is plenty of room for retries in case of medium failure and a much more relaxed need for cooperative coexistence with other wireless networks that may operate in the same area.
(b) Lower power. State of the art commercially available WSN devices still use at least 5 mA while transmitting, while they operate at less than 0.5 mA when the RF part ids turned off.
(c) The full data rate of 263 Kbps pushes some of the existing WSN protocols like BLE and ZigBee close to their theoretical limits. Using only 12 Kbps has a much higher chance of achieving reliable operation in real-life conditions.

3   Design and Implementation

In order to design and test the hardware accelerators we first created a test-bench that feeds actual measured signals to our Verilog code. The test-bench consists of the following parts:

- EDF file parser, a utility that reads the sensor data as stored in the standard EDF format. The files are then stored in a "data.txt" file which is simply structured as: Time Sig1 Sig2 Sig3 Sig4 ....0.000000-31.062271 109.987790 - 39.267399 237.362637 ...0.003906 0.195360 0.195360 0.195360 0.195360 ...
- Data_Provider.v, a verilog module that wraps the actual hardware accelerator and feeds a number of feature extraction blocks.
- The actual code of the accelerators (Verilog modules).
- An output file which stores the detected features of each signal and the classifier result if a classifier is used.

In the form of a diagram this is illustrated in Fig. 3:

4   Performance Evaluation

4.1   Functional Verification

The first step in decision making is the extraction of features from the signals. A Matlab model has been created that extracts these features and is used in the ARMOR project for algorithm evaluation and optimization [14]. In parallel, an FPGA implementation based on Verilog code has been developed, which allows feature extraction on hardware – saving power and reducing communication bandwidth while reducing the overall workload of the main Micro Controller Unit (MCU) of the sensor.

This section presents the output of the Verilog feature extraction engine as compared to the Matlab model.

4.1.1   Example Charts by Verilog and Matlab

In order to perform the comparison with the theoretically calculated values, we run a Matlab based script over the same source data, which yields a text file called "*temp_FeaturesPerFrame.txt*". We limit the size of the file by running the script over

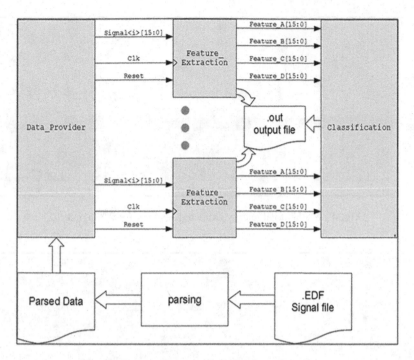

Fig. 3. Design diagram of the hardware accelerator

only a few first frames as this file contains the extracted features for all signals and frames. To begin with, we isolate one signal, and create a list of all extracted features for all frames. We arrange values of each frame in one row, with columns for features ZC (zero crossing), EN (total energy), and B1...B5 (energy per band).

The procedure described above has to be performed for each signal and for each feature, and the resulting charts are compared.

What is important to notice from the respective comparisons is that – smaller or bigger - there are some differences between the feature values calculated by the FPGA code and the values theoretically extracted by the Matlab model (In this case we notice that the maximum "error" is at 1 %). In order to minimize or even eliminate these differences, we should have to use complex floating point arithmetic in the FPGA – something that would require a much larger FPGA part to fit and would consume much more power, thus degrading the benefits of a hardware accelerator. We expect these differences to play no role at all at classification accuracy, due to the nature of the decision making algorithm. To make sure that the theoretically extracted features do not affect decision making, we do not train the classification system with feature vectors extracted by the Matlab model (Fig. 4). Instead, we will use the FPGA-generated feature vectors for training (Fig. 5).

After normalization, we again compare every individual result (Fig. 6):

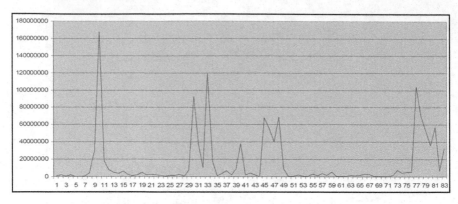

Fig. 4. Matlab total energy extracted features for 2nd signal

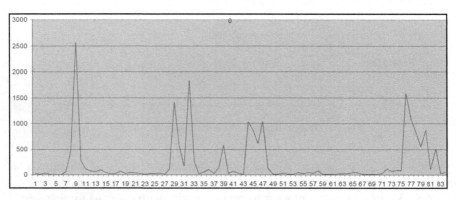

Fig. 5. Hardware module total energy extracted features for 2nd signal

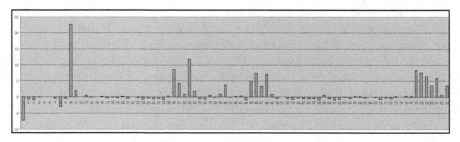

Fig. 6. Total energy extracted features for 2nd signal deviation

4.2   Implementation Characteristics

Taking into account the nature of the targeted application domain, the implementation characteristics of proposed accelerator are summarized as follows.

- **Speed and Low Power:** The reason for offering an FPGA implementation is that we expect a hardware solution to combine higher speeds with lower power consumption while at the same time alleviate respective workload from the main MCU of the sensor.
- **Cost:** In practice, having an FPGA next to a microcontroller for performing hardware acceleration is not always an optimal solution, at least in terms of material cost. However, if we can prove - via our FPGA tests - that hardware accelerators are performing as expected, a future microcontroller targeting embedded sensors for multi-signal classification and decision making could implement such functions as dedicated hardware blocks inside the same package, thus achieving also low cost. In any case the benefits and performance enhancements offers by respective implementation outweighs any relative cost disadvantages.

4.2.1 Speed at Various FPGA Clock Frequencies

To calculate the speed at various FPGA clock frequencies, we can directly measure the number of clock cycles required for:

- t_s: Processing of each sample (128)
- t_f: Frame-level processing in order to calculate features (1,275,620 for the 512-samples frame we used)

The number of clock cycles is multiplied with the clock period that corresponds to each frequency. To that calculation we are adding the delay for getting all signals of each sample out of the serial port (which is fixed, as the data rate of the serial port does not depend on FPGA clock frequency). In this implementation we used an 115200 bps serial connection:

- t_p = Number_of_Signals $* (11 + 5) * 8.680$ ns $= 4444.160$ ns for 32 signals.

These calculations are based on our implementation where each transferred byte uses 8 data bits, 1 stop bit, 2 start bits (a total of 11) and there is an average distance of five clock periods between the bytes.

We make the assumption - based on observations - that each byte will use 8 data bits, 1 stop bit, 2 start bits (a total of 11) and that there will be an average distance of five clock periods between the bytes.

We are interested into how fast can the accelerator process a single frame, as this is the rate at which the wireless network will be used for transmission of the feature vectors. Thus, the results can be plotted as a frame rate vs. frequency chart, as depicted in Fig. 7.

For the application of the ARMOR project [15], the sampling rates need at most 2 or 4 frames per second, which means that the accelerator can operate at frequencies as low as 3 MHz. If this accelerator is used for other types of signals, the currently used FPGA can support frequencies up to 128 MHz, which means that it will run up to 63 frames/second.

To further speed-up processing we could use a double-buffering scheme, which would parallelize frame processing (tf) with sample processing (ts). But this would only

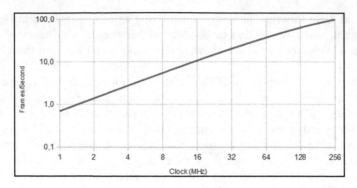

Fig. 7. Throughput performance of the hardware module wrt to clock frequency

save 0.4 % of total time in the low frequencies and 8 % at the maximum speed. On the other hand, it would require the double number of local memory buffers in the FPGA.

4.2.2   Power Consumption Estimations

The power consumption calculation is done using the estimator tools provided by the FPGA vendor (Xilinx), and specifically the Xpower Analyzer. The Xpower analyzer uses detailed data about clock trees, logic utilization etc. in order to generate a good estimation of the power consumption in the FPGA. Using this tool, we resynthesized the feature extractor for various clock frequencies and got the results presented in Fig. 8.

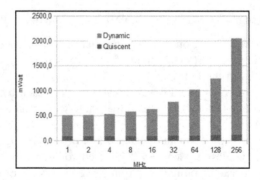

Fig. 8. Feature Extraction hardware module power consumption performance (Color figure online)

The power consumption results are - as expected - higher for higher clock frequencies. Quiescent power is around 60 mWatt for all speeds, but - even at small speeds of 1 MHz the dynamic consumption is almost half a Watt. We must remember however that these numbers correspond to an FPGA implementation, if we target the same hardware on a custom ASIC we would get even lower consumption.

4.2.3   Comparison to a Software-Only Architecture

In order to compare the proposed accelerators against a software-only architecture, we calculate a number of scenarios with the following assumptions:

- *Software Speed at a high-end microcontroller, if we need to run all in software*: 100 MIPS
- *Software Speed at a mid-end microcontroller, required if we have hardware acceleration*: 25 MIPS
- *Clock frequencies in the feature extraction acceleration unit*: 8 MHz
- *Clock frequencies in the classification acceleration unit*: 16 MHz
- *Software Overhead for forwarding signals to the accelerator*: 30 %

Comparison is primarily done in terms of speed as the power benefit mainly simply stems from the fact that we can reduce the CPU clock frequency. Assuming the mid-end microcontroller, we performed calculations for the time required to analyze signals from 1 s of captured data. The following diagrams in Figs. 9 and 10 and show the calculated comparison as computation time (in msec) vs number of signals for three window sizes, 64 and 256 respectively.

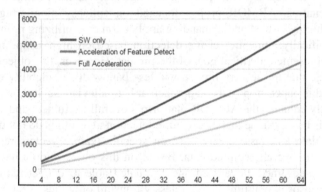

Fig. 9. Window size 64 samples (Color figure online)

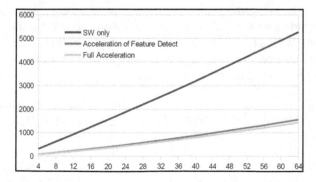

Fig. 10. Window size 256 samples (Color figure online)

When a window has many samples, the processing done in hardware takes a larger proportion of the overall processing which also includes communication, feature evaluation etc. Indeed, as expected the benefit of hardware acceleration is more significant if we have large window sizes. Specifically, and considering 64 number of signals hardware accelerator compared to software execution, leads to a drastic ~70 % is exhibited for Windows Size equal to 256.

Another significant observation is that for the larger window size, the extra benefit of the full hardware acceleration option (which includes classification) is not as noticeable as is in the smaller window sizes. This can be attributed to the fact that classification operates on the extracted features, so it does not depend on window size, making its contribution to overall speed-up smaller for large windows than for small windows. Thus for 256 Window Size full acceleration offers negligible benefits compared to Acceleration of feature extraction.

5   Conclusions and Future Work

Cyber Physical systems comprise a rapidly evolving area being able to combine the physical world with ICT domains in order to effectively address demanding real life application scenarios. ARMOR project focused on epilepsy monitoring and study representing a highly critical and demanding application case utilizing prominent WSN solutions. Specifically, epileptic seizure detection based on high sampling frequency EEG signals represented a critical goal of the project. However, this objective posed a critical challenge due to the very limited wireless bandwidth availability of WSNs.

Therefore, this paper proposed an approach able to alleviate such shortcomings and thus significantly enhance the ARMOR platform's overall usefulness and added value. The main idea is based on the fact that seizure detection algorithms do not utilize all the EEG acquired data and instead rely only on specific feature vectors representing a merely 5 % of the overall acquired data. Based on this observation a hardware component has been designed, developed and evaluated able to extract required feature vectors on the sensor in real time and wirelessly transmit only these vectors effectively yielding significant reduction of wirelessly transmitted data by 95 %, which can be translated to drastic improvement in term of power consumption and wireless bandwidth requirements.

As future work, the authors aim to transfer more intelligence on the sensor implementing, apart from the feature vector extraction algorithms, the classification algorithms as well. By implementing the classification on the monitored person, there is little, if any, delay between signal capture and reaction, so very urgent decisions can be made even if the host is temporary unreachable.

Acknowledgments. This study is partially funded by the European Commission under the Seventh Framework Programme (FP72007-2013) with grant ARMOR, Agreement Number 287720.

References

1. Hellbruck, H.: Name-centric service architecture for cyber-physical systems. In: IEEE 6th International Conference on Service-Oriented Computing and Applications (SOCA), 16–18 December 2013
2. Li, W., et al.: Collaborative wireless sensor networks: a survey. In: IEEE International Conference on Systems, Man, and Cybernetics (SMC 2011), 9–12 October 2011
3. Alemdar, H., Ersoy, C.: Wireless sensor networks for healthcare: a survey. Comput. Netw. **54**, 2688–2710 (2010). Elsevier
4. Lecointre, A., et al.: Miniaturized wireless sensor networks. In: International Semiconductor Conference, Sinaia, pp. 13–17 (2006)
5. Jin, M.-H., et al.: Sensor network design and implementation for health telecare and diagnosis assistance applications. In: 11th ICPADS, Fukuoka (2005)
6. Goyal, D., et al.: Routing protocols in wireless sensor networks: a survey. In: Second International Conference on Advanced Computing & Communication Technologies (ACCT), Rohtak, Haryana, 7–8 January 2012
7. Pei, H.: The evolution of MAC protocols in wireless sensor networks: a survey. IEEE Commun. Surv. Tutorials **15**(1), 101–120 (2013)
8. Dong, W., et al.: Providing OS support for wireless sensor networks: challenges and approaches. IEEE Commun. Surv. Tutorials **12**(4), 519–530 (2010)
9. Mporas, I., et al.: Seizure detection using EEG and ECG signals for computer-based monitoring, analysis and management of epileptic patients. Expert Syst. Appl. **42**(6), 3227–3233 (2015). Elsevier
10. Zhang, Y., et al.: Ubiquitous WSN for healthcare: recent advances and future prospects. IEEE Internet Things J. **1**(4), 311–318 (2014)
11. Conradsen, I., Beniczky, S., Hoppe, K., Wolf, P., Sorensen, H.B.: Automated algorithm for generalized tonic-clonic epileptic seizure onset detection based on sEMG zero-crossing rate. IEEE Trans. Biomed. Eng. **59**(2), 579–585 (2012). doi:10.1109/TBME.2011.2178094
12. Correa, A.G., et al.: An energy-based detection algorithm of epileptic seizures in EEG records. Conf. Proc. IEEE Eng. Med. Biol. Soc. **2009**, 1384–1387 (2009). doi:10.1109/IEMBS.2009.5334114
13. Blanco, S., et al.: Comparison of frequency bands using spectral entropy for epileptic seizure prediction. ISRN Neurol. (2013). Article ID 287327. doi:10.1155/2013/287327
14. Mporas, I., Tsirka, V., Zacharaki, E.I., Koutroumanidis, M., Megalooikonomou, V.: Online seizure detection from EEG and ECG signals for monitoring of epileptic patients. In: Likas, A., Blekas, K., Kalles, D. (eds.) SETN 2014. LNCS, vol. 8445, pp. 442–447. Springer, Heidelberg (2014)
15. ARMOR FP7 Project. http://armor.tesyd.teimes.gr/welcome

Video and Image Processing

Computing to the Limit with Heterogeneous CPU-FPGA Devices in a Video Fusion Application

Jose Nunez-Yanez[✉]

Department of Electrical and Electronic Engineering, University of Bristol,
MVB Building, Woodland Road, Bristol, BS8 1UB, UK
j.l.nunez-yanez@bristol.ac.uk

Abstract. This paper presents a complete video fusion system with hardware acceleration and investigates its performance and energy optimization. The video fusion application is based on the Dual-Tree Complex Wavelet Transforms (DT-CWT). Video fusion combines information from different spectral bands into a single representation and advanced algorithms based on wavelet transforms are compute and energy intensive. In this work the transforms are mapped to a hardware accelerator using high-level synthesis tools for the FPGA resulting in an increase of performance of the system by a factor of 3. In a second stage the hardware engine is transformed with a set of tools and detector blocks that allow the CPU device to monitor and pre-detect timing failures in the FPGA fabric. The CPU device can control the voltage and frequency of the FPGA and obtain a new working point with reducing power requirements by approximately 70 % with an equivalent performance level. This results in an energy proportional computing system in which only the energy required to maintain a required level of performance is used.

1 Introduction

Multi-sensor video data with visible and infrared images is increasingly being utilized in applications such as medical imaging, remote sensing and security applications. Multi-sensor data presents complementary information about the region surveyed and fusion provides an efficient method to combine the complementary information for better data analysis. Video fusion is just a special case of image fusion when two or more frames of different video sources are fused together continuously into a single fused video [1]. Image fusion can be performed based on wavelet transform techniques [2]. Compare to other schemes [3], wavelet transform achieves better signal to noise ratios and improved perception with no blocking artefacts. Moreover, among all the wavelet transform that applied to multifocal, remote sensing and medical image fusion, the use of the Dual-Tree Complex Wavelet Transform (DT-CWT) has been shown to produce significant fusion quality improvement [4]. The algorithm described in [4] is used in this paper which consists in applying DT-CWT to infrared and visible frames, combining the obtaining coefficients using a fusion rule and then proceeding to perform the inverse DT-CWT for reconstruction.

© Springer International Publishing Switzerland 2016
V. Bonato et al. (Eds.): ARC 2016, LNCS 9625, pp. 41–53, 2016.
DOI: 10.1007/978-3-319-30481-6_4

The proposed system is based on the ZYNQ System-on-Chip and the CPU and the FPGA work together to run the algorithm. The whole system runs under the Linux OS with a customized kernel level Linux driver. The main contributions of this paper are:

1. We create an open-source complete fusion system including processing engine, drivers, hardware interfaces and cameras. The most compute intensive parts of the algorithm are accelerated based on HLS tools using the FPGA.
2. We demonstrate the performance and energy advantages of using a heterogeneous platform for video fusion comparing to a software-only solution.
3. We extend this system with energy proportional techniques that maintain the same level of performance but they reduce power and energy significantly.

The remaining of this paper is organized as follows. Section 2 lists related work in this research area. Section 3 provides some fundamental knowledge of the DT-CWT based fusion algorithms and Section 4 discusses the energy proportional implementation flow. Section 5 introduces our hardware architecture to implement the DT-CWT with a customized kernel level Linux driver, followed by Section 6, which presents our system architecture to capture and fuse multi-sensor data. Section 7 compares the performance, power and energy consumption of the fusion application running in the ARM CPU and FPGA configurations including the use of the energy proportional approach. Finally, Sect. 8 concludes the paper.

2   Related Work

Previous research on FPGA-based fusion systems is available in recent literature. Jasiunas et al. [5] presented a wavelet based image fusion system for unmanned airborne vehicles. This is a very early attempt to develop image fusion systems on reconfigurable platform alone that achieved latency of 3.81 ms/frame for visible and infrared 8-bit images of 512×512 pixel resolution. Sims and Irvine [6] presented an FPGA implementation of pyramidal decomposition based video stream fusion. This framework can achieve a 30 frame/s, real-time fuse of video streams in grayscale video graphic arrays (VGA). Yunsheng et al. [7] presents a real-time image processing system to combine the video outputs of an uncooled infrared imaging system and a low-level-light TV system. Song et al. [8] proposed an image fusion implementation based on Laplacian pyramid decomposition of two-channel VGA video for a better fusion quality and reasonable frame rate of 25 frame/s. Mohamed and El-Den [9] applied five different measures to evaluate the performance of several different fusion techniques and the hardware implementation of DCT, DWT and PCNN-based fusion algorithms are studied. However, although these designs achieves performance enhancement to do image fusion on FPGA, the fusion algorithms they used are not state-of-the-art.

Tao et al. [10] proposed an image enhancement and fusion system to improve visibility. In this paper, two videos are captured by CCD and LWIR cameras and fused by implementing DT-CWT fusion algorithms in Xilinx Virtex-II environment. Gudis et al. [11] built an embedded vision service framework on ZYNQ SoC with a "plug-and-play" capability to allow the service-based software to take advantage of the hardware acceleration blocks available and perform the remainder of the processing in software. These designs share some similarities with our system but focus on the fusion quality more than the performance and energy efficiency.

3   The DT-CWT Based Fusion Algorithm

The aim of the wavelet transformation is to represent signals using a superposition of wavelets. The Discrete Wavelet Transform (DWT) is a spatial-frequency decomposition of a signal, which ensures the signal being decomposed into normalized wavelets at octave scales [12]. When applied to two-dimensions, signals are separately filtered and down-sampled in the horizontal and vertical directions. This creates four sub-bands at each scale, namely high-high (HH), high-low (HL), low-high (LH) and low-low (LL), as shown in Fig. 1. The name of each sub-band denotes the horizontal frequency first and then the vertical frequency. A multi-resolution decomposition of image can then be achieved by recursively applying filtering to the low-low sub-band.

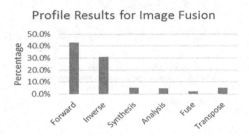

Fig. 1. Profiling results of fusing two input images

The DT-CWT transforms signals use two separate DWTs and apply spatial filters recursively to create frequency sub-bands. The application of DT-CWT to 2-D image is achieved by separable complex filtering in two dimensions. The DT-CWT is able to distinguish between positive and negative orientations and divides the horizontal and vertical sub-bands into six distinct sub-bands at each scale with the orientations of $\pm 15°$, $\pm 45°$ and $\pm 75°$. Moreover, the DT-CWT gives perfect reconstruction due to the biorthogonal nature of the filters and also delivers approximate shift-invariance.

In this paper, the whole fusion algorithm with the forward and inverse DT-CWTs is written in C++ and executed by the ARM Cortex A9 Processor. The profiling results of the fusion process, as shown in Fig. 1, indicate that the forward and inverse DT-CWT are the most compute- and energy intensive tasks. Therefore, these parts of the algorithm are the ones selected for acceleration in the FPGA. The FPGA fabric available in the ZYNQ device can be made coherent with processor caches using the (Acceleration Coherence Port) ACP and this is the option that has been selected in this paper. To achieve the FPGA acceleration, the forward and inverse DT-CWT were mapped to the PL (FPGA) side of ZYNQ to create a hardware wavelet engine controlled by the PS (CPU) side. This means that the input images are decomposed and reconstructed in hardware. The hardware accelerator has been created using the VIVADO_HLS high-level synthesis tools increasing productivity compared with a traditional RTL design. This also enables a fast exploration of the design space. The original C++ code makes use of float data types and operators. Figure 2 shows the results of the design space exploration phase in which the floats have been replaced with fixed point data types with different number of fractional bits maintaining the integer bits constant at 12 to avoid overflows. These exploration can be done in a few hours and shows that there are important benefits in terms of performance and complexity by using the fixed point data types as expected. Figure 2 also shows how PSNR reduces as accuracy reduces but this happens linearly In this research the results based around <24,12> accuracy (36 bits accuracy) have been selected since PSNR remains about 40 which is considered high quality while the number of DSP blocks required reduces significantly.

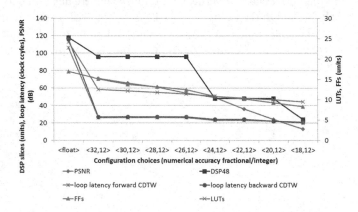

Fig. 2. Design space exploration as a function of accuracy

4   Energy Proportional Implementation Flow

The energy proportional implementation flow introduces the in-situ detectors in the design netlist guided by post place & route timing information. The core of the flow is the Elongate tool [13] that transforms the original design netlist into a new netlist with identical functionality and additional power management IP and in-situ detectors. Figure 3 shows the overall flow that can be decomposed into three distinct phases. During the first phase the original netlist goes through a full implementation run to obtain post place & route timing data in the form of a text file. In the second stage the Elongate tool takes as input the obtained timing data, the original netlist and Elongate component library that describes the power management core and in-situ detectors and produces the new power adaptive netlist. The third stage consists of a final implementation run of the power adaptive netlist to obtain the device bitstream ready to be downloaded in the device.

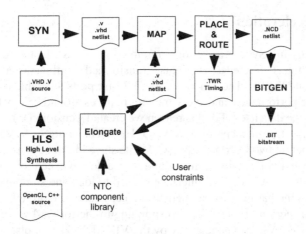

Fig. 3. Energy proportional implementation flow

The input into the flow in Fig. 3 is a C++ description of the forward and inverse DT-CWT that are initially compiled with Vivado HLS tools to obtain a netlist in either VHDL or Verilog format. This netlist is then synthesized by the Synplify synthesis tool to obtain a new VHDL netlist based on the implementation primitives available in the target technology. These initial synthesis steps are required to obtain the netlist that will be processed by Elongate. The need for this initial pre-processing is because the Elongate transformation does not take place at source level directly. The reason is that slight changes in the source can have a large effect on timing and also because it is possible to annotate the critical paths found after static timing analysis with the physical flip-flops in the netlist. The timing information is critical to allow Elongate to replace the end-point flip-flops in the critical paths with new soft-macro flip-flops that incorporate the in-situ detection logic. Each primitive flip-flop component in the technology library has a corresponding soft-macro flip-flop stored in the Elongate component library with identical functionality. Part of the user constraints input to Elongate indicate the level of coverage requested for the critical paths in the design. The coverage must be sufficient so that the critical paths of the final design have as endpoints the newly inserted soft macro flip-flops.

If there is not enough coverage then the final implementation netlist could have critical paths not protected by the soft macros and the design could not operate reliably across the range of frequencies and voltages considered. To detect this situation the tool analyzes the final timing data to verify that the critical paths end in soft-macro flip-flops and that the slowest main flip-flop is located inside a soft-macro. If these constraints are not met the designer is informed so that a new run can be launched using a different path coverage value. As a rule of thumb our experiments have indicated that a coverage level of 10 % of the total number of flip-flops is sufficient but this is ultimately dependent on how balanced the signal paths in the design are. The addition of the detectors results in a largely unaffected critical path while complexity increases by around 5 %.

5   FPGA Acceleration

The ZYNQ Processing System and Programmable Logic (PS-PL) interface is created to transfer commands, filtered coefficients, transformed coefficients and pixel data between the PS and the PL. The general purpose 32-bit ports available in Zynq do not obtain the require performance and every transfer requires around 25 clock cycles with the CPU moving the data itself. For this reason we created a custom DMA engine using the synthesis support of memcpy by VIVADO_HLS. The code for VIVADO_HLS is configured to generate two interfaces. An AXI4Lite slave interface is used to load filter coefficients and send commands to the engine to enable the execution of the forward and inverse transform. An AXI4 M interface is used to load and store pixel and transformed data using the hardware implemented memcpy function through the ACP port. Figure 4 shows a section of the code corresponding to the forward wavelet transform synthesized into FPGA logic and memory by the VIVADO_HLS tools.

```
//read data
memcpy(buff_in, (float *)(memory + in_offset), (outwidth * 2 + 12)*sizeof(float));

wav_engine_master_label0:for (int i = 0; i<(outwidth + 6); i++)
{
        input_a = (data_t)buff_in[i * 2];
        input_b = (data_t)buff_in[i * 2 + 1];

        hpMult = coeff_register_hp[0] * shift_register[0];
        lpMult = coeff_register_lp[0] * shift_register[0];
        hpAcc = hpMult;
        lpAcc = lpMult;

        wav_engine_master_label1:for (int j = 1; j < 11; j++)
        {
                lpMult = coeff_register_lp[j] * shift_register[j];
                hpMult = coeff_register_hp[j] * shift_register[j];
                hpAcc += hpMult;
                lpAcc += lpMult;
                shift_register[j - 1] = shift_register[j + 1];
        }
        lpMult = coeff_register_lp[11] * shift_register[11];
        hpMult = coeff_register_hp[11] * shift_register[11];
        hpAcc += hpMult;
        lpAcc += lpMult;
        shift_register[10] = input_a;
        shift_register[11] = input_b;
        if (i > 5)
        {
                buff_out[i * 2 - 12] = (float)hpAcc;
                buff_out[i * 2 + 1 - 12] = (float)lpAcc;
        }
}
//write data
memcpy((float *)(memory + out_offset), buff_out, (outwidth * 2)*sizeof(float));
```

Fig. 4. Sample code Extraction for FPGA synthesis

The memcpy's move data between the external DDR memories and internal BRAMs and the for loops create the filters with the help of an internal shift register. The final if makes sure that only the correct outputs are written to the output buffers. Additional pragmas are used to ensure that the tool adds the require AXI interfaces and pipeline registers to obtain an initialization interval of one clock cycle so a new input enters the pipeline in each clock cycle. Notice that the current VIVADO_HLS tools do not pipeline the memcpy's that need to complete before the loop processing can start. It is important to note that all the logic required to implement these functions is created on the PL side by VIVADO_HLS. Control variables not shown in this sample code activate one of three possible modes that correspond to (1) filter coefficient loading, (2) forward transforms and (3) inverse transform. With this setup, we wrote a kernel level Linux driver to allocate memory that can be accessed by the accelerator with physical addresses and by the processor with virtual addresses. The driver uses the standard "memcpy" function, implemented in this case in software at the user level, for data transfer. For this to work, it is necessary to obtain the physical addresses at which the memory is created by the "kmalloc" calls in the kernel driver, and then use the memory-map calls "mmap" to obtain remapped virtual addresses in user space that can be used by standard "memcpy". Additionally, the Linux driver implements the "ioctl" function, which can be used to control how the data movements take place. In our case, we used this to create different read and write offsets to the kernel allocated memory. To increase the performance of the system we divided the kernel memory into two areas or buffers. This double buffering mechanism is used to parallelize the transfer and processing of data from user space to kernel space as illustrated in Fig. 5. This approach reduces latency and hardware complexity compared with buffering the whole image in the FPGA memory. The input and output buffers have a size of 4096 32-bit, divided into two areas of 2048 32-bit, which is suitable for an image width up to 2048 pixels. Table 1 shows the implementation complexity of this hardware wavelet engine.

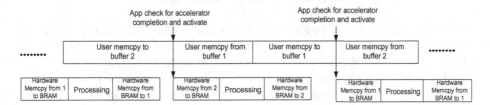

Fig. 5. Design of the kernel level Linux driver

Table 1. Implementation complexity of wavelet engine

Wavelet engine	Implementation complexity part: *xc7z020clg484-1*		
	Unitization	Available	Percentage
Registers	23412	106400	22 %
LUTs	17405	53200	32 %
Slices	7890	13300	59 %
BUFG	3	32	9 %

6   The System Architecture

This section describes the overall system architecture we implemented to capture and fuse the multi-sensor data. In this paper, we have used the ZYNQ-based ZC702 Evaluation Board running UBUNTU Linux OS. The overall architecture are shown in Fig. 6.

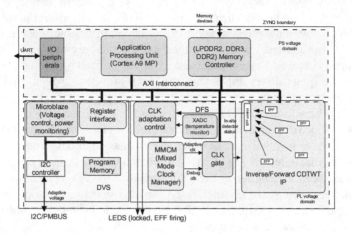

Fig. 6. Overview of the system design

The data transfer between the PS and the PL is done through the AXI interface. Both input videos are decoded into continuous pixel frames and sent to the wavelet hardware on the PL side for DT-CWT decomposition. The transformed coefficients are sent to the PS for fusion and then sent back to the wavelet hardware for inverse DT-CWT reconstruction. Since the whole system is running under Linux OS, the decoded and the fused videos are shown on screen using OpenCV funtions, with no external video connectors or cables required. Figure 7 demonstrates the video frame captured by the web-camera and the thermal-camera and the fused frame of the two. The original video captured by the web-camera was gray-scaled before fusing. A video demonstration is available as video 2^1 and a demo package available for the ZC702 board at[2].

---

[1] http://www.bris.ac.uk/engineering/research/microelectronics/enpower/demonstrations.html.
[2] https://drive.google.com/file/d/0B-8fEeeC7UJvR1FTRy1mUUVuS2c/view?usp=sharing.

7(a)Web-cam frame   7(b) Thermal-cam frame   7(c) fused frame

Fig. 7. Demonstration of the designed fusion system

7   Results Analysis and Comparison

This section compares the fusion performance and power consumption when the forward
and inverse DT-CWTs are executed by the ARM processor and the FPGA including
configurations that are voltage and frequency scale. Figure 8 shows the result of profiling
the application with and without hardware acceleration. The accelerator is run at two
frequencies of 200 MHz and 100 MHz and the bars represent the time used in seconds
by the corresponding functions. The CDTW functions are the most time consuming in
the ARM only version while they do not show up once the hardware is accelerated. This
analysis has been done with GNU GPROF function and indicates that the hardware
functions after acceleration cannot be detected by GPROF. Since these functions represent 70 % of total computation time this means that a total computation time of 1.5 s per
frame is reduced to 0.4 s with means that the whole fusion application is accelerated by
a factor of 3 when the FPGA performs the CDTW functions in parallel with the ARM
processor. It is important to note that while the accelerator is running the software needs
to prepare the next group of pixels and this task is done by the ARM that must move
data to an area that can be accessed by the hardware engine as shown in the upper part
of Fig. 5. This data movement is the performance limiting factor and not the hardware
computation and this means that the hardware configurations at 100 and 200 MHz obtain
the same performance level. The conclusion is that if we run the hardware slower we
can maintain the same level of performance but we can save power and energy by
decreasing the frequency and voltage levels. Figure 9 shows how reducing the FPGA
frequency from 200 MHz to 100 MHz and its voltage from 1 V to 0.8 V reduces power
and energy and increases the amount of time required to complete the DT-CWT transforms but this time still remains below the amount of time required by the processor to
prepare the next group of pixels so there is no negative effect. Figure 10 includes both
the PS and PL side of the Zynq device. Once the accelerators start working power
consumption increases compared with the software only solution however processing
time reduces by a factor of 3 and there is a similar effect on energy.

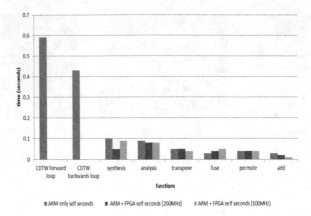

Fig. 8. Performance advantage of the hardware accelerated fusion algorithm for one frame (Color figure online)

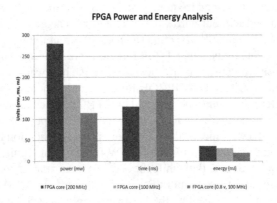

Fig. 9. Power and energy used by FPGA PL side (excluding processor PS side) (Color figure online)

The final step consists in exploring the further gains possible by computing to the limit and letting the PL to find its optimal frequency and voltage levels with the PS as the monitoring unit. To do this we enable the fully adaptive mode so that once the software tasks of moving and preparing the next data block are completed the PL reads a register in the wavelet engine to check for completion. The idea is that if the hardware engine has already completed it is running to fast. Then the voltage is reduced by the DVS and the DFS unit shown in Fig. 6 proceeds to find the maximum frequency that can be supported at that voltage level using the status of the detector flip-flops to guide this search. The process repeats until the software finds that the hardware wavelet is still working when it is checked. This indicates the point in which the software and hardware are running at approximately the same speed and not waiting for each other. Figure 11 shows the voltage and frequency points detected during this search from 1 V to a

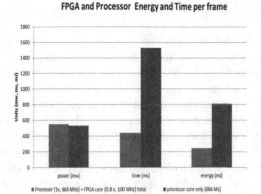

Fig. 10. Overall comparison of hardware accelerated and software only fusion (Color figure online)

minimum of 0.72 V and the corresponding optimal frequencies and power at each point. The voltage drops are done in 2 mV intervals by the DVS unit and the DFS unit determines the optimal frequency for each voltage level. The PL moves from operating at 1 V/168 MHz and 315 mW to 0.72 V/69 MHz and 79 mW which represents a reduction of power of 75 % without a negative performance effect. If there is a change in the operating conditions or workload size (e.g. frame size) then a new adaptation cycle can be started and a new voltage/frequency point will be found by the Elongate system that remains part of the bitstream.

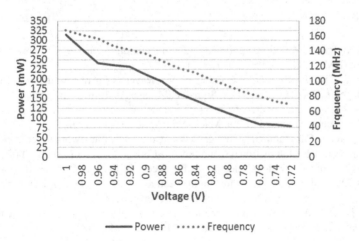

Fig. 11. Adaptive frequency and voltage search

8   Conclusions and Future Work

This paper has presented an energy efficient video fusion system based on the DT-CWT designed using high-level synthesis tools. In our design, the most compute intensive tasks, namely the forward and inverse DT-CWT were mapped to a closely coupled FPGA with a customized Linux kernel level driver to release the processor load. The performance and energy consumption of fusing input frames was compared considering configurations when the fusion process was executed by only the ARM processor and the ARM with FPGA accelerators scaled to different levels of voltage and frequency. Comparing to the execution using the ARM processor only, using the FPGA can save 70 % of the execution time of the forward and inverse DT-CWT execution respectively. Once the whole application is taking into account a speed factor of 3 is obtained compared with the ARM only solution. The experiments also show that the FPGA is generally too fast and the limiting factor is the preparation of data in memory for the wavelet engines that must be executed by the ARM processor. Exploiting this characteristic and the Elongate adaptive voltage scaling technology it is possible to reduce power and energy without affecting overall performance. The results with this additional option show a reduction in power by up to 75 % compared with running the FPGA at full throttle.

Acknowledgements. We would like to thank the support received from EPSRC for this work part of the ENPOWER project: http://www.bris.ac.uk/engineering/research/microelectronics/enpower/.

References

1. Sahu, D.K., Parsai, M.P.: Different image fusion techniques – a critical review. Int. J. Mod. Eng. Res. (IJMER) **2**(5), 4298–4301 (2012)
2. Nikolov, S., Hill, P., Bull, D., Canagarajah, N.: Wavelets for image fusion. In: Petrosian, A.A., Meyer, F.G. (eds.) Wavelets in Signal and Image Analysis: From Theory To Practice, pp. 213–241. Springer, Dordrecht (2001)
3. Toet, A.: Hierarchical image fusion. Mach. Vis. Appl. **3**, 1–11 (1990)
4. Hill, P., Bull, D., Canagarajah, C.: Image fusion using a new framework for complex wavelet transforms. In: IEEE International Conference on Image Processing (ICIP 2005), Genova, Italy. Institute of Electrical and Electronics Engineers (IEEE), pp. II–1338–II–1341 (2005)
5. Jasiunas, D., et al.: Image fusion for uninhabited airborne vehicles. In: Proceedings of the International Conference (FPT), pp. 348–351, December 2002
6. Sim, O., Ivine, J.: An FPGA implementation of pattern-selective pyramidal image fusion. In: Proceedings of the International Conference (FPL), pp. 1–4 (2006)
7. Yunsheng, Q. et al.: The real-time processing system of infrared and LLL image fusion. In: Proceedings of the International. Symposium on Photoelectron Detection Image process, pp. 66231Y–1–66231Y–9 (2008)
8. Song, Y., et al.: Implementation of real-time Laplacian pyramid image fusion processing based on FPGA. In: Proceedings of the SPIE, vol. 6833, pp. 16–18 (2007)
9. Mohamed, M.A., El-Den, B.M.: Implementation of image fusion techniques using FPGA. Int. J. Comput. Sci. Netw. Secur. **10**(5), 95–102 (2010)

10. Tao, L., et.al.: A multi-sensor image fusion and enhancement system for assisting drivers in poor lighting conditions. In: Proceedings of the Applied Imagery and Pattern Recognition Workshop pp. 1–6 (2005)
11. Gudis, E., et al.: An embedded vision services framework for heterogeneous accelerators. In: Proceedings of the Computer Vision and Pattern Recognition Workshops, pp. 598–603 (2013)
12. Singh, R.P., Dwivedi, R.D., Negi, S.: Comparative evaluation of DWT and DT-CWT for image fusion and de-noising. Int. J. Appl. Inf. Syst. (IJAIS) **4**, 40–45 (2012)
13. Nunez-Yanez, J.L.: Adaptive voltage scaling with in-situ detectors in commercial FPGAs. IEEE Trans. Comput. **64**(1), 45–53 (2015)

An Efficient Hardware Architecture for Block Based Image Processing Algorithms

Tomasz Kryjak$^{(\boxtimes)}$, Marek Gorgon, and Mateusz Komorkiewicz

AGH University of Science and Technology,
Al. Mickiewicza 30, 30-059 Kraków, Poland
{tomasz.kryjak,mago}@agh.edu.pl, komorkiewicz@gmail.com

Abstract. In this paper a novel method for data reordering in a video stream is presented. It can be used in high performance vision algorithms that require block based image processing. For case study a block based optical flow histogram computation application was selected. The proposed solution allows for a 2.3x and 6.3x speed-up for fixed-point and floating-point calculations respectively. This enables real-time operations for 1920 × 1080 pixels or higher resolutions.

Keywords: FPGA · Image processing · Block processing · Block histogram · HOG · Optical flow histogram · Data reordering

1 Introduction

Block based image processing is an often used technique in image processing and analysis. This approach is used in algorithms like: HOG (Histogram of Oriented Gradients) [5], HOOF (Histogram of Optical Flow) [12], GLCM (Gray-Level Co-occurrence Matrix) [1], image comparison in CBIR (Context Based Image Retrieval) systems [15] and face detection and recognition using LBP (Local Binary Patterns) [3,4]. These algorithms are often used in vision systems that require real-time image processing. A good example is pedestrian detection using HOG features and SVM (Support Vector Machine) classifier in ADAS (Automated Driver Assistance Systems) and advanced automated video surveillance applications.

FPGA (Field Programmable Gate Arrays) devices are a proven platform for implementing high-performance vision systems. Their main advantages are fine-grained computation parallelization, energy efficiency and the ability to work with multiple input and output devices. Moreover, heterogeneous solutions, referred to as SoC (System on Chip), are gaining more and more attention recently. They combine reconfigurable logic resources with a quite efficient ARM processor in one housing and allow the creation of integrated hardware-software data processing systems.

In a typical embedded vision system pixels from the input device (usually a digital camera) are transmitted as stream, pixel by pixel, line by line, frame by frame. Thus, in a single line data which belongs to different blocks (e.g. block

© Springer International Publishing Switzerland 2016
V. Bonato et al. (Eds.): ARC 2016, LNCS 9625, pp. 54–65, 2016.
DOI: 10.1007/978-3-319-30481-6_5

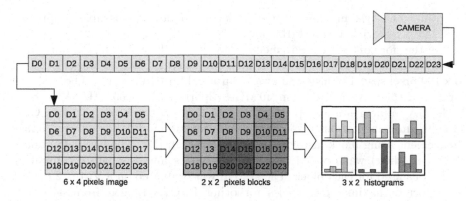

Fig. 1. Image acquisition, serial transmission, image forming, dividing pixels into blocks and histograms computation (Color figure online)

histograms), is present. This is illustrated in Fig. 1. The computation of the block histogram requires gathering the context of size corresponding to the used block (4×4 in the example) or storing intermediate results between the lines.

To assure real-time image processing, it is required that all operations for a single pixel are performed in one pixel clock cycle (with a certain simplification). In some cases it is possible to use clock multiplication inside the FPGA, however only for lower video stream resolutions. It should be noted that HD video (High Definition – 1920 × 1080 @ 60 fps) uses a pixel clock of 148.5 MHz. Doubling this frequency results is possible, but requires very careful hardware design. Increasing it four times exceeds the capabilities of modern reconfigurable devices. Another possibility is the use of two or more computing elements (algorithm parallelization). However, it has several disadvantages: more logic resources are required and additional, quite complicated logic, which allows to integrate the data stored in different computing elements has to be designed.

In the literature several works related to embedded image block processing systems, mainly histogram computation, can be found. One of the first was [9], where the histogram was computed in 9 non-overlapping regions of the image with the use of 9 separate FPGA devices. In-unit and multi-module methods used for 20 × 20 histogram block computation parallelization were presented in [6].

An adaptive histogram equalization system was described in [7]. Histograms were computed in overlapping blocks. A novel technique with horizontal and vertical buffers for temporary histogram values storage was proposed, which allowed for data reuse. The system was implemented in a Virex 4 FPGA and worked with 640 × 480 pixel video stream (maximal operating frequency 209 MHz). The main disadvantage was the high memory utilization. Histogram computation in 5 × 5 pixel blocks for HOG based people detection was proposed in [10]. Groups of 5 pixels belonging to consecutive blocks were processed in parallel. Then partial results for a block were gathered in a context and combined into the final histogram. The system implemented in Virtex 5 device was able to process 320×240 pixels with a 44.85 MHz clock.

A system for contrast enhancement in low vision, based on histogram equalization was described in [2]. The whole image was divided into 35 blocks (7×7) of 100×100 pixel size. The histogram was computed for 64 bins only. The achieved operating frequency ranged from 40 MHz (Spartan 3) to 69 MHz (Virtex 6). The FPGA implementation speed-up was 15 and 7.5 times compared to CPU and GPU implementations respectively. A hardware module for infrared image enhancement using block histogram was proposed in [13]. The 640×480 image (14 bit encoding) was divided into 80×60 blocks and a separate computing module was used for each block. The system was evaluated on a Virtex 2 device. The reported maximal frequencies for other FPGAs ranged from 44.7 MHz (Spartan 6) to 101 MHz (Virtex 5).

Analysis of the presented work reveals that the dominant method of obtaining real-time processing involves parallelization of histogram computation modules (one module per block). However, this approach has two major drawbacks. Firstly, it can be used only for a small number of blocks, due to usually limited logic resources. Second, during operation, in a given clock cycle only one module is preforming data processing and the rest is idle. This leads to very suboptimal resource utilization.

In this paper a different solution for block image processing acceleration is proposed. It assumes very fast computations for consecutive pixels from the incoming data stream. However, for HD resolution and beyond, where the spacing between pixels is less than 7 ns, this is quite problematic due to latencies of FPGA modules e.g. arithmetic units or block RAM memories. Especially, when the operation requires incrementing or adding values from the same memory location. The main contribution of this work is the proposed data reordering scheme. After applying it, data belonging to the same block, which may require storing in the same memory location, are separated from each other.

The rest of this paper is organized as follows. A detailed analysis of the block image processing issue using as example the block histogram computation is presented in Sect. 2. The proposed data reordering solutions are discussed in Sect. 3 and their hardware implementations are described in Sect. 4. An exemplary application of optical flow block histogram calculation is shown in Sect. 5. The article ends with a short summary.

2   Block Histogram Calculation Issue

As already mentioned in order to process the data stream and compute the block histogram it is necessary to perform all computations in a single clock cycle. In case of a high throughput video stream it may by problematic or even impossible. The discussed task involves the following steps: reading from the memory, data updating (e.g. incrementation or aggregation) and writing back to the memory. Assuming the use of an asynchronous element for data processing, two memory accesses are required. For the most commonly used synchronous RAM this results in two clock cycles latency. Thus, when using a typical single-port RAM module, it is difficult the meet the one pixel per cycle requirement[1].

Another solution is the use of a dual port block RAM memory (BRAM) available in FPGA devices. In this case, reading and writing is carried out independently. However, the designer must ensure correct handling of possible collisions (read and write from/to the same memory cell). It should be noted, that the latency of the computing element in this architecture must be zero[2]. In order to deeper investigate this issues, a simple testbench consisting of two BRAM modules connected to adder inputs and one BRAM connected to its output was used. All presented in this paper results were obtained using the ISE Design Suite and post place & route reports for Virtex 6 (XC6VLX240T) FPGA device.

The available in Xilinx FPGAs BRAM memory can work with latencies of 1 (default), 2 or 3 clock cycles. In addition, it is possible to configure the use of output registers: the lack of registers (REG NO), core type registers (CORE REG), primitive type registers (PRIO REG) or full registers (FULL REG) [14]. The simplest configuration (latency 1, NO REG) allows for a 213 MHz frequency, and the most complex (latency 3, FULL REG) 402 MHz. Of course, at the expense of logic resources.

A similar experiment can be performed for a 32-bit, fixed-point adder. For a module implemented directly in reconfigurable logic the following values were obtained: latency 0, 1, 2 – frequency respectively 318 MHz, 368 MHz, 409 MHz. For a DSP based solution: latency 0, 1, 2 – frequency respectively 257 MHz, 360 MHz, 539 MHz. Even bigger differences are visible for single precision floating-point adders. For latency 0 and 1 the frequency is 64 MHz, for 4–235 MHz, 8–341 MHz and 12–411 MHz.

The presented data indicates, that for high throughput video stream processing in algorithms based on block histograms or, more generally, on image block operations, the possibility of using high latency modules, especially for floating-point operations, would be very advantageous.

3   The Proposed Data Reordering

The main performance limitation of the block histogram computation module is the one clock cycle update requirement. It origins from the case when processing two consecutive pixels belonging to the same image block and also having the same value (i.e. belonging to the same bin) requires access to the same memory cell. This is shown is Fig. 2(a) – pixels DO and D1 (D0 = D1), D2 and D3 (D2 = D3) etc. The potential conflict could be avoided if the adjacent pixels in the data stream would belong to different image blocks, as then they can not share the same memory. Therefore, the proposed solution is based on data reordering. An example is shown in Fig. 2(b). In this solution, pixels belonging to the same block are no closer than three clock cycles from each other. Thus,

---

[1] In some cases, mainly for lower image resolutions, it is possible to use frequency multiplication.

[2] Otherwise it is not possible to handle a collision.

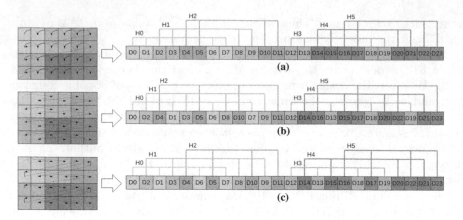

Fig. 2. Example of data reordering: (a) standard order, (b) line reordering, (c) two blocks reordering (Color figure online)

computation modules with latency 3 can be used resulting in higher maximal frequency. It should be emphasized that the presented reordering does not interfere with vertical block arrangement i.e. pixels of the first three blocks (D0–D11) are not "mixed" with pixels from the next three blocks (D12–D23). This is important for logic reuse, as usually the basic image processing unit in these types of applications is a single line of blocks (in this example two image lines).

Another data reordering scheme is presented in Fig. 2(c). It is less intuitive, since the changes do not take place within a single line but in smaller groups of pixels – in the presented case twice the width of the block (i.e. 4). Within a group (D0–D3), first the even (D0, D2) and then the odd pixels (D1, D3) are transmitted. This scheme allows for a maximum latency of 2. However, compared to the solution presented in Fig. 2(b), it is simpler to implement in hardware as it requires fewer logic resources.

The discussed reordering schemes do not include all possibilities. However, the biggest challenge is to find such a solution that on the one hand is simple to implement in hardware (high speed, low use of resources), and on the other hand provides adequate separation of data from each other.

4   Hardware Architecture for Data Reordering

The most intuitive solution is the use of FIFO buffers in number equal to the number of image blocks. Each incoming pixel is stored in the buffer corresponding to the block to which it belongs. The readout is performed cyclically – one pixel from each buffer. Unfortunately, the main disadvantages of this approach are the high logic and memory utilization and the need to implement a complex multiplexer for data extraction from various buffers (Fig. 3).

In this work a different architecture is proposed. It uses a single BRAM memory module capable of buffering one line of the image. Through appropriate address sequence generation and the use of the READ_FIRST mode (enables to read the old value and store the new one at same address in one clock cycle) it is possible to perform data reordering. In the example the image width is equal to 6 pixels, thus it is necessary to use a memory consisting of 6 cells (designated A0–A5). The module's operation is broken down into epochs i.e. processing data from one line.

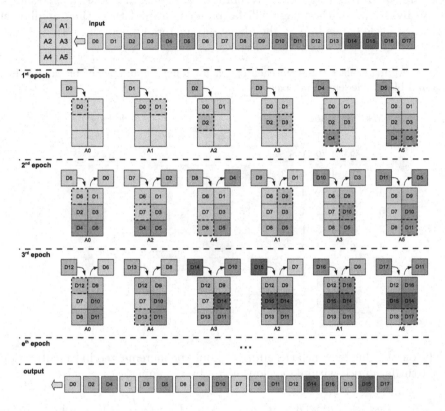

Fig. 3. First three epochs of memory data storage for pipelined stream reordering (Color figure online)

In the first epoch, the input data is stored in the memory. No memory reads are required. In the second epoch, the data must be read form top to bottom of each memory column. This allows to obtain the desired reordering. In this case, addresses are incremented by two (offset 2) with modulo 6 + 1. As a result, the input sequence (D0, D1, D2, D3, D4, D5) is reordered to (D0, D2, D4, D1, D3, D5).

In the third epoch, it is necessary to use another address generation method – the offset equals 4. This allows to obtain the sequence (D6, D8, D10, D7, D9, D11). In subsequent epochs (not presented in the figure) addresses are incremented by 3 (epoch four) and 1 (epoch five). Offset value 1 means the return to the memory configuration after the first epoch i.e. end of the cycle. The output sequence is presented in the bottom of the image. Neighbouring pixels (e.g. D0 and D1) are now split by two other pixels (e.g. D2 and D4). Therefore, the presented reordering solves the above described problem with histogram computation.

Let M denote the image width, K the block width (it is assumed that the blocks are square) and $M_B = M/K$ number of blocks in a line (it is assumed that K divides M or the image will be padded to fulfil this). The number of epochs in a cycle depending on the above parameters are shown in Table 1.

Table 1. Address offset values in each epoch for different number of blocks per line (M_B) and block side length in pixels (K)

M_B	K	Epoch										Cycle length
		0	1	2	3	4	5	6	7	8	9	
2	2	1	2	1	...	...	...	...	...	...	...	2
3	2	1	2	4	3	1	...	...	...	...	...	4
4	2	1	2	4	1	...	...	...	...	...	...	3
5	2	1	2	4	8	7	5	1	...	...	...	6
3	3	1	3	1	...	...	...	...	...	...	...	2
4	3	1	3	9	5	4	1	...	...	...	...	5
5	3	1	3	9	13	11	5	1	...	...	...	6
4	4	1	4	1	...	...	...	...	...	...	...	2
5	4	1	4	16	7	9	17	11	6	5	1	9

The offset value by which the address should be incremented in each iteration of a particular epoch within a cycle is given by the equation:

$$offset(e) = mod(K^e, M - 1) = K^e - floor(\frac{K^e}{M-1})(M-1) \qquad (1)$$

In real-life applications the block width may take different values (8, 16, or even 32). For such parameters, the number of epochs may be even greater than 1000. This causes considerable difficulties in the calculation of the Eq. (1)[3].

A scheme of the proposed hardware module for the data reordering shown in Fig. 2(b) is presented in Fig. 4. It consists of a *BRAM memory* and address sequence generation logic. On the basis of the dv (data valid) signal the iteration and epoch number is determined. The values given by Eq. (1) have been precomputed and are stored in a LUT (look up table). The current address is stored in the register and is incremented by a certain value (obtained from LUT) in each iteration. The remaining logic is responsible for checking whether the calculated

---

[3] In the work a special numeric package PariGP [11] and a variant of Eq. (1) with function *floor* was used.

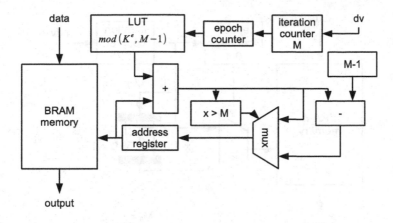

Fig. 4. General hardware module for data reordering

address does not exceed the size of the memory and, if necessary, for performing a modulo operation (by subtraction).

One potential drawback of the proposed architecture is its complexity, which may result in reduced maximum operating frequency. For example, a module designed for HD i.e. 1920 × 1080 image resolution and 16 pixel wide blocks obtains 183 MHz maximum operation frequency and provides a 120 clock cycles "gap" between data belonging to the same blocks. Comparing this with the maximum frequency of adders it can be concluded that for fixed-point operations this approach does not lead to any improvement. However, for floating-point arithmetic it is enables real-time processing of a HD video stream.

The other proposed architecture (reordering scheme from Fig. 2(c)) allows to reorder the data in fewer number of blocks. The resulting "gap" between samples belonging to the same block may be different, but it is always at least N clock cycles. In the spacial case, when the number of blocks is equal to the block width and additionally both numbers are powers of 2, the full cycle involves only two epochs. This allows a significant simplification of architecture – Fig. 5.

The simplified architecture consists of an *iteration counter* and a one-bit *epoch counter*. In the first epoch the iteration value is directly used as the address. In the second, the number is split into two equal parts, which are then swapped. Two configurations were analysed: 8 blocks 8 pixels wide (8 × 8) and 16 blocks 16 pixels wide (16 × 16). Their maximum frequencies are very high, respectively 463 MHz and 432 MHz and the resource usage is very low (<150 FF, 40 LUT6, 1 BRAM)[4]. It is worth noting that most algorithms involving block based processing can operate on blocks with size equal to powers of 2 (or can be implemented in this way without a significant loss of effectiveness).

---

[4] Basic hardware resources available in an FPGA: FF – flip-flops, LUT6 - six-input LUT modules, BRAM – block RAM memory of size 18 or 36 kB, SLICE – unit grouping logic resources in Xilinx FPGA, DSP48 – hardware arithmetic unit.

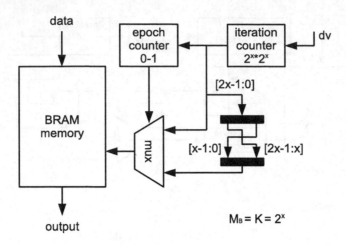

Fig. 5. Simple hardware module for data reordering

5   Case Study – Block Histograms of Optical Flow

The term optical flow refers to a vector field describing the displacement of pixels between two consecutive video frames. It is widely used in many vision systems, among others, for moving object detection and their speed and direction analysis, object classification (e.g. cars versus people), structure from motion algorithms, tracking, human behaviour analysis and UAV (Unmanned Aerial Vehicle) navigation. This subject is discussed in details in [8].

The characteristics of optical flow computations algorithms, which discussion is beyond the scope of this article, results in unreliable information about direction and speed of single pixels movement. Also, using averaging over a given area (e.g. a single object) does not always provide good results – mainly due to noise, the final value may be disturbed. A good solution seems to be the use of histograms calculated for separate image blocks. To reduce the impact of noise, in addition to the direction, the length of the vector (magnitude) should be used.

For this case study, the following parameters were used: block size 16×16, maximal image resolution 1920×1088 (additional 8 lines due to used block size). Also it was assumed that the optical flow between two consecutive frames was computed in another module and only the output i.e. magnitude values were analysed. Schematically, the proposed module is shown in Fig. 6.

The inputs are the *magnitude value* and histogram *bin number* (quantized angle). The module *block address resolver* generates addresses (`block`) using video synchronization signals – *video sync*. In addition, it returns a flag indicating the *first* and *last* sample in a block. The *readback unit* is responsible for reading the resulting bin values after completing the computations (i.e. *result*). Also, a *clear* operation is necessary to reset the memory values to 0.

If the adder latency is 0 and memory latency 1, than the *reorder unit* is not necessary. However, in the "worst case" the maximum latency can reach

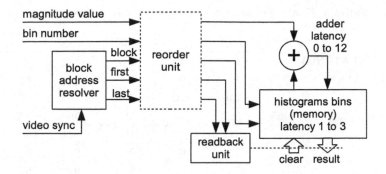

Fig. 6. Hardware architecture for efficient histogram computation

15 (12 adder + 3 memory). In this case, the *reordering module* with a minimum "gap" of at least 16 clock cycles is required. During the experiment a variety of configurations were evaluated: fixed-point adders with latency 0, 1, 2, single precision floating-point adders with latency 0, 1, 4, 8, 12 and BRAM memory with latency 1, 2 or 3. In total 58 different architectures were generated. The most important results are summarized in Tables 2 and 3.

Table 2. Fixed point histogram computation architectures – 32 bit adder

	LUT			DSP48		
MEMORY LATENCY	1	1	2	2	3	3
ADDER LATENCY	0	1	0	1	0	1
FF	92	237	205	237	493	525
LUT 6	114	150	182	179	242	220
SLICE	47	62	64	65	212	242
BRAM 18	0	0	0	0	0	0
BRAM 36	8	9	9	9	9	9
DSP48	0	0	0	0	0	0
MAX CLK	170 MHz	236 MHz	216 MHz	329 MHz	276 MHz	396 MHz
Speedup	1x	1.4x	1.3x	1.9x	1.6x	2.3x

In the case of fixed-point calculations (Table 2) the basic architecture allows for a maximum frequency of 170 MHz. The best results were obtained for an adder with latency 1 and memory with latency 3 (speed-up 2.3x).

For single-precision floating point arithmetic (Table 3) the best results were obtained for an adder with latency 12 and memory with latency 3 (speed-up 6.3x). It should be noted that the basic architecture (without data reordering) allows only for 61 MHz maximum frequency and does not meet real-time requirements for a 1920 × 1080 pixels video stream.

Table 3. Floating point histogram computation architectures

	LUT			DSP48		
MEMORY LATENCY	1	1	2	2	3	3
ADDER LATENCY	0	12	0	12	0	12
FF	92	746	205	746	493	1034
LUT 6	465	509	520	557	568	585
SLICE	149	211	177	195	321	401
BRAM 18	0	0	0	0	0	0
BRAM 36	8	9	9	9	9	9
DSP48	0	0	0	0	0	0
MAX CLK	61 MHz	252 MHz	65 MHz	369 MHz	71 MHz	383 MHz
Speedup	1x	4.1x	1.1x	6.0x	1.2x	6.3x

The obtained results show that the proposed data reordering scheme allows to create a block based image processing architecture capable of operating at higher frequencies. It should be noted that the related increase in the logical resource utilization is relatively small, especially in absolute terms due to the large number of available logical resources in today's FPGA devices. Furthermore, a solution using a simple parallelization scheme would be much more expensive due to required logical resources.

6   Summary

In this paper a concept and a hardware architecture for data reordering in video stream, which enables the acceleration of block based image processing operations, is presented. Two reordering schemes are proposed, and the second one is used in a case study – a system for calculating block histograms of optical flow. For fixed point calculations (32 bit) a 2.3x speed-up and for single precision floating point a 6.3x speed-up is achieved. The designed module uses very few logic resources.

The data reordering technique can be used not only for block histogram applications, but also for other block based algorithms e.g.: minimum and maximum in the block, SVM classification, calculating sums or averages in blocks, encryption, compression etc. It should also be noted that the extension of the maximum latency also allows the use RAM modules with a longer access time. Separation of pixels within the same block allows to perform more complex operations on a single data sample, which may be important in many advanced embedded vision algorithms. Additionally, the obtained clock frequency indicates the possibility of implementing this type of operation for images with resolutions greater than HD.

Acknowledgments. The work presented in this paper was supported by AGH University of Science and Technology project number 15.11.120.476 (first) and 11.11.120.612 (second author).

References

1. Akoushideh, A., Shahbahrami, A., Maybodi, B.-N.: High performance implementation of texture features extraction algorithms using FPGA architecture. J. Real-Time Image Process. **9**(1), 141–157 (2014)
2. Cañada, P.M., Morillas, C., Ureña, R., Gómez López, J.M., Pelayo, F.J.: Embedded system for contrast enhancement in low-vision. J. Syst. Archit. **59**(1), 30–38 (2013)
3. Cavalcanti, G.D.C., Tsang, I.R., Reis, J.R.: Recognition of partially occluded face using Gradientface and Local Binary Patterns. In: IEEE International Conference on Systems, Man, and Cybernetics (SMC), pp. 2324–2329 (2012)
4. Chiu, C.-T., Cyuan-Jhe, W.: Texture classification based low order local binary pattern for face recognition. In: 18th IEEE International Conference on Image Processing (ICIP), pp. 3017–3020 (2011)
5. Dalal, N., Triggs, B.: Histograms of oriented gradients for human detection. In: IEEE Computer Society Conference on Computer Vision and Pattern Recognition (CVPR), vol. 1, pp. 886–893 (2005)
6. Jamro, E., Wielgosz, M., Wiatr, K.: FPGA implementaton of strongly parallel histogram equalization. In: IEE Design and Diagnostics of Electronic Circuits and Systems, pp. 1–6 (2007)
7. Kokufuta, K., Maruyama, T.: Real-time processing of contrast limited adaptive histogram equalization on FPGA. In: International Conference on Field Programmable Logic and Applications (FPL), pp. 155–158 (2010)
8. Komorkiewicz, M., Kryjak, T., Gorgon, M.: Efficient hardware implementation of the Horn-Schunck algorithm for high-resolution real-time dense optical flow sensor. Sensors **14**(2), 2860–2891 (2014)
9. Kotoulas, L., Andreadis, I.: Colour histogram content-based image retrieval and hardware implementation. IEE Proc. Circ. Devices Syst. **150**(5), 387–393 (2003)
10. Negi, K., Dohi, K., Shibata, Y., Oguri, K.: Deep pipelined one-chip FPGA implementation of a real-time image-based human detection algorithm. In: International Conference on Field-Programmable Technology (FPT), pp. 1–8 (2011)
11. The PARI Group: ARI/GP, version 2.5.0 (2011). http://pari.math.u-bordeaux.fr/
12. Perš, J., Sulić, V., Kristan, M., Perše, M., Polanec, K., Kovačič, S.: Histograms of optical flow for efficient representation of body motion. Pattern Recogn. Lett. **31**(11), 1369–1376 (2010)
13. Schatz, V.: Low-latency histogram equalization for infrared image sequences: a hardware implementation. J. Real-Time Image Proc. **8**(2), 193–206 (2013)
14. Xilinx: Virtex-6 FPGA Memory Resources, User Guide, UG363 v1.6. (2011)
15. Zhu, J., Hoi, S.C.H., Lyu, M.R., Yan, S.: Near-duplicate keyframe retrieval by semi-supervised learning and nonrigid image matching. ACM Trans. Multimedia Comput. Commun. Appl. **7**(1), 4:1–4:24 (2011)

An FPGA Stereo Matching Processor Based on the Sum of Hamming Distances

Abiel Aguilar-González$^{(\boxtimes)}$ and Miguel Arias-Estrada

Instituto Nacional de Astrofísica Óptica y Electrónica (INAOE),
Luis Enrique Erro # 1, Tonantzintla, 72840 Puebla, Mexico
{abiel,ariasmo}@inaoep.mx
http://www.inaoep.mx/

Abstract. Stereo matching is a useful algorithm to infer depth information from two or more of images and has uses in mobile robotics, three-dimensional building mapping and three-dimensional reconstruction of objects. In area-based algorithms, the similarity between one pixel of an image (key frame) and one pixel of another image is measured using a correlation index computed on neighbors of these pixels (correlation windows). In order to preserve edges, the use of small correlation windows is necessary while for homogeneous areas, large windows are required. In addition, to improve the execution time, stereo matching algorithms often are implemented in dedicated hardware such as FPGA or GPU devices. In this article, we present an FPGA stereo matching processor based on the Sum of Hamming Distances (SHD). We propose a grayscale-based similarity criterion, which allows separating the objects and background from the correlation window. By using the similarity criterion, it is possible to improve the performance of any grayscale-based correlation coefficient and reach high performance for homogeneous areas and edges. The developed FPGA architecture reaches high performance compared to other real-time stereo matching algorithms, up to 10 % more accuracy and enables to increase the processing speed near to 20 megapixels per second.

Keywords: Stero matching · FPGA · Sum of Hamming Distances · CAPH

1 Introduction

The perception of depth from images is an important task of computer vision systems and has been used in several applications such as recognition, detection, three-dimensional reconstruction and positioning systems for mobile robots [12,16]. There are several techniques to compute depth from images, such as matching all pixels using correlation windows [13,21], matching interest points or features [19,24] and optimization techniques based on dynamic programming or graph cuts [9,10]. In case of matching all pixels with windows, the correspondence between stereo pairs and the geometrical configuration of the stereo camera allows obtaining dense disparity maps. To obtain a dense disparity map it is necessary to measure the similarity of all points in the stereo pair.

© Springer International Publishing Switzerland 2016
V. Bonato et al. (Eds.): ARC 2016, LNCS 9625, pp. 66–77, 2016.
DOI: 10.1007/978-3-319-30481-6_6

1.1 Related Work

In this research, we are interested in dense disparity maps. There are several dense stereo matching algorithms in the literature. To reach real-time processing, stereo matching algorithms are often implemented in FPGA devices. [6] presents an FPGA module for computing dense disparity maps. The developed module enables a hardware-based cellular automata (CA) parallel-pipelined design. The presented algorithm provides high processing speed at the expense of accuracy, with large scalability in terms of disparity levels. In [4] a fuzzy approach for computing dense disparity maps is presented. The FPGA architecture determines the similarity between pixels using a Fuzzy Inference System. Although the proposed algorithm increases the accuracy in the computed disparities, it is sensible to the untextured pixels and their performance in untextured regions is limited. In [5] an FPGA module for computing dense disparity maps using a vergence control is proposed. Different to previous work, the developed module constantly estimates the required range of disparity levels upon a given stereo image set using a vergence control. In [1] a correlation-edge distance approach is described. By using a geometric feature (the Euclidean distance between the selected point and the nearest left edge), the developed FPGA architecture has low utilization of hardware resources, high speed processing and offers high performance for low disparity levels. However, the accuracy decreases for large disparity values. In [14] an adaptive window algorithm based on the SAD algorithm is proposed. The developed FPGA architecture offers more accuracy with respect to other FPGA-based stereo matching algorithms in the literature and allows to increasing the processing speed but large correlation window's sizes are required and hardware resource consumption is high.

1.2 Motivation and Scope

The main disadvantage of matching all pixels with windows is selecting the correlation window's size. Large window size values allow determining the correct correlation values in untextured areas. However, large window sizes imply high computational demand and erroneous values due to the averaging effect of comparing an object and the background. On the other hand, small window sizes imply low computational demand but the correlation coefficient measurement is sensitive to noise hence, erroneous values at untextured regions are generated. If a correlation window large enough to avoid noise is used, high accuracy in untextured areas must be reached. However, edges be slightly blurred and erroneous values at depth discontinuities are generated. If the objects and the background in the correlation window are separated, it is possible to compute the correlation index using pixels of the same object to the reference pixel. This allows maintaining high performance at untextured areas whilst blurring edges are avoided. i.e., it allows retaining the high performance characteristics of the small and large window sizes. To separate the objects and background from a correlation window, we propose the use of a grayscale-based similarity criterion.

The rest of the article is organized as follows: Sect. 2 presents the proposed algorithm. In Sect. 3, the FPGA architecture for the proposed algorithm is described. Experimental results for different synthetic stereo pairs and performance comparisons regarding to other algorithms in the literature are detailed in Sect. 4. Finally, Sect. 5 concludes this article.

2   The Proposed Algorithm

Figure 1(a) shows many objects at different depths. When any correlation coefficient is computed using all the pixels of the correlation window the averaging effect yields errors on the estimated disparity as shown in Fig. 1(b). On the other hand, Fig. 1(c) shows a neighborhood in which only the pixels that are the projections of the same object are used. In this case retained pixels are similar to the central pixel and they have the same disparity as shown in Fig. 1(d). Although separating objects and background can improve the accuracy of the stereo match algorithms, in previous work it has been addressed via segmentation algorithms or super pixels which have high mathematical complexity and whose real-time implementation is complex, [3, 7, 22]. However, in this research, we separate objects and background using a similarity criterion based on the grayscale levels of the correlation window. The proposed similarity criterion allows implementing in dedicated hardware for real-time processing with low hardware resource consumption and parallel-pipelined design.

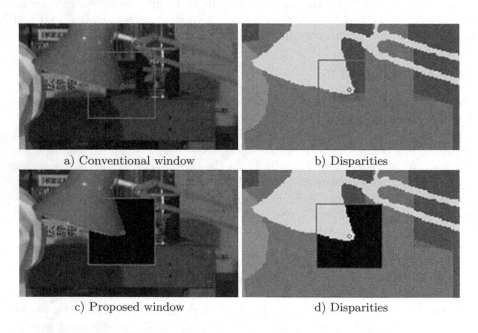

a) Conventional window   b) Disparities

c) Proposed window   d) Disparities

Fig. 1. Tsukuba scene

In the proposed algorithm, a fixed size window is centering on each pixel of the reference image, but only the pixels selected by the similarity criterion are used to compute the correlation coefficient. Any grayscale-based correlation coefficient such as Sum of Absolute Differences (SAD), Sum of Squared Differences (SSD), Normalized Cross Correlation (NCC) and so on can be modified using this technique. However, to reach real-time processing, the proposed algorithm is inspired by the Sum of Hamming Distances (SHD) [8] since it consists in binary register operations and it can be implemented in FPGA devices with low hardware resource consumption and parallel-pipelined design. In this case, we propose to use Eqs. 1 and 2,

$$C(x, y, z) = \sum_{i=-w, j=-w}^{i=w, j=w} \mathcal{H}\{Q\},$$
(1)

$$Q = \text{XOR}(I_l(x + i, y + j) \cdot \lambda(x, y, i, j),$$
$$I_r(x + z + i, y + j) \cdot \lambda(x, y, i, j)),$$
(2)

where the parameter $\lambda(x, y, i, j)$, is equal to one for all pixels in the correlation window which correspond to same object that the center pixel, zero otherwise. $(2 \cdot w + 1)^2$ is the correlation window size. z is range from 0 to $z_{\max}$ (maximum expected disparity). $I_l(a, b)$, $I_r(a, b)$ are binary registers for the pixels from the left and right images, respectively and the $\mathcal{H}$ operator is defined as shown in Eq. 3,

$$\mathcal{H}\{Q\} = \sum_{k=1}^{k=\text{bpp}} q(k),$$
(3)

where Q is a binary register and bpp is the size of the register Q, i.e., the bits per pixel for the input images.

2.1   Technique to Define the Similarity Criterion

We can assume that two pixels have different disparity levels when there is a significant difference between their greyscale values. Hence, we define $\lambda(x, y, i, j)$ as one only when the grey level $I_l(x+i, y+j)$ is close to the grey level of the pixel $I_l(x, y)$, as shown in Eq. 2. Where $\varphi(x, y)$ is the maximum acceptable difference between the greyscale values defined as shown in Eq. 4,

$$\lambda(x, y, i, j) = \begin{cases} 1, & |I_l(x + i, y + j) - I_l(x, y)| \leq \varphi(x, y) \\ 0, & \text{otherwise}, \end{cases}$$
(4)

the value of the φ parameter must be related to the uniformity of the greyscale values in the correlation window. To compute the φ value it is proposed to use Eq. 5.

$$\varphi(x, y) = \frac{\sum_{i=-w}^{i=w} \sum_{j=-w}^{j=w} |I_l(x, y) - I_l(x + i, y + j)|}{(2 \cdot w + 1)^2}$$
(5)

2.2   Disparity Computation

In standard stereo algorithms, the disparity $d_l(x, y)$ is defined as the shift z which gives the maximum (or minimum) of the correlation values in Eq. 1. To detect occlusions, the left-right consistency is used [17]. For each pixel, if the disparity $d_l(x, y)$ computed using the left image as a reference is equal to the disparity $d_r(x + z_{\max}, y)$ computed using the right image as the reference, use Eq. 6 instead of Eq. 2,

$$Q = \mathrm{XOR}(I_l(x + i, y + j) \cdot \lambda(x, y, i, j), \qquad (6)$$
$$I_r(x - z + i, y + j) \cdot \lambda(x, y, i, j)),$$

the solution is considered as correct. Otherwise the pixels are marked as occluded, however, the disparity can be assigned as the minimum value between $d_l(x, y)$ and $d_r(x + z_{\max}, y)$.

3   The FPGA Design

In Fig. 2, an overview of the FPGA design is shown. This design has five inputs, clk_pixel as the pixel clock for the input stereo pairs, left_image [7:0] and right_image [7:0] as grayscale values of the pixels from the images of left and right, respectively. x_resolution [10:0] as the horizontal resolution of the input images. n [4:0] as the number of lines in the correlation window. On the other hand, the design has one output, final_disparity [7:0], corresponding to disparity values for the output image. Its general behavior can be described as following: first, the **stereopair_buffer** module stores the grayscale values for all pixels in the correlation windows from 0 up to $z_{\max}$. Then, the proposed similarity criterion is computed. Then, left-disparity and right-disparity modules compute the disparity value using the left and right image as reference. Finally, a multiplexer (**mux**) sets the final disparity value as the minimum value between the left and right disparity values.

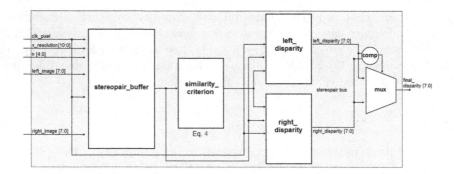

Fig. 2. General diagram for the FPGA design

3.1   The Stereopair_Buffer Module

The **stereopair_buffer** module manages an array of $n + 1 \cdot 2$ BRAM cores which store n lines of two images as shown in Fig. 3. The **RAM_controller** module assigns to each BRAM core their corresponding address and write-read values. The **RAM_controller** module has two inputs, x_resolution [10:0] as the horizontal resolution of the input images and n [4:0] as the number of lines in the correlation window. There are two outputs, where w/r [n + 1:0] consist on a logic vector with $n + 1$ bits of size, the write-read value of each BRAM are determined by each bit of the vector. address [10:0] consists of a logic vector, which corresponds to a read/write address for all the BRAM cores. Each BRAM core only provides the grayscale value of one pixel from one horizontal line in the correlation window. In order to store the others horizontal values necessary for the disparity computation, we used the **line_vector** module. Using the **line_vector** module, the value of the first horizontal pixels of the $n + 1$ BRAMs are read in parallel form and, the pixels of the n BRAMs in read mode are placed in the bits 7-0 of n storage vectors, respectively. Then, the first horizontal pixels are placed in the bits 15-8 and the second horizontal pixels are placed in the bits 7-0. This process is repeated until all horizontal pixels necessary for computing all disparity levels are stored.

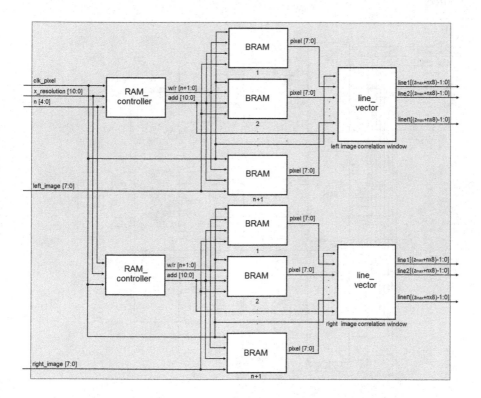

Fig. 3. FPGA design for the **stereopair_buffer** module

3.2   The Disparity Module

For the computation of the disparity map via the proposed algorithm, a pixel-parallel and window parallel architecture was designed. The architecture of the **disparity** module is presented in Fig. 4, its general behavior is as follows: first, the **XOR** modules compute the XOR operation between the pixels from left and right images of the correlation window. This process is executed in each of the $z_{max} + 1$ **XOR** modules, implemented in parallel, which are configured for expected disparity levels from 0 until z_{max}, where each module process only one disparity level and computes the XOR operation only for pixels selected by the proposed similarity criterion (Eq. 2). Then, the output of each of the **XOR** modules are sent to its corresponding **binary_opperator** module. The **binary_opperator** module corresponds to the $\mathcal{H}$ operator (Eq. 3). Then, the **adder** module computes the sum of the values for all pixels retained in the correlation window (Eq. 1). Finally, the **mux_tree** module which consist in a multiplexer tree assigns the corresponding index for all correlation values, then, determines the minimum correlation value and set the disparity value as the index of the minimum correlation value. In the developed FPGA design, two **disparity** modules were implemented in parallel form where the first module uses the left image as reference while the second module uses the right image as reference.

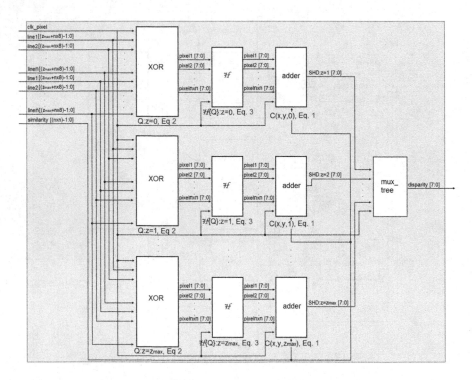

Fig. 4. FPGA design for the **disparity** module

4   Results and Discussions

The developed FPGA architecture was implemented in an FPGA Cyclone IV EP4CGX150CF23C8 of Altera. All modules were designed via the CAPH design tool, which allows high-level programing and friendly design for video stream processing [20]. Furthermore, all modules were validated via post-synthesis simulations performed in ModelSim Altera. The selected configuration for the implemented algorithm was set as: correlation window size equal to $19 \cdot 19$, i.e., $2 \cdot w + 1 = 19$ and maximum disparity level equal to 31, i.e., $z_{max} = 31$. This setup allows to read 19×19 pixels from 32 correlation windows in parallel form, i.e., it computes the correlation index value for all disparity levels in the reference pixel in the same clock cycle. The setup requires 40 BRAM cores, 64 **XOR**, $\mathcal{H}$ and **adder** modules, and two **mux_tree** module implemented in parallel-pipelined form. The hardware resource consumption of the developed FPGA architecture is shown in Table 1.

Table 1. Hardware resource consumption for the FPGA implementation

Resource (FPGA:EP4CGX150CF23C8)	Consumption
Total logic elements	62,689/149,760 (41.85 %)
Total pins	25/287 (11.48 %)
Total memory bits	242,064/6,635,920 (27.41 %)
Embedded multiplier elements	0/720 (0 %)
Total PLLs	0/6 (0 %)

In Table 2, quantitative results of the number of erroneous pixels obtained by the proposed algorithm compared with other FPGA-based stereo matching algorithms in the literature are presented. Table 2 demonstrates that the proposed algorithm improves most algorithms in the literature. The algorithms presented in [2,11,23] allow estimating dense disparity maps. However, the averaging effect due to large window sizes used generates errors at depth discontinuities. To avoid the averaging effect algorithms with small window sizes have been developed [4–6]. However, noise sensibility is increased and erroneous values in untextured regions are generated. In both cases erroneous pixels near to 12 % are reached. Other approach such as [1], which uses a geometric feature, or [15], which is inspired in the Census transform and introduces and adaptive coefficient reach erroneous pixels near to 10 %. Finally, although the algorithm presented in [14] uses a grayscale-based similarity criterion to improve the performance of the SAD algorithm, it is possible to affirm that using the similarity criterion proposed in Eqs. 1–6 of this article, allows to increase the accuracy, near to 10 % with respect to [14]. Furthermore, due to the proposed algorithm allows decreasing the correlation window size with respect to [14], the FPGA resource usage for the proposed algorithm is more efficient than [14].

In Fig. 5 the disparity maps for the Tsukuba and Venus scenes generated by the proposed method are shown. Although the obtained results retain some noise, previous algorithms in the literature [1, 4–6, 14, 15] have been improved quantitatively and qualitatively, disparity maps for the Tsukuba and Venus scenes of most algorithms compared in Table 2 can be consulted in the Middlebury Stereo Vision Page [18]. On the other hand, in Table 3 comparison of processing speed regarding to other real-time stereo matching algorithms reported in the literature is presented. It is observed high increase with respect to several FPGA-based stereo matching algorithms in the literature [2, 11, 15, 23].

Table 2. Quantitative results of FPGA-based stereo matching algorithms

Algorithm	Tsukuba$_{(all)}$	Venus$_{(all)}$	Correlation window size
Aguilar-González et al., [1]	10.9 %	6.93 %	3 · 3
Georgoulas et al., [6]	12.0 %	8.0 %	7 · 7
Alba et al., [2]	13.92 %	12.6 %	19 · 19
Georgoulas and Andreadis [4]	11 %	8 %	7 · 7
Georgoulas and Andreadis [5]	12 %	9 %	7 · 7
Perri et al., [15]	11.8 %	7.2 %	13 · 13
Ttofis et al., [23]	10.4 %	12.1 %	11 · 11
Pérez-Patricio and Aguilar-González [14]	7.6 %	3.2 %	29 · 29
Jin et al., [11]	11.57 %	5.27 %	15 · 15
Proposed	6.8 %	2.8 %	19 · 19

Table 3. Processing speed of FPGA-based stereo matching algorithms

Algorithm	Resolution	Frames/s	Pixeles/s
Georgoulas et al., [6]	1280 · 1024	65	85,196,800
Perri et al., [15]	640 · 480	68	20,889,600
Alba et al., [2]	256 · 256	100	6,553,600
Ttofis et al., [23]	1280 · 1024	50	65,536,000
Aguilar-González et al., [1]	1280 · 1024	75	98,304,000
Georgoulas and Andreadis [5]	1024 · 1024	102	106,954,752
Georgoulas and Andreadis [4]	384 · 288	833	92,123,136
Pérez-Patricio and Aguilar-González [14]	450 · 375	592	99,900,000
Jin et al., [11]	640 · 480	630	70,656,000
Proposed	1280 · 720	117	107,827,200

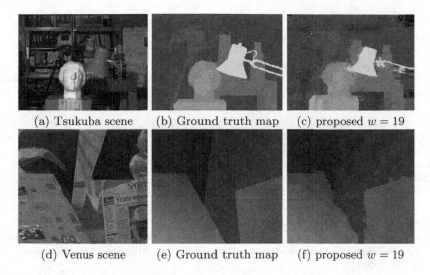

(a) Tsukuba scene   (b) Ground truth map   (c) proposed $w = 19$

(d) Venus scene   (e) Ground truth map   (f) proposed $w = 19$

Fig. 5. Disparity maps generated for different test synthetic stereo pairs

5   Conclusions

In this article an area-based algorithm for stereo matching using a similarity criterion, which is used as pixel selector in the correlation window was presented. It was demonstrated that using the modified Sum of Hamming Distance algorithm proposed in this article, it is possible to increase the accuracy of most real-time FPGA-based stereo matching algorithms in the literature and reach parallel-pipelined design that increases the processing speed. The best performance of the proposed algorithm was obtained with a large window, appropriated for untextured areas. However, due to only pixels of the same object are used in the correlation window, blurring effects are avoided, and therefore, erroneous values at depth discontinuities are reduced.

References

1. Aguilar-González, A., Pérez-Patricio, M., Arias-Estrada, M., Camas-Anzueto, J.L., Hernández-De León, H.R., Sánchez-Alegría, A.: An FPGA correlation-edge distance approach for disparity map. In: Proceedings of IEEE International Conference on Electronics, Communications and Computers (CONIELECOMP 2015), pp. 21–28. IEEE Press, Cholula (2015)
2. Alba, A., Arce-Santana, E., Aguilar-Ponce, R.M., Campos-Delgado, D.U.: Phase-correlation guided area matching for realtime vision and video encoding. J. Real-Time Image Proc. **9**, 621–663 (2012)
3. Bleyer, M., Rother, C., Kohli, P., Scharstein, D., Sinha, S.: Object stereo—joint stereo matching and object segmentation. In: IEEE International Conference on Computer Vision and Pattern Recognition (CVPR), pp. 3081–3088. IEEE Press, Providence (2011)

4. Georgoulas, C., Andreadis, I.: A real-time fuzzy hardware structure for disparity map computation. J. Real-Time Image Proc. **6**, 257–273 (2011)
5. Georgoulas, C., Andreadis, I.: FPGA based disparity map computation with vergence control. Microprocess. Microsyst. **34**, 259–273 (2010)
6. Georgoulas, C., Kotoulas, L., Sirakoulis, G.C., Andreadis, I., Gasteratos, A.: Real-time disparity map computation module. Microprocess. Microsyst. **32**, 159–170 (2008)
7. Gerrits, M., Bekaert, P.: Local stereo matching with segmentation-based outlier rejection. In: 2006 IEEE The 3rd Canadian Conference on Computer and Robot Vision, pp. 66–72, IEEE Press (2006)
8. Hamming, R.W.: Error detecting and error correcting codes. Bell Syst. Tech. J. **29**(2), 147–160 (1950)
9. Hu, T., Qi, B., Wu, T., Xu, X., He, H.: Stereo matching using weighted dynamic programming on a single-direction four-connected tree. Comput. Vis. Image Underst. **116**, 908–921 (2012)
10. Kalomiros, J.A., Lygouras, J.: Design and hardware implementation of a stereo-matching system based on dynamic programming. Microprocess. Microsyst. **35**, 496–509 (2011)
11. Jin, S., Cho, J., Pham, X.D., Lee, K.M., Park, S.K., Kim, M., Jeon, J.W.: FPGA design and implementation of a real-time stereo vision system. IEEE Trans. Circ. Syst. Video Technol. **20**, 15–26 (2009)
12. Parrilla, E., Torregrosa, J.R., Riera, J., Hueso, J.L.: Fuzzy control for obstacle detection in stereo video sequences. Math. Comput. Model. **54**, 1813–1817 (2011)
13. Pérez-Patricio, M., Aguilar-González, A., Arias-Estrada, M., Camas-Anzueto, J.L.: A fuzzy logic approach for stereo matching suited for real-time. Int. J. Comput. Appl. **113**, 1–8 (2015)
14. Pérez-Patricio, M., Aguilar-González, A.: FPGA implementation of an efficient similarity-based adaptive window algorithm for real-time stereo matching. J. Real-Time Image Proc., 1–17 (2015). doi:10.1007/s11554-015-0530-6
15. Perri, S., Corsonello, P., Cocorullo, G.: Adaptive census transform: a novel hardware-oriented stereo vision algorithm. Comput. Vis. Image Underst. **117**, 29–41 (2013)
16. Rong, X., Huanyu, J., Yibin, Y.: Recognition of clustered tomatoes based on binocular stereo vision. Comput. Electron. Agric. **106**, 75–90 (2014)
17. Scharstein, D., Szeliski, R.: A taxonomy and evaluation of dense two-frame stereo correspondence algorithms. Int. J. Comput. Vis. **47**(1), 7–42 (2002)
18. Scharstein, D., Szeliski, R., Hirschmller, H.: Middlebury Stereo Vision Page. http://vision.middlebury.edu/stereo/
19. Schauwecker, K., Klette, R., Zell, A.: A new feature detector and stereo matching method for accurate high-performance sparse stereo matching. In: IEEE/RSJ International Conference on Intelligent Robots and Systems (IROS), pp. 5171–5176. IEEE Press, Vilamoura (2012)
20. Serot, J., Berry, F., Ahmed, S.: CAPH: a language for implementing stream-processing applications on FPGAs. In: Athanas, P., Pnevmatikatos, D., Sklavos, N. (eds.) Embedded Systems Design with FPGAs, pp. 201–224. Springer, New York (2012)
21. Stefano, L.D., Marchionni, M., Mattoccia, S.: A fast area-based stereo matching algorithm. Image Vis. Comput. **22**, 983–1005 (2004)
22. Trinh, H.: Efficient stereo algorithm using multiscale belief propagation on segmented images. In: Proceedings of the British Machine Vision Conference, pp. 33.1–33.10, BMVA Press (2008)

23. Ttofis, C., Hadjitheophanous, S., Georghiades, A.S., Theocharides, T.: Edge-directed hardware architecture for real-time disparity map computation. IEEE Trans. Comput. **62**, 690–704 (2013)
24. Wang, L., Liu, Z., Zhang, Z.: Feature based stereo matching using two-step expansion. Math. Probl. Eng. **2014**, 1–14 (2014)

FPGA Soft-Core Processors, Compiler and Hardware Optimizations Validated Using HOG

Colm Kelly[1]([✉]), Fahad Manzoor Siddiqui[2], Burak Bardak[2],
Yun Wu[2], Roger Woods[2], and Karren Rafferty[2]

[1] Thales, Belfast, UK
colm.kelly@uk.thalesgroup.com
[2] Queens University, Belfast, UK
{f.siddiqui,b.bardak,yun.wu,r.woods}@qub.ac.uk,
k.rafferty@ee.qub.ac.uk

Abstract. There is demand for an easily programmable, high performance image processing platform based on FPGAs. In previous work, a novel, high performance processor - IPPro was developed and a Histogram of Orientated Gradients (HOG) algorithm study undertaken on a Xilinx Zynq platform. Here, we identify and explore a number of mapping strategies to improve processing efficiency for soft-cores and a number of options for creation of a division coprocessor. This is demonstrated for the revised high definition HOG implementation on a Zynq platform, resulting in a performance of 328 fps which represents a 146 % speed improvement over the original realization and a tenfold reduction in energy.

Keywords: FPGA · Memory · Image processing · HOG

1 Introduction

High performance image processing platforms performing Embedded Vision and Video Analysis are found in systems such as security surveillance, automated inspection, smart phone, medical research and diagnosis to name but a few. Increased intelligence within these applications implies more intelligent processing of image data. It is desirable to process the data nearer to the camera in order to reduce the data flow throughout the system as quickly as possible, whilst preserving the information content [1]. This suggests the need for higher performance, embedded solutions such as those based on FPGA. After studying the literature and industry the need to develop a new approach which leveraged both the high performance and low power requirements of FPGA, and

---

C. Kelly—Please note that the LNCS Editorial assumes that all authors have used the western naming convention, with given names preceding surnames. This determines the structure of the names in the running heads and the author index.

© Springer International Publishing Switzerland 2016
V. Bonato et al. (Eds.): ARC 2016, LNCS 9625, pp. 78–90, 2016.
DOI: 10.1007/978-3-319-30481-6_7

specifically the ease of programming associated with sequential processor was identified. In [2], the IPPro architecture was created with the aim of leveraging these FPGA advantages but avoiding long FPGA development cycles. By designing around the DSP48E1 block and minimizing supporting logic our core achieves 530MIPS. IPPro outperforms all other current FPGA based soft-core solutions [3–5].

The vast on-board (XC702) FPGA bandwidth, potentially $80\,\mathrm{Tbs}^{-1}$ [6], allows large amounts of data to be passed between arrays of Processing Elements (PE), thus reducing the need for accessing off-chip memories. In contrast, the designer is challenged by very limited local FPGA storage capacity, typically of 10's of Mbits, which must be handled carefully to ensure high throughput rates.

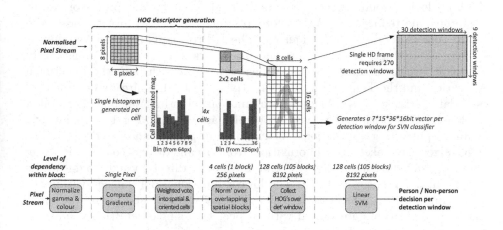

Fig. 1. HOG data dependencies as per Dalal and Triggs implementation [7]

Development of IPPro has taken this into account by carefully considering algorithm mapping and decomposition. The impact is that the IPPro instruction set is limited to maximize data throughput performance [2]. Profiling the HOG algorithm identifies the impact of a limited instruction set on IPPro performance. The absence of an explicit division operation is found to be the largest issue as 70 % of the processing time is spent on an algorithm based division operation.

This paper applies the following known and novel optimizations to improve the IPPro soft-core processor performance, applicable to any soft-core design:

– Determination of the optimal method of realizing the division function in IPPro acting to increase speed and reduce overall energy consumption.
– Register file capacity modification to reduce recurring memory access for the same data whilst having minimal resource impact on IPPro core size.
– Novel mathematical expression which maximizes data reuse within the processor through optimal selection of input pattern for windowing functions.
– Instruction level power profiling is possible with our approach and is a novel method of establishing the impact of optimizations on energy consumption.

The paper describes these optimizations in detail making use of a Zynq based HOG implementation to investigate the effect of these changes for both measured speed and power. Section 2 highlights the remaining bottlenecks in the processing path of the HOG algorithm. Three optimizations are identified and realized in Sect. 3. Section 4 compares the performance of our new architecture against state-of-the-art solutions and introduces instruction level power profiling for the IPPro. Finally Sect. 5 summarizes our findings.

2   Detailed Algorithm Profiling

The IPPro system processing core, based upon the DSP48E1 DSP block utilises the hard logic resource as the Arithmetic Logic Unit for our processor. Cores are interconnected using BRAMs before interfacing to the Zynq ARM host. The IPPro core is detailed by Siddiqui [2]. The IPPro mapping and scheduling is split into four stages: Partitioning, Allocation, Translation and Mapping [8]. In this paper we focus on the optimisations associated with both the Functional Allocation and the Translation stage since partitioning has already been defined by Dalal and Triggs [7] and Mapping is a function of our in development compiler.

The HOG algorithm, the elements of which are shown in Fig. 1, is used widely in image processing applications, for example in pedestrian detection [7]. The HOG algorithm takes pixel information from a camera and converts it to an image of gradients, where the gradients have both direction and magnitude as per the first two stages of Fig. 1. The lowest functional dependency within the algorithm is a 64×128 pixels detection window which is slid across the input frame. Improvements are viewed with respect to a single detection window as this is considered the fundamental element in HOG and can be used to tile any frame size. Each of the detection windows is divided into 8×8 pixels cells which are translated into histograms (9×16 bit vectors) representing the 64 gradients (one per input pixel) in the cell as per the third stage in Fig. 1. The histograms from 2×2 cells (256 pixels) are then normalised with each other to generate a 36×16 bit vector as shown in the fourth stage in Fig. 1. Collation of the normalised 36×16 bit vectors over the detection window (7×15 blocks) in stage five of Fig. 1 produces the HOG descriptor. In the final stage a pre-trained off-line Support Vector Machine (SVM) receives the 3780 ($7 \times 15 \times 36$) vectors and multiplies with its set weights to achieve the human detection chain.

In [8], the HOG was implemented on the IPPro where two of the six functional blocks were accelerated and the non-native IPPro functions were offloaded to the Zynq ARM cores. Here in addition we also implement a third functional block (Normalise over overlapping spatial blocks) in the IPPro system. Reducing the division operation latency makes it efficient to realise this function in the IPPro System, thus further accelerate the implementation. The full design is not realised on IPPro as further less computational demanding functions predominantly only require memory re-organisation. Doing this at the host level is the most efficient method as it avoids passing large volumes of data between Programmable Logic and the ARM cores, thereby avoiding costly transport delays.

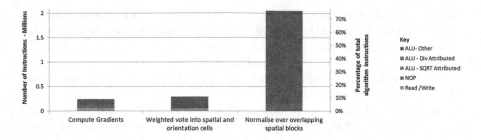

Fig. 2. IPPro instruction profile for generating the HOG descriptor for a single detection window

The code was compiled from standard IPPro Instruction Set Architecture (ISA) and analysed to examine the instruction length profile of each function. The cumulative number of instructions (Fig. 2) is 2,597,976 and generates the HOG descriptors required for a single detection window. 701M instructions generate HOG descriptors for one HD frame (270 detection windows). Input data in this instance is 8 bit grey-scale. The most efficient way to achieve the first functional block, Normalize Gamma &Colour function, is to use a 256 × 8 bits look up table as it requires a square root function as opposed to IPPro operations.

3 IPPro Optimisations

3.1 Mapping Strategy, Register Capacity

The current mapping strategy implemented in [8] aims to reduce the transfer of data in and out of the core registers whilst reserving adequate register locations to execute intermediate calculations before forwarding processed results to the next functional stage. This increases utilization of cores for processing as opposed to data transfer, thus increasing the ratio of processing to memory access which we view as processing efficiency. Whilst the soft-core would benefit from larger local registers, this would have a negative impact on the FPGA clock rate. Current mid-range FPGAs provide 5–15 Mb of on-chip memory tiled across their fabric which does not permit a full HD frame (33 Mb) to be stored in chip memory. Implementing a single core that functions sequentially with such a large register would lose the advantages of the spatial parallelism offered by FPGA.

The Zynq DSP48E1 module can operate up to 741MIPS in isolation [9]. The IPPro core is however limited to 530 MHz by the supporting control logic of the core. Whilst Zynq supports external DDR memory access, our strategy is to minimize its interaction due to its relatively low bandwidth and high latency with the aim of minimizing FPGA to host data transportation.

Due to the above issues we believe that DDR transfers should be limited to the start and end of the algorithm data path. Unfortunately, as we can see from Fig. 1, some HOG functions require a large number of pixels and are difficult to sub-divide into smaller more manageable functions. The initial IPPro 32 × 16-bit register configuration can only read blocks of 16 input pixels as 5 data values are generated for each processed input pixel during the Compute Gradients function. The limit is bounded by the IPPro core register size [2]. A maximum of 6 pixels of interest (6 pixels × 5 = 30 data points) generating 30 values can be stored prior to output during a single program memory (PM) loop as the register file size is limited to 32, 16 bit locations.

In our improved IPPro, we reconfigure the 32×16 bit kernel register storage such that it is part of the 32×16 bit local memory thus doubling its size to 64×16 bit. In the Compute Gradients function this enables the generation of a maximum of 12 pixels of interest (12 pixels × 5 = 60 data points). The increase in register size from 32 to 64 improves data reuse in the Compute Gradients function by reducing the total instructions per detection window for this function by 4 % from 242,176 to 232,544 whilst producing the same output data required for a detection window by increasing the read/write to ALU ratio.

In the Normalize function, the cell of interest is normalized with its three surrounding cells by splitting into three consecutive, identical loops, one per surrounding cell due to the limitation of the IPPro register size. To store a block (4 cells), the histogram needs $4 \times 9 \times 16$ bit register locations. The existing IPPro core cannot support this as the algorithm requires a minimum of 36 register locations. More significantly in the Normalize function an increase from 32 to 64 register locations (by providing random access to the existing 32×16 bit kernel locations), the instructions are reduced by 35 % from 2,051,280 to 1,333,920.

3.2   Mapping Strategy, Input Data Pattern

When mapping the HOG algorithm to IPPro, all valid permutations of input data patterns were explored arriving at the most efficient core in terms of data processing. The highest efficiency pattern resulted in a high ratio of data computation to data movement instructions. The main objective was to establish the ideal configuration of the input data pattern to efficiently use the limited number of register spaces. This is specific to windowing operations only as these generally occur with an overlapping behaviour where a chosen pixel of interest uses a limited number of pixels in the area of interest. The main limitation is the amount of available registers, REG. If we calculate the number of required registers, FR, to store the outputs of the window operations by estimating the algorithmic requirements, the number of outputs per filter window can be calculated. $NOFW$ is an integer representing the number of outputs per filter window.

$$NOFW = [REG/FR] \tag{1}$$

Equation (1) represents the main optimization target where the use of the REG is maximized within the given windowing function and image data. High $NOFW$ is desirable. The next step estimates register usage by considering the window function as well as input image size. The image size is important where aspect ratio will define the amount of surplus computation executed in generating "wasted" pixels that are required to be read, computed and stored due to the overlapping behaviour and pixel packet processing of the algorithm mapping in IPPro. Given an input window of X by Y pixels where most windowing operations use overlapping elements, an overlapping constant O_v is an important feature. The input window height and width are respectively HI and WI and define the input pixel pattern whereas processed pixels output pattern height and width are HO and WO respectively.

$$HI = HO + (O_v \times 2) \tag{2}$$

$$WI = WO + (O_v \times 2) \tag{3}$$

where WO and $HO's$ maximum number is defined by the $NOFW$ as

$$NOFW = HO \times WO \tag{4}$$

Then the main aim becomes to find the optimum HO and WO considering the input window size and the register use.

$$OptimumReadWindow = \left\{ \left\lfloor \frac{X}{WO} \right\rfloor \right\} * \left\{ \frac{Y}{HO} \right\} \tag{5}$$

where WO and HO are the biggest integers that realize (4). The pixel wastage is defined as the rounding error which is calculated as shown in (6) and (7). The most optimum result for efficient register and execution time can be achieved by choosing the least wastage where the smallest rounding errors should be chosen by interchanging WO and HO values if the result minimizes Δ_X and Δ_Y.

$$\Delta_X = \left\{ \frac{X}{WO} - \left\lfloor \frac{X}{WO} \right\rfloor \right\} \tag{6}$$

$$\Delta_Y = \left\{ \frac{Y}{WO} - \left\lfloor \frac{Y}{WO} \right\rfloor \right\} \tag{7}$$

With the new 64×16 bit IPPro register configuration, it is possible to generate a maximum of 60 output data values from the 12 input pixels of interest for the Compute Gradients task. Only six possible combinations of input pattern achieve this maximum output and are detailed in Table 1.

Table 1. Instruction profile for Compute Gradient function for all possible patterns

Input pattern		Reads	Instructions per PM	PM's per detection window		Instructions per detection window
x-axis	y-axis			x-axis	y-axis	
14	**3**	**38**	**350**	**5.33 (6)**	**128**	**268,800**
3	14	38	350	64	10.67	246,400
8	4	28	340	10.67 (11)	64	239,360
4	8	28	340	32	21.33 (22)	239,360
6	**5**	**26**	**338**	**16**	**42.67 (43)**	**232,544**
5	6	26	338	21.33 (22)	32	237,952

In this instance, the Compute Gradients function can have a worst case pattern requiring 268,800 instructions or a best case pattern requiring 232,544 instructions per detection window. Concious pattern choice has potential to reduce the instruction count by 13.5 % in this function without architecture changes.

3.3   Inclusion of Division to the IPPro ISA

In [8], it was established that by only using the existing native IPPro instructions to explicitly translate the HOG algorithm from mathematical expressions into IPPro instructions that only two of the six functional blocks of the HOG algorithm could be implemented. This was primarily due to the absence of division and square root instructions in the IPPro ISA. Profiling demonstrated that long hand methods are very time consuming and therefore not practical if frequently required. From a bespoke logic perspective the non-restoring division algorithm [10] is the fastest and has less complexity amongst other radix-2 division algorithms [11]. As this supports our requirement of retaining a high throughput yet simple architecture, the non-restoring algorithm was chosen. Prior to re-profiling the following two methods of division using IPPro ISA were considered.

Addition of Bespoke 32bit Register: requires the addition of a 32-bit register to facilitate the left shift where a single 16 bit division would require 151 instructions. This could be formed by a real-time copy of the top two registers R30 and R31 but requires the entire data-path to become 32-bit wide. Such increase in the interconnect for the data-path significantly reduces the operational frequency and increases resource usage.

Use Existing 16bit Datapath Architecture: uses the compare flags at the output of the ALU stage of IPPro to determine whether or not to add 0×01 to the adjacent remainder register. The algorithm loops 16 times through a routine to compute the required quotient and remainder. This realization requires 167 instructions, 16 more than the aforementioned solution as a consequence of the additional write into the second 16-bit register. We conclude that by using the current DSP48E1 on its own it is not possible to significantly reduce the number of clock cycles required to execute a 16-bit division or square root function.

Division Impact on Initial Profiling Exercise. In our profiling exercise, we compromised and assumed each division and square root function would require 160 IPPro instructions. As identified in the profiling instance of the HOG algorithm in Fig. 2, 79 % of the total processing time is attributed to the Normalize over Overlapping Spatial Blocks operation and 70+% of the total algorithm time is spent on division. As the most significant contributor to instructions per detection window, the division function is the prime candidate for acceleration.

3.4   Implementation of Co-Processor

We implement the division as a coprocessor in order to provide a speed up. Two architectural approaches have been considered, one of incorporating a single co-processor shared temporally by an array of IPPro cores and the other as a single co-processor assigned to each IPPro core (see Fig. 3). In both cases, a non-restoring integer, radix-2 divider which operates on 16 bit signed data was chosen as it provided a lightweight, fast implementation for small bit widths. For wider data-paths e.g. 32 bit, the SRT algorithm which requires a lookup table or an approximation algorithm such as Newton Raphson or Gold Schmidt, provide better performance at further FPGA resource expense but in the instance of 16 bit data they do not [12]. Simple integer CORDIC dividers were also found to require significantly more LUTs than non-restoring methods when implemented.

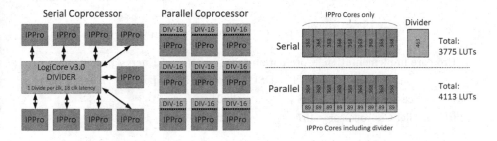

Fig. 3. Serial and Parallel coprocessor topology and associated recource costs

Serial Co-processor: The key advantage of using a serial co-processor is that any core can implement division at any time, whereas the shared resource of a parallel coprocessor needs careful scheduling. Sharing the co-processor does however potentially provide better resource utilization if it is only occasionally requested. Table 2 details our four LogiCore Divider (v3.0) [13] implementations.

Table 2. LogiCore Divider (Radix-2 integer based) implementation performance

Clks per division	Latency (clks)	LUTs	Fmax	Divisions per sec
1	**18**	**463**	**328 MHz**	**328M**
4	9	228	264 MHz	66M
4	4	385	125 MHz	31.25M
8	19	146	267 MHz	33.4M

A serial architecture can afford to consume more resources as it is shared across many IPPro cores, therefore a heavily pipelined architecture is viable.

High throughput comes with disadvantages; in particular where single spurious divisions are required, a high latency of 18 cycles. As this type of coprocessor is highly pipelined, a larger footprint of 463 LUTs is required. In order to service many IPPro cores, a high coprocessor fan-out is required which impacts the overall clock speed. The 328 MHz result in Table 2 refers to the speed of the LogiCore v3.0 Divider when placed and routed in isolation and not connected to an array of 9 cores making these connections shall further reduce the Fmax.

Parallel Co-Processor. The main advantage of a parallel divider topology is local computation and therefore minimal penalty for data transportation. Here scheduler effort is light and there is no possibility of inter-core contention as there is with a serial divider. The parallel coprocessor also has a small footprint of 89 LUTs (including control and interfacing logic) which is just greater than one ninth of the footprint of the serial coprocessor. It also has a higher Fmax.

Table 3. Divider coprocessor resource and power

IPPro core implementation	Core parameters			Energy power	
	LUTS	DSPs	Clock (MHz)	Latency	Energy (nJ)
Non-coprocessor	368	1	530	183	4.3
With Parallel Coprocessor	457	1	530	18	0.6

Unfortunately, these advantages are challenged by the fact that the divider is not pipelined and requires 19 cycles per division. Unlike the serial divider logic which will potentially be employed very regularly during a typical algorithm execution, the logic which makes up the parallel divider shall be dormant for longer durations. We view this as an inefficient use of the resources thus driving the decision to exclude the co-processor from cores with no division requirement.

Architecture Choice. An 8 % difference in the total LUT resource is not deemed significant enough to influence choosing one implementation over the other. The coprocessor architecture choice influences the overall algorithm implementation performance due to the overhead of interconnection and scheduling. For the normalization function in HOG, the serial processor both requires division at the same instance and also for the majority of the processing time within that functional block without stalling the IPPro Cores for considerable periods. Whilst a serial coprocessor has very high standalone potential in the instance of HOG, it will be impossible due to required concurrent access. This can be considered to be a general case for most SIMD targeted parallelized image processing algorithms. In addition to reducing the division instruction count from 160 to 20 instructions, a parallel solution also allows the IPPro core to continue operation.

Using a coprocessor to offload the division effort of the Normalize over Overlapping Spatial function shows that our preferred parallel co-processor implementation reduces the associated IPPro Core instructions by 82 % from 1,344,420 to 246,120 for the Normalisation function for a single detection window. This saving is attributed to the introduction of the co-processor at the cost of 89 LUTs per core as shown in Table 3.

The impact on energy consumption was measured on our Zynq ZC702 development board (based around an XC7Z020 chip) by comparing the power of two 70 core implementations, the first array included coprocessors and the second used the original IPPro core with native instructions only. Measurements were achieved by averaging the on-board I2C (Texas Instruments UCD9248) power module results over thousands of division operations. The almost tenfold reduction in energy consumption per division operation due to faster execution time is recorded in Table 3.

4   Optimisations Impact Discussion

Whilst re-profiling the HOG algorithm, three key optimisations were made reducing the total required IPPro processor instructions from 2,590,416 to 705,224 per HOG detection window. Our solution used 120 IPPro cores and maintained a 530 MHz clock rate. Our results detailing the achieved performance and resource usage for the existing and revised IPPro are summarised in Table 4. To minimise resource usage we only implement the coprocessor in the cores where required (Fig. 4).

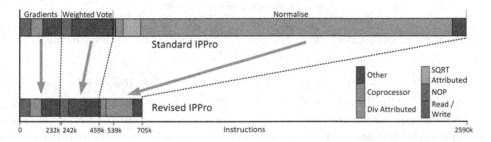

Fig. 4. Instruction profile of standard and optimised IPPro for single detection window

Table 4 highlights that the bottleneck in the standard implementation is in the normalisation stage as an array of 42 standard cores achieves only 40 fps. The coprocessor optimisation in this instance enables a greater than times 8 performance to 335 fps. For a single core implementation it was necessary to use a coprocessor equipped core so the implementation could not avail of the overall LUT savings by only using a coprocessor when required.

A total increase of 7.5 % in LUTs for the 120 core implementation (Fig. 5) achieves the following increases in performance; Gradient and Binning functions, 4 % and 31 % respectively and Normalise by 737 % (predominately coprocessor).

Whilst it wasn't possible to contrast our HOG IPPro implementation against one which had exactly the same performance and/or resource profile we can

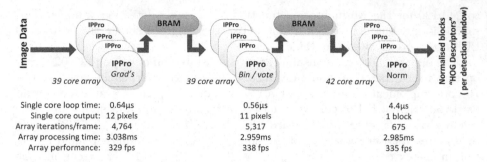

Single core loop time:	0.64µs	0.56µs	4.4µs
Single core output:	12 pixels	11 pixels	1 block
Array iterations/frame:	4,764	5,317	675
Array processing time:	3.038ms	2.959ms	2.985ms
Array performance:	329 fps	338 fps	335 fps

Fig. 5. 120 IPPro core architecture generating HOG descriptors from a stream of gamma corrected pixels - performance quoted per HD frame generated

Table 4. Resource and performance of IPPro in generation of HOG descriptors

IPPro core architecture	Performance: HD fps		Resource: LUTs	
	Single	120 Core array	Single	120 Core array
Standard	0.75	316 (Grad' 39 cores) 258 (Vote' 39 cores) **40 (Norm' 42 cores)**	368	44,160
Optimised	2.78	329 (Grad' 39 cores) 338 (Vote' 39 cores) 335 (Norm' 42 cores)	457 (368+ 89)	47,720

Table 5. Resources usage of 120 core IPPro design and recent FPGA implementations

Ref	Device	Clock	LUTs	DSPs	BRAMs	Resolution	fps
Our	XC7Z020	530 MHz	47,720	120	7	1920 × 1080	328
[14]	XC5VFX200T	270 MHz	3,642	12	26	1920 × 1080	64
[15]	XC6VLX760	150 MHz	92,477	191	95	640 × 480	68
[16]	XC5VLX50	44.85 MHz	17,383	no data	36	640 × 480	112

see that [14] is similar in terms of performance per resource cost. Unlike all other implementations in current literature IPPro offers considerable ease of programmability, re-programmability and design space exploration that is not so evident in the traditional hand crafted designs of [14–16].

5   Conclusions

The work describes three methods of increasing the performance possible by IPPro, all of which have been employed to more efficiently generate HOG descriptors whilst furthering the scope of application in implementing the HOG algorithm beyond [8]. Our optimized solution offers further choice over, area, power and processing speed than existing approaches whilst being easily programmed in a fast manner. Our design targets a modest size and cost FPGA comparable to current high performance GPU and CPU offerings demonstrating that this FPGA approach is practical for smart camera and similar low power &cost applications. The prime advantage of IPPro is the ease and speed at which design iterations can be produced with predictable, high performance outcomes.

Acknowledgments. This work has been undertaken in collaboration with Heriot-Watt University in a project funded by the Engineering and Physical Science Research Council (EPSRC) through the EP/K009583/1 grant.

References

1. Gat, Y., Kozintsev, I., Nestares, O.: Fusing image data with location and orientation sensor data streams for consumer video applications. In: 2010 IEEE Computer Society Conference on Computer Vision and Pattern Recognition Workshops (CVPRW), pp. 1–8 (2010)
2. Siddiqui, F., Russell, M., Bardak, B., Woods, R., Rafferty, K.: Ippro: FPGA based image processing processor. In: 2014 IEEE Workshop on Signal Processing Systems (SiPS), pp. 1–6 (2014)
3. Andryc, K., Merchant, M., Tessier, R.: Flexgrip: a soft GPGPU for FPGAs. In: 2013 International Conference on Field-Programmable Technology (FPT), pp. 230–237 (2013)
4. Cheah, H.Y., Fahmy, S., Kapre, N.: Analysis and optimization of a deeply pipelined FPGA soft processor. In: 2014 International Conference on Field-Programmable Technology (FPT), pp. 235–238 (2014)
5. Severance, A., Lemieux, G.: Venice: a compact vector processor for FPGA applications. In: 2012 International Conference on Field-Programmable Technology (FPT), pp. 261–268 (2012)
6. Xilinx Inc. San Jose. UG473: 7 Series FPGAs Memory Resources (2014). http://www.xilinx.com/support/documentation/user_guides/ug473_7Series_Memory_Resources.pdf
7. Dalal, N., Triggs, B.: Histograms of oriented gradients for human detection. In: IEEE Computer Society Conference on Computer Vision and Pattern Recognition, CVPR 2005, vol. 1, pp. 886–893 (2005)
8. Kelly, C., Siddiqui, F., Bardak, B., Woods, R.: Histogram of oriented gradients front end processing: an FPGA based processor approach. In: 2014 IEEE Workshop on Signal Processing Systems (SiPS), pp. 1–6 (2014)
9. Xilinx Inc. San Jose. DS183: Viretx-7 and XT FPGAs Data Sheet: DC and AC Switching Characteristics, May 2015. http://www.xilinx.com/support/documentation/data_sheets/ds183_Virtex_7_Data_Sheet.pdf
10. Oberman, S., Flynn, M.: Division algorithms and implementations. IEEE Trans. Comput. **46**(8), 833–854 (1997)
11. Sutter, G., Deschamps, J.-P., Bioul, G., Boemo, E.: Integrated Circuit and System Design. Power and Timing Modeling, Optimization and Simulation. Springer, Berlin (2004)

12. Deschamps, J., Sutter, G., Cantó, E.: Guide to FPGA Implementation of Arithmetic Functions. Lecture Notes in Electrical Engineering. Springer, The Netherlands (2012)
13. Xilinx Inc. San Jose. LogiCORE IP Divider Generator v3.0 (2011). http://www.xilinx.com/support/documentation/ip_documentation/div_gen_ds530.pdf
14. Hahnle, M., Saxen, F., Hisung, M., Brunsmann, U., Doll, K.: FPGA-based real-time pedestrian detection on high-resolution images. In: 2013 IEEE Conference on Computer Vision and Pattern Recognition Workshops (CVPRW), pp. 629–635 (2013)
15. Ma, X., Najjar, W., Roy-Chowdhury, A.: Evaluation and acceleration of high-throughput fixed-point object detection on FPGAs. IEEE Trans. Circ. Syst. Video Technol. **25**(6), 1051–1062 (2015)
16. Negi, K., Dohi, K., Shibata, Y., Oguri, K.: Deep pipelined one-chip FPGA implementation of a real-time image-based human detection algorithm. In: 2011 International Conference on Field-Programmable Technology (FPT), pp. 1–8 (2011)

A Comparison of Machine Learning Classifiers for FPGA Implementation of HOG-Based Human Detection

Masahito Oishi$^{(\boxtimes)}$, Yoshiki Hayashida, Ryo Fujita,
Yuichiro Shibata, and Kiyoshi Oguri

Nagasaki University, 1-14 Bunkyo-machi, Nagasaki 852-8521, Japan
{oishi,yoshiki,fujita}@pca.cis.nagasaki-u.ac.jp,
{shibata,oguri}@cis.nagasaki-u.ac.jp

Abstract. In this paper, we demonstrate and compare FPGA implementations of Real AdaBoost classifiers and linear SVM classifiers for image-based human detection using histograms of oriented gradients (HOG) features, in terms of performance, hardware amount and accuracy of detection. In both architectures, a deep-pipelined stream structure and fixed-point arithmetic are employed. The evaluation results show the comparative analysis of the performance, resources, accuracy of detection between Real AdaBoost and the SVM. While FPGA resources required for Real AdaBoost designs are increased with the number of weak classifiers, the largest Real AdaBoost design with $1,737$ weak classifiers can be implemented using approximately 60% LUTs compared to the SVM counterpart. Although software implementation of the Real AdaBoost is much slower than the SVM due to serial evaluation of weak classifiers, the AdaBoost achieves a slightly better throughput on an FPGA, taking an advantage of parallel processing. For the detection accuracy, the AdaBoost designs are better than the SVM designs when the same number of training data is utilized. As regards the embedded use with low power requirements, the AdaBoost approach is suitable, while the linear SVM approach has a possibility to achieve a high degree of accuracy on rather large high-end FPGA systems.

1 Introduction

Nowadays, image-based object recognition, especially human detection, is actively addressed in a wide range of applications such as advanced driving assistant systems (ADAS), surveillance system, robotics and so on. In human detection systems, histograms of oriented gradients (HOG) features [1] are widely used as image features for machine learning. Extraction of HOG features needs a large amount of computation for vast amount of image data. FPGA-based stream computing has been proven to be a promising approach for real-time, low-power and compact implementation.

Recent advances in machine learning techniques have also played an important role in enabling efficient FPGA-based image detection systems. When it

© Springer International Publishing Switzerland 2016
V. Bonato et al. (Eds.): ARC 2016, LNCS 9625, pp. 91–104, 2016.
DOI: 10.1007/978-3-319-30481-6_8

comes to HOG-based human detection, AdaBoost or a support vector machine (SVM) is typically utilized. Mizuno et al. presented unified FPGA implementation of HOG feature extraction and an SVM classifier [2]. This implementation achieved the throughput of 72 fps for 800×600-pixel images. Cao et al. have implemented a traffic stop sign recognition system with HOG feature extraction and AdaBoost-based classifiers [3]. Komorkiewicz et al. have implemented HOG feature extraction and SVM classifiers using single precision floating point arithmetic on an FPGA [4]. The system can detect multiple objects at 60 fps for 640×480-pixel images. Hahnle et al. have implemented HOG feature extraction with SVM classifiers using different clock domains for calculation and image interface [5] and achieved 64 fps for 1920×1080 pixels. Hsiao et al. have implemented human detection system on a MaCube platform using a combination of AdaBoost and SVM classifiers [6]. We also implemented a unified HOG feature extraction and AdaBoost classifiers on one FPGA [7,8], with a stream processing architecture without any external memory [9–11]. By making the best use of deep-pipelined hardware, our system can operate 112 fps for 640×480-pixel images at a moderate clock frequency of 25 MHz, achieving high energy efficiency.

  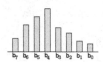

Fig. 1. Gradient orientation   **Fig. 2.** Binarization

These works have demonstrated effectiveness of FPGAs in image detection with HOG features and machine learning techniques. However, it has not been revealed which machine learning approach is suitable for FPGA implementation. In this paper, we compare a Real AdaBoost technique and a linear SVM technique on the same FPGA-based image detection platform in terms of required hardware resources and quality of detection. Furthermore, we discuss the tradeoff between the two approaches in FPGA implementation.

2   Algorithms

2.1   HOG Feature Extraction

Histogram Generation. First of all, the central differences of luminance intensity in the x direction $g_x(x, y)$ and the y direction $g_y(x, y)$ are calculated. Then, the gradient orientation θ and the gradient magnitude m are calculated as:

$$\theta(x, y) = \tan^{-1} \frac{g_y(x, y)}{g_x(x, y)} \tag{1}$$

$$m(x, y) = \sqrt{g_x(x, y)^2 + g_y(x, y)^2}. \tag{2}$$

Histograms of the gradient orientations and the gradient magnitudes are calculated for each *cell*, which is a square region consisting of $p \times p$ pixels ($p = 5$ in this implementation). When the given image size is $w \times h$, the number of cells is $\frac{w}{p} \times \frac{h}{p}$ because the cells are not overlapped. For the gradient orientation θ, we are interested only in its orientation but not in the direction. Therefore, it ranges from 0 to π and is quantized into 8 orientations as shown in Fig. 1. Consequently, 8-bin histograms are generated by voting the gradient magnitudes m for the 8 orientations.

Histogram Normalization and Binarization. The histograms are then normalized for each *block*, which is a square region consisting of $q \times q$ cells ($q = 3$ in this implementation). Each cell has an 8-bin histogram expressed as $\boldsymbol{f} = (f_0, f_1, f_2, f_3, f_4, f_5, f_6, f_7)$ where f_n ($n = 0, 1, \cdots, 7$) means the sum of gradient magnitudes of bin b_n. The block feature $\boldsymbol{v}$ at the i-th row and the j-th column is expressed as:

$$\boldsymbol{v} = (\boldsymbol{f}(i,j), \boldsymbol{f}(i+1,j), \boldsymbol{f}(i+2,j), \tag{3}$$
$$\boldsymbol{f}(i,j+1), \boldsymbol{f}(i+1,j+1), \boldsymbol{f}(i+2,j+1),$$
$$\boldsymbol{f}(i,j+2), \boldsymbol{f}(i+1,j+2), \boldsymbol{f}(i+2,j+2))$$

where $\boldsymbol{f}(i,j)$ means the feature vector for the cell at the i-th row and the j-th column. The normalized histogram $\boldsymbol{v}_n$ is calculated as

$$\boldsymbol{v}_n = \frac{\boldsymbol{v}}{||\boldsymbol{v}||_1 + \varepsilon} \quad (\varepsilon = 1) \tag{4}$$
$$||\boldsymbol{v}||_1 = \sum ||\boldsymbol{f}(i,j)||_1 \tag{5}$$

where $||\boldsymbol{f}(i,j)||_1$ means the sum of f_n in cell (i,j), and $\boldsymbol{v}$ means a feature amount for a block. The same cell is normalized many times because the focused block slides on the array of cells. Since the blocks that cross the frame edges are ignored, a total of $(\frac{w}{5} - 2) \times (\frac{h}{5} - 2)$ blocks are processed.

The amount of required memory for HOG feature extraction is $(\frac{w}{5} - 2) \times (\frac{h}{5} - 2) \times 8$ dimensions $\times$ 9 cells $\times$ 8 bytes and is not suitable for compact FPGA implementation. The HOG feature amount can be effectively reduced by binarization:

$$\boldsymbol{v}_b = \begin{cases} 1 & \text{if } \boldsymbol{v}_n \geq t_b \\ 0 & \text{otherwise} \end{cases} \tag{6}$$

where t_b is the binarization threshold [12]. Figure 2 shows this detail.

2.2 Real AdaBoost Classifier

A Real AdaBoost classifier is generated by combining weak classifiers, each of which returns true or false. A weak classifier is expressed as $C_w = \{P, H\}$, where P and H are a block coordinate and a HOG feature amount, respectively.

A weak classifier returns true if a given image has the HOG feature H at the block coordinate P. A strong classifier C_s is consisted of multiple weak classifiers: $C_s = \{C_{w1}, C_{w2}, \cdots, C_{wi}\}$. The number of weak classifiers that returns true corresponds a likelihood of the detection target. Weak classifiers that forms a strong classifier are serially generated through an iterative learning process by changing weight values. This learning process is separated from the FPGA hardware and is processed offline. Let us consider the following variables:

- Index of learning data: $s = 1, 2, \cdots, S$
- Index of learning iterations: $n = 1, 2, \cdots, N$
- Block coordinate for learning data: $P = 1, 2, \cdots, B$
- HOG feature amount: $H = 0, 1, \cdots, 255$
- Row index of cells in block: $i = 1, 2, 3$
- Column index of cells in block: $j = 1, 2, 3$

where S is the number of learning data, N is the number of learning iterations, and B is the number of blocks. First, we prepare a total of S learning image data including both positive samples that show a human and negative samples that do not. Then, we extract HOG features for each block of each data. We also assign a weight value D_s for each data, which is initialized to $\frac{1}{S}$.

We generate distribution of occurrence probability of HOG feature amount $W_+{}^{H(S,P,i,j)}$, $W_-{}^{H(S,P,i,j)}$ for each block coordinate P, using learning data weights D_s. HOG feature values in sample data are converted to bins, and the corresponding occurrence probability of the HOG feature is calculated as:

$$W_+{}^{H(S,P,i,j)} = \sum_{\text{positive samples}} D_s \tag{7}$$

$$W_-{}^{H(S,P,i,j)} = \sum_{\text{negative samples}} D_s. \tag{8}$$

In addition, we calculate the differences between the two functions $W_+{}^{H(S,P,i,j)}$ and $W_-{}^{H(S,P,i,j)}$. If the difference is larger, it would be a better criterion. Accordingly, the combination of H and P which maximizes

$$W_{\text{diff}} = W_+{}^{H(S,P,i,j)} - W_-{}^{H(S,P,i,j)} \quad (H \neq 0) \tag{9}$$

is selected as a weak classifier. We do not select weak classifiers with $H = 0$, since a lot of zero values are produced by the feature binarization.

Before repeating the aforementioned flow, the weight values D_s of the data are changed. With respect to the sample images that have the same HOG feature amount H at the corresponding block coordinate P as those of the selected weak classifier, the weight values are unchanged. For the other samples, the weight values are multiplied by $\exp(\frac{1}{2})$. Afterwards, the updated weight values are normalized. Eventually, the weight values of the sample images for which the selected weak classifier returns true are decreased whereas the other weight values are increased. We repeat this learning process N times and select one weak classifier for each iteration of the process. However, as the same weak classifiers may be selected multiple times, the total number of the weak classifiers is not necessarily N.

2.3 SVM Classifiers

The basic idea of the SVM technique is to find a border line (hyperplane), which discriminates positive samples and negative samples distributed in a feature space. According to HOG-based human detection, each binarized histograms in the detection window span a multidimension feature space. Each training data consisting of positive and negative samples is converted to a HOG vector x_i and mapped on the feature space. This problem is formalized as an L2-regularized L2-loss support vector classification with the following primal problem:

$$\min_{w} \frac{1}{2} w^T w + C \sum_{i=1}^{l} (\max(0, 1 - y_i w^T x_i))^2 \tag{10}$$

where $y_i \in \{+1, -1\}$ show labels of training data (+1 for positive samples and −1 for negative samples), $C > 0$ is a penalty parameter, and w is a weight vector of the discriminant hyperplane.

In order to increase the accuracy of classification, the discriminant function of the classifier may introduce a bias term. By choosing a appropriate constant value B, the dimension of training vectors can be increased as: $x_i^T \leftarrow [x_i^T, B]$. Moreover, the dimension of the discriminant hyperplane solved by the SVM technique is also increased as: $w^T \leftarrow [w^T, b]$. The detection process is performed by using following discriminant function:

$$f(x) = [w^T, b][x^T, B]^T \tag{11}$$

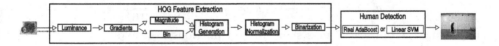

Fig. 3. Overview of our human detection system

where x represents a HOG vector extracted from the detection window. When the value of Eq. (11) is larger than 0, the window is detected as a human.

3 Implementation

We used an OmniVision Technologies OV9620 CMOS camera as an input device, which generates 8-bit Bayer pattern image data with 800×500 pixels, consisting of 640×480 valid pixels and a synchronization region. Figure 3 illustrates an overview of the system. This system actively employed the stream architecture pattern which consists of shift registers and FIFOs as shown in Fig. 4. With each arrival of a new data item, the item is shifted into the architecture so that the window of shift registers holds the data to be processed. On-chip BRAM blocks are used as FIFOs for line buffers. As the input data stream is processed in a deeply pipelined way, any external memory units are not required.

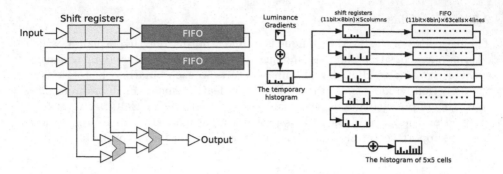

Fig. 4. Stream architecture pattern   **Fig. 5.** Histogram generation

3.1   Histogram Generation

Luminance data are calculated with a 2×2 mean filter for noise reduction. A total of 640×8 bits of on-chip memory is required for buffering and luminance data of 320×240 pixels are produced in a pipelined manner. The stream architecture pattern is also used for this calculation, requiring 3×3 shift registers and 2 lines of FIFOs to store $317(= 320 - 3)$ cells. The calculation of the gradient magnitude shown in Eq. (2) needs square arithmetic and square root arithmetic. These arithmetic units were generated by Xilinx CORE Generator. In order to make the hardware compact, direct calculation of the inverse tangent function was avoided by modifying the calculation for the gradient orientation shown in Eq. (1) into:

$$g_x \cdot \tan(\frac{n}{8}\pi - \frac{\pi}{16}) \leq g_y < g_x \cdot \tan(\frac{n}{8}\pi + \frac{\pi}{16}) \tag{12}$$

simplifying the bin selection as shown in our previous work [8].

Figure 5 shows the stream architecture for histogram generation, which needs 8 bins $\times$ 5 shift registers and four lines of FIFO buffers. Note that the histograms need not to be calculated every clock cycle because the cells are not overlapped each other. We accumulate the gradient magnitudes of five columns of cells to generate the temporary histograms. Once the temporary histograms are calculated, they are stored in the FIFO and the accumulated registers are initialized to 0. After five rows of temporary histograms are obtained, they are summed up in the column direction to make the final histogram of each cell.

3.2   Histogram Normalization

We employed an approximate method using the shift operations, where $||v||_1 + \epsilon$ was replaced by 2^α such that $||v||_1 + \epsilon$ to $2^{\alpha-1} < (||v||_1 + \epsilon) \leq 2^\alpha$. To alleviate the approximation error, piecewise approximation was performed by the following four intervals: $\left(2^{\alpha-1}, (1 + \frac{1}{4})2^{\alpha-1}\right], \left((1 + \frac{1}{4})2^{\alpha-1}, (1 + \frac{2}{4})2^{\alpha-1}\right], \left((1 + \frac{2}{4})2^{\alpha-1}, (1 + \frac{3}{4})2^{\alpha-1}\right], \left((1 + \frac{3}{4})2^{\alpha-1}, 2^\alpha\right]$. The comparison results of our method and a naive method using power-of-two divisions (shift operations) are shown in [8].

In spite of the approximation avoiding division arithmetic, these modules still occupy large part of LUT resources. Considering the fact that the module of the histogram generation does not output the results for each clock cycle as described above, there is room for improvement of the operation rates of the modules by resource sharing. In addition, focusing on the fact that the stream of histograms is not continuously flowed due to the synchronization regions of video images, we use on-chip memory buffering to optimize the pipeline scheduling and further improve the resource sharing.

3.3 Human Detection Using AdaBoost Classifier

Training for AdaBoost classifiers is performed by software in advance. The generated feature vectors H and the block coordinates P are stored in on-chip registers. We used 100×210 pixels sample images for machine learning, and the resolution is compressed to $\frac{1}{4}$ by a noise reduction mean filter, resulting in 50×105 pixels. Thus, the whole image contains 8×19 blocks.

Figure 6 shows the detection architecture with Real AdaBoost classifiers. The extracted HOG features of given input image are also stored in the stream architecture with shift registers and line buffers. The HOG features shown in the detection window are compared with weak classifiers. The comparisons are parallelly performed for every classifier. Then, the strong classifier circuit counts up the number of weak classifiers which match the extracted HOG features. The window regions where this count exceeds a threshold are detected as a human. In our architecture, this comparison and summation processes are performed in a pipelined manner with a latency of 3 clock cycles.

3.4 Human Detection Using Linear SVM

For the training of a linear SVM, we used liblinear [13] which is open source library for large-scale linear clustering. We used 100×210-pixel sample images for machine learning, thus the amount of HOG feature extracted from training data is $8 \times 19 \times 9 = 1,368$. As a result of training, the weight vector w of $1,369$ dimensions including a bias term were obtained. The detection hardware corresponding to Eq. (11) was implemented on the FPGA using the obtained weight vector. In order to simplify the circuit, we employed fixed-point arithmetic for the FPGA implementation of the SVM classifier. As shown in Fig. 7, we evaluated the calculation accuracy while changing the number of bits of fraction part. From the results, we decided 8-bit integers for HOG features and a fixed point numbers with a 6-bit integer part and a 22-bit fraction part for weight vector w.

We also employed the stream architecture with 72bits $\times 8 \times 19$ shift registers and 18 lines FIFOs to store 72bits $\times 54$ blocks for the detection window. The inner product is calculated by the HOG features of detection window and the weight vector. First, every column of the extracted features in the detection window is calculated by MAC operators, and then the results are accumulated as shown in Fig. 8.

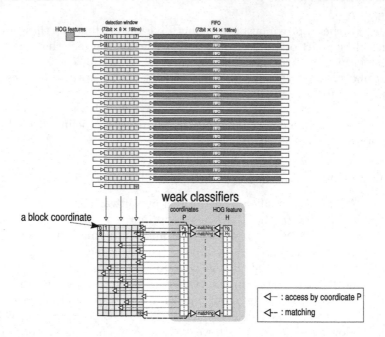

Fig. 6. Human detection using stream architecture

4   Evaluation and Discussion

We implemented the aforementioned architectures on a Kintex-7 XC7K325T FPGA using Xilinx ISE design tools 14.7. For training of both classifiers of AdaBoost and SVM, we used training images of NICTA Pedestrian Dataset (Positive Train Set and Negative Train Set) [14]. For comparison, we evaluated the designs changing the number of positive and negative samples: 1,000, 2,000, 3,000, 4,000, 5,000, 6,000, and 7,000. Besides, we evaluated with 28,000 positive and negative samples for the linear SVM, which was possible due to a high-speed solver in the liblinear library [15]. Table 1 summarizes implementation results of these designs.

4.1   Required Hardware Amount

In order to compare the resource utilization of Real AdaBoost and the SVM, we illustrate Table 1. It shows that required FPGA resources of Real AdaBoost tend to increase as long as the number of training images increases. The reason is that the more training images are available, the more weak classifiers are generated even with the same number of training iterations. On the other hand, required resources for the SVM designs are not changed much, since the dimensions of the weight vector w of the linear SVM do not depend on the number of training data.

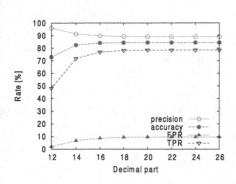

Fig. 7. Calculation accuracy using the type of fixed point

Fig. 8. Calculation architecture of linear SVM

Table 1. Resource utilization

Classifier	Slice regs	LUT	BRAM (18 Kb)	BRAM (36 Kb)	DSP48E	Frequency(MHz)	FPS
Real AdaBoost487 (p1000_n1000)	19,776	17,372	6	33	0	62.5	156
Real AdaBoost850 (p2000_n2000)	20,220	22,524	6	33	0	62.2	156
Real AdaBoost1123 (p3000_n3000)	20,514	26,321	6	33	0	62.4	156
Real AdaBoost1323 (p4000_n4000)	20,733	31,404	6	33	0	60.8	152
Real AdaBoost1488 (p5000_n5000)	20,949	33,348	6	33	0	57.2	143
Real AdaBoost1611 (p6000_n6000)	21,099	36,325	6	33	0	61.5	154
Real AdaBoost1737 (p7000_n7000)	21,257	38,155	6	33	0	60.3	151
Linear SVM (p1000_n1000)	65,984	68,164	4	29	840	51.4	129
Linear SVM (p2000_n2000)	66,247	69,039	4	29	840	54.1	135
Linear SVM (p3000_n3000)	65,906	67,901	4	29	840	51.7	129
Linear SVM (p4000_n4000)	64,380	65,656	4	29	840	52.2	130
Linear SVM (p5000_n5000)	63,856	64,841	4	29	840	54.3	136
Linear SVM (p6000_n6000)	63,388	63,950	4	29	840	48.6	122
Linear SVM (p7000_n7000)	63,059	63,516	4	29	840	52.8	132
Linear SVM (p28000_n28000)	60,292	65,413	4	29	613	56.9	142

In our implementation, the Real AdaBoost designs are more compact than the SVM designs. Since the weight vector has 1,369 dimensions and each of which needs 28-bit multiplier, the linear SVM designs require a relatively large amount of resources. Meanwhile, a weak classifier of our Real AdaBoost needs only 8-bit comparators for both feature patterns and block coordinates. Since the major task of the SVM classifier is an inner-product operation, DSP48E blocks are actively utilized by the SVM designs. However, even the largest Real AdaBoost design with 1,737 weak classifiers was implemented by about 60 % LUTs compared to the SVM counterpart.

Table 2. Detection rates

classifier	TP	TN	FP	FN	Accuracy	True positive rate	False positive rate	Precision
Real AdaBoost(p1000_n1000)	2564	2473	527	436	0.84	0.85	0.18	0.83
Real AdaBoost(p2000_n2000)	2661	2458	542	339	0.85	0.89	0.18	0.83
Real AdaBoost(p3000_n3000)	2675	2477	523	325	0.86	0.89	0.17	0.84
Real AdaBoost(p4000_n4000)	2617	2480	520	383	0.85	0.87	0.17	0.83
Real AdaBoost(p5000_n5000)	2614	2521	479	386	0.86	0.87	0.16	0.85
Real AdaBoost(p6000_n6000)	2653	2541	459	347	0.87	0.88	0.15	0.85
Real AdaBoost(p7000_n7000)	2636	2545	455	364	0.86	0.88	0.15	0.85
Linear SVM(p1000_n1000)	2243	2132	868	757	0.73	0.75	0.29	0.72
Linear SVM(p2000_n2000)	2264	2114	886	736	0.73	0.75	0.30	0.72
Linear SVM(p3000_n3000)	2300	2192	808	700	0.75	0.77	0.27	0.74
Linear SVM(p4000_n4000)	2367	2385	615	633	0.79	0.79	0.21	0.79
Linear SVM(p5000_n5000)	2359	2510	490	641	0.81	0.79	0.16	0.83
Linear SVM(p6000_n6000)	2369	2566	434	631	0.83	0.79	0.14	0.82
Linear SVM(p7000_n7000)	2403	2545	466	597	0.82	0.80	0.15	0.84
Linear SVM(p28000_n28000)	2354	2712	288	646	0.84	0.78	0.10	0.89

4.2   Performance

Table 1 also shows the maximum clock frequencies and the maximum throughput values in terms of frames per second (FPS) for the evaluated designs. Since our design policy was to make the entire system synchronized with the camera device clock, real-time frame rates were achieved by moderate clock frequencies, suggesting high energy efficiency. Compared to the SVM designs, the AdaBoost designs achieved slightly better performance, reflecting the advantage of the simple architecture of AdaBoost classifiers. The maximum frequency achieved by the Real AdaBoost designs with 1,737 weak classifiers was a 60.3 MHz, which corresponds to 151 fps, while the maximum frequency for the linear SVM designs was 56.9 MHz, which corresponds to 142 fps.

For comparison, we also implemented the same algorithms as an embedded software system on a Raspberry Pi Model B+ platform [16], equipped with an ARM 1176JZFS processor and a dedicated camera module. For video image handling, we used the OpenCV 2.4.1 library [17]. The measured frame rates of 0.23 fps and 1.06 fps were achieved by the Real AdaBoost and the linear SVM, respectively. The interesting point is that the SVM design was 4.6 times faster than the AdaBoost counterpart, because the comparisons with a lot of AdaBoost weak classifiers need to be serially performed in software implementation. This is one of major reasons why the SVM approach is more popular in software. In contrast, the AdaBoost can be efficiently implemented with the parallel processing property offered by FPGAs.

4.3   Quality of Detection

Next, we evaluated the quality of detection, comparing the two machine learning algorithms. In the validation test, we used 3,000 images of Positive Valid Set and 3,000 images of Negative Valid Set in NICTA Pedestrian Dataset.

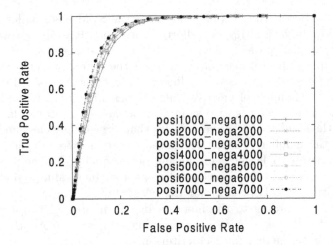

Fig. 9. ROC evaluation result of Real AdaBoost

First, by changing the threshold parameter of the Real AdaBoost, we plotted receiver operating characteristic (ROC) curves in Fig. 9, where the x-axis and y-axis show the false positive rate and true positive rate, respectively. The better quality of detection the system achieves, the closer to the upper left corner the curve goes. When the number of positive and negative training images was increased from 1,000 to 7,000, the detection accuracy was also improved. Obviously, this quality improvement requires additional hardware resources as we discussed before.

We also plotted ROC curves for the best SVM design in Fig. 10, by changing the bias parameter of the linear SVM. Compared to the threshold parameter

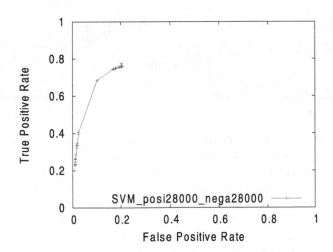

Fig. 10. ROC evaluation result of linear SVM

of the Real AdaBoost, the bias parameter for the SVM has smaller impact on the detection quality, resulting in a shorter trajectory. It is also shown that the better detection quality was achieved by the AdaBoost designs.

Table 2 depicts the comparison results on the detection qualities between the Real AdaBoost designs and the linear SVM designs. Here, TP, TN, FP, and FN show the number of positive samples that are successfully classified as a human, the number of negative samples that are successfully classified as a non-human, the number of positive samples that are wrongly classified as a non-human, and the number of negative samples that are wrongly classified as a human, respectively. A larger value means better quality for the accuracy, the true positive rate, and the precision, whereas a smaller value is preferable for the false positive rate. Especially for the SVM designs, the criteria values are much improved according to the increase in the number of training samples. Nevertheless, for the same number of training samples, the AdaBoost designs tend to show better quality for each criterion.

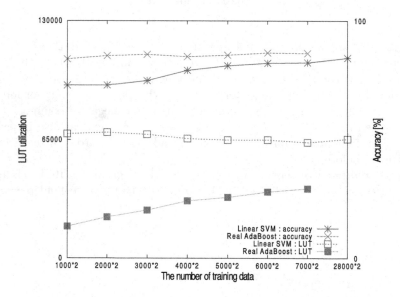

Fig. 11. The relation of resources (LUT) and detection rate (accuracy)

Figure 11 illustrates the tradeoff relationship between the two machine learning approaches, focusing on the number of utilized LUTs and the accuracy of the detection. The number of LUTs in the Real AdaBoost increases depending on the numbers of training data, but the LUTs in the SVM is still stable. However, the AdaBoost designs tend to be smaller as far as the data size we evaluated. With regard to the accuracy, the AdaBoost designs show better results than the SVM counterparts, especially for small training data size. Therefore, for embedded systems with severe requirements of power consumption, the compact architecture of the Real AdaBoost is preferable for FPGA implementation.

On the other hand, when we consider rather high-end systems compromising the hardware size to some extent, the SVM approach with a vast amount of training images could be a good solution for achieving high degree of accuracy.

5 Conclusion

This paper discussed the comparison of Real AdaBoost classifiers and linear SVM classifiers in terms of FPGA implementation of HOG-based human detection. While the FPGA resources required for Real AdaBoost designs were increased according to the improvement of the detection accuracy, resource requirements for SVM designs were stable. However, for the same number of training data, AdaBoost designs showed better accuracy with smaller hardware compared to SVM counterparts. Unlike software implementation, performance bottleneck of the Real AdaBoost classifiers was eliminated by FPGA implementation, achieving slightly better frame rates than the SVM classifiers. On the other hand, the dimensions of an SVM weight vector do not depend on the number of training data. Hence, the SVM approach have the advantage that a classifier can be updated without circuit reconfiguration, by just changing the weight values. Our future work includes hardware reduction of inner-product operations in SVM classifiers with a method such as a nested residue number system [18].

References

1. Dalal, N., Triggs, B.: Histograms of oriented gradients for human detection. In: Proceedings of IEEE Computer Society Conference on Computer Vision and Pattern Recognition, CVPR 2005, pp. 886–893 (2005)
2. Mizuno, K., Terachi, Y., Takagi, K., Izumi, S., Kawaguchi, H., Yoshimoto, M.: An FPGA implementation of a HOG-based object detection processor. IPSJ Trans. Syst. LSI Des. Methodol. 6, 42–51 (2013)
3. Cao, T.P., Elton, D., Deng, G.: Fast buffering for FPGA implementation of vision-based object recognition systems. J. Real-Time Image Process. 7(3), 173–183 (2012)
4. Komorkiewicz, M., Kluczewski, M., Gorgon, M.: Floating point HOG implementation for real-time multiple object detection. In: Proceedings of 22nd International Conference on Field Programmable Logic and Applications(FPL), pp. 711–714 (2012)
5. Hahnle, M., Saxen, F., Hisung, M., Brunsmann, U., Doll, K.: FPGA-based real-time pedestrian detection on high-resolution images. In: Proceedings of IEEE Conference on Computer Vision and Pattern Recognition, CVPR, pp. 629–635 (2013)
6. Hsiao, P.-Y., Lin, S.-Y., Huang, S.-S.: An FPGA based human detection system with embedded platform. Microelectron. Eng. 138, 42–46 (2015)
7. Negi, K., Dohi, K., Shibata, Y., Oguri, K.: Deep pipelined one-chip FPGA implementation of a real-time image-based human detection algorithm. In: Proceedings of International Conference on Field-Programmable Technology (FPT), pp. 1–8. IEEE (2011)
8. Dohi, K., Negi, K., Yuichiro, S., Kiyoshi, O.: FPGA implementation of human detection by HOG features with AdaBoost. IEICE Trans. Inf. Syst. 96(8), 1676–1684 (2013)

9. Matsubayashi, H., Nino, S., Aramaki, T., Shibata, Y., Oguri, K.: Retrieving 3-d information with FPGA-based stream processing. In: Proceedings of the 16th International ACM/SIGDA Symposium on Field Programmable Gate Arrays, p. 261. ACM (2008)

10. Dohi, K., Yorita, Y., Shibata, Y., Oguri, K.: Pattern compression of FAST corner detection for efficient hardware implementation. In: Proceedings of International Conference on Field Programmable Logic and Applications (FPL), pp. 478–481. IEEE (2011)

11. Dohi, K., Hatanaka, Y., Negi, K., Shibata, Y., Oguri, K.: Deep-pipelined FPGA implementation of ellipse estimation for eye tracking. In: Proceedings of 22nd International Conference on Field Programmable Logic and Applications (FPL), pp. 458–463. IEEE (2012)

12. Yamauchi, Y., Matsushima, C., Yamashita, T., Fujiyoshi, H.: Relational HOG feature with wild-card for object detection. In: Proceedings of IEEE International Conference on ComputerVision Workshops(ICCV Workshops), pp. 1785–1792 (2011)

13. Fan, R.-E., Chang, K.-W., Hsieh, C.-J., Wang, X.-R., Lin, C.-J.: LIBLINEAR: a library for large linear classification. J. Mach. Learn. Res. 9, 1871–1874 (2008)

14. NICTA Pedestrian Dataset. https://www.nicta.com.au/category/research/computer-vision/tools/automap-datasets/

15. LIBLINEAR library. http://www.csie.ntu.edu.tw/~cjlin/liblinear/

16. Raspberry Pi Model B+ platform. https://www.raspberrypi.org/products/model-b-plus/

17. OpenCV 2.4.1. http://opencv.org/documentation/opencv-2-4-1.html

18. Nakahara, H., Sasao, T.: A deep convolutional neural network based on nested residue number system. In: Proceedings of 25th International Conference on Field Programmable Logic and Applications, FPL 2015, pp. 1–6. IEEE (2015)

A Scalable Dataflow Accelerator for Real Time Onboard Hyperspectral Image Classification

Shaojun Wang[1,2]($^{\boxtimes}$), Xinyu Niu[2], Ning Ma[1], Wayne Luk[2], Philip Leong[3], and Yu Peng[1]

[1] Harbin Institute of Technology, Harbin 150008, China
wangsj@hit.edu.cn
[2] Imperial College London, London SW7 2NZ, UK
[3] University of Sydney, Sydney 2006, Australia

Abstract. Real-time hyperspectral image classification is a necessary primitive in many remotely sensed image analysis applications. Previous work has shown that Support Vector Machines (SVMs) can achieve high classification accuracy, but unfortunately it is very computationally expensive. This paper presents a scalable dataflow accelerator on FPGA for real-time SVM classification of hyperspectral images. To address data dependencies, we adapt multi-class classifier based on Hamming distance. The architecture is scalable to high problem dimensionality and available hardware resources. Implementation results show that the FPGA design achieves speedups of 26x, 1335x, 66x and 14x compared with implementations on ZYNQ, ARM, DSP and Xeon processors. Moreover, one to two orders of magnitude reduction in power consumption is achieved for the AVRIS hyperspectral image datasets.

1 Introduction

Hyperspectral image (HSI) classification aims to assign a categorical class label to each pixel in an image, according to the corresponding spectral and/or spatial features [1]. In satellite onboard processing, real-time HSI classification can significantly reduce download bandwidth and storage requirements, as well as enable greater autonomy due to improved real-time decision making ability. Moreover, improved processing speeds are necessary to match the higher spectral, spatial and temporal resolutions associated with improved sensors.

While there is a clear need for real-time HSI classification, it is challenging to meet both the required computational ($\approx 3 \times 10^{10}$ operations/second [10]) and power (< 20 W) constraints. In this paper we propose an FPGA-based SVM processor which fully meets these requirements. To the best of our knowledge, this is the first reported system that addresses this challenge.

Support vector machines (SVM) are a supervised non-linear machine learning technique which can effectively deal with the Hughes phenomenon [9], caused by

This work was partially supported by the Fundamental Research Funds for the Central Universities (Grant No. HIT.NSRIF.201615) and China Scholarship Council.

© Springer International Publishing Switzerland 2016
V. Bonato et al. (Eds.): ARC 2016, LNCS 9625, pp. 105–116, 2016.
DOI: 10.1007/978-3-319-30481-6_9

the high spectral dimensionality of HSI data. For this reason it has been widely used for HSI classification [3]. SVM classification is computationally intensive task, with computational complexity being linear with the number of support vectors (SV), the dimensionality of SVs, and the dimensionality of the problem [11]. Furthermore, a multi-class classifier is required for most remote sensing applications. In this paper, we focus on acceleration of the classification phase, and assume that training has been performed off-line.

FPGAs have been widely used to accelerate applications in a number of different fields usually achieving low power consumption [8]. Due to its importance, several FPGA-based implementation of SVMs have been reported using techniques such as Logarithmic Number Systems [4], Cascade SVM [11,14], systolic architectures [4,6], mixed-precision [12], coprocessor [2], and data flow architectures. Most of these studies focused on binary classifiers and were tailored to special applications. This work addresses the multi class classification problem in which strategies for dealing with data dependencies between binary classifiers are explored.

This paper proposes a scalable SVM multi-class classifier accelerator for HSI classification which achieves real-time on-board classifications under strict power and volume constraints. The main contributions are:

- A scalable accelerator architecture which utilises dataflow programming technology to maximize performance.
- Models to predict and optimise the proposed architecture.
- An implementation of the accelerator on a Maxeler MPC-X1000 dataflow node. The runtime, energy consumption and classification accuracy are evaluated and compared to ARM, ZYN, DSP and Xeon on real HSI datasets.

2   Background

Hyperspectral Images are typically represented as a data cube [1], $Z \in R^{n_1 \times n_2 \times n_b}$, with spatial information collected in the X-Y plane containing $n_1 \times n_2$ pixels, and spectral information represented in the Z-direction with n_b spectral bands.

Each pixel can be represented as a vector $z \in R^{n_b}$ in spectral space. Similar materials on the earth's surface have similar spectral feature, making the pixels separable. Multi-class classifiers are built from multiple binary classifiers and strategies can be parallel or hierarchical. Parallel approaches usually provide higher accuracy and less data dependencies, but require more binary classifier instances compared to hierarchical approaches [9]. Thus they are more suitable for FPGA based implementation. Parallel approaches label a new sample according to the result of a discriminant function whose inputs are the output of several parallel binary classifiers. The One-Against-One (OAO) parallel strategy usually provides higher accuracy when used with a proper discriminant function such as Hamming distance.

In OAO, a K class classification uses $K (K - 1) / 2$ binary classifiers to compute all pair-wise values. Each binary classifier is trained with the same number

---

Algorithm 1. Multi class SVM classifier with Hamming Distance as discriminant function

---

1: input a test pixel z;
2: **for** Iteration j from 1 to $K(K-1)/2$ **do**
3:    compute the jth Hamming Code bit with SVM binary classifier as

$$R\_code(j) = sign\left[\sum_{i=1}^{l} \alpha_{(j,i)} K(z, x_{(j,i)}) + b_j)\right] \qquad (1)$$

4: **end for**
5: **for** Iteration j from 1 to K **do**
6:    compute the Hamming distance with each class's mask and identifying code as

$$T\_res(j) = (R\_Code\&mask(j)) \oplus I\_code(j) \qquad (2)$$

7:    **for** Iteration i from 1 to $K(K-1)/2$ **do**
8:       accumulate the total none zero bits as hamming distance

$$H(j) = (T\_res_{(j,i)} == 1)?H(j) + 1 : H(j) \qquad (3)$$

9:    **end for**
10: **end for**
11: label the pixel with the index of $minH(j)$

---

of samples from two different classes. After training, the classification of a new pixel vector, $z \in R^{n_{b1}}$, involves the process as shown in Algorithm 1.

For each new test data, $K(K-1)/2$ binary classifiers can generate the corresponding $K(K-1)/2$ bit Hamming code, using Eq. (1), in which $x_{(j,i)} \in R^{n_{b1}}$ is the ith support vector in the jth SVM binary classifier, n_{b1} is the support vectors's dimension which is usually much less than the number of spectral bands n_b, l is the total number of support vectors in each SVM binary classifier, $\alpha_{(j,i)}$ is the ith Lagrange multiplier in j^{th} SVM binary classifier, b_j is a real constant, and $K(z, x_{(j,i)})$ is the kernel function. In this work, we employ the widely-used radial basis function (RBF) kernel:

$$K(z, x_j) = exp\left\{- \| z - x_j \|_2^2/\sigma^2\right\} \qquad (4)$$

where σ is the width parameter. The values of the hyperparameters, σ, α and b are ascertained by cross validation during training.

Each class also has an identifying code formed in the training process. By computing the Hamming distances between the test data's Hamming code and each classes' according to Eqs. (2) and (3), the test data is labelled with the class with the minimum corresponding Hamming distance.

In Eq. (2), $mask(j)$ and $I\_Code(j)$ are the mask code and identifying code of the jth class. Table 1 shows an example in which these codes are generated for a 4 class classification problem. In this example, we use $C_4^2 = 6$ binary classifiers, with the binary classifier for classes 1 and 2 being labelled as $1vs2$. The outputs can have values of 1, 0, and x, where 1 and 0 indicate whether the processed

Table 1. The identifying and mask codes for a 4-classification problem

	1vs2	1vs3	1vs4	2vs3	2vs4	3vs4	Identifying code	Mask code
Class 1	1	1	1	x	x	x	111000	111000
Class 2	0	x	x	1	1	x	000110	100110
Class 3	x	0	x	0	x	1	000001	010101
Class 4	x	0	0	x	0	0	000000	001011

datum is in this class, and x indicates the output is not related to this class. In Table 1, the outputs of $2vs3$, $2vs4$, and $3vs4$ are labelled x for class 1, since class 1 is not used in these classifiers. To support efficient hardware operators, the mask code sets the bit that corresponds to x to be 0 to only use relevant outputs, and the identifying code contains the classifier outputs.

3   Accelerator Architecture

3.1   Architecture Overview

The data flow accelerator architecture is shown in Fig. 1. We implement a data flow engine (DFE) on an FPGA chip. The DFE takes newly sampled data, and outputs classification results to the decision system or downlink system of satellites. Several binary classification kernel (BC kernel) groups are instantiated on the FPGA, each of which can generate the Hamming code for an image pixel. With the Hamming distance kernel following each BC kernel group, each pixel is assigned a class label. The collection kernel combines the results of the Hamming distance kernel to a certain bit width and finally outputs the results for all the pixels processed in the DFE.

The number of BC kernel groups in the DFE can be adjusted according the classification problem size and the hardware resources available on the FPGA. The whole system is scalable and flexible, and can fit different application. Moreover, no data dependencies exist between different BC kernels. All BC kernel groups operate simultaneously to achieve the best performance under memory and interface bandwidth constraints.

3.2   Memory and Computation Data Flow

As shown in Fig. 1, different BC kernel groups have separate image data RAM and share preload SVM model ROMs. A single DFE contains M BC kernel groups, and M image data RAMs are instantiated. The preload SVM model ROMs store the parameters for each binary SVM classifier that comprise the support vectors and corresponding alpha parameter. For each binary SVM model, a support vector (SV) ROM and corresponding Alpha parameter ROM are instantiated. For the BC kernel group containing N BC kernels, N SV ROMs and N Alpha ROMs are needed. The data in each SV ROM and each Alpha ROM

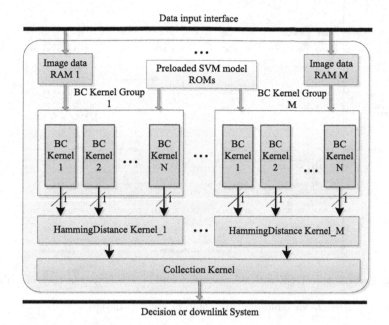

Fig. 1. Architecture of multi class classifier for HSI classification

are shared by M BC kernel with the same index in M BC kernel groups. All the data are stored as 32 bit single precision values for compatibility with software, but computations are in fixpoint (16,16) to save DSP resources and decrease computing latency. The data flow in DFE is shown in Fig. 2. In Fig. 2, $z(i,j)$ is the jth element of ith test pixel vector, $SV\_t(i,j)$ is the jth element of ith support vector in t^{th} binary classifier, $Alpha\_t(i)$ is the ith Lagrange multiplier in the tth binary classifier, l is the total number of support vectors for each binary classifier and n_{b1} is the dimension of support vector.

As shown in Fig. 2, M BC kernel groups, containing total $M \times N$ BC kernels, work simultaneously. Each kernel inputs one element of the support vector and one element of the test pixel vector in each clock tick. So M test pixels can get their corresponding N bits hamming codes in $l \times n_{b1}$ ticks.

3.3 Design Models

In this section, we analyze the performance of the aforementioned architecture. We use a resource specification file to indicate the number of available resources in the target platform. The available resources include on-chip logic resources and off-chip bandwidth resources.

In order to eliminate performance bottlenecks, we develop design models to estimate resource usage based on application variables and design parameters, as listed in Table 2.

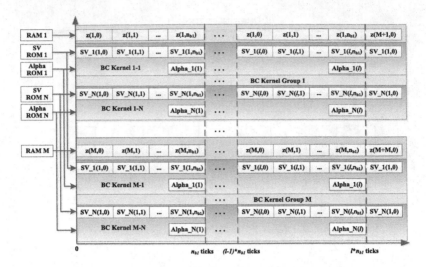

Fig. 2. Data flow in DFE with M classifiers and N BC kernel in each classifier

Table 2. Variables and parameters used by design models.

Design parameters	
na_i	Number of arithmetic operators of type i
$r_{i,L/F/D}$	Resource usage of a type i arithmetic operator on LUTs, FFs, or DSPs
r_M	Number of bits can be stored in a BRAM
$A_{L/F/D/M/BW}$	Available logic, memory, and memory bandwidth resources
Application variables	
K	The number of classes
N	The number of BC kernels in each group and equals to $K(K-1)/2$
M	The number of BC kernel Groups in single DFE
l	The number of support vectors for each binary classifier
n_{b1}	The dimension of each support vector
Clk_Fren	The system clock frequency for the kernels

Bandwidth Analysis. ROM initialization is one-time process which is prior to the computation process and has no strict bandwidth requirements.

The off-chip data transfer only involves the data interface (PCIe, Ethernet, 1394) through which CPU or Spectral meter transfers test pixel data to RAMs and reads back classification results during computation process.

According to Fig. 2, M single precision pixel vectors should be transferred to RAMs in one clock in each first n_{b1} clock ticks starting from each integer times of $l \times n_{b1}$ clock ticks. The peak bandwidth is $32 \times M \times Clk\_Fren$. The pixel vector data will be stored in RAM and repeatedly used in total $l \times n_{b1}$ clocks.

The BC kernel group needs $l \times n_{b1}$ clock cycles to process one pixel, and the result is 4bits (for the maximum 16 classes situation), even M BC kernel groups work simultaneously, the output bandwidth is $4 \times M/(l \times n_{b1})$ bits/s. Therefore, we express the total bandwidth requirements (bits/s) as:

$$BW = 32 \times M \times Clk\_Fren + 4 \times M/(l \times n_{b1}) \tag{5}$$

Hardware Utilisation Analysis. The logic cells, on-chip memory and DSP blocks are the main resources consumed in the design. We list the data-path structure for BC kernels in Fig. 3. Most of the on-chip resources are consumed by arithmetic operators in BC kernels.

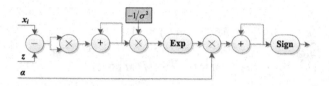

Fig. 3. Data path of binary classifier kernel

The proposed architecture contains $N \times M$ BC kernels. We express the on-chip logic resource usage as

$$R_{L/F/D} = \sum_{i \in \odot = +,-,*,\ldots} na_i \cdot r_{i,L/F/D} \cdot N \cdot M \tag{6}$$

where na_i indicates the number of arithmetic operators of type i, and $r_{i,L/F/D}$ indicates the resources (LUTs, FFs, or DSPs) consumed by the operator. As an example, as shown in Fig. 3, a BC kernel contains 3 multipliers ($na_\times = 3$) and each multiplier uses 1 DSP block ($r_{\times,D} = 1$).

The direct on-chip memory requirements involve the SV ROMs, Alpha ROMs and RAMs. We map these memory into Block RAMs (BRAMs) in FPGAs.

In Table 3, we list the number of bits the total on-chip memory architecture needs to store, and use r_M to indicate the memory capacity of a BRAM. As shown in the table, the number of total memory blocks can be expressed as:

$$R_M = 32 \times \lceil (N \times l \times n_{b1})/r_M + N \times l/r_M + (M \times n_{b1})/r_M \rceil \tag{7}$$

Performance Model. As shown in Fig. 1, a DFE can process M pixels in $l \times n_{b1}$ clock cycles when the bandwidth and hardware requirement are both satisfied. The system performance is $M \times Clk\_Fren/(l \times n_{b1})$ pixel/s. For real time image processing, the sampling rate S must satisfy the following formula.

$$M \times Clk\_Fren/(l \times n_{b1}) \geq S \tag{8}$$

Table 3. Memory requirements

	SVROM	Alpha ROM	RAM
Width (bits)	32	32	32
Depth	$l \times n_{b1}$	l	n_{b1}
Number	N	N	M
Total (bits)	$32 \times N \times l \times n_{b1}$	$32 \times N \times l$	$32 \times M \times n_{b1}$
Block memory	$\lceil (32 \times N \times l \times n_{b1})/r_M \rceil$	$\lceil (32 \times N \times l)/r_M \rceil$	$\lceil (32 \times M \times n_{b1})/r_M \rceil$

s.t.

- $32 \times M \times Clk\_Fren + 4 \times M/(l \times n_{b1}) \leq A_{BW}$
- $R_{L/F/D} = \sum_{i \in \odot = +,-,*,\dots} na_i \cdot r_{i,L/F/D} \cdot N \cdot M \leq A_{L/F/D}$
- $R_M = 32 \times \lceil (N \times l \times n_{b1})/r_M \rceil + \lceil N \times l/r_M \rceil + \lceil (M \times n_{b1})/r_M \rceil \leq A_M$

where A_{BW} indicates the available off-chip memory bandwidth, and $A_{L/F/D}$ and A_M indicates the available on-chip logic and memory resources.

4   Experiments and Results

In this section the performance of the proposed accelerator is compared to systems using radiation hardened and state-of-the-art commercial multi core CPUs.

4.1   Experimental Setup

The accelerator is implemented on a Maxeler MAX4 DFE which is equipped with an Altera Stratix V 5SGSMD8N2F45C2 FPGA. Although the DFE board is connected to a server via PCIe, our accelerator can operate without an external server, thus making it more suitable for space applications. We used the MAXJ language to express the accelerator design. The MaxCompiler maps the design to the FPGA and provides APIs for the host application running on the CPU.

The HSI data sets used are the well-known Airborne Visible Infra-Red Imaging Spectrometer (AVIRIS) Northwestern Indiana scene and Salinas Valley scene. These images data contain 224 spectral bands. However, because of water absorption and information redundance, only a few spectral bands, e.g. 9 in this study, are used for training and classification. Both images contain 16 classes.

4.2   Classification Accuracy and Hardware Occupation

LS-SVM[1] is adopted in training phase to keep the number equality of support vectors in each binary classifier. We evaluate the overall accuracy of our accelerator in the aforementioned two image data sets. For both images, we try to classify 6 classes from totally 16 classes. Each binary classifier is trained with

---

[1] The source code can be found from http://www.esat.kuleuven.be/sista/lssvmlab/.

100 samples containing 9 spectral bands, and 15 binary classifiers are used to realize the 6 class classification problem. 540 pixels in each image are used as the test pixel vectors. The overall accuracy and comparison with some recent research are shown in Table 4.

Table 4. Overall accuracy (OA) comparison

Methods	OA on first image (%)	OA on second image (%)
Approach in this paper	98.3	97.8
ANN based Adaboost [13]	98.02	-
MLRsub [5]	92.5	-
HA-PSO-SVM [15]	98.2	-
SdA [7]	91.9	95.5

From Table 4, the overall accuracy of the multi classifier based on Hamming distance is almost the same or better than other methods on these two data sets. We did not realize 16 classes because the other 9 classes did not have enough labeled samples for training. Many approaches have been proposed to solve this problem [15]. These methods are implemented during the training phase, and can be combined with the Hamming distance method of this study during the classification phase. The only problem is that we need more BC kernels in a group to realize multi classification.

Eight BC kernel groups each containing 15 BC kernels, 8 Hamming Distance kernels, 8 RAM kernels, 15 SV ROM kernels and 15 Alpha ROM kernels and one Collection kernel are instantiated in a single DFE. The target operating frequency is set to 120 MHz. The hardware utilisation after map and routing using Altera Quartus II 13.1 tool set is shown as in Table 5.

Table 5. FPGA resource utilization

Resources	Logics	FFs	DSPs	Block memory
Used	234666	443688	1680	1715
Avaiable	262400	524800	1963	2567
Utilization	89.43 %	84.55 %	85.58 %	66.81 %

From Table 5, we can see that hardware resources are almost fully utilized and Utilization is balanced between logic, flip-flops, DSPs and memory.

4.3 Performance Comparison with Other Processors

Radiation harden processors are the traditional option for satellite on-board computers, and performance of the most advanced space grade CPU, e.g. RAD750 from BAE systems, is just about 400 DMIPS @ 200 MHz. Other processors, such as ARM and DSP are also used in some low cost space missions, especially in some experimental micro satellites. In this context, we compare the run time and energy consumption between our DFE accelerator and some available commercial processors whose performances are similar with space grade CPUs. These processors include ZYNQ XC7Z020, ARM Cortex A9 and TMS320C6678 DSP. Xilinx ZYNQ XC7Z020 chip runs at 100 MHz frequency. Six binary SVM classifiers are instantiated in the PL part with HLS design and computation flow and data transfer management are performed with the ARM processor. The ARM Cortex-A9 processor runs at 666.7 MHz, and employs the Vector Floating Point Unit and 32 KB Cache to speed up the computing. TMS320C6678 DSP is one of the most advanced multicore DSP chips from Texas Instruments. It runs at 1 GHz and 8 cores are programmed in parallel. One million test pixel vectors are used for the evaluation. We also compare the performance of the accelerator with state-of-the-art dual Intel Xeon E5-2650 CPUs to demonstrate its performance advancement. The Xeon CPUs has 12 cores and 12 threads parallel programming are designed with OpenMP library. Eight millions test pixel vectors are used for duel CPUs performance evaluation. The detailed result is shown as in Table 6.

From Table 6, the accelerator on DFE gets 26x, 1334.5x, 66.4x and 14.2x speed up compared to the ZYNQ, ARM, DSP and Xeon processors respectively, while consuming two orders of magnitude less energy than the ARM, DSP and Xeon processors. However, less hardware resource in radiations harden FPGA chips and other reliability related measures, such as triple module redundancy (TMR) and configuration scrubbing, can decrease the performance in real space application compared to this study. The most advanced space grade FPGA chip, Xilinx Virtex-5QV XQR5VFX130, has about 1/7 hardware resources of the FPGA chip in this research. Taking the extra hardware consumption for TMR into account, the performance in space grade FPGA may decrease about 21 times compared to FPGA in this paper. Nevertheless more than 60x and 3x speed up compared to ARM and DSP respectively can be achieved.

4.4   Performance Comparison with Design Model

To evaluate the accuracy of the design model proposed in Sect. 3, we compare the real performance of accelerator with the theoretical performance from design model in terms of the average processing time for one pixel as shown in Fig. 4.

Table 6. Runtime and energy consumption comparison

Platform	ZYNQ	ARM	DSP	Xeons	DFE
T(μs/pixel)	25.8	1321.2	65.8	14.1	0.99
Power (W)	3.9	3.3	16	95	26.3
E(mJ/pixel)	0.1	4.3	1.05	1.33	0.03
Speedup	26.0	1334.5	66.4	14.2	1

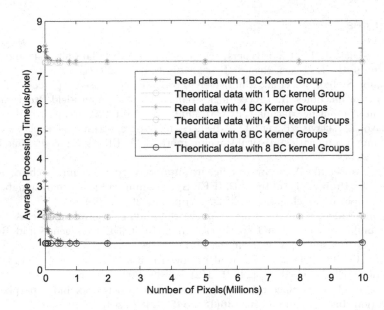

Fig. 4. Performance comparison between the models and real implementation

From Fig. 4, the real performances are similar to the theoretical results especially when the amount of pixels are larger than 1 M. When the pixels are less than 1 M, the real performance is lower than theoretical value. It's caused by kernel initialization which is a relatively fixed period but has more influences on the average performance for small datasets. The results demonstrate the accuracy of the design model is good enough for performance prediction and optimization.

5   Conclusion

This paper proposes a novel accelerator architecture for real time hyperspectral image classification which is a bottleneck for on-board hyperspectral image analysis. The Hamming distance based SVM is adopted as the multi class classifier which provides high accuracy and avoids data dependency between different binary classifiers. The accelerator uses the advantages of dataflow programming to achieve high performance and can be easily scaled to fit different applications. The accelerator is implemented on the Maxeler MAX4 DFE board. Experimental results on real HSI data sets show that Hamming Distance based multi classes SVM classifier can achieve higher or equal accuracy compared to other approaches, with 26x, 1334.5x, 66.4x and 14.2x speed up over ZYNQ, ARM, DSP and Xeon processors, while consuming one or two orders of magnitude lower energy. These results show for the first time, the feasibility of real-time on-board HSI classification. Future work involves accelerating the multi class classifiers with feature extraction, and extending the accelerator architecture to other state-of-the art classifiers, such as convolutional neural networks.

References

1. Bioucas-Dias, J.M., et al.: Hyperspectral remote sensing data analysis and future challenges. IEEE Geosci. Remote Sens. Mag. **6**, 6–36 (2013)
2. Cadambi, S., Igor, D., et al.: A massively parallel FPGA-based coprocessor for support vector machines. In: Proceedings - IEEE Symposium on Field Programmable Custom Computing Machines, FCCM 2009, pp. 115–122 (2009)
3. Gustavo, C., Davis, T., et al.: Advances in hyperspectral image classification: earth monitoring with statistical learning methods. IEEE Sig. Process. Mag. **31**(1), 45–54 (2014)
4. Irick, K.M., et al.: A hardware efficient support vector machine architecture for FPGA. In: Proceedings of the 16th IEEE Symposium on Field-Programmable Custom Computing Machines, FCCM 2008, pp. 304–305 (2008)
5. Khodadadzadeh, M., et al.: A new framework for hyperspectral image classification using multiple spectral and spatial features. In: IEEE Geoscience and Remote Sensing Symposium, pp. 4628–4631 (2014)
6. Kyrkou, C., Theocharides, T.: SCoPE: towards a systolic array for SVM object detection. IEEE Embed. Syst. Lett. **1**(2), 46–49 (2009)
7. Liu, Y., et al.: Hyperspectral classification via deep networks and superpixel segmentation. Int. J. Remote Sens. **36**(13), 3459–3482 (2015)
8. Lopez, S., et al.: The promise of reconfigurable computing for hyperspectral imaging onboard systems: a review and trends. Proc. IEEE **101**(3), 698–722 (2013)
9. Melgani, F., Bruzzone, L.: Classification of hyperspectral remote sensing images with support vector machines. IEEE Trans. Geosci. Remote Sens. **42**(8), 1778–1790 (2004)
10. Montenegro, S., et al.: Hyperspectral monitoring data processing, pp. 1–4 (2003). ISBN 3-89685-569-7
11. Papadonikolakis, M., Bouganis, C.S.: Novel cascade FPGA accelerator for support vector machines classification. IEEE Trans. Neural Netw. Learn. Syst. **23**(7), 1040–1052 (2012)
12. Papadonikolakis, M., Bouganis, C.S.: A heterogeneous FPGA architecture for support vector machine training. In: 18th IEEE Annual International Symposium on Field-Programmable Custom Computing Machines (FCCM), pp. 6–9 (2010)
13. Sami, Q., et al.: Neural network based adaboosting approach for hyperspectral data classification. In: International Conference on Computer Science and Network Technolgoy, pp. 241–245 (2011)
14. Christos, K., et al.: Embedded hardware-efficient real-time classification with cascade support vector machines. IEEE Trans. Neural Netw. Learn. Syst. **26**(1), 99–112 (2016)
15. Xue, Z., et al.: Harmonic analysis for hyperspectral image classification integrated with PSO optimized SVM. IEEE J. Sel. Top. Appl. Earth Observations Remote Sens. **7**(6), 2131–2146 (2014)

Fault-Tolerant Systems

A Redundant Design Approach with Diversity of FPGA Resource Mapping

Yudai Shirakura[1]([✉]), Taisei Segawa[1], Yuichiro Shibata[1], Kenichi Morimoto[2],
Masaharu Tanaka[3], Masanori Nobe[1], Hidenori Maruta[1], and Fujio Kurokawa[1]

[1] Nagasaki University, Nagasaki 852-8521, Japan
yudai@pca.cis.nagasaki-u.ac.jp
[2] Mitsubishi Hitachi Power Systems, Ltd., Yokohama 220-8401, Japan
[3] Mitsubishi Heavy Industries, Ltd., Tokyo 108-8225, Japan

Abstract. When applying FPGAs to control systems for industrial infrastructures such as thermal power plants, triple module redundancy (TMR) which is simple redundant design approaches is not enough in terms of functional safety. To cope with this problem, this paper proposes a novel dissimilar redundant design approach, focusing on the diversity offered by modern FPGA architectures. By mapping the same logic functionality to different FPGA resources, diversity is easily introduced in module redundancy using the same RTL description. In order to evaluate the effectiveness of the proposed approach, timing analysis of netlists and empirical experiments with a real FPGA chip are performed under an overclock situation as an example of common cause errors. The evaluation results show our approach effectively improves the error detection rate compared to conventional redundancy approaches.

1 Introduction

For recent control systems in industrial infrastructures such as thermal power plants, demands for high speed responsiveness, intelligent communication, and high performance arithmetic are increasingly growing. While use of multi-core processors is a mainstream of implementation, product cycles of multi-core processors are becoming quite shorter than plant facilities. Thus, it is becoming difficult to utilize the same architecture in a long term. From these viewpoints, FPGAs are receiving growing attention as a promising implementation approach of industrial control systems. Since FPGAs can offer an overlay architecture between application logic and physical devices, the problem of long-term succession of running application assets can be solved. Higher energy efficiency compared to multi-core processors is another merit of FPGAs in industrial infrastructures.

One of the major challenges of applying FPGA technologies for control systems in industrial infrastructures is reliability. Industrial plants need to meet the requirements of the functional safety standard IEC-61508 [1]. Here, enough risk management is required to face with both systematic failure due to deterministic factors such as algorithmic defects and random failure owing to accidental factors such as device deterioration. A conventional approach to the reliability

© Springer International Publishing Switzerland 2016
V. Bonato et al. (Eds.): ARC 2016, LNCS 9625, pp. 119–131, 2016.
DOI: 10.1007/978-3-319-30481-6_10

issues is redundant design such as triple module redundancy (TMR), where the same submodules are simply replicated. However, there is still a large possibility that all the redundant subsystems are affected by a common cause error at the same time. Therefore, IEC-61508 recommends to introduce diversity in redundant design, by combining different approaches to the same functionality. While a lot of work is performed for redundant design on FPGAs, how we should introduce diversity in FPGA redundant design has not been addressed so far.

This paper proposes a novel approach to introduce diversity in redundant design, focusing on a variety of hardware resources that modern FPGAs offer. The major contributions of this paper include:

- A novel FPGA redundant design approach, which introduces diversity in a resource mapping level.
- Analysis of error detection rates of the proposed designs with netlist simulation.
- Empirical evaluation of error detection rates of the proposed design with a real FPGA chip.

2   Background

2.1   Functional Safety and Dissimilar Redundancy

Frequency of failure occurrence in modern computer systems is increasing, in association with a recent rapid increase in its system size, performance and complexity and a basic risk management scheme in functional safety is to be able to detect errors and move to a safe state. One of the most popular approaches is redundant design, where an entire system can continue to operate even if an error occurs in part of the system.

However, even in a redundant system, the probability of a dangerous failure on demand (PFD) does not necessarily decrease, due to common cause errors. Therefore, introduction of diversity in redundant design is strongly recommended by the functional safety standard [1]. Diversity is to take different multiple approaches to obtain the same result. For example, different algorithms can be adopted to the same problem at the same time. Hereafter, redundancy with diversity is called dissimilar redundancy, while conventional redundancy without diversity is called similar redundancy.

Figure 1 shows the concepts of similar and dissimilar redundant designs. In similar redundant design, all the redundant submodules may be affected by a common cause error at the same time (e.g. temperature, humidity and radioactivity). Since the error will affect each module in the same manner, the same wrong values may be output. In this case, the similar redundant design cannot detect the error occurrence.

On the other hand, in dissimilar redundant design, each redundant submodule operates for the same functionality but in different mechanisms. Thus, the common cause error is expected to affect each submodule in different ways. Since each submodule will produce a different wrong output value, the error can be

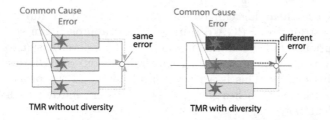

Fig. 1. Common cause error in similar and dissimilar redundant systems

detected by comparing these output values. In this way, dissimilar redundant designs achieve higher functional safety compared to similar redundant designs.

2.2 Related Work

Reliability improvement on FPGA designs has been mainly addressed in a context of a countermeasure for soft errors caused by radiation. Since soft errors hardly trigger common cause errors to redundant modules, the main approach is similar redundant design where the identical modules are simply replicated. The most common method is triple module redundancy (TMR) [2,3]. Partial and dynamic reconfigurability of FPGAs are also advantageous for recovery from soft errors in TMR designs [4]. Various granularity of reconfiguration including a tile-base approach has been proposed [5]. A comprehensive comparison was carried out in [6]. Simple redundancy on FPGAs was also discussed from a practical viewpoint of a control application [7]. Although the importance of diversity in redundancy has been pointed out in terms of software design [8], dissimilar redundant FPGA design with diversity has not been addressed so far. For soft error, a novel way of error detection and correction circuit for embedded reconfigurable systems has been proposed [9].

3   Proposed Approach

This paper proposes a novel method to implement dissimilar redundancy on FPGAs, focusing on diversity offered in resource mapping. While early FPGAs had rather simple and regular architecture mainly consisting of LUTs and FFs, modern FPGAs are composed of various specialized hardware primitives such as DSP blocks and memory blocks to enable more efficient implementation of circuits. This variety of hardware resources can provide diversity at a resource mapping level.

For example, an integer multiplier is typically implemented with DSP blocks on modern FPGAs. In addition, the same functionality of the multiplier can be implemented with conventional logic fabrics consisting of LUTs. As for memory functionality, we also have alternative resources such as memory blocks BRAMs and LUTs (distributed RAMs). In other words, modern FPGA architectures can offer diversity in mapping between logical functionality and physical hardware resources. Our proposal is to utilize this diversity for dissimilar redundant designs.

Since resource mapping can be generally controlled by directives in HDL files or as constraints to FPGA design tools, our approach can share the same HDL descriptions among redundant modules. Therefore, designers can easily introduce diversity, without preparing multiple versions of HDL descriptions for the same functionality. This is a practical advantage of the proposed method, compared to other approaches such as using different hardware algorithms for the same calculation.

4   Simulation Analysis

4.1   Evaluated Method

First, we carried out simulation analysis to evaluate how the error detection rate was improved by the proposed approach. We assumed timing violation caused by abnormality of the clock signal as a common cause error, and simulated this situation with overclocking. We evaluated five types of 32-bit pipelined arithmetic circuits, Arithmetic (1) to Arithmetic (5) illustrated in Fig. 2.

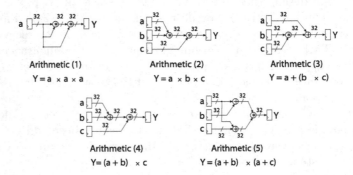

Fig. 2. Evaluated arithmetic circuits

The circuits were mapped on a Xilinx Kintex-7 xc7k325t-2 FPGA using an ISE-14.7 tool. For each arithmetic circuit, we prepared two versions of implementation: DSP version and LUT version. Both versions share the identical Verilog-HDL RTL description. While DSP versions were mapped on the FPGA with a default setting of the ISE tool, LUT versions were implemented with the additional directive of "(*use_dsp48 ="no"*)". Using these two versions, we evaluated the following three types of dual redundant designs for comparison:

- *DIVERSITY:* proposed dissimilar redundant design with a pair of DSP and LUT versions as shown in Fig. 3 (a)
- *DSP2:* similar redundant design using only DSP versions as shown in Fig. 3 (b)
- *LUT2:* similar redundant design using only LUT versions as shown in Fig. 3 (c)

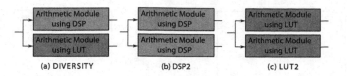

(a) DIVERSITY   (b) DSP2   (c) LUT2

Fig. 3. Evaluated redundant approaches

After FPGA mapping, the post-map netlists with timing information were generated and simulated while changing the clock frequency by 2 MHz. For each frequency, a total of $1,000,000$ random input test vectors were evaluated. When the given clock frequency is too high for design, either one of redundant modules or both modules may produce wrong output values (error occurrence). This error can be detected if the two redundant modules output different values (error detection). However, if the two modules output the same wrong values, the error cannot be detected (error overlooking). An error detection rate is defined as the number of detected errors divided by the number of error occurrences.

When an error occurs, the number of different bits (Hamming distance) between two output values is likely to related to the detectability of the error. Thus, we also evaluated the average Hamming distance between error values, which is defined as

$$H = \frac{\sum_{i=1}^{N} d(\boldsymbol{x_i}, \boldsymbol{y_i})}{B \cdot E} \tag{1}$$

where $d(\boldsymbol{x_i}, \boldsymbol{y_i})$ is the Hamming distance between the two redundant output values of the i-th execution trial, N is the total number of trials executed, E is the number of errors occurred, and B is the bit width of output values. In this experiment, $N = 1,000,000$ and $B = 32$ as aforementioned.

4.2 Simulation Results

Figure 4 describes the simulation results for Arithmetic (1). In Fig. 4 (a), different tendencies of error occurrences were shown by redundancy approaches. While the number of errors for LUT2 was gradually changed according to an increase in the clock frequency, a sudden increase in errors was shown for DIVERSITY and DSP2. This suggests that propagation delays of the LUT version have larger variance than the DSP version and strongly depend on input values. On the other hand, the delays of the DSP version are almost fixed for any operand values. Note these results are for $1,000,000$ trials with random input operands and are not for total inspection. Hence, errors of the LUT version were not observed for low clock frequencies, although the LUT version actually has a larger critical path delay than the DSP counterpart.

Figure 4 (b) suggests DSP2 overlooked many errors while DIVERSITY and LUT2 successfully detected most errors. However, comparing the error detection rates in Fig. 4 (c), it is revealed that LUT2 also overlooked many errors around 150 MHz. In fact, LUT2 overlooked 15, 923 errors at 152 MHz. Whereas,

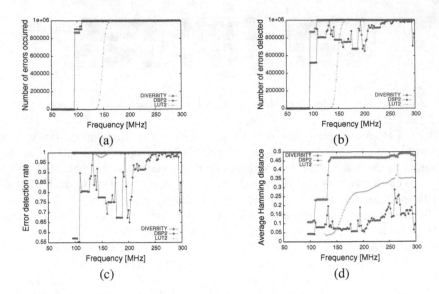

Fig. 4. Simulation results for Arithmetic (1)

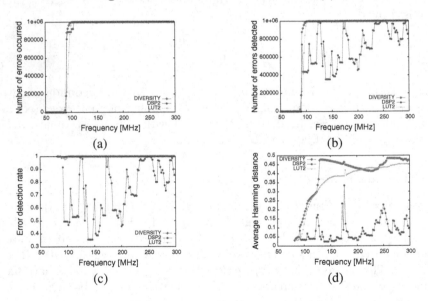

Fig. 5. Simulation results for Arithmetic (2)

DIVERSITY overlooked only 3 errors even in the worst-case frequency. In addition, the advantage of DIVERSITY is also shown as an improvement in the average Hamming distance as depicted in Fig. 4 (d).

The similar trends were observed for the results of the other arithmetic circuits (Figs. 5, 6, 7 and 8), demonstrating that the diversity introduced by the proposed method effectively improves error detection rates compared to

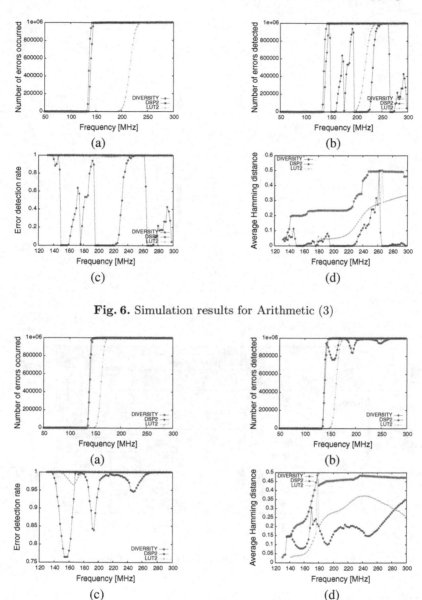

Fig. 6. Simulation results for Arithmetic (3)

Fig. 7. Simulation results for Arithmetic (4)

conventional similar redundant approaches. Comparing LUT2 with DPS2, LUT2 showed much better results. Since an LUT versions of arithmetic circuits is composed of multiple LUTs, certain diversity might be naturally introduced at different levels, such as LUT clustering or allocation to logic slices.

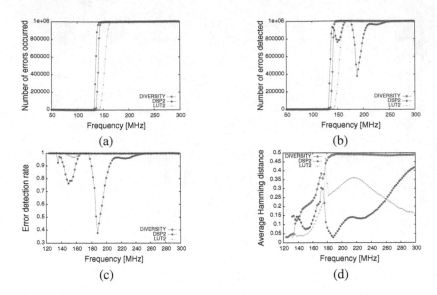

Fig. 8. Simulation results for Arithmetic (5)

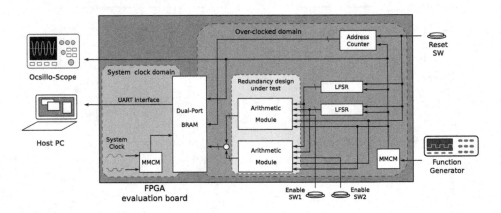

Fig. 9. Overview of empirical evaluation framework

5   Empirical Evaluation

5.1   Setup for Experiments

In the aforementioned simulation analysis using post-map netlists, timing models provided by the FPGA design tool did not reflect some practical issues such as on-chip variation of delays. Moreover, probabilistic behaviors caused by metastability were not also considered. Accordingly, we carried out empirical experiments with the same circuits as the simulation analysis by actually overlocking a real Kintex-7 xc7k325t-2 FPGA chip.

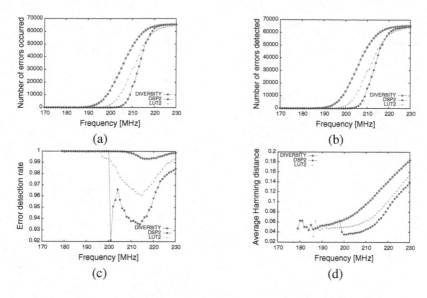

Fig. 10. Experimental results for Arithmetic (1)

Figure 9 shows an overview of a setup for the experiments. A function generator was utilized to feed a clock signal with a desired frequency, and this frequency was multiplied by 10 using an on-chip clock manager (MMCM). The output clock of this MMCM was used in a overclocked domain. Operand values to be fed to the arithmetic circuits were generated by random number generators implemented with a linear feedback shift register (LFSR). All the output values of arithmetic circuits were once stored in dual-port BRAM, and they were read back to a host PC using serial interface after execution. This data capturing mechanism was implemented in a system clock domain, which is not influenced by the frequency of the external function generator. After reading back all the results, comparison and analysis of the output values were performed offline on the host PC. The overclocked frequency was changed by 1 MHz. A total of 65, 535 operands were processed for each frequency.

5.2   Experimental Results

The result of the experiments for Arithmetic (1) is summarized in Fig. 10. Some differences with the simulated trend of error occurrence were shown in Fig. 10 (a). Errors on the real FPGA chip were observed with higher clock frequencies compared to the simulation results, since the timing models in the simulation assumed a pessimistic operational environment. Another difference is that the number of error of the DSP version was also gradually changed with the frequency, reflecting diversity introduced by practical environments such as on-chip variety of delays. Effects of this practical diversity were also shown in the trends of error detection. Comparing Fig. 4 (b) with Fig. 10 (b), fewer errors were overlooked by DSP2 in the empirical experiments.

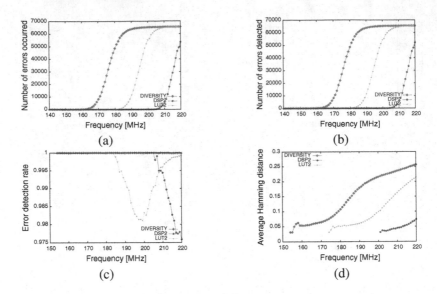

Fig. 11. Experimental results for Arithmetic (2)

Table 1. Summary of empirical evaluation results

Circuit	Worst-case error detection rate			Average error detection rate			Average Hamming distance		
	DIVERSITY	DSP2	LUT2	DIVERSITY	DSP2	LUT2	DIVERSITY	DSP2	LUT2
$a \times a \times a$	99.330	92.105	96.075	99.826	95.943	98.389	0.0931	0.0710	0.0752
$a \times b \times c$	99.988	97.584	98.113	99.999	99.046	99.365	0.1494	0.0480	0.1050
$a + (b \times c)$	99.985	98.989	98.384	99.997	99.905	99.567	0.0949	0.3947	0.1232
$(a + b) \times c$	99.436	97.872	97.802	99.833	98.809	99.345	0.0754	0.0601	0.0904
$(a + b) \times (a + c)$	99.846	98.765	99.464	99.986	99.563	99.938	0.0530	0.0506	0.0520

Nevertheless, the advantage of the proposed dissimilar redundancy was still shown in error detection rates as illustrated in Fig. 4 (c). DIVERSITY showed the best results and LUT2 was the second, which is the same order with the simulation results. Similar tendencies were observed for the other arithmetic circuits as depicted in Figs. 11, 12, 13 and 14. However, unlike the simulation results, LUT2 showed larger average Hamming distances for Arithmetic (3) and Arithmetic (4), reflecting the diversity introduced in LUT mapping to slices.

Table 1 summarizes the results of the empirical experiments. For all the arithmetic circuits, DIVERSITY achieved the highest worst-case error detection rate as well as the highest average error detection rate. While LUT2 showed larger Hamming distances in some cases, it was the second best in terms of the detection rates. As like in the simulation analysis, these empirical results have also revealed that the proposed dissimilar redundant approach effectively improves reliability of FPGA circuits.

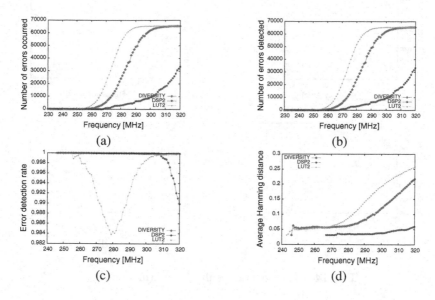

Fig. 12. Experimental results for Arithmetic (3)

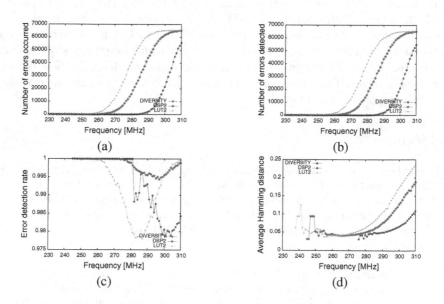

Fig. 13. Experimental results for Arithmetic (4)

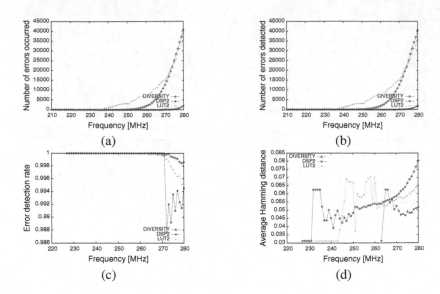

Fig. 14. Experimental results for Arithmetic (5)

6   Conclusion

This paper proposed and discussed a novel dissimilar redundant design approach using diversity of FPGA resources, to improve reliability from the perspective of a high degree of functional safety. We demonstrated the proposed approach effectively improved error detection rates for timing violation compared to conventional approaches, through simulation analysis and empirical experiments. Our future work includes evaluation with more practical application circuits with various type of common cause errors and further expansion of diversity using other resource mapping alternatives.

References

1. International Electrotechnical Commission: Functional safety of electrical/electronic/programmable electronic safety related systems, IEC 61508 (2000)
2. Ichinomiya, Y., Tanoue, S., Ishida, T., Amagasaki, M., Kuga, M., Sueyoshi, T.: Memory sharing approach for TMR softcore processor. In: Becker, J., Woods, R., Athanas, P., Morgan, F. (eds.) ARC 2009. LNCS, vol. 5453, pp. 268–274. Springer, Heidelberg (2009)
3. Hayek, A., Al-Bokhaiti, M., Borcsok, J.: Design and inplementation of an FPGA-based 1oo4-archtecture for safety-related system-on-chip. In: Proceedings of IEEE 25th International Confierence on Microelectronices(ICM), pp. 1–4 (2013)
4. Bolchini, C., Miele, A., Santambrogio, M.D.: TMR and partial dynamic reconfiguration to mitigate SEU faults in FPGAs. In: Proceedings of 22nd IEEE International Symposium on Defect and Fault-Tolerance in VLSI Systems, DFT 2007, pp. 87–95. IEEE (2007)

5. Kanamaru, A., Kawai, H., Yamaguchi, Y., Yasunaga, M.: Tile-based fault tolerant approach using partial reconfiguration. In: Becker, J., Woods, R., Athanas, P.,
   Morgan, F. (eds.) ARC 2009. LNCS, vol. 5453, pp. 293–299. Springer, Heidelberg
   (2009)
6. Konoura, H., Imagawa, T., Mitsuyama, Y., Hashimoto, M., Onoye, T.: Comparative
   evaluation of lifetime enhancement with fault avoidance on dynamically reconfigurable devices. IEICE Trans. Fund. Electron. Commun. Comput. Sci. **97**(7), 1468–
   1482 (2014)
7. Kocur, M., Kozak, S., Dvorscak, B.: Design and implementation of FPGA-digital
   based PID controller. In: Proceedings of International Carpathian Control Conference (ICCC), pp. 233–236 (2014)
8. Lovric, T.: Systematic and design diversity—software techniques for hardware fault.
   In: Echtle, K., Powell, D.R., Hammer, D. (eds.) EDCC 1994. LNCS, vol. 852, pp.
   307–326. Springer, Heidelberg (1994)
9. Zhao, Q., Ichinomiya, Y., Amagasaki, M., Iida, M., Sueyoshi, T.: A novel soft
   error detection and correction circuit for embedded reconfigurable systems. IEEE
   Embedd. Syst. Lett. **3**(3), 89–92 (2011)

Method to Analyze the Susceptibility of HLS Designs in SRAM-Based FPGAs Under Soft Errors

Jorge Tonfat[⊠], Lucas Tambara, André Santos, and Fernanda Kastensmidt

Instituto de Informática – PGMICRO,
Universidade Federal do Rio Grande do Sul (UFRGS), Porto Alegre, Brazil
{jltseclen, latambara, afdsantos, fglima}@inf.ufrgs.br

Abstract. SRAM-based FPGAs are attractive to critical applications due to their reconfiguration capability, which allows the design to be adapted on the field under different upset rate environments. High level Synthesis (HLS) is a powerful method to explore different design architectures in FPGAs. In this paper, we analyze four different design architectures implemented in a 28 nm SRAM-based FPGA under fault injection to analyze the probability of errors of them. We compare the information of essential bits provided by Xilinx with the susceptible bits obtained by fault injection. The dynamic cross section, soft error rate and mean work between failures are calculated based on the experimental results. There is a trade-off in the number of errors classified as silent data corruption and timeout errors according to the architecture and DSP blocks usage. The proposed characterization method can be used to guide designers to select the most efficient architecture concerning the susceptibility to upsets and performance efficiency.

Keywords: FPGA · Soft error · Fault injection · HLS

1 Introduction

Integrated circuits operating in high radiation environments are well known to be susceptible to errors due to particle ionization. However, circuits operating on Earth can experience transient faults too caused by the interaction of low and high-energy neutrons with the silicon [1]. Field Programmable Gate Arrays (FPGAs) are flexible components that can be customized and reconfigured to implement a large variety of designs. FPGAs are attractive devices for use in particles accelerators, automotive industry, aircrafts and satellites systems due to their high density and capability of integrating many designs into a single chip and still achieving high performance due to the process parallelism.

Transient ionization may occur when a single radiation-ionizing particle strikes the silicon, creating a transient voltage pulse, or a Single Event Effect (SEE). This effect affects integrated circuits by modifying values stored in the sequential logic, known as Single Event Upset (SEU), or by changing the function of a circuit in the combinational

V. Bonato et al. (Eds.): ARC 2016, LNCS 9625, pp. 132–143, 2016.
DOI: 10.1007/978-3-319-30481-6_11

logic, known as Single Event Transient (SET). SRAM-based FPGAs are mainly susceptible to Single Event Upset (SEU) in their configuration memory bits and embedded memory cells. When energy is collected by a sensitive junction of an SRAM cell transistor that composes the configuration memory bits of the SRAM-based FPGA bitstream, a bit-flip (SEU) can occur. This bit-flip can change the configuration of a routing connection or the configuration of a LUT or the configuration of the BRAMs. This bit-flip has a persistent effect, which can only be corrected when a new bitstream is loaded to the FPGA. Bit-flips can also occur in the flip-flop of the CLB used to implement the user's sequential logic. In this case, the bit-flip has a transient effect and the next load of the flip-flop can correct it. Thus, the majority of the errors observed in harsh environments come from bit-flips in the configuration memory bits. Fault injection in the bitstream can be performed in the laboratory, and it is useful for analyzing the logical vulnerability of a design to bit-flips in the configuration memory.

Depending on the design's architecture, more or less configuration bits are used and more or less susceptible bits may be responsible for provoking an error in the design output. However, it is not only the number of used bits that determine the sensitivity, the masking effect of the application algorithm plays an important role and for that there are tradeoffs in the architecture such as area, performance, execution time in clock cycles and types of resources utilized that may direct contribute to the soft error rate analysis in FPGAs.

This work presents a method to evaluate the susceptibility of designs generated by High Level Synthesis (HLS) tools by using fault injection in SRAM-based FPGAs. Essential bits and critical bits are obtained and compared for four different design architectures of a matrix multiplication algorithm. Static and dynamic cross sections were estimated and also the Mean Workload Between Failures metric is discussed. Previous works on HLS focus on the generated design quality in terms of area, performance or power consumption but not in analyzing their susceptibility under upsets in SRAM-based FPGAs [2, 3]. So, it is mandatory to propose a methodology to analyze the impact of using different architectures provided by HLS tools in the error rate of the design.

This paper is organized as follows: Sect. 2 describes the proposed methodology to analyze the susceptibility of HLS designs. Section 3 presents the fault injection results for the selected case-study designs. Finally, Sect. 4 presents the conclusions and future work.

2   Proposed Methodology

The susceptibility analysis of a design implemented in an SRAM-based FPGA under soft errors is not a straightforward task. It depends on the characteristics of the design and the susceptibility of the underlying FPGA platform. This section presents the metrics to analyze the susceptibility and the methods to obtain them.

2.1   Analyzed Metrics for Estimating Susceptibility

The following parameters should be used to characterize a design into SRAM-based FPGA under soft errors. We first define each one of these parameters that we suggest using in our proposed method. The first group of parameters include *Area* and *Performance*. The area of an implemented design can be expressed in terms of the number of used resources such as LUTs, flip-flops, BRAM blocks, DSP blocks, etc. Also, it is possible to express the area in terms of configuration frames. A configuration frame is the smallest addressable memory segment of the configuration memory (bitstream). Since each frame is related to a specific resource and position in the floorplan [4], it is possible to calculate the number of configuration frames used by a design. The performance of a design can be expressed in terms of the execution time, operational frequency and the processed workload. The execution time can be defined by the number of clock cycles to perform the operation. According to the FPGA and design architecture, a maximum clock frequency is achieved. Another important parameter is the workload processed by the design. The workload is the amount of data computed in one execution. In terms of reliability, the performance information is helpful to know how much time the design is exposed to soft errors during the execution of the implemented function.

The second group of parameters includes the *Essential bits*, *Error* and *Critical bits*. The essential bits are defined by Xilinx [5], and they refer to the amount of configuration bits associated to a design mapped in a certain FPGA. Essential bits are a subset of the total configuration bits, and they depend on the area of the implemented design. The errors are defined as any deviation from the expected behavior. They can be classified as Silent Data Corruption (SDC) errors and timeout errors. The critical bits are also defined by Xilinx [5] as the amount of configuration bits that once flipped they cause an error in expected design behavior (SDC or timeout). The critical bits are a subset of the essential bits.

The third group of parameters includes radiation measurements such as static and dynamic cross sections. The static cross section (σ_{static}) is an intrinsic parameter of the device usually expressed in terms of area (usually cm^2/device or cm^2/bit) and is related to the minimum susceptible area of the device to a particle species (e.g. neutron, proton, heavy ion, etc.). The expression to obtain the static cross section per bit of a device is:

$$\sigma_{static} = \frac{N_{SEU}}{\Phi_{particle}} \tag{1}$$

$$\sigma_{static-bit} = \frac{\sigma_{static}}{N_{bit}} \tag{2}$$

Where N_{SEU} is the number of SEU in the configuration memory bits, $\Phi_{particle}$ is the particle fluence. The fluence is measured by particle per cm^2, and it is calculated by multiplying the particle flux by the time the device has been exposed to that flux. The cross section per bit is calculated by dividing the static cross section by the total number of bits in the device (N_{bit}). In SRAM-based FPGAs the most important static cross section per bit is the one from the configuration memory and the user embedded memory (BRAM).

The dynamic cross section ($\sigma_{dynamic}$) is defined as the probability that a particle generates an error in the design. The expression to obtain the dynamic cross section is:

$$\sigma_{dynamic} = \frac{N_{ERROR}}{\Phi_{particle}} \qquad (3)$$

Where N_{ERROR} is the number of errors observed in the design behavior and $\Phi_{particle}$ is also the particle fluence.

The fourth group of parameters include the metrics used based on the radiation measurements and estimations in the laboratory. They are *Soft Error Rate* (SER) and *Mean Workload Between Failures* (MWBF). SER is expressed in Failure in Time (FIT) units, and is defined as the expected amount of errors per 10^9 device operation hours in a determined radiation environment. It can be obtained multiplying the dynamic cross section with the particle flux in the radiation environment. The metric MWBF was proposed in [6], and it evaluates the amount of data (workload) processed correctly by the design before the appearance of an output error. It is defined as:

$$MWBF = \frac{w}{\sigma_{dynamic} * flux * t_{exec}} \qquad (4)$$

Where w is the workload processed in one execution, $\sigma_{dynamic}$ is the dynamic cross section, *flux* is the particle fluence per unit time and t_{exec} is the execution time of the design.

2.2 Xilinx Analysis Tools

By using the Xilinx Vivado design tool, we can obtain the following metrics: area in terms of resource utilization after the design is placed and routed, the performance of the design in terms of clock cycles and execution time, and also the essential bits of a particular design. The essential bits are calculated using a proprietary algorithm of the Xilinx tool after the bitstream is generated. Excluding essential bits, all the other mentioned metrics can be obtained with tools from other FPGA manufacturers.

2.3 Fault Injection Method

Fault injection (FI) by emulation is a well-known method to analyze the reliability of a design implemented in an SRAM-based FPGA. The original bitstream configured into the FPGA can be modified by a circuit or a computer tool by flipping one of the bits of the bitstream, one at a time. This flip emulates an SEU in the configuration memory cells. Fault injectors take advantage of dynamic partial reconfiguration capabilities of SRAM-based FPGAs to reduce the time to inject bit-flips.

The produced data output of the design under test (DUT) can be constantly monitored to analyze the effect of the injected fault into the design. If an error is detected, this means that this configuration memory bit is a critical bit. It is possible to inject faults in all the configuration bits and obtain the critical bits of the design. The entire fault injection campaign can spend from few hours to days depending on the amount of bits that are going to be flipped and the connection to the fault injection control circuit. The fault injection method provides us the error analysis, classification and the critical bits.

2.4   Accelerated Radiation Method

The accelerated radiation method consists in exposing the device in front of a particle accelerator beam and monitor the design behavior. This method is employed to obtain the device sensitivity to a determined range of particles and also to obtain a soft error rate of a circuit. In the case of FPGAs, the test can be static or dynamic. The basic procedure consists on programming the FPGA with a known (golden) bitstream, irradiate the device and continuously readback the bitstream from the FPGA, to compare to the golden bitstream and to count the number of bit-flips. From the static test, it is possible to calculate the static cross section of the FPGA configuration memory. The static cross section can be given per bit. In case the target FPGA has already been tested for a particular particle, the static cross section can be found in papers or in datasheets. The static cross section per bit for many Xilinx FPGAs can be obtained from the Xilinx Reliability Report [7]. In this work, the static cross section of each circuit is estimated using the static cross section per bit from the Xilinx Reliability Report under neutron and the number of configuration bits (frames) the design uses.

The dynamic test analyzes the design output mapped into the FPGA, and from this test is obtained the dynamic cross section and soft error rate. In this case, the expected soft error rate is much lower than the obtained from the static test. In this work, we calculate the dynamic cross section by a method proposed in [8]. The details are shown in next section.

3   Experimental Results

In order to evaluate the effects of using High Level Synthesis (HLS) in the design for SRAM-based FPGAs in the susceptibility to soft errors, we use the method proposed in Sect. 2. The idea is to have a straightforward method to predict the susceptibility and in early design phase being able to select the designs that will present the highest reliability and efficiency when synthesized into SRAM-based FPGAs.

3.1   Case-Study Designs Using HLS from Xilinx

The evaluated case-study algorithm is the matrix multiplication. The algorithm is shown in Fig. 1. Each input matrix is a 6×6 8-bits array generating a 6×6 16-bits array output. Two architectural versions were generated using the Xilinx HLS tool from the algorithm C source code.

```
void matrixmul(
        mat_a_t a[MAT_A_ROWS][MAT_A_COLS],
        mat_b_t b[MAT_B_ROWS][MAT_B_COLS],
        result_t res[MAT_A_ROWS][MAT_B_COLS])
{ // Iterate over the rows of the A matrix
   Row: for(int i = 0; i < MAT_A_ROWS; i++) {
       // Iterate over the columns of the B matrix
       Col: for(int j = 0; j < MAT_B_COLS; j++) {
           res[i][j] = 0;
           // Do the inner product of a row of A and col of B
           Product: for(int k = 0; k < MAT_B_ROWS; k++) {
               res[i][j] += a[i][k] * b[k][j]; }}}}
```

Fig. 1. Matrix multiplication algorithm.

The HLS tool requires a validated algorithm source code and a set of constraints and directives to generate an RTL synthesizable netlist. The design flow is presented in Fig. 2.

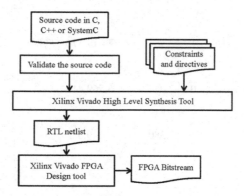

Fig. 2. FPGA design flow using Xilinx High Level Synthesis (HLS) tool.

The first design is generated by using no optimization directives in the tool. So the generated circuit implements the hardware for the inner product loop (Fig. 1) and an FSM to control the data flow. The second design uses the pipeline directive, so the three iteration loops are unrolled, and many instances of the hardware inner product are generated. The generated circuit implements a pipeline version of the inner product loop hardware (Fig. 1) and it presents a pipeline of 37 stages depth. Each architectural version has two different synthesis map implementations in the FPGA matrix. One uses the DSP48E resources to implement the adders and multipliers of the FPGA and the other not, consequently the adders and multipliers are implemented by Lookup Tables (LUTs). The four design versions are named: *No opt., No DSP48E*; *No opt., with DSP48E*; *Pipeline opt., No DSP48E*; and *Pipeline opt., with DSP48E*.

The matrix inputs A and B are stored in two embedded memories (BRAM) and the output matrix C is stored in other BRAM for all the architectures. Each element of the input matrixes is fixed to the value 0×55 that resembles a checkerboard pattern. So, the output matrix is also fixed for all the executions.

The designs were synthesized into SRAM-based FPGA Artix-7 XC7A100TCSG324 from the 7-series family. The configuration frame size varies among FPGA families; and in the case of the Xilinx Artix-7 FPGA, each frame has 101 words of 32-bits [4]. Table 1 shows the area implementation results and the performance analysis of the four design versions. Performance is presented in terms of execution time measured in clock cycles and in time when a 100 MHz clock is used. The workload is given in bits. In this work, the workload is two matrixes of 36 elements each and each element is an 8-bit data.

Table 1. Area details in terms of FPGA resources and configuration bits. Performance results in terms of execution results and workload.

	Area					Performance		
Matrix Mult. version	# 6-input LUTs	#User FFs	DSP 48E	#Config. frames in design area	#Config. Bits in design area	Exec. time (clk cycles)	Exec. time (ns) @ 100 MHz	Workload (bits)
No opt., No DSP48E	155	70	0	2,044	6,569,416	733	7,330	576
No opt., with DSP48E	50	38	1	2,184	7,019,376	733	7,330	576
Pipeline opt., No DSP48E	18,910	5,735	0	2,044	6,569,416	36	360	576
Pipeline opt., with DSP48E	1,117	1,327	198	2,380	7,649,320	36	360	576

The versions with the pipeline optimization use more resources and have a better execution time than the versions without optimization since the HLS tool unrolls the loops, generating more hardware instances and incrementing the parallelism. Also, it is possible to see that the use of DSP resources reduces the number of LUTs since the multipliers and adders are better implemented in dedicated DSP resources.

3.2   Obtaining Critical Bits from Fault Injection

The fault injector platform used in this work is based on the fault injection platform first presented in [9]. The fault injection core controls the Internal Configuration Access Port (ICAP) to be able to read and write frames of the bitstream of the FPGA. The original fault injection core handled frames from the Virtex-5 bitstream, so modifications were performed to adapt the core to handle frames from the Artix-7 bitstream that is from Series 7 FPGA family.

The fault injection campaign is defined by the flow diagram of Fig. 3a. The first step is to setup the injection campaign that includes the injection area and the type of fault injection campaign. In this case, the critical bits of each design version are obtained by an exhaustive fault injection in all the configuration bits of the injection area one at a time and identifying the ones that cause the matrix multiplication behavior differs from the golden execution.

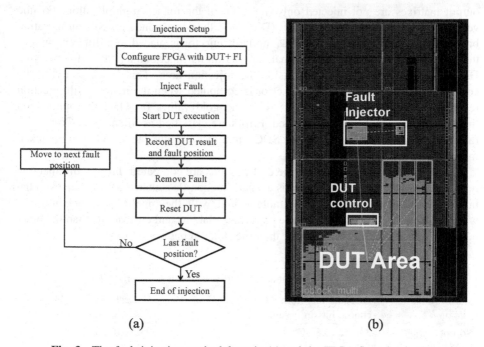

(a)   (b)

Fig. 3. The fault injection methodology in (a) and the FPGA floorplan in (b).

The next step is to configure the FPGA with the DUT and the fault injector (FI). Then, the first fault is injected, and it is done before the execution of the DUT. Afterwards, the DUT starts executing its function and when the DUT execution is finished, the DUT result is analyzed. The DUT result analysis and fault position are saved. Finally, the fault is removed and the DUT is taken to its initial good known condition, prepared for the next fault injection. This process is done until all the configuration bits of the DUT area are evaluated. The required time to complete a fault injection campaign depends on the DUT area and the time to inject and remove a fault. The time to inject a fault is constant and is in the order of few microseconds for this device. But to remove a fault, it is used two approaches. The first one is to insert again a fault in the same bit, restoring its original value, and then the DUT is run again to verify that the fault was removed successfully. When the error is not removed, a second approach is used. The monitor PC reconfigures the whole FPGA to ensure that all configuration bits are restored. The latter approach is the main reason why some of our fault injection campaigns last more than one day. This approach can be improved by using dynamic partial reconfiguration on the DUT.

In the monitor PC, it is defined the injection area, as shown on the floorplan in Fig. 3b. The DUT area is the injection area where the matrix multiplication designs are placed, and this area remains constant for the four designs. In this area are only injected the configuration bits related to CLBs (LUTs, user FFs and interconnection) and clock distribution interconnection. BRAM configuration bits are not injected, so the input and output matrixes are not injected only the logic of the matrix multiplication. For the versions which include DSP resources (DSP48E), the correspondent DSP configuration bits were added to the injection area. The fault injector is placed in a different area of the FPGA to avoid fault injections that can disrupt its functionality. It is also shown a DUT control block that is also outside the injection area. This block analyzes the correctness of the output matrix. An error is computed when the matrix multiplication results stored in the memory differs from the gold values or when the application finished in a different time as expected. Errors are classified as Silent Data Corruption (SDC) errors and timeout errors. The SDC can affect a single data element in the result matrix, or it can affect a set of them.

In Table 2, the critical bits and the essential bits are compared. From fault injection results, it can be observed that there is a small fraction (less than 10 %) of the essential bits that are critical. The version implemented with the pipeline optimization and without using the DSP resources have more essential bits and critical bits than the other designs since it uses more resources than the other versions.

Table 2. Xilinx essential bits and critical bits comparison.

Matrix Mult. version	Essential bits from Xilinx tool (% of config. bits in design area)	Critical bits from FI (% of Essential bits)
No opt., No DSP48E	34,862 (0.53 %)	2,434 (6.98 %)
No opt., with DSP48E	18,208 (0.26 %)	1,740 (9.56 %)
Pipeline opt., No DSP48E	3,494,735 (53.20 %)	170,929 (4.89 %)
Pipeline opt., with DSP48E	834,967 (10.92 %)	66,758 (8.00 %)

The proposed method presented by Velazco R, et al. [8] was used to estimate the neutron dynamic cross section. In this method, the dynamic cross section is calculated by multiplying the static cross section by masking upset effect probability as shown in Eq. 5. The masking upset effect probability can be considered by using the information of essential bits or by the critical bits achieved by fault injection.

$$\sigma_{dynamic-est} = \sigma_{static} * \frac{\#bits_{essential}|\#bits_{critical}}{bits_{injected}} \tag{5}$$

Table 3 shows the estimated dynamic cross section, SER and MWBF based on essential bits and critical bits. The SER is calculated using the average neutron flux at sea level, i.e. 13 n/(cm^2 × h) [10].

Table 3. Estimated dynamic cross section, SER and MWBF based on Xilinx essential bits and critical bits.

	From Xilinx report	From essential bits			From critical bits		
Matrix Mult. version	σ_{static} (cm^2)	$\sigma_{dynamic}$ (cm^2)	SER @ NYC (FIT)	MWBF (bits)	$\sigma_{dynamic}$ (cm^2)	SER @ NYC (FIT)	MWBF (bits)
No opt., No DSP48E	4.6E-08	2.4E-10	31.7	8.9E + 19	1.701E-11	2.2	1.3E + 21
No opt. with DSP48E	4.9E-08	1.3E-10	16.5	1.7E + 20	1.216E-11	1.6	1.8E + 21
Pipeline opt., No DSP48E	4.6E-08	2.4E-08	3175.7	1.8E + 19	1.195E-09	155.3	3.7E + 20
Pipeline opt. with DSP48E	5.4E-08	5.8E-09	758.7	7.6E + 19	4.666E-10	60.7	9.5E + 20

The use of essential bits to estimate the susceptibility of a design in terms of dynamic cross section or MWBF gives a good approximation comparing those metrics calculated by using fault injection critical bits. We would like to point out that by only analyzing the dynamic cross section one can say: by using the DSP block the dynamic cross section can reduce from 0.4x to 0.7x according to the architecture, and that by using pipeline optimization the cross section can increase from 40x to 70x according to the use of not of DSP resources.

However, the MWBF gives us the susceptibility analysis taking into account not only the area bits but also the performance (execution time and workload) of the application. When the trade-off of the performance is considered, one can see that the differences between designs are drastically reduced. The best design in terms of MWBF is the version without optimization and using DSP as expected because it presents the lowest number of essential bits and critical bits. Although this design version has the highest MWTF, the pipeline version using DSP may also be in some cases a good solution as well because it presents a MWBF reduction in only half while reducing the absolute execution time value in 20x, which can be interesting at system level. These results also match with the results presented in [11].

3.3   Classifying the Errors by Fault Injection

Although the use of essential bits can early determine the trend behavior of a design under soft errors, the fault injection is essential to classify the errors and to help designers to analyze the efficiency of fault tolerant techniques once they are applied in the design. Errors are classified as Silent Data Corruption (SDC) errors and timeout. The SDC can affect a single data word in the result matrix, or it can affect a set of them.

Figure 4 presents the error histograms of the four designs obtained by fault injection. Each histogram shows the number of times that a set of SDC and timeout errors occurs in the fault injection campaign. The set of SDC errors spans from one erroneous data value of the output matrix to all erroneous data values (36) of the output matrix. One can see that the non-optimized versions have a different pattern when compared to the pipeline optimized versions. The non-optimized versions have more percentage of errors related to the control flow of the algorithm because the control finite state machine in those architecture versions occupies a larger area of the

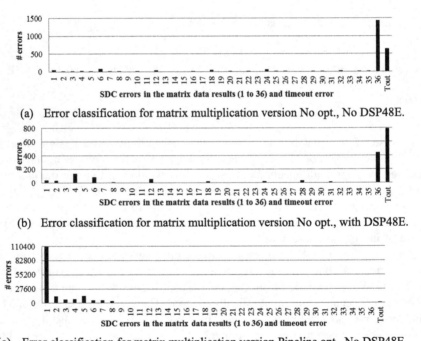

(a) Error classification for matrix multiplication version No opt., No DSP48E.

(b) Error classification for matrix multiplication version No opt., with DSP48E.

(c) Error classification for matrix multiplication version Pipeline opt., No DSP48E.

(d) Error classification for matrix multiplication version Pipeline opt., with DSP48E.

Fig. 4. Error classification in the four matrix multiplication design versions.

architecture, which leads to a high number of timeouts errors and errors in all data values of the output matrix. The pipeline versions have more errors related to the data flow, which leads to a high number of errors in single or few data values of the output matrix. These results are mainly driven by the architecture of the design, which in the case of the pipeline optimization explores more the parallelism of the algorithm.

4   Conclusions

It was presented a method to analyze the susceptibility of designs generated by HLS. The method takes into account not only the susceptible area details of the design but also the efficiency of the design architecture to process data. A comparison between essential bits and critical bits obtained by fault injection is done. Even that metrics obtained from essential bits are a good approximation to estimate the soft error rate of a design; the fault injection method gives us a better analysis of the errors. It was shown that the architecture has a key influence on the error type.

References

1. Wang, F., Agrawal, V.D.: Single event upset: an embedded tutorial. In: 21st International Conference on VLSI Design, pp. 429–434 (2008)
2. Skalicky, S., Wood, C., Lukowiak, M., Ryan, M.: High level synthesis: where are we? a case study on matrix multiplication. In: 2013 International Conference on Reconfigurable Computing and FPGAs, pp. 1–7 (2013)
3. Windh, S., Xiaoyin, M., Halstead, R.J., Budhkar, P., Luna, Z., Hussaini, O., Naijar, W.A.: High-Level language tools for reconfigurable computing. Proc. IEEE 103(3), 390–408 (2015)
4. Xilinx Inc. 7 series FPGAs configuration - user guide, UG470 (v1.10) (2015)
5. Xilinx Inc. Soft error mitigation using prioritized essential bits, XAPP538 (v1.0) (2012)
6. Rech, P., Pilla, L.L., Navaux, P.O.A., Carro, L.: Impact of GPUs parallelism management on safety-critical and HPC applications reliability. In: 44th Annual IEEE/IFIP International Conference on Dependable Systems and Networks, pp. 455–466 (2014)
7. Xilinx Inc. Device reliability report, UG116 (v9.4) (2015)
8. Velazco, R., Foucard, G., Peronnard, P.: Combining results of accelerated radiation tests and fault injections to predict the error rate of an application implemented in SRAM-based FPGAs. IEEE Trans. Nucl. Sci. 57(6), 3500–3505 (2010)
9. Tarrillo, J., Tonfat, J., Tambara, L., Kastensmidt, F., Reis, R.: Multiple fault injection platform for SRAM-based FPGA based on ground-level radiation experiments. In: 16th IEEE Latin American Test Symposium, pp. 1–6 (2015)
10. JEDEC (2006). Measurement and reporting of alpha particle and terrestrial cosmic ray-induced soft errors in semiconductor devices JEDEC standard [Online]. http://www.jedec.org/sites/default/files/docs/jesd89a.pdf
11. Tambara, L.A., Rech, P., Chielle, E., Tonfat, J., Kastensmidt, F.L.: Analyzing the failure impact of using hard- and soft-cores in all programmable SoC under neutron-induced upsets. In: 2015 European Conference on Radiation and Its Effects on Components and Systems (2015)

Low Cost Dynamic Scrubbing
for Real-Time Systems

Leonardo P. Santos[1,2(✉)], Gabriel L. Nazar[2], and Luigi Carro[2]

[1] Instituto Federal de Educação Ciência e Tecnologia do Rio Grande do Sul,
Porto Alegre, Brazil
`leonardo.santos@restinga.ifrs.edu.br`
[2] Instituto de Informática, Universidade Federal do Rio Grande do Sul,
Porto Alegre, Brazil
`{glnazar,carro}@inf.ufrgs.br`

Abstract. Field-programmable gate arrays (FPGAs) offer several desirable characteristics, such as high speed and flexibility. These characteristics come at a cost, however, as high performance FPGAs use SRAM-based configuration memories that are susceptible to Single Event Upsets (SEUs). The conventional approach is to use some form of redundancy with a periodic scrubbing of the configuration memory, thus removing accumulated SEUs. In this paper we propose a novel approach to scrubbing FPGAs in real-time systems, by using diagnostic information based only on the primary outputs of the circuits, in the form of a coarse-grained DMR, and a specialized scrubbing mechanism to avoid missing real-time deadlines.

Keywords: Field-programmable gate arrays (FPGA) · Scrubbing · Fault diagnosis · Fault tolerance · Real-time

1 Introduction

Field-Programmable Gate Arrays (FPGAs) have seen widespread adoption in several industries as they offer high density, high flexibility, high performance and low cost on a range of applications where both software and Application Specific Integrated Circuit (ASIC) solutions fall short. FPGAs are able to offer those characteristics because most devices use a RAM to store the configuration. The application of FPGAs in critical real-time systems is limited by their susceptibility to Single-Event Upsets (SEUs)-induced errors [1], especially for space and defense applications. SEUs pose a major reliability concern to logic designers for real-time systems, as soft-errors caused by SEUs might not only cause a failure in the user application circuit, but may also change the device's configuration, altering its functionality until explicit repair countermeasures are taken. Therefore, in this context, ensuring that repair can be concluded before real-time deadlines are missed is crucial. Because Commercial Off-the-Shelf (COTS) SRAM FPGAs offer far greater density, speed and lower costs than other technologies more resilient to radiated environments, such as Antifuse or flash-based devices, it is very important develop techniques to increase their reliability. To this end, different

© Springer International Publishing Switzerland 2016
V. Bonato et al. (Eds.): ARC 2016, LNCS 9625, pp. 144–156, 2016.
DOI: 10.1007/978-3-319-30481-6_12

techniques have been proposed to mitigate the effects of SEUs in FPGAs by guaranteeing that the configuration memory remains correct.

One of the most widespread techniques used to mask errors in RAM-based FPGAs is Triple Module Redundancy (TMR). If the device to be protected supports partial reconfiguration, it is possible to ally TMR with a periodic re-write of the device configuration memory, allowing for extended periods of error-free operation. The re-writing of the configuration memory is called scrubbing [2, 3] and it can be either periodic or triggered by an error-detection mechanism [4]. After a device's memory is scrubbed, it is correct until a fault is generated by an SEU. While TMR is effective to mask a single error, it has a serious drawback in that it uses over 300 % of the unprotected circuit's area [5] and this cost might not be acceptable to low power or low budget applications.

This paper presents a protection technique that achieves a lower cost than TMR, by using Coarse-Grained Double Module Redundancy (CG-DMR), while maximizing the probability of repairing a fault given a time window in a real-time system. The use of CG-DMR allows for effective diagnostic information that is already available in DMR, by comparing only the Primary Outputs (POs) of circuits. With this information, we anticipate the best scrubbing starting position as to maximize the repair probability given a fixed time, depending on the slack time of the system, as not to miss those deadlines even in the presence of an error. The use of CG-DMR is a significant change from previous approaches such as [6, 7] which artificially introduce numerous comparators to obtain additional diagnosis information, increasing the critical path delay and thus reducing the circuit's performance and the repair time available, as will be explained in Sect. 3.1. The remainder of this paper is organized as follows: in Sect. 2 we discuss related works. Section 3 presents the proposed technique. The validation and measurement setup is explained in Sect. 4, while Sect. 5 contains the results and their discussion. We end this paper with the conclusions in Sect. 6.

2 Related Work

Dynamic partial reconfiguration, by means of scrubbing, has been explored as a way to repair SEU-induced soft-errors in FPGAs [2, 3]. In [8], the configuration bitstream in the FPGA is read back frame-by-frame and its CRC is compared with a CRC table stored in a hardened medium. In case of an error the faulty frame is repaired. Other works try to circumvent permanent faults in components by partitioning the FPGA and creating different versions of each component, while maintaining a common interface [4]. It uses DMR to detect faults with a coarse granularity, as each duplicated component defines a partition.

The work in [9] proposes a design flow in which reliability constrains for different components are used to automatically explore the design space and reduce resource overheads, offering also different granularity levels for TMR and DMR. DMR and TMR are used to detect faults and start the device scrubbing. It uses floorplaning to statically map areas in the FPGA that will be used by each component, to correctly map the components to configuration frames in the FPGA.

The authors of [7] make use of DMR and divide the FPGA in a static and a dynamic region. The static region is assumed to be protected by TMR. The dynamic region is protected by DMR with different error detection granularity levels, CG-DMR and Fine-grained DMR (FG-DMR). In order to know the relation between an error signal and its corresponding configuration frame, all components are placed under constraints. Different benchmarks are then analyzed and the Mean Time to Repair (MTTR) and area overhead are compared. The paper does not indicate the delay overhead that is incurred by placing so many comparators.

A combination of checkpointing and on-demand scrubbing for real-time systems with softcore processors is demonstrated in [10]. That work uses a readback of the configuration memory to detect errors, halting the processor and then starting a scrubbing process. The computation is continued from the last correct checkpoint. The number of checkpoints is indirectly bound by the time required to perform a readback. The number of checkpoints is also bound by the fact that saving a checkpoint consumes computation time, thus reducing the available time to repair the fault. So while checkpointing is a sound idea, preferably it should use fast diagnostic information to trigger the repair process, such as CG-DMR.

By using FG-DMR, the paper in [11] maximizes the probability of repairing a fault within the slack time of the tasks in a real-time system. But differently from reducing MTTR, the goal is the maximization of the repair probability, thus the algorithm to choose the best starting frame is different. Because it uses a fine-grained, LUT-level DMR, it degrades the critical path's delay, severely reducing the circuit's operating frequency and the available repair time, increasing the probability of missed deadlines in case of a fault. The use of FG-DMR also increases the number of critical bits.

The solutions available in the literature suffer from different problems, as small reconfigurable partitions to achieve a fast repair time or many comparators in the critical path, increasing the delay, or by placing severe routing restrictions. The work in this paper uses CG-DMR in order to use a less intrusive diagnostic technique, minimizing the impact on the clock cycle period. While allowing making use of an intelligent scrubbing process, this also leaves a large slack time to repair the circuit, thus maximizing the available repair window. It can be used along with previous partition-based repair procedures, such as [4, 9], thereby building upon previous works to improve real-time repair properties with small costs.

3   Proposed Work

3.1   Challenges

To understand the challenges of fault-tolerance in real-time systems, we first must consider the standard definition of a real-time system. One or more computational tasks must be executed within a bounded time, called time slot. A correct system will be able to execute all designed tasks during their respective time slots. An execution timeline for a given task T_A is shown in Fig. 1(a), where T_A is always finished before the deadlines, represented by t_1, t_2 and t_3. The remaining time between the end of T_A and the deadline is called slack. Figure 1(b) shows an execution where two errors occurred.

For the first error, the repair process was able to recover the system fast enough so T_A could finish before the deadline for t_2. For the second error the repair process could not recover fast enough, so the failure caused a deadline violation for t_3. In hindsight, a designer might want to minimize the MTTR, as to leave the most remaining slack possible. However, just as a real-time system is normally more concerned with worst-case execution time than with average execution time, the mechanism herein proposed aims at maximizing the repair probability within a given timeframe, rather than minimizing the MTTR. As in [11], the expression "target repair time" will be used meaning the remaining slack time, which is the upper bound for the time interval the repair mechanism has to repair the circuit and not create a deadline violation.

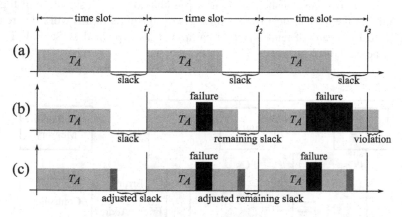

Fig. 1. Correct execution (a), execution with errors (b), execution with repair (c)

Besides repairing the circuit, the diagnostic and repair technique might cause a longer delay in the critical path, thus requiring a lower clock frequency, shown in Fig. 1(c) as the darker area to the right of the task's execution, reducing the available slack. If the available slack is reduced, so does the repair probability, which is contrary to this paper's objective of effective diagnostics and repair. So it is very important that the proposed technique tries to preserve the clock cycle length as much as possible. In order to not degrade the clock frequency, we propose in this paper to use CG-DMR, as opposed to FG-DMR, leaving a longer slack available for repair procedures. CG-DMR also has the advantage that it leads to fewer sensitive bits than FG-DMR, which is important for Failure-In-Time (FIT) results presented in Sect. 5.2.

Any error correcting technique using partial reconfiguration faces the challenge of mapping a detected error to where in the FPGA the circuit that generated the error is implemented. Ideally, one would be able to pinpoint a single configuration memory position (i.e., a frame) as the fault's location. However, this is unfeasible, since multiple errors in multiple frames can lead to faults with identical behavior on the user circuit. In this work we make use of an error injection platform [12] to simulate SEUs and track the relation between configuration memory errors and their effects on the user circuit. The standard DMR would compare each of the POs bits of each copy and generate a single error bit (e_0 and e_1 in Fig. 2). We extended the standard DMR to also make available the output of each comparison, i.e., one error-indicating signal will be generated for each PO bit. We call the concatenation of these bits as the error signature (sig_0 and sig_1 in Fig. 2). As can be seen in Fig. 2, we use dual rail comparison to generate the error signatures. As the comparators are subject to SEU errors themselves, this architecture allows us to detect SEUs in the comparators. In Fig. 2, copy_0 and copy_1 indicate the original unhardened circuit that was duplicated. It could also indicate different reconfigurable partitions within a larger design. Finally, in Fig. 2 the non-volatile memory and low-complexity scrubbing controller are implemented externally, using a hardened technology such as anti-fuse or flash-based FPGAs, as assumed in other works as [8, 9]. The relation between error signatures and configuration frames in error is stablished, making it possible to create a signature histogram, thus identifying the most critical frames for a given signature. In this work this relation is discovered by means of fault-injection campaign, as explained in Sect. 4. The ST block will be explained in Sect. 3.3.

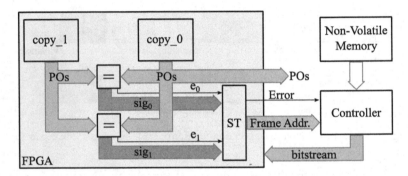

Fig. 2. System architecture

3.2   Shifted Scrubbing

The concept of shifted scrubbing is based on the realization that the actual time to repair any fault depends on how many frames we have to write until reaching the faulty frame. The standard approach is to start at beginning of the configuration addressing space (or the beginning of a reconfigurable partition). In this case, we are oblivious as to where the error most likely occurred and the repair time will depend on whether the error is located near the beginning or the end of the area being scrubbed. The basic idea behind shifted scrubbing is that, by starting the scrubbing operation at an appropriately chosen frame, the repair time will be smaller than that of the standard technique. The approach herein proposed attempts to dynamically choose an improved starting frame without the need for costly fine-grained checkers as in [6, 7, 11]. To illustrate the concept of shift scrubbing, the following histogram for an arbitrary signature of the *pdc* benchmark circuit is shown (Fig. 3):

The figure shows that as the errors only occur on later frames, the standard scrubbing will take a long time to repair a frame that actually matters. The two vertical marks on the X axis indicate the best frame to start the intelligent scrubbing for different deadlines, the solid line for a deadline of 10 μs and the dotted line for a deadline of 600 μs.

3.3   Signature Translator

A block called signature translator (ST in Fig. 2) receives as input the error signature and outputs an error flag and the chosen frame address to start scrubbing in order to maximize the probability that the error is repaired given the slack available. The translation between an error signature and a single configuration frame is not straightforward. A single error might lead to several signatures, depending on the circuit's input stimuli and masking affects. The same signature could also manifest itself from different injected errors. This can be seen in Fig. 2, if either the same bit in the POs of copy_0 or copy_1 are wrong, that bit in the signature will be a logic 1. Others factor such as routing play an important role, as demonstrated in [13].

To map the relation between configuration frames and error signatures, a histogram $h_s[k]$ for signature S can be built, based on the number of times S was generated when errors were injected in configuration frame k. This histogram is then built for all configuration frames. The probability of repairing the system when S is generated by scrubbing frame k is the number of times S happens for all frames divided by the number of time S happens for frame k. In other words, this probability is the proportion of errors in frame k responsible for generating S among all S-generating errors. The probability of repairing an error for a given signature S when starting scrubbing by frame f and scrubbing at most K frames is the sum of the repair probability of all frames that were scrubbed:

$$P_s(f) = \sum_{k=f}^{f+K-1} \frac{h_s[k \bmod N]}{O_s} \tag{1}$$

O_s is the sum of all occurrences of S for all frames and N is the number of frames of the partition's configuration. The modulo division is present because if the scrubbing process reaches the end of the configuration space for that partition before scrubbing K frames, it should wrap around and start scrubbing at the beginning of the configuration space.

In order to repair a frame, a number of bits must be written in the FPGA. If FS is the configuration frame size in bits and BR is the configuration memory port bit rate, the time to scrub K frames is given by C + K·FS/BR, where C is the overhead associated with interfacing with the Internal Configuration Access Port (ICAP) interface, which is negligible for most devices, including the one used as a case study in this work. Given a real-time task slack of SL, in this time at most K frames can be scrubbed:

$$K = \left\lfloor \frac{(SL - C) \cdot BR}{FS} \right\rfloor \tag{2}$$

The heuristic then must try to maximize $P_S(f)$ for a given K. This is done iteratively, by calculating $P_S(f)$ for all N frames of the partition's configuration. When the optimum answer is found, it is recorded. When all optimum starting frames for all signatures have been found, it is possible to build the signature translator circuit, shown as ST in Fig. 2. It has as inputs the error signatures and the error flags and as outputs an error signal and the frame address. We call the translator that generates the optimum starting frame for all signatures the Perfect Signature Translator (PST). As the PST is not implementable for circuits with long signatures (or it may be excessively costly), a heuristic to compact the signatures to manageable sizes is needed. In this paper we will use the heuristic presented in [11] to create a Real-time Heuristic Signature Translator (RHST).

3.4   Real-Time Heuristic Signature Translator

The RHST is built on a compressed signature table. The compression algorithm must preserve as much as possible a precise mapping between signatures and configuration frames. The following algorithm tries do maintain this balance. This is not the only possible algorithm and future work could de carried to evaluate the effectiveness of the presented algorithm versus other alternatives. It is presented as one possible way to achieve manageable area costs for the RHST.

First a real-time slack must be defined, based on the available time slot and expected computation time. In this work we are considering a fixed slack, resulting from modules with constant workload and deterministic performance. Dynamically dealing with variable slacks is considered a promising future work, as it can be both challenging and relevant. It could be done, for example, with different translating tables, i.e., several RHSTs optimized to deal with different slacks, chosen at runtime according to current system parameters. Nonetheless, in this work we use a range of different slacks to evaluate our technique. After the slack has been defined, the algorithm starts by building a table with all signatures and their histograms, called *sigTable*, and another table with the optimum mapping between the signatures and the frame addresses, called *addrTable* (in the first iteration this table is the translation table for PST) using (1). Then iteratively it groups every two bits, using a criteria that will be explained shortly. This proceeds for all signatures in *sigTable*. The algorithm then checks for collisions in the new *sigTable* created with the compressed signatures, merging the histograms from the old *sigTable*. Then a new *addrTable* is built using (1), considering the new compressed signatures. This process continues while the signature length in bits is greater than a parameter called *maxSize*. After the round finishes, the last calculated *addrTable* is used to build the RHST circuit.

The RHST is built with a compression heuristic that compresses the potentially large signatures until a pre-specified *maxSize* parameter is reached. The compression heuristic groups signature bits by applying the OR function onto them, thereby reducing the signature size to half after each iteration. The choice of which bits must be grouped is extremely sensitive to the overall quality of the final solution. We build a complete graph in which each vertex is a bit (or group of bits) and edge is weighted according to the frequency with which those bits are activated by errors in nearby regions. Then, the maximum weighted matching, implemented in [14], is computed on this graph. The vertices linked by the chosen edges are then contracted, becoming a single vertex in the new graph, to be used by the next iteration. Once *maxSize* is reached, the final compressed signature is used to build a table of much reduced dimensions, when compared to the PST. For more details on the compression heuristic, please refer to [11].

4 Experimental Setup

The case studies used in this paper were taken from the MCNC benchmark suite found in [15] and modified ALU circuits compatible with a MIPS processor (alu 32b and alu 64b). All the benchmarked circuits are combinational, as the comparison of POs does not allow for detecting an error and halting a sequential circuit before the error is captured. The proposed technique must then be used in combinational blocks before the inputs of flip-flops. In this case, the error signals (e_0 and e_1) could be used with a rollback mechanism as in [10]. The unhardened benchmark circuits were first synthesized and then processed by the netgen tool from Xilinx ISE 13.4. The resulting VHDL is then processed by a C++ application that creates a new VHDL file with part of the architecture shown in Fig. 2, excluding the ST block, configuration memory and configuration controller. Both copies of the CUT (copy_0 and copy_1 in Fig. 2) and the PO's comparators are placed under constrains to emulate the real-word use of devices, in which designs usually have a high device occupation due to the use of FPGAs that are as small and low-cost as possible. The target occupation was 85 %, which is a high occupation scenario [16]. Moreover, ensuring a high occupation gives a fairer comparison against the standard scrubbing approaches, as they are benefitted by partitions that are as small as possible. The placement constraints were created in a way that the CUT would be placed in the beginning of a configuration row (in the case of a Virtex 5 device, the Y placement coordinate is a multiple of 20) and in an integer number of CLB columns (X placement coordinate is a multiple of 2). The 0.0 attained occupations are shown in Table 1. The column designated "DMR" shows the results for standard

Table 1. Benchmark area occupation

Benchmark	Area occupation		Benchmark	Area occupation	
	DMR	*RHST*		*DMR*	*RHST*
alu 4b	84.58 %	87.50 %	*ex1010*	87.86 %	90.71 %
alu 32b	89.00 %	82.81 %	*ex5p*	96.25 %	92.29 %
alu 64b	85.06 %	85.26 %	*misex3*	88.13 %	82.44 %
apex2	83.23 %	84.43 %	*pdc*	83.55 %	86.45 %
apex4	82.75 %	85.94 %	*seq*	82.79 %	86.73 %
des	80.88 %	85.10 %	*spla*	75.31 %	90.63 %

DMR and the column "RHST" shows the results for the architecture in the FPGA shown in Fig. 2.

The synthesized test circuit was programmed in a Xilinx Virtex 5 XC5VLX110T FPGA contained in a Xilinx XUPV5-LX110T board. Errors are then injected in the CUT, as per [12], generating error signatures. After all signatures were captured, they were analyzed using C++ applications.

The captured signatures are split in two groups, a training group and a testing group. The training group is used to build the RHST tables and the verification group is used to test the effectiveness of the generated RHST. The unhardened circuits and the protected circuits were processed with Xilinx tools to evaluate area costs and delay values. With the increased clock delay values of the hardened circuits, the training signatures were processed in a C++ application that implements (1) and (2), creating tables for different metrics the RHSTs, for different time-slot occupation scenarios and for an arbitrary *maxSize* parameter of 7. This value is considered according to [6] due to technological and implementation characteristics of the Virtex 5 devices. This step already considers that the available repair slack is reduced in the hardened circuit. The effectiveness of the generated RHST tables is verified with the testing signature group, ensuring the generality of the solution as this group was not used to create the RHST tables. Finally, the RHST tables were evaluated for area costs.

5   Experimental Results

5.1   Area and Delay Costs

Table 2 shows the results for area and delay. The increases in area and in the clock cycle period are also compared. It can be seen that for some benchmark circuits, the area overhead over standard DMR is less than 10 %, while for the other circuits the area overhead is greater, specially in the case of the *alu 32b*, *exp5* and *des* circuits. This is

Table 2. Area and Delay results

Benchmark	# POs	Area (LUTs)			Delay (ns)		
		DMR	RHST		DMR	RHST	
alu 4b	9	812	1049	29.19 %	6.49	6.58	1.34 %
alu 32b	34	712	1107	55.48 %	8.14	8.16	0.22 %
alu 64b	66	1497	1732	15.70 %	9.62	10.64	10.56 %
apex2	4	1598	1715	7.32 %	7.28	7.57	4.08 %
apex4	19	1324	1375	3.85 %	7.34	7.85	7.00 %
des	246	1294	1803	39.34 %	6.91	7.86	13.82 %
ex1010	11	984	1015	3.15 %	6.44	6.45	0.23 %
ex5p	64	308	560	81.82 %	5.39	5.30	−1.61 %
misex3	15	1410	1550	9.93 %	7.01	7.31	4.16 %
pdc	41	2540	2628	3.46 %	8.71	9.05	3.99 %
seq	36	1722	2147	24.68 %	7.24	7.60	4.89 %
spla	47	482	579	20.12 %	6.18	6.47	4.69 %

due the relation between the number of POs and the area of the standard DMR. We choose to use one LUT for every compared bit on the RHST circuits and one LUT for every three compared bits for standard DMR. The average area overhead for all circuits is 24.5 %. The area results for the RHST already account for the signature translation tables. We choose to use the worst case for each circuit, among all synthesized tables (with different target slacks). The average delay overhead is 4.07 %, which shows that our expectation was justified in that CG-DMR does not introduce a large clock cycle overhead. For the *ex5p* and *pdc* circuits the RHST circuit was actually faster than the standard DMR, which is likely due to the random optimizations of the implementation heuristics. It is important to compare these results with those obtained in [11], in which the average clock cycle overhead over standard DMR was 23.6 % and the average area overhead was 10.2 %. Even though the average area overhead is smaller in [11], this is due to four circuits that present high PO counts for their sizes (*alu 32b*, *des*, *ex5p* and *seq*), which presented the higher costs in this work. For the other eight circuits, area overheads were smaller in this work. Using mixed solutions combining both approaches is a possible future work to mitigate such costs. In terms of delay, the mentioned averages faithfully show the significant reductions, since the proposed approach had shorter delay for all the circuits. In this paper we also managed to find usable solutions (i.e., that still respect all real-time deadlines in the absence of faults) in all occupation scenarios for all circuits, differently from [11].

5.2   Failure-in-Time Results

We calculated the expected FIT values for each circuit. As the FIT value takes into account the number of sensitive bits in a circuit, it consists in an appropriate metric to compare circuits with different sizes implemented on the same technology. The FIT results are shown in a series of graphics in Fig. 4, for each of 15 deadlines, ranging from 10 μs to 600 μs. We also considered three scenarios in which the task computing time occupies 25 %, 50 % and 75 % of the time slot, adjusted for the reduced slack due to the delay overhead (Fig. 1(c)). Note that, for higher occupations, delay penalties

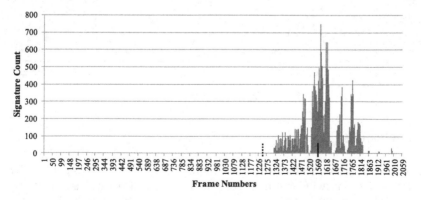

Fig. 3. Signature histogram and best starting frames

have a larger impact in slack reduction. The FIT value for each circuit was calculated according to:

$$\text{FIT} = F \cdot \sigma \cdot SB \cdot (1-Pr) \cdot 10^9 \qquad (3)$$

F is the neutron flux. At sea level a value of 13 n/cm^2·h was used as typical for neutrons with energy above 10 MeV [17]. σ is the cross section per bit, as reported in [18]. SB is the number of sensitive bits for each circuit and was measured in the fault injection experiments. Finally, Pr is the repair probability, obtained with (1) and considering the frame chosen for each signature by the synthesized ST circuit. FITs calculated through (3), therefore, take into account any costs the introduced techniques may have both in terms of area (by means of an increased SB) and delay (which reduce the available slack time to conclude repair). Benefits observed in FIT come from an increased Pr, obtained through the described low-cost diagnostic and repair mechanism.

The technique was able to achieve relevant FIT reductions, when compared to the standard approach, for a wide range of target repair times. For some circuits the gains were smaller; in the case of *des* this is due to larger delay penalty (therefore reducing the available slack), which is more noticeable for the 75 % occupation scenario.

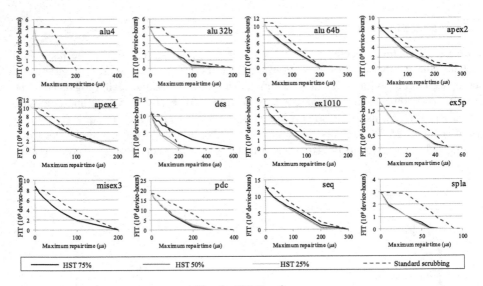

Fig. 4. FIT Results

6   Conclusions

In this work we have presented a novel technique that aims at improving the probability of repairing systems with real-time constraints before deadlines are violated. The proposed technique differs from previous works because it is able to make dynamic diagnosis of faults without needing costly comparators spread throughout the circuit, which introduce severe delays in the clock cycle. Thereby, reduced area and performance penalties are attained for most circuits, while still providing a reduced FIT when compared to standard partitioned scrubbing. Future works include taking into account variable slack times and identifying interesting intermediate granularities that may further improve reliability while maintaining reduced costs.

References

1. Lesea, A., Drimer, S., Fabula, J.J., Carmichael, C., Alfke, P.: The rosetta experiment: atmospheric soft error rate testing in differing technology FPGAs. IEEE Trans. Device Mater. Reliab. **5**, 317–328 (2005)
2. Carmichael, C., Caffrey, M., Salazar, A.: Correcting Single-Event Upsets Through Virtex Partial Configuration
3. Carmichael, C., Tseng, C.W.: Correcting single-event upsets in Virtex-4 FPGA configuration memory
4. Psarakis, M., Apostolakis, A.: Fault tolerant FPGA processor based on runtime reconfigurable modules. In: Proceedings - 2012 17th IEEE European Test Symposium, ETS 2012 (2012)
5. Carmichael, C.: Virtex Series Triple Module Redundancy Design Techniques for Virtex FPGAs, 197, 1–37 (2006)
6. Nazar, G.L., Santos, L.P., Carro, L.: Fine-grained fast field-programmable gate array scrubbing. IEEE Trans. Very Large Scale Integr. Syst. **23**, 893–904 (2014)
7. Reorda, M.S., Sterpone, L., Ullah, A.: An error-detection and self-repairing method for dynamically and partially reconfigurable systems. In: Proceedings - 2013 18th IEEE European Test Symposium, ETS 2013 (2013)
8. Gokhale, M., Graham, P., Johnson, E., Rollins, N., Wirthlin, M.: Dynamic reconfiguration for management of radiation-induced faults in FPGAs. In: 18th International Parallel Distributed. Processing Symposium 2004, Proceedings (2004)
9. Bolchini, C., Miele, A., Sandionigi, C.: A novel design methodology for implementing reliability-aware systems on SRAM-based FPGAs. IEEE Trans. Comput. **60**, 1744–1758 (2011)
10. Sari, A., Psarakis, M., Gizopoulos, D.: Combining checkpointing and scrubbing in FPGA-based real-time systems. In: Proceedings of IEEE VLSI Test Symposium (2013)
11. Nazar, G.L.: Improving FPGA repair under real-time constraints. Microelectron. Reliab. **55**, 1109–1119 (2015)
12. Nazar, G.L., Carro, L.: Fast single-FPGA fault injection platform. In: 2012 IEEE International Symposium on Defect and Fault Tolerance in VLSI and Nanotechnology Systems (DFT), pp. 152–157 (2012)
13. Kastensmidt, F.L., Kinzel Filho, C., Carro, L.: Improving reliability of SRAM-based FPGAs by inserting redundant routing. IEEE Trans. Nucl. Sci. **53**, 2060–2068 (2006)
14. Dezso, B., Jüttner, A., Kovács, P.: LEMON - an open source C++ graph template library. Electron. Notes Theor. Comput. Sci. **264**, 23–45 (2011)
15. Minkovich, K.: Kirill Minkovich's Home Page. http://cadlab.cs.ucla.edu/~kirill/
16. DeHon, A.: Balancing interconnect and computation in a reconfigurable computing array (or, why you don't really want 100 % LUT utilization). In: Symposium Field Programmable Gate Arrays, pp. 69–78 (1999)

17. JEDEC: Measurement and Reporting of Alpha Particle and Terrestrial Cosmic Ray Induced Soft Error in Semiconductor Devices (2006)
18. Xilinx Inc.: Device Reliability Report. http://www.xilinx.com/support/documentation/user_guides/ug116.pdf

Tools and Architectures

Analytical Delay Model for CPU-FPGA Data Paths in Programmable System-on-Chip FPGA

Mohammad Tahghighi[✉], Sharad Sinha, and Wei Zhang

Hong Kong University of Science and Technology,
Kowloon, New Territories, Hong Kong
mtahghighi@ust.hk

Abstract. The CPU hard cores in programmable System-on-Chips (SoC) often communicate with the soft IP cores in reconfigurable fabric through some dedicated ports. The various data paths corresponding to different ports have different performance characterizations which make them suitable for various applications. This article studies the analytical performance model for transferring data stored in CPU side to FPGA side and vice versa through all different communication ports and data paths available in a typical programmable SoC. The proposed methodology for extracting the cycle accurate delay models is applicable to other similar programmable SoCs. Evaluation experiments identified that the error rate of proposed models are within an acceptable rate of 5%.

Keywords: High-performance ports · Performance modelling · All programmable systems-on-chip · Heterogeneous architectures

1 Introduction

FPGA based programmable System-on-Chip (SoC) refers to the architectures with both general purpose Central Processing Units (CPU) and Field Programmable Gate Arrays (FPGA). CPU and FPGA are usually connected to each other through several different communication links in such architectures. Each of these communication links has specific performance features which make the interface suitable for a specific category of applications. The engineers who design the applications on such systems, need to be aware of the characteristics of different interfaces in order to efficiently utilize them in their design. It is crucial since the highest potential speedup achievable in such architectures is basically limited by the data communication rate between software in the CPU and accelerators in the FPGA fabric [9]. Moreover, the CAD and Automation tools need to be aware of the performance model of various communication links within the SoC for efficiently porting the software kernels to the hardware designs. Furthermore, for a specific interface, different parameters like data size, burst length and data width may affect the overall performance. Hence, studying the delay model which relates the design parameters to the interface performance is an important step for creating the automatic performance tuning tools.

© Springer International Publishing Switzerland 2016
V. Bonato et al. (Eds.): ARC 2016, LNCS 9625, pp. 159–170, 2016.
DOI: 10.1007/978-3-319-30481-6_13

Zynq 7000 [11] as an example of FPGA based programmable SoC, integrates an ARM dual core Cortex A9 [13] in the Processing Subsystem (PS) and Xilinx 7 series FPGA in the Programmable Logic (PL). This paper studies the performance of different interfaces in Zynq, however, we believe that the methodology is applicable to other similar FPGA based programmable SoCs currently available in the market. This is because all currently available FPGA based programmable SoCs have ARM processors besides the FPGA on the same chip. Therefore, the SoC vendors find it naturally reasonable to employ the ARM Advanced Microcontroller Bus Architecture (AMBA) to connect the ARM Processors to the FPGA within the SoC chip. This makes all SoC FPGAs available in the market almost similar in terms of CPU-FPGA interfacing. More specifically, Xilinx and Altera FPGA SoCs, are exploiting the same variation of AMBA specification, which is AXI protocol, for CPU-FPGA data transfers. In view of these facts, the products of Xilinx and Altera companies are similar in terms of CPU-FPGA performance model so that, the principles behind the analytical methodology described in this article for Zynq is applicable to all other FPGA based programmable SoCs already manufactured by these two companies.

2   Related Work

There are many literature [6–8] which study the performance of multi-processor systems sharing the main memory between the processing cores, but this subject is not yet studied thoroughly in FPGA based programmable SoCs. In [3], the authors studied the effect of sharing the DDR memory between ARM dual cores in PS side and many core accelerators in PL side in Zynq. The authors in [4], implemented scale invariant feature transform (SIFT) algorithm as a case study to investigate the speedup achievable using different interfaces for exchanging data between PL and PS in Zynq. In [10], the authors investigated how the granularity of data exchanging between the accelerator and memory may affect the overall performance of system. An implementation of FFT application on Zynq is presented in [5] which utilized the Accelerator coherency port. Two closely related works to this paper are [1,2] which studied the performance of different interfaces in Zynq. In [1], the authors developed some part of an application in FPGA and other part in software. They utilized ACP and HP ports for exchanging data between accelerator and software. Their results however, are related to some specific instances of design space and are applicable to the specific application example they chose. There is no clue on how their results can be generalized for designing other applications in Zynq. Moreover they did not provide the analytical explanation for the graphs they presented. In [2], the authors examined almost all Zynq interfaces and accomplished the performance benchmarking for different ports. They also examined the effect of data size on performance, however, their work is limited to some specific design parameters. For example, they chose specific data bus width, and clock frequencies but, as we will show in this paper, changing these parameters can affect the performance severely. Moreover, similar to [1], this work also lacks the analytical explanations for different cases.

3 Background

This section briefly provides the reader with some background information.

AMBA AXI protocol [14] is a communication protocol which supports designing the systems with high performance and high frequency requirements. AXI4 defines several write and read channels which can be employed concurrently by applications. These channels use VALID/READY handshake signalling mechanism to transfer information.

Zynq is equipped with three types of slave interfaces, all support the AXI protocol. The First, General Purpose (GP) 32 bits data bus width port, is suitable for general and low speed applications. The Second, High Performance (HP) port with internal FIFOs for data buffering, supports both 32 and 64 bits data bus and is designed for high performance data exchange between PL masters and PS memories. The third type is Accelerator Coherency Port (ACP) which is a 64 bits bus and is designed to provide the cache coherent access directly from PL. There are two types of memories available to Zynq device: On-chip Memory (OCM) contains 256 KB of RAM and DDR which provides the larger capacity but relatively slower access time. Hence, there are 6 possible paths between PS and PL in Zynq. Figure 1 shows all such different data paths.

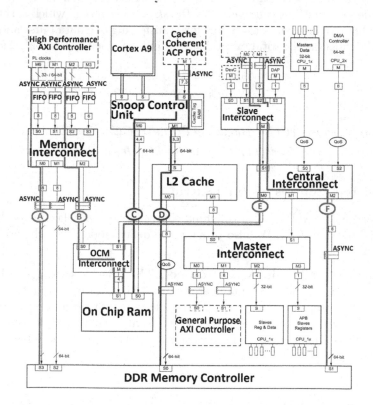

Fig. 1. All various data path between PL and PS in Zynq [11]

4   Analytical Delay Model

In this section we will explain our methodology for building the analytical delay model. We will first define some terms related to the data transfer delay, then we will describe the models for components resided in the data path. Finally, we will sum all delay up to find an expression for the total delay.

4.1   BurstTransferCC, BurstNetTransferCC and BurstExtraCC

Typically one DMA transaction is divided into several smaller data transfers called Burst. For each burst the transferred data size is calculated by Burst Length multiplying by Burst Size. Burst Size is defined as data width of DMA controller while Burst Length is the number of data pieces (each piece as large as burst size bytes) transferred. Hence, $NumberofBursts$ can be defined as (1):

$$NumberofBursts = \frac{TransferredDataSize}{BurstLength \times BurstSize} \tag{1}$$

We also define the $TotalCC$ as the total number of clock cycles necessary for exchanging the data between the source and destination in (2). The $BurstTransferCC$ is defined in (3) as summation of $BurstNetTransferCC$ which is the minimum number of clock cycles necessary for transferring one data burst and $BurstExtraCC$ defined as the total extra delay in unit of clock cycles for performing one Burst transfer.

$$TotalCC = NumberofBursts \times BurstCC \tag{2}$$

$$BurstTransferCC = BurstNetTransferCC + BurstExtraCC \tag{3}$$
$$= BurstLength \times 1\ ClockCycles + BurstExtraCC$$

4.2   Different Sources of BurstExtraCC

In this section, we will explain different sources of extra delay for each burst transfer (BurstExtraCC). We also provide the delay model for each case.

Handshake Signalling in AXI Protocol. The BRAM controller in PL side and ports in PS side both communicate using AXI protocol. The AXI protocol defines a set of steps for initiating and completing the read and write transactions. These steps specify a sequence of handshake signalling between Master and Slave parts which incurs some fixed extra delays denoted as C1 in the rest of this paper.

AXI Interconnect Delay. AXI Interconnect Module [15] is basically an inter-connect module including some sub modules which make specific AXI based design scenarios possible. For example, in applications that number of compo-nents in either side of slave or master, is more than one an AXI Crossbar IP core is necessary to be inside the AXI Interconnect to make the connections possible. Another example is for the applications that the AXI protocol version of master side does not match with that of slave (such as PS section of Zynq which only supports the AXI-3, while in PL side the modules typically are using AXI-4), in such cases an AXI Protocol converter IP must be located between master and slave sides for applying the necessary changes. The extra delay associated with the modules inside the AXI Interconnect is fixed but the total delay of this unit depends on the type of blocks used for a specific design. We use the parameter C2 for representing this delay.

Additional Components in PS Section. According to the Zynq diagram in Fig. 1, for all data paths between PL and PS, there are some extra compo-nents, e.g. ASYNC and interconnects, which may add extra delay to one burst transfer. Each of these extra components is clocked by different clock source and frequency. The delay associated with these blocks is fixed because it is indepen-dent of the amount of data transferred in each burst (e.g. Delay of ASYNC is not a function of data size and is fixed). This total delay is represented by T1. Here T1 is the absolute time in seconds.

Memory Controller and Memory Read/Write Access Time. Memory controllers usually have state machines and some other logic circuits which con-trol the signalling of transactions between the internal memory cells and outside. Moreover, each read/write access to the memory cells takes some time to com-plete. This delay varies for different burst lengths and basically increases for larger burst length. We uses *T2(Burst Length)* to express this delay.

4.3   Complete Model for BurstExtraCC

The complete model for BurstExtraCC in (4) is the summation of the delay model for all major components explained in previous sections:

$$BurstExtraCC = C1 + C2 + \lceil (T1 + T2) \times PLFreq \rceil \qquad (4)$$

4.4   Extending the Model for Sequence of Bursts

The delay expressed by (4) is the extra delay for transferring one burst of data. However, the DMA Controller initiates two bursts at beginning, and later ini-tiates the next burst as soon as the previous one is completed. Therefore, two burst transactions are always active concurrently which causes the extra delay of the second burst partially overlapped with the transferring time of the previous burst. The Fig. 2 shows the sequence of transactions. The rows in this figure show how two DMA transactions can be overlapped. PLDelay is defined as the part of delay (in clock cycles) due to PL components while PSDelay is defined as delay (in clock cycles) due to the components in PS section.

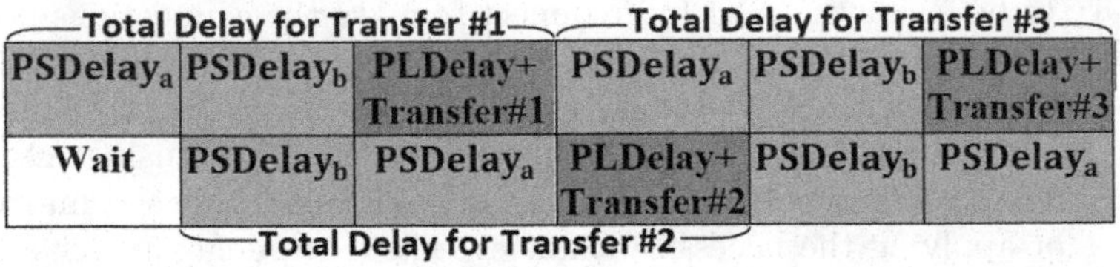

Total Delay for Transfer #1			Total Delay for Transfer #3		
PSDelay$_a$	PSDelay$_b$	PLDelay+ Transfer#1	PSDelay$_a$	PSDelay$_b$	PLDelay+ Transfer#3
Wait	PSDelay$_b$	PSDelay$_a$	PLDelay+ Transfer#2	PSDelay$_b$	PSDelay$_a$

Total Delay for Transfer #2

Fig. 2. CDMA initiates two DMA transactions concurrently

We divided the PSDelay into two parts, PSDelay$_a$, defined in (5), is part of the delay hidden by PL Data Transfer time, since the PSDelay and PLDelay are overlapped during data transfer. PL Data Transfer time is composed of two parts: *BurstTransferCC* which is the number of clock cycles required for transferring the data piece of size Burst Length; and some extra delay, expressed as PLDelay. The PLDelay is described in (6) as summation of C1, the extra delay due to handshake signalling in AXI protocol, and C2, AXI interconnect delay. At the same time, the PSDelay is composed of the memory read/write access time, T2(Burst Length), and extra delay required along the data transfer path, T1. We convert the PSDelay time into the PL clock cycle numbers by timing the PL frequency, as shown in (7). PSDelay$_b$, defined in (8), is part of the delay not covered by PL Data Transfer time. By considering the overlap of two data transfers depicted in Fig. 2, it can be understood that the value for PSDelay$_b$ is 0 for the cases that whole PSDelay, (the summation of PSDelay$_a$ and PSDelay$_b$) can be overlapped by PL Data Transfer time, otherwise it would be PSDelay–PSDelay$_a$ as described in (8). It is clear from Fig. 2 that for each two burst transfers, the BurstExtraClockCycles besides the data transfer time is equal to one unit of PSDelay$_b$ and two units of PLDelay. Consequently, the AverageBurstExtraClockCycles per burst transfer can be averaged over two and expressed in (9).

$$PSDelay_a = PLDelay + BurstTransferCC = BurstLength + C1 + C2 \quad (5)$$

$$PLDelay = C1 + C2 \quad (6)$$

$$PSDelay = \lceil (T1 + T2(BurstLength)) \times PLFreq \rceil \quad (7)$$

$$if\ (PSDelay - (PLDelay + BurstTransferClockCycles)) > 0)$$

$$PSDelay_b = PSDelay - (PLDelay + BurstTransferCC) \quad (8)$$

$$= \lceil (T1 + T2(BurstLength)) \times PLFreq \rceil - BurstLength + C1 + C2$$

$$otherwise$$

$$PSDelay_b = 0$$

$$\text{if } (PSDelay_b > 0)$$

$$AverageBurstExtraCC = \frac{PSDelay_b}{2} + PLDelay = \frac{C1 + C2}{2} \tag{9}$$
$$+ \frac{\lceil (T1 + T2(BurstLength)) \times PLFreq \rceil}{2} - \frac{BurstLength}{2}$$

$$\text{otherwise}$$
$$AverageBurstExtraCC = PLDelay = C1 + C2$$

4.5 Extending the Model for Different Data Bus Width

The model described in (9) is valid for the cases that master and slave data bus width are the same. However, sometimes the designers prefer to increase the master data width in PL to match the application requirements. In such cases AXI Interconnect delay, C2, will include the delay of AXI Data width converter which is responsible for unifying the data width of master and slave in AXI communications. We will use C2$'$ to distinguish this case. Another difference with the previous case is the extra clock cycles necessary for building the larger data width from smaller pieces. If W_{ratio} expresses the ratio of PL datawidth over PS datawidth, the extra delay due to buffering in PL side can be defined as BurstLength $\times$ ($W_{ratio} - 1$). Hence, PLDelay for this case can be described in (10):

$$PLDelay = C1 + C2' + BurstLength \times (W_{ratio} - 1) \tag{10}$$

By substituting (10) in (8) and (9) we can find the adapted model for this case:

$$\text{if } (PSDelay_b > 0)$$

$$AverageBurstExtraCC = \frac{PSDelay_b}{2} + PLDelay = \frac{C1 + C2'}{2} \tag{11}$$
$$+ \frac{\lceil (T1 + T2(BurstLength)) \times PLFreq \rceil}{2} + \frac{BurstLength \times W_{ratio}}{2}$$
$$- \frac{BurstLength}{2}$$

$$\text{otherwise}$$
$$AverageBurstExtraCC = PLDelay = C1 + C2' + BurstLength \times (W_{ratio})$$

4.6 Experimental Setup and Measurement of Parameters

Equations 9 and 11 express the delay as a function of several parameter, (C1, C2, T1, and T2). In order to measure the parameters values and finally extract the cycle accurate equations for delay of each path, a vast number of experiments have been performed on Zedboard [12], which is a complete development board equipped with Zynq.

We designed an application on Zynq to measure the speed of data transfers and wide range of data transfer sizes, 32 B (small) to 32 KB (large) were examined (transfer size larger than 32 KB has no impact on derived models). In the hardware section of application, the data would be read from or written to the BRAM in FPGA. DMA controller IP Core (CDMA) was utilized to initiate the DMA transactions and control the flow of bursts. The software was mainly responsible for initiating the configurations for the whole experiments, such as the Cache controllers, interrupt handler routines, internal registers of PLL for changing the clock frequency, DMA controller and AXI Timers. We ran a complete set of experiments over a complete set of design parameters listed as follows:

- PL frequency: a complete range of clock frequencies starting from 1 MHz up to 250 MHz which includes 95 different frequencies assigned as PL frequency for driving the HP/GP/ACP ports.
- Burst Length: the complete burst lengths range in AXI-4, 2, 4, 8, 16, 32, 64, 128, 256, were examined.
- W_{ratio}: Since the ports width are fixed (e.g. 32 bits for GP), the PL side datawidth is chosen from a complete set of valid data width. The corresponding set of examined W_{ratio} is 2, 4, 8, 16 and 32.

5   Results and Evaluations

In this section we will present and discuss the results of parameters measurements and provide the cycle accurate delay models for all data paths between PL and PS in Zynq. Moreover, we will show the graph for average and maximum error rate evaluation of models.

5.1   Complete Cycle Accurate Model

The complete cycle accurate models of AverageBurstExtraCC for different data paths are presented in Table 1. For each path two models are given, since read and write access delay to OCM/DDR memories are not symmetric. This is because write access delay increases linearly by increasing the burst length (writing larger data chunks take larger amount of time). However, the read access delay is fixed and does not change with the burst length, since the memory controller always read a fixed amount of data to fill in a fixed size row buffer and if the read data size is larger than burst length, the extra data would be ignored. The OCM/DDR write access delay is given as a linear function of burst length in all models. The given linear models are based on aggregating the linear functions extracted by curve fitting techniques.

The components in PL side communicate using AXI-4 protocol which supports the burst length up to 256, however, in the PS side all components communicate through AXI-3 protocol which supports smaller Burst Length range of up to 16. Hence, the data transfers with burst size larger than 16 in PL side will be divided into several data transfers with burst length equal to 16.

By comparing the finalized models in Table 1 for burst length no larger than 16 with the analytical models in (9), the quantitative values for different parameters in (9) can be identified. For example, the values for $\frac{C1+C2}{2}$ and $\frac{T1+T2}{2}$ in (9) for DDR to BRAM transactions through HP port, are 4.75 and 0.0567 respectively.

Paths Through HP Port. The HP Port is equipped with 1 KB FIFOs for buffering the read/write commands and data, which is the unique feature of this port type. FIFO size is big enough to buffer the large burst length transfers. As a result of buffering capability, for burst length larger than 16, the overhead of initial signalling for the next sub-transaction of size 16 is overlapped with the data transfer time of previous sub-transaction. Hence, the model shown in Table 1, shows the fixed delay for the cases that burst length is larger than 16, i.e. 2 clock cycles for read and 3 clock cycles for write access.

Paths Through GP Port. For most of the cases the GP models looks pretty similar to the corresponding models presented for HP port. The difference between HP model and corresponding GP model in parameters, e.g. the slope of the linear parts, is because of the difference in components resided in each path. The GP model for BRAM to OCM/DDR paths for burst length larger than 16 are the only cases which look different from the corresponding models in HP port. The explanation for these cases are given in the following.

Unlike the HP port, the GP port has no FIFO for buffering the data. Therefore, the transactions with burst size larger than 16, will be automatically divided into several smaller sub-transactions of burst size equal to 16, each of which needs to be completed before the next one can be initiated. Therefore, the next write burst transaction cannot be initiated before the response signal corresponding to the previous write transaction is received. In fact, a transaction with burst size equal to BL, is divided to BL/16 number of sub-transactions each of which adds 2 more clock cycles for initiation. But, there is no such extra delay for the transactions in reverse paths (OCM/DDR to BRAM) since in reverse path the data should be read from OCM/DDR while there is no response channel for read transactions. This implies that for OCM/DDR to BRAM transactions, the next burst can be initiated one or two clock cycles ahead of completion of the previous burst transaction, so that the extra delay of initiating a new transaction could be hidden.

Paths Through ACP Port. The path from ACP port to OCM/DDR memories is going through Snoop Control Unit. This unit provides the coherency between L1/L2 Caches and OCM/DDR memories. Despite of communicating with cache controllers instead of memory controllers, the OCM/DDR read access through the ACP follows our analytical model and are quite similar to OCM/DDR read access models of HP. This is because each memory read transaction first brings data to the cache from memory which incurs some delay

Table 1. The cycle accurate average delay models (AverageBurstExtraCC) for CPU-FPGA data paths in Zynq. The W_{ratio} is fixed to 1 for these models and the frequency is in MHz unit in all equations.

Source	Destination	Conditions	Port	Model
DDR	BRAM	BL$\leq$ 16	HP	$Max(2, 0.0567 \times Freq + 4.75 - \frac{BL}{2})$
			GP	$Max(2, 0.076 \times Freq + 3.25 - \frac{BL}{2})$
			ACP	$Max(2, 0.052 \times Freq + 3.75 - \frac{BL}{2})$
DDR	BRAM	$32 \leq$ BL$\leq$ 256	HP	2
			GP	2
			ACP	2
BRAM	DDR	BL$\leq$ 16	HP	$Max(3, (0.0015 \times BL + 0.0305) \times Freq$ $+5.25 - \frac{BL}{2})$
			GP	$Max(3, (0.0034 \times BL + 0.0513) \times Freq$ $+4.75 - \frac{BL}{2})$
			ACP	$Max(3, 0.0105 \times Freq + 5.25 - \frac{BL}{2})$
BRAM	DDR	$32 \leq$ BL$\leq$ 256	HP	3
			GP	$Max(1 + 2 \times \frac{BL}{16},$ $\frac{BL}{16} \times (0.038 \times Freq - 1)$
			ACP	$\begin{cases} 3, \text{if Freq} <150 \\ 3 + \frac{1}{2} \times \frac{BL}{16}, \text{if Freq} = 150 \\ 3 + \frac{BL}{16}, \text{if Freq} >150 \end{cases}$
OCM	BRAM	BL$\leq$ 16	HP	$Max(2, 0.042 \times Freq + 4.75 - \frac{BL}{2})$
			GP	$Max(2, 0.042 \times Freq + 4.75 - \frac{BL}{2})$
			ACP	$Max(2, 0.015 \times Freq + 3.75 - \frac{BL}{2})$
OCM	BRAM	$32 \leq$ BL$\leq$ 256	HP	2
			GP	2
			ACP	2
BRAM	OCM	BL$\leq$ 16	HP	$Max(3, (0.0021 \times BL + 0.0366) \times Freq$ $+5.25 - \frac{BL}{2})$
			GP	$Max(3, (0.0034 \times BL + 0.0396) \times Freq$ $+4.75 - \frac{BL}{2})$
			ACP	$Max(3, 0.0014 \times Freq + 5.25 - \frac{BL}{2})$
BRAM	OCM	$32 \leq$ BL$\leq$ 256	HP	3
			GP	$Max(1 + 2 \times \frac{BL}{16},$ $\frac{BL}{16} \times (0.026 \times Freq + 0.4))$
			ACP	$\begin{cases} 3, \text{if Freq} <150 \\ 3 + \frac{1}{2} \times \frac{BL}{16}, \text{if Freq} = 150 \\ 3 + \frac{BL}{16}, \text{if Freq} >150 \end{cases}$

similar to memory access through HP. Similar to the GP port, the difference between the ACP model parameters and those of HP, is because of the difference between the components resided in these paths. For writing to the OCM/DDR memories with burst length larger than 16, the delay model is more complicated than corresponding models through HP and GP ports. The special complexity of ACP models and particularly three segmented function for BRAM to OCM/DDR transactions of Burst Length larger than 16, is because of the complexity of the interactions between Cache controllers and OCM/DDR Memory controllers which is not completely clear to us. However, it is presumed that similar to GP port, the term BL/16 represents the extra delay for initiating the sub-transactions of fixed size 16.

5.2 Evaluation of Models

We performed a vast number of experiments to verify the validity and evaluate the accuracy of the constructed models. Each of the experiments is repeated 10 times and the averaged result of experiments were considered for evaluations. We calculated the percentage of average (AVG) and maximum (MAX) error rate of models with respect to the corresponding measurements of transfer time in real application for each of data paths in Zynq. The graph in Fig. 3 summarizes the results of our evaluations.

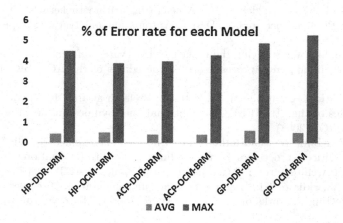

Fig. 3. Average and maximum error rate for different models

6   Conclusion

The data exchange rate between CPU cores and FPGAs in FPGA based SoCs is a key performance limitation factor [9]. Performance models which quantitatively express the performance of different interfaces as a function of design parameters can be used by designers and automation tools for tuning the design parameters so that the overall performance improves significantly. In this paper the analytical performance models for all possible data paths between programmable logic and processing sub system in Zynq are studied. The key elements of performance models are specified using the analytical approach and later on, using the practical methods, the parameters of analytical models are measured. The cycle accurate models extracted by our methodology were evaluated by huge number of experiments. The experiment results verified that the average and maximum error rate of presented models are less than 1 and 5 % respectively.

References

1. Sadri, M., Weis, C., When, N.: Energy and performance exploration of accelerator coherency port using xilinx ZYNQ. In: 10th FPGAWorld Conference, Copenhagen, Denmark, September 2013
2. Silva, J., Sklyarov, V., Skliarova, I.: Comparison of on chip communications in Zynq-7000 all programmable systems-on chip. IEEE Embed. Syst. Lett. 7, 1 (2015)
3. Vogel, P., Marongiu, A., Benini, L.: An evaluation of memory sharing performance for heterogeneous embedded SoCs with many-core accelerators. In: Proceedings of the 2015 International Workshop on Code Optimisation for Multi and Many Cores (2015)
4. Ding, H., Huang, M.: Improve memory access for achieving both performance and energy efficiencies on heterogeneous systems. In: Field-Programmable Technology (FPT) (2014)
5. Giefers, H., Polig, R., Hagleitner, C.: Accelerating arithmetic kernels with coherent attached FPGA coprocessors. In: Design, Automation and Test in Europe (DATE), Germany (2015)
6. Liu, F., Solihin, Y.: Studying the impact of hardware prefetching and bandwidth partitioning in chip-multiprocessors. In: Proceedings of the ACM SIGMETRICS (2011)
7. Lee, C., Mutlu, O., Narasiman, V., Patt, Y.: Prefetch-aware DRAM controller. In: Proceedings of the 41th IEEE/ACM International Symposium on Microarchitecture (MICRO) (2008)
8. Rafique, N., Lim, W., Thottethodi, M.: Effective management of DRAM bandwidth in multicore processors. In: Proceedings of the 16th International Conference on Parallel Architectures and Compilation Techniques (PACT) (2007)
9. Sklyarov, V., Skliarova, I.: High-performance implementation of regular and easily scalable sorting networks on an FPGA. Microprocess. Microsyst. 38(5), 470–484 (2014)
10. Lafond, S., Lilius, J.: Interrupt costs in embedded system with short latency hardware accelerators. In: Engineering of Computer Based Systems, pp. 317–325 (2008)
11. Xilinx Co.: Zynq-7000 All Programmable SoC Technical Reference Manual (2014)
12. Avnet Co.: ZedBoard Hardware Users Guide (2014)
13. Arm Co.: Cortex-A9 MPCore Technical Reference Manual (2012)
14. Arm Co.: AMBA AXI and ACE Protocol Specification (2013)
15. Xilinx Co.: LogiCORE IP AXI Interconnect v2 (2013)

New Partitioning Approach for Hardware Trojan Detection Using Side-Channel Measurements

Karim M. Abdellatif$^{(\boxtimes)}$, Christian Cornesse, Jacques Fournier, and Bruno Robisson

Center of Microelectronics in Provence (CMP), Gardanne, France
karim.abdellatif@emse.fr

Abstract. Hardware Trojans have emerged as a security threat to many critical systems. In particular, malicious hardware components can be inserted at the foundry for implementing hidden backdoors to leak secret information. In this paper, we present a new method to partition the circuit under test into blocks in order to obtain different side-channel signatures per chip. Each signature indicates which block is off or on in terms of the dynamic power (switching activity). As a result, there are different co-existing decisions to more precisely detect the Trojan instead of one decision resulting from one side-channel signature. Moreover, this method detects in which block the Trojan exists. AES was used as an example to be divided into blocks. Sakura-G was used as an implementation target. The obtained results give four decisions to enhance Trojan existence and position. This paper also presents a methodology for Trojan detection using a cryptographic protocol to secure the detection process.

Keywords: Hardware Trojans · Hardware partitioning · FPGAs · Sakura-G

1 Introduction

Hardware piracy is a threat that is becoming more and more serious in the last few years. There are different types of threats include mask theft, illegal overproduction, as well as the insertion of malicious alterations to a circuit, known as 'Hardware Trojans' (HTs). Hardware Trojans have emerged as a major security concern for integrated circuits (ICs). An adversary can mount such an attack with an objective to cause operational failure or to leak secret information from chips (eg., the key in a cryptographic chip) [1].

HTs are typically composed of two different parts: a trigger and a payload. The HT trigger is responsible for activating the malicious functionality at a particular moment. In other words, the trigger acts like an always-on sensing circuit that waits for a particular event (internal or external) in order to activate the payload part. Figure 1 shows a simplified block diagram of a hardware Trojan, which causes a malfunction (by modifying signal S to S^-), when the activation

V. Bonato et al. (Eds.): ARC 2016, LNCS 9625, pp. 171–182, 2016.
DOI: 10.1007/978-3-319-30481-6_14

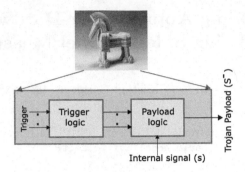

Fig. 1. Hardware Trojan

condition realized by the trigger logic is true. Such malicious inclusions effectively act as spies or terrorists on chip and can be extremely powerful, potentially leading to catastrophic consequences in diverse applications [2]. HTs can be categorized according to multiple parameters, including insertion phase, effect, location, size, etc., as shown in [3–5].

Therefore, techniques to detect hardware Trojans are in focus of IT security research [3,6]. An alternative approach is to measure a side-channel parameter, such as supply current or path delay, which can be affected due to any design modifications. The advantage of side-channel based techniques is that the Trojan can be detected even it is not activated because the trigger part is always on. Side-channel detection approaches typically require a golden design or a set of golden ICs to compare the measured values in order to identify the Trojan-infected ones [3,7,8].

Our Contribution: We propose a new method for dividing the circuit under test into blocks in order to obtain different side-channel signatures per chip in more precise. Each power signature indicates a part of the chip which is on or off in terms of the dynamic power. As a result, detecting Trojan in complex designs (complex chips) will be more efficient because of partitioning the circuit into blocks (parts). Also, the proposed methodology indicates the location of the malicious component. Furthermore, we present a secure protocol for Trojan detection between the trusted entity and the user in the field.

Section 2 shows an introduction and previous work concerning HT detection. After that, our proposed methodology is presented in Sect. 3. Then, we report our results in Sect. 4. Section 5 proposes the methodology of HT detection using two parts, the trusted one and the user in the field. Finally, Sect. 6 concludes our work.

2   Hardware Trojan Detection

There are two techniques for HTs detection, destructive and non-destructive techniques. Destructive technique involves invasive hardware reverse-engineering [9]. This technique is extremely complex, expensive, and also time consuming. It uses chip delayering, optical and/or scanning electron microscope (SEM) imaging, and netlist reconstruction [10]. HTs can then be detected by comparing the reverse-engineered netlist with the golden one.

The second technique is known as non-destructive technique. It is divided into logical and physical methods. Logic testing uses test patterns to hit the trigger mechanism to detect the presence of HT [8,11]. The efficiency of logic testing method is limited because of the stealthiness of HTs and the possibly extremely large search space of activation events. In addition, it requires not only to hit the trigger mechanism but also to notice the effect of the activated payload.

Physical methods depends on the idea that any malicious insertion or modification of a hardware design, such as an HT, should be reflected to changes of physical properties, which is called "side channels", such as leakage current, dynamic power trace, data path delay, or electromagnetic field characteristics [3,7,8]. The main advantage of side-channel based approaches is that the presence of HT can be tested without the need to hit its payload. The common requirement between logic testing and physical methods is the need to the golden model. In this paper we will present an efficient HT detection belonging to the second category, physical methods.

3   Proposed Methodology

The previous work presented in [3,7,12] has the common methodology in HT detection as shown in Fig. 2. Each chip (the golden or the DUT) has only one power signature when all chip components are always-on. Our methodology is based on dividing the chip into blocks and getting the power signature of each block separately to perform the comparison between the golden chip and the DUT.

Region-based partitioning method for HT detection was presented by [8] using associated vector generation algorithm to switch on/off a specific region. A vector is suitable if it maximizes the switching activity in one step of the selected regions. Furthermore, the vector should not activate the unselected regions. As shown in [13], it is difficult to obtain a pattern which switches on/off a specific region completely.

In our proposed method, we will focus on the hardware design issues which are more related to the power consumption. One of these issues is the dynamic power. It results from changing the switching activity which depends on the data variation activity (see Eq. 1 [14]). As a result, if the input to the combinational logic circuit is fixed (constant), this means that there is no switching activity.

$$P_{dynamic} = (\frac{1}{2} \times C \times V_{DD}^2 + Q_{se} \times V_{DD}) \times F \times N \tag{1}$$

where C, V_{DD}, Q_{se} are technology dependent parameters, F is the clock frequency, and N is the switching activity.

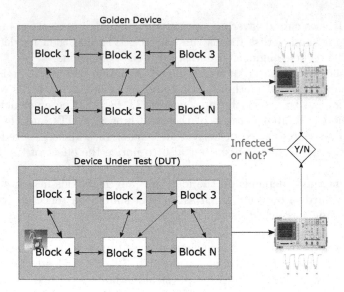

Fig. 2. Previous methodology

An example of how we are able to switch off/on a combinational logic circuit in terms of the dynamic power is presented in Fig. 3. If the input to the combinational circuit is fixed with time (for example, a vector of zeros), there is no switching activity. As a result the dynamic power is zero. This means that this combinational circuit is **off**. In contrast to the first case, if the input is variable (for example, X is variable with time), the combinational circuit is **on** because the switching activity exists.

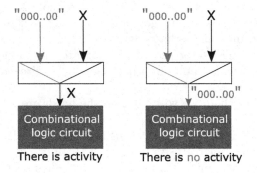

Fig. 3. Switching activity

AES [15] is used as an example for the golden and infected circuits. The most consuming parts in AES are SubBytes and MixColumns blocks. In order to switch off/on subBytes and MixColumns separately or together, we propose

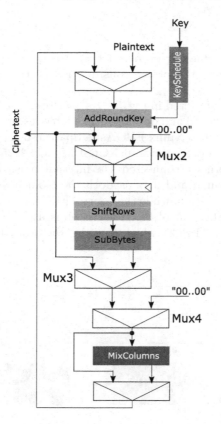

Fig. 4. Proposed architecture

the architecture shown in Fig. 4. Mux2 is used to switch on/off the block of SubBytes. When Mux2 selects zeros as an input, this means that the block of SubBytes is totally off in terms of the dynamic power (there is no switching activity). When the SubBytes is off, the value after the AddRoundKey stage is passed through Mux3 and Mux4 to keep the MixColumns block on. In case of switching off the block of MixColumns, Mux4 selects zeros as an input. Mux2 and Mux4 select zeros as an input to switch SubBytes and MixColumns blocks off together. In total, the proposed architecture has four modes of test:

- SubBytes and MixColumns are on (**Mode 0**, which is the normal mode)
- SubBytes block is off (**Mode 1**)
- MixColumns block is off (**Mode 2**)
- SubBytes and MixColumns are off (**Mode 3**)

The proposed architecture enables us to obtain four power signatures. Each power signature is related to the specific block which is on or off. The proposed method stimulates specific parts of the integrated circuitry to analyze the power consumption more precise. Therefore, scanning all the circuit area is possible with the proposed architecture.

4   Results

In this section, we describe our proposed HT detection methodology based on measuring and analyzing the power consumption of the golden and infected circuits.

Our testing setup is depicted in Fig. 5. Our platform is a Sakura-G board [16] which is specifically designed and developed to enable research on hardware security. The board features two Xilinx FPGAs: a Spartan-6 XC6SLX75-2CSG484C (main FPGA) and a Xilinx Spartan-6 XC6SLX9-2CSG225C (control FPGA). Both FPGAs are internally connected via internal pins. The main FPGA is the circuit to be measured and acts as both the Golden device and the DUT depending on its configuration, while the control FPGA acts as interface between the main FPGA and the control PC. PicoScope is used to measure the power consumption of the main FPGA which contains the desired design as shown in Fig. 5.

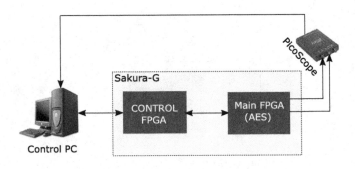

Fig. 5. Testing setup

The Trojan is inserted inside the MixColumns block. The trigger of the Trojan is 12 of 2-NAND gates and 6-AND gates. The payload is a simple XOR gate to invert one of the inputs to MixColumns block when the trigger is true.

We need to keep the same placement and routing between the golden circuit and HT infected circuit on the FPGA to imitate the HT insertion in ASICs. To insert a HT, avoiding modifying the routing, we use the following steps in the Xilinx ISE platform:

1. Synthesize and place&route the original circuit shown in Fig. 4.
2. Extract the Native Circuit Description (NCD) file which contains all the circuit, placement&routing information of the original circuit (golden model).
3. Add the HT circuit manually by editing the NCD file. The HT circuit is added in the unused LUTs and Slices of FPGA (see Fig. 6).
4. Generate bit files for both original and infected circuits with FPGA editor.

The input operands to the design, namely 128-bit plaintext and 128-bit secret key, are provided by the control FPGA to the main FPGA. The design performs

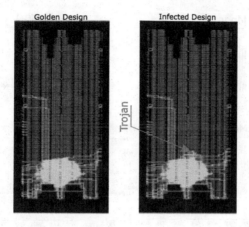

Fig. 6. Difference between golden and infected designs

the AES encryption after all input data has been received. After that, it sends the output ciphertext back to the control FPGA.

We collect four power signatures from the golden design as we described before (four modes). The infected design is the same circuit shown in Fig. 4 with the Trojan inserted in the MixColumns stage. We also collect four power signature such as the golden design.

As shown from Fig. 7, there are four different power signatures taken from the golden design shown in Fig. 4. The same will be for the infected design. For each mode, we collect 5000 traces. As a result, we have four modes with 20 k traces for each design (golden or infected).

After collecting side channel measurements from the infected design (DUT), our methodology requires to apply a statistical test to compare the measurement data with the golden reference data (golden power signatures). The main idea is that the power measurement of a DuT without HT should have similar characteristics as the golden reference. In contrast, they don't have the same characteristics if the comparison is performed between the golden and infected design.

In order to show the difference between the golden design and infected one, we use the T-test based approach for HT detection. We use Welch's two-tailed T-test to test the hypothesis that the two sets of measurements (from the golden circuit and from the DuT) have equal means. The test computes a T-score for each time sample in the measurements as follows:

$$T = \frac{\mu_0 - \mu_1}{\sqrt{\frac{\sigma_0^2}{N_0^2} + \frac{\sigma_1^2}{N_1^2}}} \qquad (2)$$

where μ_0 is the sample mean of the golden measurement set, μ_1 is the sample mean of the measurement set from the DuT, and σ^2 is the sample variance of a set.

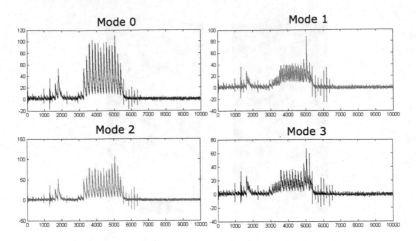

Fig. 7. Four power signatures of the golden design

The T-test was performed between the golden design and the injected one in four modes. We focus only in AES execution period. Because the Trojan exists in the MixColumns block, it is active in **Mode 0** and **Mode 1** (see Fig. 8), when MixColumns block is on. However, it is off (there is no activity) in **Mode 3** and **Mode 4**, when MixColumns block is off. As a result, the Trojan appears only when the block, where it exists, is **on** (see Table 1).

Table 1. Trojan appearance

Mode	Trojan activity
Mode 0	Yes
Mode 1	Yes
Mode 2	No
Mode 3	No

Obtaining different power signatures depending on the activity of specific blocks (**on or off**) per one design analyzes the power signature more precisely. Furthermore, it helps to locate the Trojan in the infected design. Complex designs can benefit from the presented methodology by performing an efficient scanning Trojan searching.

Table 2 shows the effect of our proposed methodology on the performance of the AES. It presents the performance of AES before and after adding the testing Multiplexers (Mux2, Mux3, and Mux4). To our knowledge, there is no any previous methods about scanning to do the comparison. However, previous work such as [17,18] presented online monitoring which is based on additional of reconfigurable logic in a given SoC to enable real-time functionality monitoring

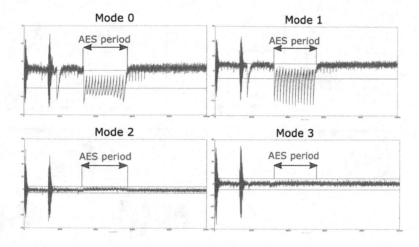

Fig. 8. T-test scores

using security monitors. It is indeed more expensive than our approach. In terms of the effect of adding testing Muxs on the frequency of the design, this effect is reduced in parallel architectures, where Muxs will not be added in a row, but added in parallel.

Table 2. Hardware comparison

Design	Area (Slices)	Frequency (MHz)	Target
AES (Before)	2040	127	Spartan-6
AES (After)	2555	55.642	Spartan-6

5   Secure Hardware Trojan Detection

In addition to HT detection techniques, we are also interested to secure the HT detection process. Therefore, in this section, we will present a secure environment for Trojan detection.

The two interesting entities in HT detection are the user in the field, who wants to verify the originality of the device and the authorized entity, who has the golden model (golden curves). In the presented scenario, we call the user in the field as Server2 and the authorized entity as Server1.

The user in the field needs the golden power signatures (golden curves) in order to evaluate the DUT if it is infected or not. Therefore, he has to send a request for an authorized (trusted) entity to send the golden curves.

In the presented scenario, we use Elliptic Curve Digital Signature Algorithm (ECDSA) in order to verify the authenticity. Server1 must send the golden curves

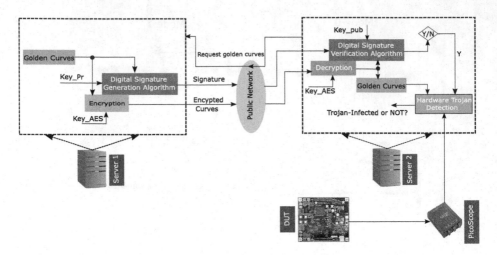

Fig. 9. Secure hardware Trojan detection

signature to Server2 to ensure the authenticity. Sending the golden curves into the public network without encryption raise the problem of learning attacks because attackers can learn from the golden curves to design a Trojan which is not activated during the golden measurements. Therefore, encryption (for example: AES [15]) and authentication must be performed.

Our proposed scenario is as follows (see Fig. 9):

– Server2 sends a golden curves request to Server1.
– Server1 encrypts the golden curves using AES by Key_AES. Also, it generates the signature of the curves using ECDSA by Key_pr.
– Server1 drops encrypted golden curves with its signature through the public network.
– Server2 decrypts the received data by Key_AES and verifies its signature by Key_pr.
– After signature verification is true, Server2 performs Trojan detection process.

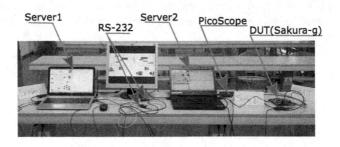

Fig. 10. Overall setup

The overall setup is shown in Fig. 10. Encryption/decryption and digital signature generation/verification algorithms have been done in software (Python) to be run by Server1 and Server2.

6   Conclusion

We proposed a novel hardware-based partitioning (scanning) method for HT detection. With the proposed method, we can analyze the power signature of the design more precisely depending on which block is activated. Trojan location is also possible with the presented methodology. Furthermore, a secure environment for Trojan detection was highlighted. Future work includes using different chips to study the process variation.

Acknowledgment. This work was supported by the European Commission through the ICT program under contract FP7-ICT-2011-317930 HINT. The authors would like to thank Driss Aboulkassimi and David Cambon for their help in this work.

References

1. Defense Advanced Research Projects Agency (DARPA): TRUST in Integrated Circuits (TIC) (2007). http://www.darpa.mil/MTO/solicitations/baa07-24
2. Bhunia, S., Abramovici, M., Agrawal, D., Bradley, P., Hsiao, M., Plusquellic, J., Tehranipoor, M.: Protection against hardware Trojan attacks: towards a comprehensive solution. IEEE Des. Test **30**(3), 6–17 (2013)
3. Agrawal, D., Baktir, S., Karakoyunlu, D., Rohatgi, P., Sunar, B.: Trojan detection using IC fingerprinting. In: IEEE Symposium on Security and Privacy, SP 2007, pp. 296–310. IEEE (2007)
4. Wolff, F., Papachristou, C., Bhunia, S., Chakraborty, R.S.: Towards Trojan-free trusted ICs: problem analysis and detection scheme. In: Proceedings of the Conference on Design, Automation and Test in Europe, pp. 1362–1365. ACM (2008)
5. Tehranipoor, M., Koushanfar, F.: A Survey of Hardware Trojan Taxonomy and Detection (2010)
6. Tehranipoor, M., Koushanfar, F.: A survey of hardware Trojan taxonomy and detection. IEEE Des. Test **27**(1), 10–25 (2010)
7. Balasch, J., Gierlichs, B., Verbauwhede, I.: Electromagnetic circuit fingerprints for hardware Trojan detection. In: IEEE International Symposium on Electromagnetic Compatibility (EMC 2015), pp. 246–251. IEEE (2015)
8. Du, D., Narasimhan, S., Chakraborty, R.S., Bhunia, S.: Self-referencing: a scalable side-channel approach for hardware Trojan detection. In: Mangard, S., Standaert, F.-X. (eds.) CHES 2010. LNCS, vol. 6225, pp. 173–187. Springer, Heidelberg (2010)
9. Torrance, R., James, D.: The state-of-the-art in semiconductor reverse engineering. In: Proceedings of the 48th Design Automation Conference, pp. 333–338. ACM (2011)
10. Bao, C., Forte, D., Srivastava, A.: On application of one-class SVM to reverse engineering-based hardware Trojan detection. In: 15th International Symposium on Quality Electronic Design (ISQED 2014), pp. 47–54. IEEE (2014)

11. Chakraborty, R.S., Wolff, F., Paul, S., Papachristou, C., Bhunia, S.: *MERO*: a statistical approach for hardware Trojan detection. In: Clavier, C., Gaj, K. (eds.) CHES 2009. LNCS, vol. 5747, pp. 396–410. Springer, Heidelberg (2009)
12. Liu, Y., Huang, K., Makris, Y.: Hardware Trojan detection through golden chip-free statistical side-channel fingerprinting. In: Proceedings of the 51st Annual Design Automation Conference, pp. 1–6. ACM (2014)
13. D'Souza, A.L., Hsiao, M.S.: Error diagnosis of sequential circuits using region-based model. In: Fourteenth International Conference on VLSI Design, 2001, pp. 103–108. IEEE (2001)
14. Sanno, B.: Detecting Hardware Trojans. Ruhr-University Bochum, Bochum (2009)
15. Chown, P.: Advanced Encryption Standard (AES) Ciphersuites for Transport Layer Security (TLS) (2002)
16. SAKURA-G Quick Start Guide. http://satoh.cs.uec.ac.jp/SAKURA/doc/SAKURA-G_Quik_Start_Guide_Ver1.0_English.pdf
17. Xiao, K., Tehranipoor, M.: BISA: built-in self-authentication for preventing hardware Trojan insertion. In: IEEE International Symposium on Hardware-Oriented Security and Trust (HOST 2013), pp. 45–50. IEEE (2013)
18. Abramovici, M., Levin, P.: Protecting Integrated Circuits from Silicon Trojan Horses, January/February 2009

A Comprehensive Set of Schemes for PUF Response Generation

Bilal Habib$^{(\boxtimes)}$ and Kris Gaj

Electrical and Computer Engineering Department,
George Mason University, Fairfax, VA, USA
{bhabib,kris}@gmu.edu

Abstract. In this work we present a comprehensive set of schemes to generate Physical Unclonable Functions (PUF) responses. Software scripts have been developed to generate the PUF IDs using five different schemes. We also propose a new set of PUF metrics that are based on the Worst Case (WC) PUF performance. Values of these metrics, for the Ring Oscillator (RO) PUF and SR-Latch PUF, have been presented and analyzed in the paper.

Keywords: FPGA · PUF · Analysis

1 Introduction

Extensive research has been going on to develop new hardware primitives for security. PUF is one of such primitives that can efficiently solve several problems in hardware security. These problems range from reverse engineering and counterfeiting to detection of pirated devices. For this purpose the two important applications where PUF can be used are: key generation and device authentication. The input to PUF is called a challenge and the output is called a response. In the past researchers used only one scheme to generate the PUF responses. For more in-depth analysis we need to generate responses using more than one scheme. This approach gives us the flexibility to control the response bit size. We present five most popular schemes in this work. In Sect. 2, we describe the previous work. Section 3 explains the PUF schemes; methodology is covered in Sect. 4. In Sect. 5, we discuss the results. The conclusion and future study are described in Sect. 6.

2 Previous Work

The previously reported schemes for PUF response generation from raw data included: comparing the counts of neighboring ROs [1], Lehmer-Gray encoding method [3], Identity-mapping [4] and S-ArbRO method [5]. Quantitative and statistical performance evaluations of Arbiter PUF and RO-PUF were presented in [2,6], respectively. In this work we analyze PUF responses generated using five different schemes. Each scheme is described in detail using a pseudocode. For evaluation of responses, PUF metrics have been developed.

© Springer International Publishing Switzerland 2016
V. Bonato et al. (Eds.): ARC 2016, LNCS 9625, pp. 183–194, 2016.
DOI: 10.1007/978-3-319-30481-6_15

3   PUF Schemes for ID Generation

PUF responses are generated from the raw PUF data as shown below in Fig. 1,

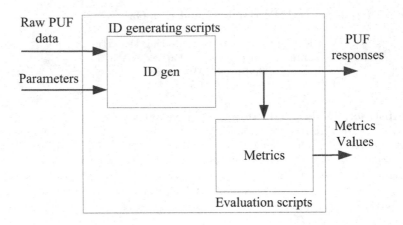

Fig. 1. PUF ID generation and evaluation

As shown above in Fig. 1, the raw PUF data is the input to our PUF generation module. In case of RO-PUF raw input consists of the number of ring-oscillator periods within a predefined fixed time interval. Similarly in case of SR-Latch PUF, raw input consists of the number of oscillations of a latch during metastable state. In this work we used three data sets; Spartan-3 data-set for ROs [7], Spartan-6 data-set for SR-Latches [8] and Zynq data-set for SR-Latches. Devices used for Zynq data belongs to (XC7Z010) family. Five schemes are explained below.

(i) Comparing the Neighboring Components (CNC). In this scheme raw data from the neighboring components of FPGA are compared. Figure 2 shows this scheme on the left side. In this figure C_0, C_1,...,C_{M-1} shows the physical location of components on the FPGA fabric. The comparison of (C_0,C_1), (C_1, C_2), (C_2, C_3),...,(C_{M-2},C_{M-1}) is carried out. Therefore for M components the total number of PUF response bits will be equal to M-1. Response array stores the PUF response of M components.

(ii) Pairwise Comparison (PC). In this comparison each component is compared only once with its neighbor. The comparison of (C_0, C_1), (C_2,C_3), (C_4, C_5),...,(C_{M-2}, C_{M-1}) is carried out. Therefore for M components the total number of PUF response bits will be equal to $\lfloor M/2 \rfloor$. Figure 2 shows this scheme on the right.

Algorithm 1. Comparing the Neighboring Components

```
CNC( F[] , M):    // F[] is the input array of M components.
for ( i = 0; i< M−1; i++)
        if (F[ i ] > F[ i +1])
                Response [ i ] = 1
        else
                Response [ i ] = 0
        end if
end for
```

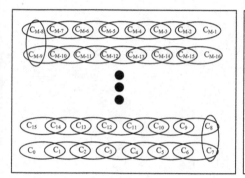 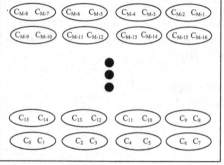

Fig. 2. Comparison of neighboring Components (Left). Pairwise comparison with neighbors (Right).

Algorithm 2. Pairwise Comparison

```
PC(F[] , M):    // F[] is the input array of M components
for ( i =0; i < 2 * ⌊M/2⌋ ; i+=2)
        if (F[ i ] > F[ i +1])
                Response [ i ] = 1
        else
                Response [ i ] = 0
        end if
end for
```

(iii) Binary Lehmar-Gray (BLG) Encoding. In LG encoding, all components are divided into sets of size S. Encoding the ordering of S component measurements $F^s = (F_0, \ldots, F_{s-1})$ results into an L-bit response. It represents the sorted ordering of F components as a coefficient vector $L^{s-1} = (L_1, \ldots, L_{s-1})$ with $L_i \in [0, 1, ..., i]$. It is clear that L^{s-1} can take $2 * 3 * \ldots * S = S!$ possible values which is exactly the number of possible orderings. The Lehmer coefficients are calculated from F as $L_j = \sum_{i=0}^{j-1} gt(Fj, Fi)$ with gt (x, y) = 1 if x > y and 0 otherwise. The total number of bits generated for each set is: $\sum_{i=2}^{S} \lceil log_2 i \rceil$.

Below is a pseudocode for converting counts of M components into an $\lfloor M/S \rfloor$ *L -bit response denoted by Response.

Algorithm 3. Binary Lehmer Gray Encoding

```
BLG (F[] , M, S):    // S=Set size.
for(t=0; t < ⌊M/S⌋ ; t++)
Response= Response || Lehmer(F[t*S:(t+1)*S−1], S)
end for

Lehmer(array[] , S):
for(j=1; j< S ; j++)
   sum = 0
   for(i=0; i<j ; i++)
            if (array [j] > array [i])
            sum= sum + 1
            end if
   end for
L_Response = L_Response || (Gray(bin(sum, ceil(log₂(j+1)))))
end for
return L_Response

Gray(bin_bits)://array of binary bits is passed to Gray().
Len_bits=len(bin_bits)              //Length of an array
G[0] = bin_bits[0]
for(i=1; i< Len_bits; i++)
        G[i] = XOR(bin_bits [i], bin_bits [i−1])
end for
```

Above a function named bin(p,t), converts a decimal number p to t binary bits. In [3], set size S, is 16. Similarly, a function named Gray() is used for encoding the Lehmer co-efficients. Where bin_bits is an array of binary bits. G is an array of corresponding Gray encoded bits.

(iv) S-ArbRO-2. This scheme is described in [5]. In this design the number of CRPs have been increased. Components are divided into elements. Each element has a pair of components associated with it as shown in Fig. 3 on the left side,

The difference between the counts of components in each element is the respective count associated with that element (r1-r2 or r2-r1). The next step is to select a group size for elements. This is done by selecting a value for parameter K. Inside this group, elements are added with each other. The range of K is $2 \leq K \leq N$.

Algorithm 4. S-ArbRO-2

```
S−ArbRO−2(E[] , K):        //K is the parameter passed.
combo =[]
//It will hold all the possible combinations
                        //of groups of Elements.
sums =[]     //It will hold the result of all the additions.
Kp= 2^(K−1)              // power(2, K−1).
i = 0
for x in combinations(E,K): // Generate all combinations
                        // of K out of N elements.
          combo [i]= x
          i = i + 1
end for
for(i=0; i< len(combo); i++):
  for(j = 0; j< Kp; j++):
   temp =[]
   p=bin(j,K)                //convert j into K binary bits.
    for(s=0; s<len(p); s++):
     if(p[s] =='0')
        temp = temp||(combo[i][s][0] − combo[i][s][1])//r1−r2
      else
        temp = temp||(combo[i][s][1] − combo[i][s][0])//r2−r1
      end if
     end for
    sums= sums || (sum(temp))
   end for
end for
for(i=0; i< len(sums); i++):
  if(sums[i]> 0)
        Response[i]=1
   else
        Response[i]=0
   end if
end for
```

If the result of adding elements is positive, the response is 1, otherwise it is 0. The total Challenge Response (CR) space is,

$$\text{Total CR space} = \frac{N!}{K! * (N - K)!} * 2^{K-1} \tag{1}$$

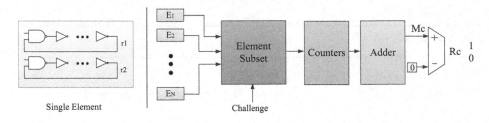

Fig. 3. Single element having two components (Left). S-ArbRO-2 showing the relationship between Challenge Response Pairs (Right)

As evident from the Fig. 3, the total number of elements is N. In the pseudocode, E[ ] is an input array of N elements.

Each Element has 2 components. K is the subset size. Combo holds all the possible combinations of $\binom{N}{K}$ elements. Sums will hold all the sums for K elements. Combination (N,K) calculates the $\binom{N}{K}$, sum (array) adds all the elements of an array. The response of S-ArbRO-2 is returned by an array Response[ ]. The pseudocode will generate all the possible CRPs. Assume that the component raw data is [10,5,6,4,17,11]. Therefore the three elements formed are $E_1 = [10,5]$, $E_2 = [6,4]$ and $E_3 = [17,11]$. The possible number of combinations for K = 2 is $\binom{3}{2} = 3$. Hence three groups of elements formed will be $\{E_1, E_2\}$, $\{E_1, E_3\}$ and $\{E_2, E_3\}$. Combo will contain $[\{E_1, E_2\}, \{E_1, E_3\}, \{E_2, E_3\}]$ or $[\{[10,5], [6,4]\}, \{[10,5], [17,11]\}, \{[6,4], [17,11]\}]$. If the group challenge is (01), it will select group $[E_1, E_3]$. Similarly inside each group if the challenge is (00), It will result in $0 \implies E_1[r1{-}r2] = 10{-}5 = 5$ and $0 \implies E_3[r1{-}r2] = 17{-}11 = 6$. Sums will hold $5 + 6 = 11$. Since 11>0, therefore the final PUF response will be 1.

(v) Identity Mapping (Id-Map). This scheme is described in [4]. In identity mapping M components can generate 2^M - M - 1 response bits. In this method, t component counts are selected from M component counts where $2 \leq t \leq M$. Initially all the pairs and triplets of component counts are determined by $| S_2 | = \binom{M}{2}$ and $| S_3 | = \binom{M}{3}$ respectively.

Likewise,

$$| S_t | = \binom{M}{t} \tag{2}$$

Then a random variable Q_t is defined that assigns a real number X to each outcome of S_t, $Q_t : S_t \longrightarrow X$ such that

$$Q_t(f_{x1}, f_{x2}, ..f_{xt}) = \sum_{u=1}^{t-1} \sum_{v=u+1}^{t} w_{(xu)(xv)} \cdot \| f_{xu} - f_{xv} \|^e \tag{3}$$

where $1 \leq x1, x2, x3,..., xt \leq m$.

And, $x1 \neq x2 \neq x3 \neq .. \neq xt$ and $2 \leq t \leq M$. The weight factor $w_{(xu)(xv)}$ can depend on a particular design. However, in our script it is equivalent to 1. Response R from Q is generated by using the following equation:

$$R = mod(Q[i]/q, 2) \; for \; i = 0, 1, 2, ... \tag{4}$$

q is the bucket size. The size of array Q depends on the value of t selected. For instance if $t = 2$, the total elements of Q are $\binom{M}{2}$. If $t = 3$, then total length of Q will be $\binom{M}{2} + \binom{M}{3}$, and so on. In addition to the response bits, a set of helper data is also generated. This helper data is used to reduce the effect of noise in the field.

Algorithm 5. Identity Mapping

```
Identity_map (components[], q, t, e):
                    //q, t and e are parameters.
S=[]                //It will hold the (M t) component counts.
Q=[]                //It will hold the Qs.
i = 0
for x in combinations(components,t)
          S[i]= x
          i = i + 1
end for
j = 0
for a,b in combinations(S,2)
          Q[j]= (|a − b|)^e
          j = j + 1
end for
for (i=0; i< len(Q); i++)
          Response_enrollment[i]= (Q[i]/q) mod 2
          Wt[i] = (0.5 * q)−(Q[i]−  ⌊(Q[i]/q)⌋ * q)
end for
for (i=0; i< len(Q'); i++) //Q' is generated in the field.
          temp[i]= ( Wt[i] + Q'[i])        //error correction
          Response_field[i]= (temp[i]/q) mod 2
end for
```

Helper data W_t is calculated using the following equation,

$$W_t = \binom{q}{2} - (Q[i] - q * \lfloor \frac{Q[i]}{q} \rfloor) \; for \; i \; = 0,1,2,3... \tag{5}$$

In (5), q is the bucket size. In the pseudocode, components[] is an input array that contains the counts of components, parameter e is any real number $\neq 1$. Parameter t can hold values , such that $2 \leq t \leq m$. PUF Response during enrolment is stored in an array Response_enrollment. While W_t is the array that contains the helper data. In the field, each response bit is recalculated using W_t and noisy Q values. Response_field[] contains the PUF response generated at the field.

4   Methodology

We use three properties of PUF to rank the schemes. These properties are Average uniformity, WC uniqueness and WC reliability. These properties are explained here, Uniformity of a PUF estimates how uniform the proportion of 0 s and 1 s are in the PUF response of a device. It is calculated using (6),

$$Uniformity(i) = \frac{1}{L} \sum_{l=1}^{L} r_{i,l} * 100\,\% \tag{6}$$

where $r_{i,l}$ is the lth binary bit in the response of a chip i. Response of each device is L bits. Average uniformity of N devices is shown in (7). The optimal value is 50 % for a set of N devices.

$$Avg \; Uniformity = \frac{1}{N} \sum_{i=1}^{N} Uniformity(i) \tag{7}$$

Worst case uniqueness is equal to minimum relative Hamming Distance between the response R(i) and response R(j), as well as between R(i) and complement of R(j). It is determined by looking at all pairs of responses from devices i and j. Its optimal value is equal to 50 %. It is calculated at the room temperature and nominal voltage. It is defined as:

$$WC \; Uniqueness = \min_{i=1,j=i+1}^{i=N-1,j=N} \left(\frac{min(HD(R_i, R_j), L - HD(R_i, R_j))}{L} \right) * 100\,\% \tag{8}$$

R_i and R_j are the responses of two FPGA devices. To determine the best scheme we chose the one that has the highest WC uniqueness. The worst case reliability is calculated using the following equation,

$$WC \; Reliability = \min_{i=1}^{N} \left(1 - \left(\frac{\overset{C}{\underset{c=0}{\max}} HD(R_i, R_{i,c})}{L} \right) \right) * 100\,\% \tag{9}$$

It describes how close to the 100 % reproduction of the PUF bits a given scheme is getting in the worst case. Optimal value is equal to 100 %. In (9), HD is the hamming distance. R_i is the response of device i at the nominal condition. $R_{i,c}$ is the response of device i in the field. L is response size in bits and C is the total number of conditions applied in the field. The best scheme in terms of WC reliability is the one that has the highest value for (9). Overall, we used the following equation to determine the optimum parameters:

$$Z = Max\{50\% - Avg\ Uniformity, 50\% - WC\ Uniqueness, 100\% - WC\ Reliability\} \quad (10)$$

We choose the parameter for any dataset which gives the smallest value for Z according to (10). These parameters are shown in Tables 4, 5, 6, 7. The input to PUF-ID generating scripts is in the chip-row format. In this format the rows contain the data for a particular device while the columns contain the M components.

5   Results

In order to generate same number of PUF response bits using different schemes, we chose the PUF response size of 128 bits. It is due to the fact that Pairwise Comparison (PC) generates only 128 bits using all the 256 components of SR-latch data (Table 1).

Table 1. Details of dataset.

	CNC	PC	BLG	S-ArbRO-2	Id-Map
Parameters			Set size = 16	K = 2	t = 2
PUF response length (L)	128	128	128	128	128
Min components required (M)	129	256	48	24	17
PUF response (L)	M-1	$\lfloor M/2 \rfloor$	(M/S)*L	$\binom{M}{K} * 2^{k-1}$	$\binom{M}{t}$

Zynq Data set: Total devices = 10, Components per device = 256
Spartan-6 Data set: Total devices = 25, Components per device = 256
Spartan-3 Data set: Total devices = 193, Components per device = 512

From Tables 2, 3 and 4, it is evident that the best scheme in terms of WC uniqueness is PC for both Zynq and Spartan-3 datasets. However for Spartan-6 data it is the CNC scheme that generates the best results. Similarly for Average uniformity the best results are offered by BLG in Zynq dataset and S-ArbRO-2 in both Spartan-6 and Spartan-3 datasets. Tables 5, 6, 7 shows the worse case reliability as defined in (9). Spartan-3 data set contains voltage and temperature data for only five devices. Similarly Zynq data set contains voltage and temperature data for ten devices. Additionally the Spartan-6 data set contains voltage and temperature data for fifteen devices. The nominal voltage of Zynq devices is 1 V on the other hand it is 1.2 V for both Spartan-6 and Spartan-3 devices.

Table 2. Zynq data.

	CNC	PC	BLG	S-ArbRO-2	Id-Map
Parameters			Set size = 16	K = 2	e = 0.5, q = 2, t = 2
Inter-chip HD mean	49.02 %	49.87 %	46.64 %	50.46 %	50.14 %
Inter-chip HD min	38.28 %	42.19 %	36.72 %	29.69 %	39.84 %
Inter-chip HD max	57.03 %	58.59 %	53.91 %	71.88 %	58.59 %
Inter-chip HD std dev	4.48 %	3.36 %	3.8 %	10.28 %	4.37 %
WC uniqueness	38.28 %	**41.41 %**	36.72 %	28.12 %	39.84 %
Avg uniformity	46.87 %	46.79 %	**47.89 %**	54.14 %	47.34 %
Std dev uniformity	1.39 %	4.49 %	4.58 %	10.19 %	12.44 %

Table 3. Spartan-6 Data

	CNC	PC	BLG	S-ArbRO-2	Id-Map
Parameters			Set size = 16	K = 2	e = 0.5, q = 1, t = 2
Inter-chip HD mean	49.36 %	49.25 %	46.12 %	49.77 %	46.37 %
Inter-chip HD min	35.16 %	33.59 %	32.81 %	25.78 %	34.38 %
Inter-chip HD max	63.28 %	60.16 %	59.38 %	83.59 %	62.5 %
Inter-chip HD std dev	5.2 %	4.45 %	4.34 %	10.41 %	4.82 %
WC uniqueness	**35.16 %**	33.59 %	32.81 %	16.41 %	34.38 %
Avg uniformity	44.03 %	44.71 %	44.65 %	**52.96 %**	63.68 %
Std dev uniformity	1.95 %	4.52 %	4.24 %	8.63 %	6.41 %

From Tables 5, 6, 7, the best scheme in terms of worst case reliability is CNC for Zynq, PC for Spartan-6 and Id-Map for Spartan-3 datasets. The bold values shown in each column shows the minimum value. For any dataset the best scheme is chosen that results in the highest bold value. The worst result is offered by S-ArbRO-2 for Spartan-3 dataset. It might be due to the fact that certain ROs are affected more by voltage and temperature variation than others. In S-ArbRO-2 if the sign of the elements change in the field. Then it results in a bit flip, hence low reliability.

Table 4. Spartan-3 Data

	CNC	PC	BLG	S-ArbRO-2	Id-Map
Parameters			Set size = 16	K = 2	e = 0.5, q = 30, t = 2
Inter-chip HD mean	46.83 %	46.61 %	45.85 %	46.13 %	48.76 %
Inter-chip HD min	28.91 %	30.47 %	26.56 %	13.28 %	24.22 %
Inter-chip HD max	65.63 %	62.5 %	66.41 %	83.59 %	64.84 %
Inter-chip HD std dev	4.86 %	4.45 %	4.76 %	10.2 %	4.47 %
WC uniqueness	28.91 %	**30.47 %**	26.56 %	13.28 %	24.22 %
Avg uniformity	49.86 %	52.25 %	47.70 %	**50.24 %**	57.80 %
Std dev uniformity	2.53 %	4.58 %	6.70 %	9.39 %	4.96 %

Table 5. CNC and PC results

	CNC			PC		
	Zynq	Spartan-6	Spartan-3	Zynq	Spartan-6	Spartan-3
PUF Type	SR-Latch	SR-Latch	RO-PUF	SR-Latch	SR-Latch	RO-PUF
Rel @ +5 % V	93.75 %	99.21 %	**87.50 %** (+10 % V)	93.75 %	97.65 %	**91.40 %** (+10 % V)
Rel @ −5 % V	93.75 %	95.31 %	91.40 % (−10 % V)	93.75 %	**96.09 %**	92.96 % (−10 % V)
Rel @ 85 C	**91.40 %**	**94.53 %**	95.31 % (+65 C)	**89.84 %**	96.09 %	92.96 % (+65 C)
Rel @ 0 C	94.53 %	96.87 %	N/A	94.53 %	96.09 %	N/A

Table 6. BLG and S-ArbRO-2 results

	BLG			S-ArbRO-2		
	Set size = 16			K = 2		
	Zynq	Spartan-6	Spartan-3	Zynq	Spartan-6	Spartan-3
Rel @ +5 % V	86.71 %	94.57 %	**83.59 %** (+10 % V)	92.18 %	96.87 %	48.14 % (+10 % V)
Rel @ −5 % V	85.93 %	90.62 %	84.37 % (−10 % V)	92.96 %	96.09 %	**38.2 %** (−10 % V)
Rel @ 85 C	**78.9 %**	**85.93 %**	90.62 % (+65 C)	**83.59 %**	**89.06 %**	39.06 % (+65 C)
Rel @ 0 C	89.84 %	92.18 %	N/A	92.96 %	93.75 %	N/A

Table 7. Identity Mapping scheme

	Zynq	Spartan-6	Spartan-3
Parameters	q = 2	q = 1	q = 30
Rel @ +5 % V	**75.81 %**	89.84 %	94.53 % (+10 % V)
Rel @ −5 % V	91.4 %	**85.93 %**	**92.96 %** (−10 % V)
Rel @ 85 C	64.84 %	89.84 %	97.65 % (+65 C)
Rel @ 0 C	92.18 %	90.62 %	N/A

6   Conclusion and Future Work

From this work we conclude that PUF responses should be generated using
multiple schemes to determine the uniformity and worst cases of uniqueness and
reliability. S-ArbRO-2, Lehmer-Gray and Identity mapping offers the ability to
use less number of components for PUF design; however the CRPs are no longer
independent. BLG scheme offers the best results in terms of uniformity in Zynq,
however it is the S-ArbRO-2 scheme that generates the best uniformity results
for both Spartan-3 and Spartan-6 datasets. In case of uniqueness PC scheme
offers best results for both Zynq and Spartan-3 datasets. In case of Reliability
we have no winner as three different schemes offer the best results for three data
sets. In the future we intend to enhance the scope of our method by including
the Arbiter PUF data set [9] in our analysis. We plan to post our scripts at [10].

References

1. Maiti, A., Schaumont, P.: Improved ring oscillator PUF: an FPGA friendly secure primitive. J. Cryptology **24**(2), 375–397 (2010)
2. Hori, Y., Yoshida, T., Katashita, T., Satoh, A.: Quantitative and statistical performance evaluation of arbiter physical unclonable functions on FPGAs. In: Proceedings of International Conference on Recongurable Computing and FPGAs (ReConFig) 2010, pp. 298–303 (2010)
3. Maes, R., Van Herrewege, A., Verbauwhede, I.: PUFKY: a fully functional PUF-based cryptographic key generator. In: Prouff, E., Schaumont, P. (eds.) CHES 2012. LNCS, vol. 7428, pp. 302–319. Springer, Heidelberg (2012)
4. Maiti, A., Kim, I., Schaumont, P.: A robust physical unclonable function with en-hanced challenge-response set. IEEE Trans. Inf. Forensics Secur. **7**(1), 333–345 (2012)
5. Ganta, D., Nazhandali, L.: Easy-to-build arbiter physical unclonable function with enhanced challenge/response set. In: 14th International Symposium on Quality Electronic Design Proceedings of Quality Electronic Design (ISQED) (2013)
6. Maiti, A., Gunreddy, V., Schaumont, P.: A systematic method to evaluate and compare the performance of physical unclonable functions. In: Athanas, P., Pnevmatikatos, D., Sklavos, N. (eds.) Embedded Systems Design with FPGAs, pp. 245–267. Springer, New York (2013)
7. http://rijndael.ece.vt.edu/puf/detailed.php
8. Habib, B., Kaps, J.-P., Gaj, K.: Efficient SR-latch PUF. In: Sano, K., Soudris, D., Hübner, M., Diniz, P. (eds.) ARC 2015. LNCS, vol. 9040, pp. 205–216. Springer, Heidelberg (2015)
9. https://staff.aist.go.jp/hori.y/en/puf/index.html
10. https://cryptography.gmu.edu/puf

Design and Optimization of Digital Circuits by Artificial Evolution Using Hybrid Multi Chromosome Cartesian Genetic Programming

Vitor Coimbra[✉] and Marcus Vinicius Lamar

Department of Computer Science, University of Brasília,
Brasília, DF 70910-900, Brazil
vitorc@aluno.unb.br, lamar@unb.br

Abstract. Traditional digital circuit design techniques are based, for the most part, on top-down methods, which use a set of rules and restrictions to assist the construction of the project. Genetic algorithms, on the other hand, haven proven themselves to be a very useful tool for solving high complexity problems, relying on a bottom-up methodology. This paper proposes a new design algorithm, named HMC-CGP, which operates by first finding a functional solution by using the MC-CGP method. Then, optimizes it by using standard CGP approach. Test circuits used include 1 and 2 bit full adders, 2 bit multiplier and 7 segment hexadecimal decoder. Obtained results show that by making use of faster convergence granted by the MC-CGP mechanism together with an optimization strategy generates novel approaches for those circuits, with results showing a logic gate and transistor usage reduction of up to 60.8 %.

Keywords: Genetic algorithm · Evolving hardware · Digital circuit · CGP

1 Introduction

Traditionally, human beings have designed high complexity systems, such as buildings, computers and cars, by making use of a complex set of rules that aim to fulfill a set of requirements. By its nature, this process is handled in a top-down manner, that is, an abstract specification is used as a starting point and, from then on, smaller and more specific systems are designed to accomplish the task [10].

This is in direct contrast with the evolutionary mechanism that resulted in the creation of the immense diversity of living beings found today. All this biodiversity is a consequence of a simple instruction set, encoded by DNA, responsible for countless chemical reactions that result in the construction of a complex organism.

Inspired by this concept, genetic algorithms have been used for a diverse range of applications. Consisting of an iteration on populations, in which each individual represents a possible solution, its primary inspiration comes from the

© Springer International Publishing Switzerland 2016
V. Bonato et al. (Eds.): ARC 2016, LNCS 9625, pp. 195–206, 2016.
DOI: 10.1007/978-3-319-30481-6_16

idea of natural selection [2]. Individuals with traits that allow it to survive longer have higher chances of reproducing and passing these traits onward. With each generation, the population converges to a desired solution. Genetic algorithms are a suitable approach for complex problems, where an heuristic approach is a better fit than traditional resolution techniques [7].

The problem of digital circuit design is commonly used for the evaluation of non-standard computation methods. It has been shown to generate novel solutions unreachable by traditional human methods [9]. Of the better known techniques, Cartesian Genetic Programming (CGP), first defined by Miller [8], describes a genotype encoding that aims to configure a two dimensional grid of interconnected nodes. Each node is responsible for executing a function on a set of inputs.

CGP has been shown to be very effective for the design of circuits, in particular those with one output. As the circuit number of outputs grows, it becomes increasingly less likely to reach a functional solution. Because of this, many techniques have been developed to circumvent this limitation. Among those, a multi-chromosome encoding technique, called Multi Chromosome-CGP (MC-CGP) [12], offers a parallel take by treating each output of the circuit as a sub-problem to be solved. Its solution is the union of all solutions for each sub-problem.

This paper addresses the main disadvantage from both aforementioned methods. As both methods terminate their execution as soon as a working solution is found, these solutions often offer inefficient usage of available resources. That is, for digital circuits, there are usually more logic gates, transistors or a longer delay between inputs and outputs than necessary. A new hybrid method is proposed which seeks to find solutions and optimize them efficiently.

The remainder of this paper is organized as the following: Sect. 2 presents the concepts behind Cartesian Genetic Programming. Section 3 describes the Multi Chromosome CGP algorithm and its advantages. The proposed hybrid technique is explained in Sect. 4. Experimental results obtained are shown and discussed in Sect. 5. Final thoughts and conclusions are discussed in Sect. 6.

2   Cartesian Genetic Programming

CGP encodes a genotype by using a fixed-length list of integers that defines how the nodes in a two dimensional grid are connected in a feed-forward manner. The example in Fig. 1 shows a genotype and its resulting phenotype below. The first part of the genotype describes each node by its inputs (in this example, its two inputs) followed by its function. The node described by the integers *0 1 2* takes inputs 0 and 1 and multiplies them. The second part details which pins are connected to the outputs of the circuit. In this case, the first output is connected to pin 10 and the second output is connected to pin 11.

Note that, while the genotype has a fixed length, its resulting phenotype may have different amounts of active nodes, that is, nodes that exert a computation on an output. These inactive genes have a neutral effect in the evaluation of

Genotype

0 1 2   3 4 2   6 2 2   7 5 2   8 9 0   8 9 1   10 11

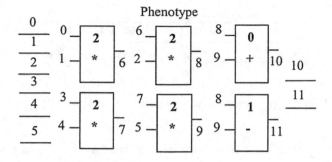

Fig. 1. A simple arithmetic circuit example encoded by CGP [8].

an individual. This property has been shown to have a positive effect in the evolutionary process by contributing to neutral drifts in the solution space [11].

Other works that make use of CGP typically use recombination strategies that don't use crossover operations, as it has been shown to have a detrimental effect on the algorithm's performance. Strategies such as $(1 + \lambda)$ [4], containing only mutation operations are employed for the selection of individuals in CGP algorithms.

3   Multi Chromosome CGP

Originally proposed by Walker *et al.* [12], this multi-chromosome encoding technique divides the genotype in k sections of equal length, where k is the number of outputs in the circuit. Each output can, thus, only take their values from distinct sections. Figure 2 has an example which shows a genotype divided in 4 different sections, (c_0, c_1, c_2, c_3) with each output connected to a specific one, indicated by its subscripts $(o_{c_0}, o_{c_1}, o_{c_2}, o_{c_3})$.

Reported results show that the method converges to a functional solution from 3 to 392 times faster compared to successful evolutions by the use of a standard CGP strategy [12]. Additionally, dividing a genotype by sections allow them to be evolved in parallel, alleviating, in part, the sequential nature of genetic algorithms.

The CGP and MC-CGP algorithms terminate their executions as soon as an individual that implements the desired functionality is found. A consequence of this is final generated circuits which, for the most part, do not efficiently make use of the available resources [1,6].

Some authors, thus, choose to use multi-objective techniques to produce optimized circuits. Hilder *et al.* [6], for instance, propose a two-step algorithm, similar to that found in this paper. The first step consists of finding a functional solution

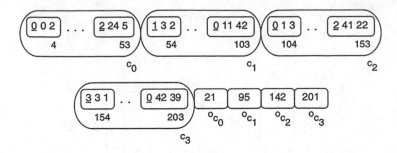

Fig. 2. Genotype division typically seen in MC-CGP [12].

for the problem. To achieve that, they used a standard CGP strategy. The second step is responsible for optimizations, by use of a evolutionary strategy called NSGA-II [5], developed with specific multi-objective goals taken into account. Results reported by the authors show highly optimized circuits, however they chose to run the optimization phase for 20 to 50 million generations, making it impossible for us to evaluate the proposed method's efficiency for lower amounts, i.e., in a practical amount of time using the available computing hardware.

4   Hybrid MC-CGP

The proposed method in this paper attempts to unite the aforementioned advantages of both CGP and MC-CGP techniques. The algorithm, entitled Hybrid MC-CGP (HMC-CGP), is composed of two sequential phases.

4.1   Functional Solution

The first step of the algorithm has, as its main objective, to find a solution that implements the desired functionality correctly. A modified MC-CGP algorithm is, then, used to achieve that goal. Each section of the chromosome division is treated as its own CGP grid. Effectively, each output consists of a distinct population with identical CGP parameters, such as number of rows and columns.

The fitness function f_1 used to verify the functionality of an individual in this first phase is defined by

$$f_1(C, D) = \frac{1}{\varepsilon_0 + \varepsilon(C, D)},\tag{1}$$

where $\varepsilon(C, D)$ is the error obtained by the phenotype of chromosome C and the desired output set D, calculated by

$$\varepsilon(C, D) = \sum_{i=0}^{\rho-1} |S_i(C) - D_i|,\tag{2}$$

where $\rho = 2^{n_{in}}$, n_{in} the number of circuit inputs and S the set of outputs calculated by the individual C.

This phase terminates once all sections have found suitable individuals, that is, once they have achieved the maximum defined fitness $\frac{1}{\varepsilon_0}$.

4.2   Optimization

An important property of parallel evolution of individuals is the prioritization of performance, in terms of number of generations, over possible solutions that use the circuit resources in a more efficient manner.

To overcome that disadvantage, this second phase has the main purpose of being an explicit optimization phase applied to the results found in the first phase. Typical attributes of interest to circuit designers, which were chosen to be the optimization parameters for the algorithm in this work are:

1. Number of logic gates (n_g);
2. Longest gate path from input to output (n_l);
3. Number of transistors (n_t).

Optimizing the number of logic gates results in a more compact final circuit. On the other hand, since logic gates are implemented with different amounts of transistors, compact circuits in terms of logic gates don't necessarily mean they are compact from a transistor standpoint as well. Because of that, the amount of transistors used, in total, by the circuit is also taken into account. Another aspect that relates directly to how quickly a circuit responds to a change to the input is the longest gate-path. The longer a path is from an input to an output, the more gates a change will propagate until it is stabilized in its output. This is one of the traits that define a circuit's maximum frequency usage.

All of the individuals that solved their own output problem in the first phase are united, by rows, in a single CGP grid, forming one population. Additionally, the population is altered by α such that $\lambda' = \lambda \cdot \alpha$ enables a higher diversity of generated individuals, broadening the search in the solution space.

Figure 3 shows a three output problem example. In the first phase, all individuals are evolved separately as denoted by each output being connected to one CGP grid. In the second phase, the correct individuals that resulted from the first are united, with each one initially being a row of the new population. This allows these independent solutions to share nodes between themselves. In this phase, therefore, we propose the use of a standard CGP approach by evaluating the aforementioned attributes of each individual.

The fitness function f_2 responsible for the optimization evaluation in this second phase is given by

$$f_2(C, D) = \begin{cases} 0, & \text{if } \varepsilon(C, D) \neq 0 \\ \frac{1}{1+n_g(C)} + \frac{1}{1+n_l(C)} + \frac{1}{1+n_t(C)}, & \text{otherwise.} \end{cases} \qquad (3)$$

where $n_g(C)$ is the number of gates of the circuit generated by chromosome C, $n_l(C)$ is the longest path, and $n_t(C)$ the number of transistors.

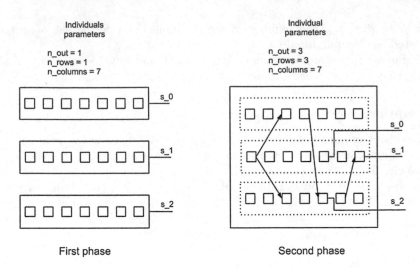

Fig. 3. An exemplified overview of the HMC-CGP method

The main difference between the first and second phase evaluations is that, in this second phase, circuits that do not implement the desired functionality receive the lowest fitness score possible, effectively removing them from next generations.

The algorithm is finished once a set number of generations has passed in this stage and the highest fitness individual found by its end is considered the final solution. Notably, however, it has no maximum achievable fitness score to be reached.

5   Obtained Results

The experiments were conducted in a manner to compare the chosen attributes after the end of the first phase and after the end of the second.

To deal with the inherent randomness of the evolution process, each experiment was repeated 30 times, using 50000 generations for the second phase and the mutation operator was set to mutate 3 genes. The initial parameters for the first phase, which uses the MC-CGP method, were set so each population's individuals were composed of 1 row and 10 columns, with the allowed logic functions *AND, OR, XOR, NOT, NAND, XNOR, NOR*. Both phases of the HMC-CGP algorithm use the evolutionary strategy $(1 + \lambda)$ with $\lambda = 4$ [13].

Logic gate implementations on transistor level are highly dependent on the technology they are based on. In this work the NOT gate uses 2 transistors, AND, OR and XOR gates are designed using 6 transistors each, NAND and NOR with 4 transistors and XNOR gate uses 8 transistors.

Four combinational circuits were chosen to verify the proposed method: 1 and 2 bit full adders, 2 bit multiplier and 7 segment hexadecimal decoder. The choice of the adder and multiplier circuits is based on the fact that they are common basic blocks for many complex modules. Optimizations found in these blocks could propagate very visible performance increases. Being a more complex circuit with many unrelated outputs, the 7 segment decoder was a good candidate for testing whether sharing gate logic allows better optimizations.

The obtained circuits are evaluated by the target attributes to optimize: n_g the number of logic gates, n_l the longest path and n_t the number of transistors. Table 1 shows the expected values of these attributes over 30 runs, and t the average time, in seconds, needed to run one experiment in a computer with an *Intel(R) Core(TM) i5-3570 CPU @ 3.40 GHz* processor and 8 GB RAM.

Table 1. Expected values of the obtained circuits' attributes.

Experiment	Phase 1			Phase 2			$t(s)$
	n_g	n_l	n_t	n_g	n_l	n_t	
1 bit full adder	8.16	3.8	47.6	5.03	3.0	25.93	99.13
2 bit full adder	18.06	5.16	107.13	11.06	4.9	60.06	709.56
2 bit multiplier	14.2	4.03	74.33	7.7	2.2	37.53	357.76
7 segment decoder	47.53	5.83	270.46	32.86	5.0	176.4	740.63

As shown by Table 1 the average of number of gates n_g of 1 bit full adder circuits is optimized by the second phase from 8.16 to 5.03, without a significant reduction of the path length n_l. On the other hand the 2 bit multiplier the length path is reduced in from $n_l = 4.03$ to 2.2 gates in average. In all of these circuits the number of transistors n_t is significantly reduced by the second phase of the proposed HMC-CGP algorithm.

For the 1 bit full adder circuit synthesis experiments, very little diversity of solutions was observed. Most individuals converged to a circuit with $n_g = 5$, $n_l = 3$ and $n_t = 24$. Figure 4 shows a comparison between the usual solution, shown in Fig. 4b and the evolved solution in Fig. 4a. The classic solution shown has $n_g = 5$, $n_l = 3$ and $n_t = 30$. Thus, even though both have the same amount of logic gates, the genetic solution shows a more efficient transistor usage.

The best optimization case for 2 bit full adder experiment, in terms of n_g and n_t, was an individual found with $n_g = 10$, $n_l = 5$ and $n_t = 52$. Another solution, more efficient for n_l, was found with $n_g = 11$, $n_l = 4$ and $n_t = 58$. It is interesting to note that this last solution has a lower gate path count than the usual method of creating a 2 bit full adder by cascading two 1 bit full adders, which has a gate path of 5. Figure 5 compares both the solution found by the genetic algorithm, seen in Fig. 5a and the traditional 2 bit adder design of cascading two 1 bit adders, seen in Fig. 5b.

In the 2 bit multiplier circuit design experiments, most runs converged to an individual with $n_g = 7$, $n_l = 2$ and $n_t = 32$ shown in Fig. 6.

Runs on the 7 segment display decoder experiments had the most diversity of solutions. In terms of n_g and n_t, the best individual found has $n_g = 29$, $n_l = 5$

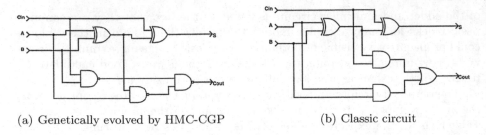

(a) Genetically evolved by HMC-CGP   (b) Classic circuit

Fig. 4. 1 bit full adder circuit found by the proposed method (a) and the classic circuit (b).

and $n_t = 152$, this circuit can be seen on Fig. 7. Of note, it is possible to observe that although no output has any dependency on another, there is a degree of logic sharing between them. In terms of n_l, the best circuit found has $n_g = 32$, $n_l = 4$ and $n_t = 170$. Even with the relative complexity inherent to the circuit specification, significant improvements over the first phase solution were found. In [6] the authors report the evolution of a solution with $n_g = 22$, $n_l = 5$, in 50 million generations. For comparison, the circuit generated by Altera's

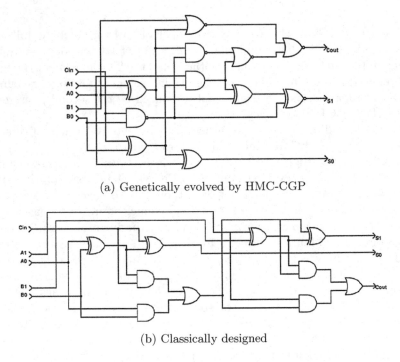

(a) Genetically evolved by HMC-CGP

(b) Classically designed

Fig. 5. 2 bit adder circuits found by the proposed method (a) and by the classic 1 bit adder cascading (b)

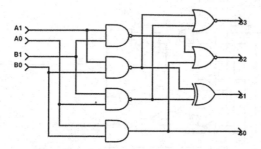

Fig. 6. Resulting evolved 2 bit multiplier solution from the HMC-CGP method.

Quartus II software ver. 13.0 [3] can be seen in Fig. 8 which uses 74 logic gates built with 352 transistors. Even though this software is designed to efficiently use the Logic Elements of an Altera FPGA, the results show the importance of internal logic sharing as opposed to independent output circuit design.

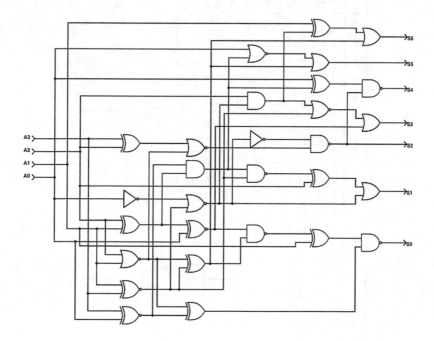

Fig. 7. Genetically evolved 7 segment display decoder circuit.

The experiments show that the proposed method offers a significant improvement in performance, mainly for relatively complex circuits such as the 7 segment decoder. By allowing the different solutions to share gates between themselves, new optimization avenues open up, making it possible for common sub-expressions to be shared and further reducing gate and transistor usage.

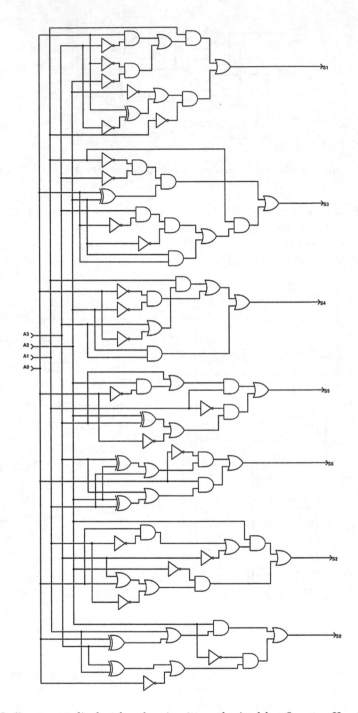

Fig. 8. 7 segment display decoder circuit synthesized by *Quartus II* software.

This kind of optimization is not taken into account on traditional optimization methods such as Karnaugh Maps and Quine-McCluskey.

6   Conclusions

The use of a genetic evolution approach to design digital circuits is in direct contrast with traditional design methods, which are guided by abstractions made to help the human designer in its design process.

This paper proposed a new hybrid method HMC-CGP to evolve digital circuits by combining the main advantages of Cartesian Genetic Programming and Multi Chromosome CGP techniques. CGP presents a low convergence rate for multiple output circuits, while MC-CGP typically converges to solutions with inefficient resource usage.

To address both issues the new method employs a two-step algorithm. First, it uses the MC-CGP technique, which prioritizes performance in finding functional solutions. In its second step, it uses the CGP method for an additional amount of generations in order to optimize the solution found according some defined criteria. In this work, the number of logic gates, the number of transistors used by the circuit and its longest gate path from an input to an output are proposed as optimization criteria.

The obtained results indicate that the proposed HMC-CGP method is capable of significant optimization of resource usage over the solutions found in the first phase of the algorithm. Experiments on classic digital circuits were performed. In the design of a 7 segment display decoder, the number of gates are reduced by 60.8 % and the number of transistors by 56.8 % when compared to the circuit obtained from the Altera's software *Quartus-II*.

One of the main optimizations observed in the experiments with HMC-CGP is common sub-circuit sharing by unrelated outputs of a circuit. This kind of optimization is usually infeasible for human designers to take into account for complex specifications.

References

1. Asha, S., Hemamalini, R.R.: Synthesis of adder circuit using cartesian genetic programming. WSEAS Trans. Circuits Syst. **14**, 83–88 (2015)
2. Greenwood, G.W., Tyrrell, A.M.: Introduction to Evolvable Hardware: A Practical Guide for Designing Self-adaptive Systems. Wiley, Hoboken (2006)
3. FPGA CPLD and ASIC from Altera. http://www.altera.com
4. Beyer, H.: Towards a theory of 'Evolution Strategies'. Some asymptotical results from the (1,+lambda)-theory. Evol. Comput. **1**, 165–188 (1993)
5. Deb, K., Pratap, A., Agarwal, S., Meyarivan, T.A.M.T.: A fast and elitist multiobjective genetic algorithm: NSGA-II. IEEE Trans. Evol. Comput. **6**, 182–197 (2002)
6. Hilder, J., Walker, J.A., Tyrrell, A.: Use of a multi-objective fittness function to improve cartesian genetic programming circuits. In: NASA/ESA Conference on Adaptive Hardware and Systems (AHS 2010), California, pp. 179–185. IEEE (2010)

7. Melanie, M.: An Introduction to Genetic Algorithms. Bradford, MIT Press, Cambridge (1999)
8. Miller, J.F.: An empirical study of the efficiency of learning boolean functions using a cartesian genetic programming approach. In: Proceedings of the Genetic and Evolutionary Computation Conference, Florida, pp. 1135–1142. Morgan Kaufmann (1999)
9. Thompson, A.: Hardware Evolution. Automatic Design of Electronic Circuits in Reconfigurable Hardware by Artificial Evolution. Springer, London (1998)
10. Torresen, J.: Evolvable hardware-a short introduction. In: Proceedings of the 1997 International Conference on Neural Information Processing and Intelligent Information Systems, pp. 674–677. Springer, New York (1997)
11. Vassilev, V.K., Miller, J.F.: The advantages of landscape neutrality in digital circuit evolution. In: Miller, J.F., Thompson, A., Thompson, P., Fogarty, T.C. (eds.) ICES 2000. LNCS, vol. 1801, pp. 252–263. Springer, Heidelberg (2000)
12. Walker, J.A., Völk, K., Smith, S.L., Miller, J.F.: Parallel evolution using multi-chromosome cartesian genetic programming. Genet. Program Evolvable Mach. **10**, 417–445 (2009)
13. Oliveira, V.C.: Design and Optimization of Digital Circuits by Use of Artificial Evolution Techniques (in Portuguese). University of Brasília, Brasília (2015). http://bdm.unb.br/handle/10483/11045

A Multi-codec Framework to Enhance Data Channels in FPGA Streaming Systems

Marlon Wijeyasinghe$^{(\boxtimes)}$ and David Thomas

Department of Electrical and Electronic Engineering,
Imperial College London, London, UK
{marlon.wijeyasinghe09,d.thomas1}@imperial.ac.uk

Abstract. We propose a framework to apply general-purpose data transforms to a data channel between a stateless FPGA kernel and a CPU, such as increasing effective bandwidth by using spare CPU and FPGA resources on a heterogeneous CPU-FPGA system. Compute-intensive transforms (codecs) such as compression are applied in real-time while maintaining the simplicity of a high-level abstraction for a PCI-express channel. Real-time encoding/decoding is accelerated by splitting the data stream into segments and having multiple codec threads processing different segments. Multi-threading on the CPU allows the overlap of encoding, data transmission and decoding thereby functioning as a software pipeline. We demonstrate this using 4 compression codecs across 3 data types, showing speed-ups ranging from 1.26x to 1.60x in a Maxeler-based system. For example, we achieve a 1.51x speed-up for delta compression, increasing the effective total input/output bandwidth of the data channel from 2509 MB/s to 3790 MB/s.

1 Introduction

Modern day FPGA streaming systems are ideal for high-performance computing (HPC) applications as they use pipeline parallelism and replicated pipelines to achieve high speed computation. Such applications have traditionally been built at the Register Transfer Level (RTL), but the time this takes is increasing due to the complexity of developing pipelines and coordinating dataflow. HPC programmers (kernel designers) now use high-level synthesis (HLS) tools to handle low-level aspects such as instantiating and re-timing pipelines in hardware kernels.

HLS tools have drawbacks despite their ability to simplify the design process – the kernel designer is restricted to using language/library primitives provided by the tool to describe logic, arithmetic and stream control. Hence they must revert to an RTL description to implement features that are not included in the streaming services provided by the tool.

A major challenge that streaming systems face is limited data bandwidth to/from the chip. FPGA kernels are capable of high-speed computation, but if the channel supplying data to the kernel is incapable of providing data at the required speed, it is not possible to make full use of the kernel's computational

© Springer International Publishing Switzerland 2016
V. Bonato et al. (Eds.): ARC 2016, LNCS 9625, pp. 207–219, 2016.
DOI: 10.1007/978-3-319-30481-6_17

capabilities. One way to mitigate the bandwidth issue in an existing high-level streaming system is for the HPC programmer to design compression at RTL or include pseudo-RTL code within the high-level code. This adds complexity to the design process in both software (SW) and hardware (HW) thereby reducing the benefits of working with HLS tools.

We propose a framework to add compute-intensive real-time codecs (e.g. compression to improve effective bandwidth) by using spare CPU cycles on the SW side and spare FPGA resources on the HW side of the channel. Software codecs must be multi-threaded and hardware codecs must be pipelined to operate at line rate (channel data rate) to avoid reducing bandwidth in the system.

Hence, the contributions of this paper are:

- A multi-threaded framework to apply compute-intensive codecs to a segmented data stream by using spare resources in software and hardware.
- A concrete implementation of the framework in a commercial platform using C code on the CPU side and OpenSPL code on the FPGA side.
- A model for predicting the end-to-end transmission latency when the framework is applied to a streaming system.
- Evaluation of data transmission performance across a bandwidth-limited PCI-express channel on a Maxeler machine with compression codecs showing up to 1.60x speed-up and comparison with model-predicted performance.

2   Background

FPGA streaming systems accelerate computationally intensive algorithms by exploiting their parallelism and/or using replicated pipelines. This is done by transmitting data along a pipelined kernel at a high throughput. Previous work on streaming applications, such as [1,2], demonstrated that FPGAs can often outperform multi-core CPUs in terms of speed and energy efficiency. Such implementations are suitable where large amounts of data are transmitted such that the total transmission time is much larger than the pipeline latency; thereby making the implementation tolerant to latency.

The bandwidth problem arises due to limitations in the capability of data channels. The I/O bandwidth of the chip is restricted by the number of I/O pins and the clock frequency of their corresponding registers. The physical characteristics of the off-chip data channel(s) which are used to access the FPGA can also limit the bandwidth with which the FPGA can be accessed externally. For example, we use the Maxeler [3] heterogeneous CPU-FPGA platform where the CPU transmits data to and from the FPGA via PCI-express with a theoretical bandwidth of 2 GB/s in either direction (total 4 GB/s). Assuming the transmission is happening in both directions simultaneously, if a pipelined computation kernel on the FPGA has a 128-bit wide data bus, the channel bandwidth is sufficient to support the kernel being clocked at up to 134 MHz. A kernel with a higher clock frequency will not run at full capacity since the channel supplying the kernel is a bottleneck.

To tackle the bandwidth issue, different compression methods have been implemented on FPGAs. Sano [4] implemented a floating point hardware compressor/decompressor to be placed at either end of a Lattice Boltzmann Method (LBM) streaming kernel to improve effective memory bandwidth, achieving a compression ratio ranging from 2.5–3.8. Similarly, in [5], sparse matrix vector multiplication, a memory-bound algorithm was accelerated by compressing redundant non-zero data and achieved a compression ratio of 1.14–2.65. These compression methods are specific to the date type being compressed and optimised for the specific algorithm they were designed for, due to the nature of the patterns of data handled by the algorithms. Additionally, the computation kernel was not modified in these two cases.

The framework that this paper presents works with a good degree of transparency, under the same principle of not modifying the kernel. However its emphasis is broader than purely accelerating bandwidth-bottlenecked HPC applications by designing state-of-the-art compression algorithms - but rather to use compression codecs to demonstrate the capability of the proposed framework. The framework aims to enhance communication between software-hardware boundaries.

Some general purpose compression algorithms have previously been implemented on FPGAs. The general purpose ZLIB algorithm [6] was implemented on FPGA and it operates at 250 MB/s. The LZMA algorithm [7] operates at up to 16 MB/s. GZIP [8] attained a compression bandwidth of up to 110 MB/s. While these implementations were on older technology (therefore they will be faster on newer technology), all three are at least an order of magnitude slower than our channel bandwidth (2509 MB/s). The existing implementations are not able to perform real-time compression on a CPU-FPGA heterogeneous system.

Other attempts at general data channel enhancements have been made, using various approaches. In previous work, we proposed the idea of transparently adding capabilities such as compression and error correction to data channels without modifying the kernel [9] but it was not implemented. Further, [10] describes a platform for simplifying communication between FPGAs and GPUs via PCIe on heterogeneous HW accelerators which use both GPUs and FPGAs. In [11], the authors describe how a high-level streaming language (Brook) can simplify the design of HW accelerators. In [12], the authors designed a customised architecture which supports streaming applications.

A related problem is network bandwidth and there is an analogy between the layers of abstraction in networks and the framework that we present. We work with an HLS tool which abstracts away the details of the function of the FPGA kernel and its communication across the CPU-FPGA data channel. In general networking, there are several abstraction layers, such as routing, packetisation, data frames and raw bits at the hardware level, and data segmentation, encoding and high-level APIs at the software level. In software, the framework functions at the encoding level and in hardware it functions at the packetisation and raw bit levels.

3   Conceptual Framework

While compression methods and other enhancements exist, they are difficult to apply to a streaming system in real-time, as discussed earlier. We want to bring the benefits of these enhancements to the user without adding a significant amount of complexity. Therefore, we require a general framework for supporting codecs, which will:

- Allow the HPC programmer to apply software and hardware codecs to the data in a streaming system with minimal changes to HW and SW.
- Make use of unused resources in software and hardware.
- Enable other independent programmers to incorporate new codecs into the framework through its extensible nature.

The framework enables the HPC programmer to add codecs by using idle CPU cycles in SW and unused FPGA resources in HW. The data to be transmitted is split into segments and each segment is processed by a software pipeline of codec threads: compression; kernel transmission and decompression. Real-time codecs must operate faster than line rate (channel data rate) in order for compression to achieve a speed-up. If c is the compression ratio, f_{kernel} the kernel frequency, w_{kernel} the kernel bus width and BW the external bandwidth of the PCIe bus via which data is supplied to the kernel, the following condition must be satisfied in order for the channel not to be a bottleneck:

$$f_{kernel} \times w_{kernel} \leq \frac{BW}{c} \tag{1}$$

The conditions required of the codecs on the hardware side are:

- Must be pipelined in hardware to operate at line rate.
- Occupy a small amount of FPGA resources.
- Must have a streaming input and output.
- Must have common interface properties.

The conditions required of the codecs on the software side are:

- Must be multi-threaded to process segmented data at line rate.
- Be able to push and pop data segments to and from a queue.
- Be fast and simple enough to operate in real-time.
- Must have common interface properties.

With the specifications of the framework defined, we will now develop a model for how the performance of a streaming system will be affected by applying compression using this framework, and this model assumes that there are an infinite number of CPU cores available. Table 1 defines the parameters we use in the model and Fig. 1 shows the interleaving of compression (C), transmission (T) and decompression (D) by different threads for 8 segments of data - it is approximate since the multi-threading is not deterministic.

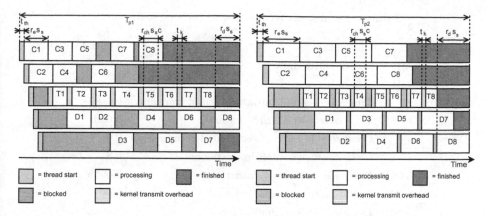

Fig. 1. Conceptual timing diagram showing interleaved compression, kernel computation and decompression with a saturated kernel operating at maximum capacity (Color figure online).

Fig. 2. Conceptual timing diagram showing interleaved compression, kernel computation and decompression where the compression is too slow to saturate the kernel (Color figure online).

1. Blue sections show the overhead in launching each software thread, so that the starting point of subsequent threads have a cumulative delay.
2. The pink sections show:
   (a) Compression threads being blocked until space is available in the input queue (a maximum queue length of 3 is chosen for this example).
   (b) The transmission thread being locked until there is data present in the input queue.
   (c) Decompression threads blocked until data is available in the output queue.
3. Green sections show threads being idle after completing their task.
4. White sections show processing taking place. In the transmission thread, the transmission time varies for each segment depending on its compression ratio.

End-to-end latency for original, unsegmented, unencoded data including overhead:

$$T_{orig} = r_{ch}S + t_k \tag{2}$$

If the entire block of data is sequentially encoded, transmitted and decoded, the end-to-end latency is:

$$T_{seq} = S(r_e + r_{ch}c + r_d) + t_k \tag{3}$$

When threaded software pipelining is applied, there are three possible cases. The ideal case is illustrated by Fig. 1, where there are as many encode/decode software threads as necessary for software codecs to work faster than the channel data rate such that the kernel to be saturated:

$$\frac{r_e}{n_e}, \frac{r_d}{n_d} < r_{ch}$$

Table 1. Parameters for model and their typical values

Name	Unit	Description	Typical value
S	MB	Size of entire data	2048
s_s	MB	Size of segment	8
t_k	s	Time overhead of initiating kernel transmit	0.0003
t_{th}	s	Time overhead of thread start	0.0002
c	-	Compression ratio of segmented compression	0.6
a	-	CPU resource contention exponent	0.8
r_{ch}	s/MB	Line rate or channel data rate	0.0005
r_e	s/MB	Encode rate in a single thread	0.001
r_d	s/MB	Decode rate in a single thread	0.001
n_e	-	Number of encode threads	3
n_d	-	Number of decode threads	3
r_e/n_e^a	s/MB	Encode rate for multiple threads	0.0004
r_d/n_d^a	s/MB	Decode rate for multiple threads	0.0004
S/s_s	-	Number of segments	256

$$T_{p1} = t_{th} + r_e s_s + (t_k + r_{ch} s_s c)\frac{S}{s_s} + r_d s_s \qquad (4)$$

The second case, where encoding (compression) does not happen fast enough is illustrated in Fig. 2. This happens if the compression is slow either because of too few compression threads or due to CPU resource contention between threads reducing the benefit of multi-threading. Then the overall end-to-end latency is:

$$T_{p2} = t_{th} + r_e s_s \frac{1}{n_e^a}\frac{S}{s_s} + n_e(t_k + r_{ch} s_s c) + r_d s_s \qquad (5)$$

The third case, which is very similar to the second case, is where decoding (decompression) is too slow:

$$T_{p3} = t_{th} + r_e s_s + (t_k + r_{ch} s_s c)n_d + r_d s_s \frac{1}{n_d^a}\frac{S}{s_s} \qquad (6)$$

Therefore, the threaded, software-pipelined end-to-end latency is defined as:

$$T_{pipe} = max(T_{p1}, T_{p2}, T_{p3}) \qquad (7)$$

When compression is applied using the framework, the end-to-end threaded time must not exceed the time for sending uncompressed data:

$$T_{pipe} < T_{orig} \qquad (8)$$

This framework is suited in applications where large amounts of data are transmitted to fully benefit from compression and ensure that the hardware pipeline latency is negligible compared to the end-to-end transmission latency.

Furthermore, while we discuss compression-based codecs, designing a state-of-the-art algorithm is not our goal; compression is considered as a useful case study. The emphasis is on a framework with the ability to add different features/codecs to a streaming system under a high degree of transparency with low effort from the programmer. Codecs such as multi-threaded encryption and error correction can potentially be added without a loss in performance. If the programmer wanted to transmit data directly without using codecs, there is a function provided by the platform for that - where pointers to the input and output arrays along with the data sizes are parameters to the function call. To transmit data while applying a codec, a different function with a similar function signature can be used; the threading and segmentation are handled internally.

We have described a multi-threaded framework to apply compute-intensive codecs to a segmented data stream by the use of spare resources and the specifications required of such a framework. We developed a model for predicting performance of streaming systems when codecs are applied without the need to do a full implementation and benchmark. We will next discuss the technical details of the implementation of the framework.

4   Concrete Realisation

Now that the conceptual framework has been proposed and a model developed to predict its performance, we will discuss technical details. The framework is built using a commercial HLS tool called MaxCompiler by Maxeler Technologies. The Maxeler machine has multiple CPU cores and an FPGA which are interfaced together via a PCI-express channel. It includes high-level libraries for building commercial heterogeneous HPC applications and allows high-speed streaming of data across the channel. This platform is an ideal match for our requirements.

Maxeler offers two modes of data transmission. The first and more commonly used mode requires a hardware interrupt to be generated for each data transfer, where the application is suspended until the interrupt is dealt with by the operating system. While this is suitable for transmitting large contiguous blocks of data, it is not suitable for our application, where the data is split into multiple smaller segments since there will be a significant latency added to each segment by the interrupts. The second mode is the 'Low latency' [3] interface, which is optimised for short and frequent data transfers - the FPGA kernel is permanently running and data segments can be transmitted to/from the kernel as and when we want. The second mode is ideal for our segmented data.

Figure 3 shows a block diagram of the system with and without codecs and Fig. 4 shows how multiple threads access data. In software: encode thread(s) compress and push segments into an input queue; the transmit thread pops data from the input queue, transmits data to the FPGA and receives processed segments from the FPGA and pushes it onto an output queue; the decode thread(s) pop segments from the output queue and perform decompression. In hardware: data passes through the decoder module at the start of the pipeline, into the kernel, then into the encoder module towards the end of the pipeline.

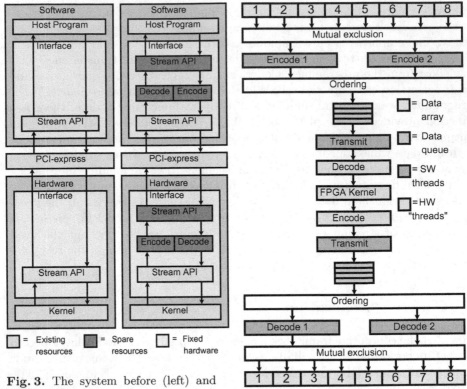

Fig. 3. The system before (left) and after (right) a codec is applied. The green blocks represent the spare resources used by the codec and the blue blocks represent existing in-use resources (Color figure online).

Fig. 4. Diagram showing how queues are managed by the threads (Color figure online).

To demonstrate the framework, a set of compression codecs are applied to the data in a streaming system, leaving the original software and hardware intact, and performance is evaluated. The methods to be tested are:

- Integer delta compression - where differences between adjacent values in smooth data are computed and represented using half the number of bytes.
- Lossless floating point - where denormal numbers and zero values in a single precision floating point data stream are packed into a single byte.
- RGB32 to RGB24 - where the alpha channel is omitted in applications where it is unused.
- Lossy double precision - where double precision values are converted to single-precision values.

For the purpose of evaluating performance, an identity kernel clocked at 200 MHz is taken as the existing hardware kernel. When codecs are used, we assume there is a high-speed stateless computation kernel in the FPGA, where the bandwidth supplying data to/from the kernel is a bottleneck. The exact computation that takes place in the kernel is irrelevant and so it is treated as a black box. An identity kernel is appropriate since it meets the requirement of transmitting data at a high throughput and 200 MHz is a typical clock frequency that FPGA kernels operate at in HPC applications. It must be noted that for the purpose of testing correctness, a blur kernel on RGB data was also used.

5   Evaluation

To demonstrate the performance of the proposed framework, the performance when different compression codecs were applied to the transmission channel was measured. The metrics we use to assess performance are end-to-end transmission time, effective bandwidth, speed-up and compression ratio.

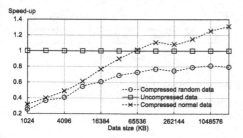

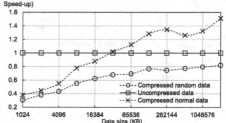

Fig. 5. Speed-up against total data size for lossless float compression.   **Fig. 6.** Speed-up against total data size for integer delta compression.

Figures 5 and 6 show how the speed-up is affected by lossless floating point and delta compression in comparison to transmitting raw data for varying total data sizes. For Fig. 5, 'normal' data is a set where there are several zero values and the random data is obtained from a random number generator (RNG). The normal data and random data saw 1.31x and 0.795x changes in speed for a data block of size 2 GB. Similarly, for Fig. 6, 'normal' data is smooth data and the random data from an RNG. The normal data and random data saw 1.51x and 0.821x changes in speed for a data block of size 2 GB. If a compression method appropriate for the type of data is used, then this shows that a small speed up can be achieved with low effort.

Figures 7, 8 and 9 compares the speed up achieved from lossless single precision floating point, lossy double precision and RGB32 image compression as the total data size is varied. The 'ideal' plots are baseline showing the theoretical best speed-up. All the curves are asymptotic towards their theoretical best

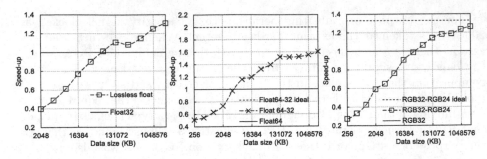

Fig. 7. Ratio of time taken for float32 compression

Fig. 8. Ratio of time taken for float64 compression

Fig. 9. Ratio of time taken for image compression

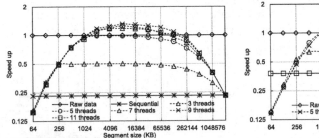

Fig. 10. Speed-up for 2 GB data against segment size for lossless float compression.

Fig. 11. Speed-up for 2 GB data against segment size for delta compression.

as the data becomes larger - the theoretical best is the reciprocal of the compression ratio. Therefore, the graph for RGB32-RGB24 tends towards 1.33x and the graph for float64-32 tends towards 2x. Lossless float also tends towards the reciprocal of its compression ratio, which is dependent on the nature of the data.

Figures 10 and 11 illustrates the speedup from different segment sizes and different threads for floating point and delta compression. It shows a slowdown of an order of magnitude for unthreaded (sequential) compression. There is always one transmit thread and an equal number of encode/decode threads - the graph shows the total threads. The best performance was achieved at 9 threads (4 encode, 4 decode, 1 transmit) at a segment size of 8192 KB for float compression and 7 threads with 16384 KB segments for delta compression. This was measured on a machine with a Xilinx Virtex 6 FPGA and 12 Intel Xeon 2.67 GHz CPU cores with hyperthreading. 11 threads performed worse than 9 threads due to resource contention as we approach the maximum number of physical cores.

Figures 12 and 13 compares the measured end-to-end execution time against the time predicted by the mathematical model. The model, while slightly under-estimating the time, is a reasonably good fit for predicting run time. The discrepancy is larger with more software threads - the maximum discrepancy for delta compression is 12.9 % and for float pack it is 13.7 %.

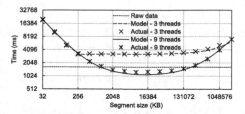

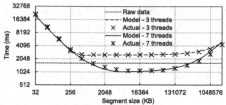

Fig. 12. Modelled/actual time for loss-less float compression with 3 and 9 threads.

Fig. 13. Modelled/actual time for delta compression with 3 and 7 threads.

The model does not consider the latency of hardware codecs. The transmit overhead in software is around 200–300 µs; equivalent to 40000–60000 clock cycles in the FPGA. Therefore the latency of hardware codecs are orders of magnitude lower than the software latency. The CPU resource contention exponent was empirically determined to be 0.82 by measuring encode time as the number of threads were varied. The model can be used to predict and evaluate the performance of a system without the need to fully build and benchmark.

Table 2 shows how the performance metrics are affected when the codecs are applied in a sequential or a threaded manner. Applying codecs sequentially does give any speed up.

Table 2. Comparing the effective bandwidth, end-to-end latency, speed-up and compression ratio for different compression techniques

Compression type	Effective BW (MB/s)	Latency (ms)	Speed-up	Ratio
Raw 2 GB data	2509	1633	1x	1
RGB32-RGB24 threaded	3170	1292	1.26x	0.750
RGB32-RGB24 sequential	1360	3011	0.542x	0.750
Delta threaded	3790	1081	1.51x	0.541
Delta sequential	952	4300	0.380x	0.541
Float lossless threaded	3286	1247	1.31x	0.625
Float lossless sequential	579	7071	0.231x	0.625
Float 64-32 threaded	4022	1018	1.60x	0.500
Float 64-32 sequential	2464	1662	0.982x	0.500

6   Conclusion and Future Work

We have proposed and implemented a multi-threaded framework that is capable of applying compute-intensive codecs to a data stream in real-time on a heterogeneous CPU-FPGA system. Multi-threading allowed encoding, transmission and decoding to be interleaved. A model was developed to predict the performance of streaming systems with codecs added, without the need for a full-scale implementation before performance is assessed. RGB32-RGB24, delta compression, lossless floating point compression and lossy double-single compression achieved speed-ups of 1.26x, 1.51x, 1.31x and 1.60x respectively. While these speed-ups are not particularly large, the significance of these results is that a speed up can be achieved with low effort.

This opens up the possibility to add other codecs such as encryption or error correction instead of just compression. We believe the work discussed in this paper will be of interest to: FPGA vendors; HPC programmers using streaming tools; providers of low-level IP services; developers of streaming compilers.

The framework could be further developed to function on streaming systems with multiple kernels, which place higher demands on bandwidth than the single kernel used in this work. The design can be made platform-independent, since it is currently built on the Maxeler platform. For example, it should be possible to seamlessly integrate such an framework onto systems that use the Avalon or AXI streaming interfaces by Altera and Xilinx. After further improvement, we aim to offer an open source release of the technology.

Acknowledgment. This work was sponsored by the UK Engineering and Physical Sciences Research Council (EPSRC) Doctoral Training Award studentship and the EPSRC Platform Grant EP/I012036/1.

References

1. Sano, K., et al.: FPGA-based streaming computation for lattice Boltzmann method. In: Field-Programmable Technology, pp. 233–236, December 2007
2. Guha, R., Al-Dabass, D.: Performance prediction of parallel computation of streaming applications on FPGA platform. In: 2010 12th International Conference on Computer Modelling and Simulation (UKSim), pp. 579–585, March 2010
3. Maxeler Technologies, Dataflow programming for networking. Technical report (2013)
4. Sano, K., et al.: Segment-parallel predictor for FPGA-based hardware compressor and decompressor of floating-point data streams to enhance memory I/O bandwidth. In: Data Compression Conference (DCC), pp. 416–425, March 2010
5. Grigoras, P., et al.: Accelerating SpMV on FPGAs by compressing nonzero values. In: Field-Programmable Custom Computing Machines, September 2015
6. Zaretsky, D., Mittal, G., Banerjee, P.: Streaming implementation of the ZLIB decoder algorithm on an FPGA. In: ISCAS 2009, pp. 2329–2332, May 2009
7. Li, B., et al.: Implementation of LZMA compression algorithm on FPGA. Electron. Lett. **50**(21), 1522–1524 (2014)
8. Ouyang, J., Luo, H., Wang, Z., Tian, J., Liu, C., Sheng, K.: FPGA implementation of GZIP compression and decompression for IDC services. In: 2010 International Conference on Field-Programmable Technology (FPT), pp. 265–268, December 2010
9. Wijeyasinghe, M., Thomas, D.: Using high-level knowledge to enhance data channels in FPGA streaming systems. In: 2014 24th International Conference on Field Programmable Logic and Applications (FPL), pp. 1–2, September 2014

10. Thoma, Y., Dassatti, A., Molla, D.: FPGA2: an open source framework for FPGA-GPU PCIe communication. In: ReConFig 2013, pp. 1–6, December 2013
11. Plavec, F., et al.: Enhancements to FPGA design methodology using streaming. In: Field Programmable Logic and Applications, pp. 294–301, August 2009
12. Alves, J., Diniz, P.: Custom FPGA-based micro-architecture for streaming computing. In: 2011 VII Southern Conference on Programmable Logic (SPL), pp. 51–56, April 2011

Signal Processing

Reconfigurable FPGA-Based FFT Processor for Cognitive Radio Applications

Mário Lopes Ferreira[✉], Amin Barahimi, and João Canas Ferreira

INESC TEC and Faculty of Engineering, University of Porto,
Rua Dr. Roberto Frias, s/n, 4200-465 Porto, Portugal
{mario.l.ferreira,amin.barahimi,joao.c.ferreira}@inesctec.pt

Abstract. Cognitive Radios (CR) are viewed as a solution for spectrum utilization and management in next generation wireless networks. In order to adapt themselves to the actual communications environment, CR devices require highly flexible baseband processing engines. One of the most relevant operations involved in radio baseband processing is the FFT. This work presents a reconfigurable FFT processor supporting FFT sizes and throughputs required by the most used wireless communication standards. By employing Dynamic Partial Reconfiguration (DPR), the implemented design can adapt the FFT size at run-time and specialize its operation to the immediate communication demands. This translates to hardware savings, enhanced resource usage efficiency and possible power savings. The results obtained for reconfiguration times suggest that DPR techniques are a viable option for designing flexible and adaptable baseband processing components for CR devices.

Keywords: Cognitive radio (CR) · Reconfigurable hardware · Fast Fourier Transform (FFT) · FPGA · Dynamic partial reconfiguration (DPR)

1 Introduction

In the wireless communications technology field, Cognitive Radio (CR) emerged as a solution for a more flexible and efficient spectrum management, enabling dynamic allocation of unoccupied frequency bands and automatic radio settings adjustment for better utilization of the available wireless channels. Regarding baseband processing, CR devices require multi-channel communication methods providing a high degree of flexibility and adaptability. Additionally, the ability to handle high data rates is required. Therefore, a strong candidate for the Physical layer (PHY) baseband processing implementation of CR devices is NC-OFDM (*Non-Contiguous Orthogonal Frequency Division Multiplexing*) [2]. NC-OFDM

M.L. Ferreira—This work was financed by the FCT - Fundação para a Ciência e a Tecnologia (Portuguese Foundation for Science and Technology) within the *CREaTION* project (EXCL/EEI-TEL/0067/2012) and through Ph.D. Grant PD/BD/105860/2014.

© Springer International Publishing Switzerland 2016
V. Bonato et al. (Eds.): ARC 2016, LNCS 9625, pp. 223–232, 2016.
DOI: 10.1007/978-3-319-30481-6_18

is a spectrally agile version of OFDM, a widely used technique which is the base of the most recent wireless communication standards (e.g.: IEEE 802.11, IEEE 802.22, WiMAX, 3GPP-LTE). An indispensable component in OFDM-based systems is the Fast Fourier Transform (FFT) processor. Particularly, in the context of OFDM-based CR applications, the implementation of a flexible and adaptable FFT processor covering the FFT requirements of a wide range of wireless communication protocols is a valuable contribution.

To cover FFT size requirements for several standards, a worst-case approach could be adopted by considering an FFT processor supporting the greatest possible FFT size. However, such a big FFT would not always be needed, leading to an inefficient use of the available resources. Ultimately, this worst-case approach could have a poor behaviour in terms of power consumption. An alternative approach consists of having an FFT processor that is able to adapt its operation and use only the necessary resources for the computational demands at a certain instant, thus improving resource usage and power efficiency. This paper presents work in progress towards the study and design of an efficient, low-power, flexible and reconfigurable FFT processor intended for NC-OFDM transceivers. The FFT processor should support FFT sizes and throughputs required by the most used wireless communication standards and be able to dynamically adapt the FFT size according to the run-time system's operation requirements. Moreover, we explore FPGA-based DPR techniques and evaluate their applicability in the context of CR hardware infrastructures.

2   Related Work

In this section, some FFT implementations for OFDM systems are highlighted. Boopal et al. [3] describe an FFT architecture for variable sizes and multiple streams intended for WiMax wireless receivers. FFT size selection is done using multiplexers. Input data interleaving is used to handle multiple streams. Venilla et al. [11] present a dynamically reconfigurable mixed-radix Single-Delay Feedback (SDF) FFT implementation supporting three FFT lengths (64, 128 and 256 points). The design was implemented on FPGA and the switching between different FFT sizes computation is done by DPR. The DPR implementation showed a better resource usage by saving about 41 % of slices and 32 % of LUTs, compared with a conventional multiplexer-based reconfigurable architecture. No power estimates are presented. Combining DPR with the concept of Time Division Multiplexing (TDM), Chao et al. [4] propose a new FFT design that allows for multiple applications to simultaneously compute variable length FFTs. Wang et al. [12] present a reconfigurable mixed-radix FFT architecture for 3GPP-LTE systems supporting non-powers-of-two FFT sizes. No DPR techniques are employed and run-time reconfiguration is achieved through bypass structures along the pipeline.

Most FFT processors for OFDM systems can be grouped according to whether the supported FFT lengths must be powers of two and according to the reconfiguration methodology employed (DPR versus multiplexing/circuit switching). To our best knowledge, there are no implementations of FFT processors supporting both powers-of-two and non powers-of-two lengths, and employing DPR.

3   Implementation

3.1   FFT Algorithm

The Cooley-Tukey FFT algorithm [6] was chosen, as it offers a systematic procedure to compute the FFT for any size (N) factorization, with a good balance between arithmetic and computational complexity. This algorithm employs a *divide-and-conquer* strategy to recursively decompose the original N-point FFT into smaller FFTs. Considering an FFT of size $N = N_1 \times N_2$, the Cooley-Tukey algorithm starts by computing N_2 FFTs of size N_1. After that, the outputs of this stage are multiplied by *twiddle factors*. The complex multiplication by these factors is also known as *rotation*. Next, the algorithm proceeds by taking the rotation results and computing N_1 FFTs of size N_2. The most common way to employ the Cooley-Tukey algorithm is to consider values of N which are powers of a base r, such that $N = r^s$. This sub-class of algorithm is commonly referred as *Radix-r FFT* algorithms and the most common radices are 2 and 4, due to their computational simplicity. In a Radix-r FFT algorithm, the basic computational block performs r-points FFTs and is usually called a *butterfly*. Radix-2 algorithms are widely used due to the simplicity of the butterfly. Using butterflies of higher radices will reduce the number of stages and butterflies, but will increase the complexity of the butterfly. However, radix-4 algorithms have some interesting properties, as a considerable number of twiddle factor multiplication consists of multiplying by -j, which is still considered a trivial multiplication. Radices higher that 4 will introduce non-trivial complex multiplications inside the butterflies, increasing the overall algorithm complexity. It is also possible to mix several radices in the same algorithm - *Mixed-Radix FFT* - and thus explore the benefits each radix has to offer.

Typically, FFT sizes are powers-of-two and a Radix-2 Algorithm would cover all required sizes. However, recent standards, as 3GPP-LTE, introduced non powers-of-two FFT sizes (e.g.: 1536-points FFT, required by 3GPP-LTE for 15 MHz bandwidth support). The implemented FFT processor addresses the most frequent FFT sizes in 3G/4G wireless standards. A list of the considered sizes and respective factorization is shown in Table 1. The Radix-4 stages mentioned in Table 1 were implemented using the Radix-2^2 FFT algorithm proposed by He and Torkelson in [7]. This algorithm has the same multiplicative complexity of the Radix-4, while keeping the simple Radix-2 butterfly structures as fundamental processing blocks. Apart from radices 2 and 4, the support for 1536-FFT introduces a Radix-3 stage. Overall, the FFT algorithm variant adopted was the Cooley-Tukey Mixed-Radix-2^2/2/3 algorithm.

3.2   FFT Architecture

There are two main types of FFT architectures: *Memory-based* and *Pipelined*. Compared with memory-based architectures, pipelined architectures require

Table 1. Implemented FFT sizes and their factorization

FFT size	Factorization	# Radix-4 stages	# Radix-2 stages	# Radix-3 stages
64	4^3	3	-	-
128	$4^3 \times 2$	3	1	-
256	4^4	4	-	-
512	$4^4 \times 2$	4	1	-
1024	4^5	5	-	-
1536	$4^4 \times 2 \times 3$	4	1	1
2048	$4^5 \times 2$	5	1	-

more resources and circuit area, but allow for better performance and the continuous flow of data. In wireless communications, data arrives continuously and FFT requirements are prone to vary with time. So, the FFT processor should have a regular and scalable architecture. Therefore, a pipelined architecture was adopted. Among the existing pipelined architectures, Single-Delay Feedback (SDF) was chosen due to its simpler implementation, lower memory requirements and acceptable throughput. In feedback architectures, the butterflies have feedback loops, so that some butterfly outputs are fed back to a memory stream in the same stage. The memory streams (shift registers) are used to correctly pair the input samples for further butterfly processing. According to the operation phase, an SDF processing element (PE) may forward input data to the feedback memory stream, keeping the butterfly in an idle state, or perform butterfly calculations, producing results to be multiplied by a twiddle factor or fed back to the local memory stream. To implement the Mixed-Radix-2^2/2/3 algorithm in a Pipelined SDF architecture, the following basic elements were considered: Radix-2^2 PE, Radix-2 PE and Radix-3 PE. Figure 1 depicts their general structure. The operation parameters in each PE are the size of the feedback memory stream(s) (grey rectangles above the butterflies) and the set of twiddle factors (W_N) used to rotate the butterfly results. Details about the butterfly operations and internal structure can be found in [5,9].

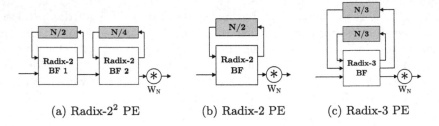

(a) Radix-2^2 PE   (b) Radix-2 PE   (c) Radix-3 PE

Fig. 1. Basic processing elements

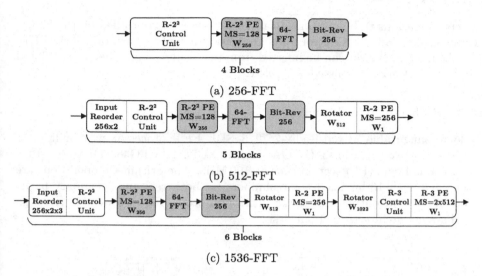

Fig. 2. FFT pipeline structure for N = 256, 512 and 1536

The number of PEs of each type, as well as their location in the pipeline is defined by the factorizations from Table 1 and the chosen FFT algorithm. Figure 2 presents some examples of how to build an FFT pipeline with the PEs previously referred and how to build bigger sizes from smaller ones by reusing some PEs.

For instance, a 256-FFT (Fig. 2a) comprises four Radix-2^2 PEs, three of which belong to the 64-FFT block. The operation of each PE is dictated by the *Radix-2^2 Control Unit*. Apart from feeding input data to the subsequent pipeline stages, this unit generates a binary counter which is propagated along the pipeline. This counter is used by each Radix-2^2 PE to determine whether it should only fed data back to the memory stream, or also perform butterfly computations. Additionally, the binary counter is used to fetch correct twiddle factors for rotation. The considered FFT algorithm receives the inputs in natural order and produces the outputs in bit-reversed order - *Decimation in Frequency*. Thus, in order to provide the outputs in natural order, a bit-reversal operation is required after the last Radix-2^2 PE.

In turn, a 512-FFT (Fig. 2b) can be built by reusing the same Radix-2^2 PEs from the 256-FFT case and adding a Radix-2 PE, whose control is also determined by the binary counter from Radix-2^2 Control Unit. As the factorization of 512 involves different radices, it is necessary to perform a reordering operation on the input data stream and also apply a rotation between the two different radix domains. The relations used in both the input reordering and inter-radix rotations are described in [10]. Similarly, a 1536-FFT (Fig. 2c) is built from the 512-FFT by adapting the reordering operation on the input data and by adding a single Radix-3 stage. Besides the Radix-3 PE and the required rotator between Radix-2 and Radix-3 domains, this later stage includes a *Radix-3 Control Unit*, as the operations to be performed cannot be correctly controlled by the binary counter from Radix-2^2 Control Unit. The structure and organization of the FFTs for the remaining sizes can be inferred from the examples provided in Fig. 2 and from the factorizations listed in Table 1.

3.3   High-Level Architecture

The reconfigurable Mixed-Radix-$2^2/2/3$ SDF FFT processor was built on a Xilinx ZedBoard platform (FPGA device: XC7Z020-CLG484-1), whose Programmable Logic (PL) section runs at 100 MHz. The arithmetic operations are computed with 16-bit fixed-point numbers for both real and imaginary parts. Both input and output values are in natural order. Figure 3 depicts the high level system architecture of our design.

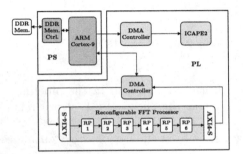

Fig. 3. High level system architecture   **Fig. 4.** RPs role for every FFT configuration

The FFT reconfigurable pipeline was implemented on the PL section of the Zynq device. As the bigger FFT sizes (1536 and 2048) are constituted by six building blocks, the pipeline comprises six Reconfigurable Partitions (RPs) embedded in an AXI4-Stream IP core. Depending on the size of the FFT to be computed, a partial bitstream is loaded for every RP using DPR. The FFT processor receives input data from DDR memory, performs computation over these data and sends the results back to DDR memory. Depending on the FFT configuration, RPs are used to perform FFT-related operations or simply propagate results along the pipeline - *bypass mode*. Figure 4 shows the role of each RP for every FFT configuration. Table 2 provides information about the size and available resources for each RP. In order to reduce the amount of data to be transferred though the FPGA configuration port, partial bitstream sizes were reduced by enabling the bitstream compression capability of the Xilinx Vivado tool.

FPGA configuration memory was accessed through the Xilinx Internal Configuration Access Port (ICAPE2) primitive. When powered on, the FPGA is configured with a boot image file stored in an SD card, and partial bitstreams

Table 2. Resources per RP and partial bitstream sizes

	RP1	RP2	RP3	RP4	RP5	RP6
Slice LUTs	400 (0.8 %)	2400 (4.5 %)	1600 (3 %)	1600 (3 %)	800 (1.5 %)	3200 (6 %)
Slice registers	800 (0.8 %)	4800 (4.5 %)	3200 (3 %)	3200 (3 %)	1600 (1.5 %)	6400 (6 %)
BRAM	10 (7.1 %)	10 (7.1 %)	10 (7.1 %)	10 (7.1 %)	10 (7.1 %)	10 (7.1 %)
DSP	0 (0 %)	20 (9.1 %)	20 (9.1 %)	20 (9.1 %)	20 (9.1 %)	20 (9.1 %)
# RM variants	5	3	3	4	3	3
Partial bitstream Max. size (KB)	42.9	156	104	98.3	73	193
Max. Reconfig. time (μs)	112	402	269	254	189	496

are copied from the SD card to the DDR memory. Then, subsequent DPR operations are controlled by the ARM processor. Apart from DDR read/write operations performed by the FFT processor, partial bitstreams need to be fetched from DDR and sent to the ICAPE2 primitive for DPR purposes. These standard bus operations require the CPU to be involved in every transaction. To speed-up both FFT and reconfiguration throughput, CPU involvement in DDR-PL communication was eliminated by using two dedicated DMA controllers for 32-bit data stream transactions: one for data transfers between DDR and ICAPE2 primitive and one for data transfers between DDR and FFT processor. Both DMA controllers were implemented using Xilinx AXI DMA IP cores. In terms of resources, the infrastructure built around the FFT reconfigurable pipeline - *static part* - uses 5410 (10.17 % of available) Sliced LUTs, 6653 (6.25 % of available) Sliced Registers and 6 (4.29 % of available) BRAMs

4   Evaluation and Discussion

The functional correctness of the implemented FFT processor was verified by comparing the system outputs with MATLAB results. For all FFT sizes, the FFT processor produced correct results. To be suitable for OFDM systems, the FFT processor should handle the data rates defined by the most used standards. In steady-state operation, the FFT pipeline throughput is about 98 MSamples/s, which is very close to the limit imposed by the employed FFT architecture at 100 MHz (100 MSamples/s). The achieved throughput is large enough to handle wireless standards as IEEE 802.11a/b/g, WiMAX or 3GPP-LTE.

A CR device should be able to control the adaptability of its PHY operation according to the communication conditions. However, if the reaction to a variation in the communication environment is too slow, interferences with licensed users may occur, thus degrading communication Quality of Service (QoS). So, when designing reconfigurable hardware infrastructures for CR base-band processing, it is important to have a reference regarding the order of magnitude of radio devices reactivity. IEEE 802.22 was the first wireless standard designed for CR environments and it determines several timing parameters to protect licensed spectrum users from interferences [1]. These timing parameters are a good reference for CR devices reactivity requirements. For instance, radio devices using this standard must be able to establish the communication on a channel in 2 s - *channel setup time* (CST). Then, during normal operation, IEEE 802.22 devices should detect the presence of a licensed user on a channel in less than 2 s - *channel detection time* (CDT). Upon licensed user detection, the device has 2 s to cease all interfering communications in the current channel - *channel move time* (CMT). In particular, events such as transmission establishment/cessation and channel features variation may involve changes in PHY parameters. For our system, the experimental worst-case DPR latency is 1.63 ms, for a reconfiguration throughput of 380 MiB/s (95 % of the ICAP theoretical limit 400 MiB/s). Obviously, NC-OFDM baseband processing does not consist exclusively of FFT computation tasks, but FFT is one of the most demanding tasks within the baseband transceiver.

Compared with the CR timing parameters defined in IEEE 802.22, the worst-case reconfiguration delay observed is within an acceptable range for CR applications. Furthermore, there is still a considerable improvement margin for the work in progress. Reconfiguration time reduction can be achieved by reducing the amount of reconfiguration data to be transferred. Until now, only modular-based DPR was exploited. But, in some situations only small changes are needed in the design and difference-based DPR may be a better option. In this case, only the information regarding differences introduced in the design is contained in the bitstream. If these differences are not large, the bitstream size can be quite small, leading to lower reconfiguration latencies. The way reconfiguration procedures are deployed should be in charge of a Management Unit capable of handling the reconfiguration in an intelligent way, mitigating the impact of reconfiguration on performance and power consumption. As the implemented FFT processor is to be integrated in a reconfigurable NC-OFDM baseband processor, DPR management must be optimized from an overall system perspective.

Resource usage efficiency can be further improved by reusing resources allocated to RPs in bypass mode. For example, instead of computing a single 64-FFT, the three RPs in bypass mode (Fig. 4) could be used to compute another 64-FFT, allowing parallel multiple stream processing and duplication of FFT throughput with the same clock frequency. In the context of an NC-OFDM transceiver, those resources could also be used for other baseband operations (e.g.: constellation (de)mapping, cyclic prefix insertion/removal).

The power consumed by the implementations of FFT processors for the sizes addressed in this work was estimated using Vivado's Power Analysis, and the results also encourage the exploitation of DPR techniques to enhance power efficiency. The estimates are presented in Fig. 5. One can observe that changes in power consumption are mainly due to FFT processor dynamic power and that dynamic power increases with the FFT size. Comparing the smallest and the largest FFT sizes cases (64 and 2048-points FFT), the dynamic power increases by a factor of approximately 3.15. The impact of DPR on power consumption has not yet been evaluated. However, in [8], Liu et al. studied the feasibility

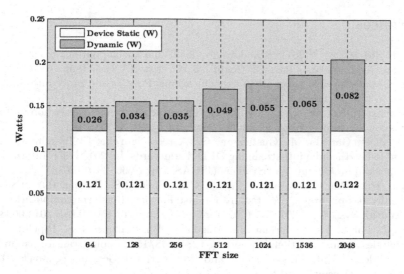

Fig. 5. Power consumption estimations. FPGA device: XC7Z020-CLG484-1; Clock freq.: 100 MHz; Analysis tool: Vivado 2015.2; Post-Implementation power analysis with high confidence level; Activity derived from simulation files (.saif).

of using DPR to improve power consumption and concluded that it can reduce both static and dynamic power. A crucial requirement to mitigate DPR power consumption overhead is the reduction of reconfiguration times.

5 Conclusions

The research work developed so far produced the implementation of a run-time reconfigurable FFT processor supporting FFT sizes and throughputs required by the most used 3G and 4G wireless standards. The FFT processor employs a Mixed-Radix-$2^2/2/3$ SDF approach and run-time reconfiguration was achieved through DPR. The measured reconfiguration times showed the viability of applying DPR techniques in the design of CR baseband processing components. Hence, the implemented FFT processor is suitable for NC-OFDM transceivers in CR applications. For some FFT sizes, there are resources not used for FFT computation purposes which can be reused for other NC-OFDM baseband operations, potentially improving resources usage efficiency. DPR latency introduced in the current design can be further reduced and, although DPR power consumption overhead was not yet studied, estimates for FFT power consumption variation with FFT size motivate the exploitation of DPR for energy-efficient operation.

References

1. IEEE Std 802.22™-2011: Standard for local and metropolitan area networks - specific requirements - Part 22: Cognitive Wireless RAN Medium Access Control (MAC) and Physical Layer (PHY) specifications: Policies and procedures for operation in the TV Bands (2011)
2. Bogucka, H., Kryszkiewicz, P., Kliks, A.: Dynamic spectrum aggregation for future 5G communications. IEEE Commun. Mag. **53**(5), 35–43 (2015)
3. Boopal, P., Garrido, M., Gustafsson, O.: A reconfigurable FFT architecture for variable-length and multi-streaming OFDM standards. In: 2013 IEEE International Symposium on Circuits and Systems (ISCAS), pp. 2066–2070 (2013)
4. Chao, H.L., Wu, C.C., Peng, C.Y., Lu, C.H., Shen, J.S., Hsiung, P.A.: Dynamic partially reconfigurable architecture for fast Fourier transform computation. Int. J. Embed. Syst. **6**(2), 207–215 (2014). http://dx.org/10.1504/IJES.2014.063818
5. Cho, I., Patyk, T., Guevorkian, D., Takala, J., Bhattacharyya, S.: Pipelined FFT for wireless communications supporting 128–2048/1536 - point transforms. In: 2013 IEEE Global Conference on Signal and Information Processing (GlobalSIP), pp. 1242–1245, December 2013
6. Cooley, J.W., Tukey, J.W.: An algorithm for the machine calculation of complex Fourier series. Math. Comput. **19**(90), 297–301 (1965). http://www.jstor.org/stable/2003354
7. He, S., Torkelson, M.: A new approach to pipeline FFT processor. In: The 10th International of Proceedings of Parallel Processing Symposium, IPPS 1996, pp. 766–770, April 1996
8. Liu, S., Pittman, R.N., Forin, A.: Energy Reduction with Run-Time Partial Reconfiguration. Tech. rep. MSR-TR-2009-2017, September 2009. http://research.microsoft.com/apps/pubs/default.aspx?id=112466
9. Löfgren, J., Nilsson, P.: On hardware implementation of radix 3 and radix 5 FFT kernels for LTE systems. In: NORCHIP 2011, pp. 1–4, November 2011
10. Meyer-Baese, U.: Digital Signal Processing with Field Programmable Gate Arrays, August 2014. http://www.springer.com/engineering/signals/book/978-3-540-72613-5
11. Vennila, C., Lakshminarayanan, G., Ko, S.B.: Dynamic partial reconfigurable FFT for OFDM based communication systems. Circuits Syst. Sign. Process. **31**(3), 1049–1066 (2012). http://link.springer.com/article/10.1007/s00034-011-9367-9
12. Wang, G., Yin, B., Cho, I., Cavallaro, J., Bhattacharyya, S., Takala, J.: Efficient architecture mapping of FFT/IFFT for cognitive radio networks. In: 2014 IEEE International Conference on Acoustics, Speech and Signal Processing (ICASSP), pp. 3933–3937, May 2014

Real-Time Audio Group Delay Correction with FFT Convolution on FPGA

Arthur Spierer[✉] and Andres Upegui

InIT Institute, hepia, University of Applied Sciences and Arts Western Switzerland - HES-SO,
Geneva, Switzerland
arthur.spierer@hesge.ch, andres.upegui@hesge.ch

Abstract. This paper describes the implementation of a digital hardware architecture for correcting the effect produced by group delay distortion on multiway loudspeakers. The correction is performed by a digital filter implemented in the form of an FFT convolution. The application imposes real-time execution on an embedded low-cost platform using a high-resolution audio format (stereo coded on 24 bits @ 96 kHz). The result is a pipelined streaming architecture composed of FFT-complex multiplication-iFFT performed on 32,768 samples using a floating-point representation. The filter computation is performed in 72 ms and the overall maximal audio latency is 169 ms running on a Cyclone V FPGA.

1 Introduction

High-resolution audio (HRA) refers to digital audio formats with higher quality than CD standards (16 bits sampled at 44,100 Hz). There is not a standard format for this high quality representation, but usually we deal with sample frequencies of 96 kHz or 192 kHz and a 24-bit resolution. For several years HRA has been mostly reserved for very high-end audio systems for privileged audiophiles, but recently it is becoming present in more affordable manners like HRA download sites and portable HRA players.

An excellent audio quality is not only determined by a high sampling frequency, another important factor to take into account is the different distortions that signal can suffer from the digital to analog conversion to the ear. One of these is the so-called group delay distortion [1]. When a signal is propagated through an amplifier, a cable or through the air, it suffers a delay which is imposed by the physical medium. This delay depends on the frequency of the signal, generating a phase misalignment on the audio signal finally perceived. This phenomenon is of particular interest in multiway loudspeakers. For a more detailed analysis on the sources and effects of group delay distortion please refer to [2].

The effect of group delay can be corrected by applying a filter in order to perform a phase correction for compensating the different phase delays. A filter implementation can be done in time or frequency domain [3, 4]. Typical time domain filters are in the form of FIR and IIR filters, which compute for every output sample a sum of weighted input samples. The computation of FIR and IIR filters is very efficient for low order filters, but for higher order filters they result very inefficient. Frequency domain filters are computed in the form of a Fourier transform performed on a set of samples, followed

© Springer International Publishing Switzerland 2016
V. Bonato et al. (Eds.): ARC 2016, LNCS 9625, pp. 233–244, 2016.
DOI: 10.1007/978-3-319-30481-6_19

by a multiplication in the frequency domain, and a final inverse Fourier transform generating a set of output samples. This FFT convolution approach is much more efficient that FIR and IIR filters for higher order filters. This is thus the approach that we will consider in this paper.

Our goal at the beginning of this project was thus to implement a phase correction for at least 32,768 samples to be performed on an audio stream coded with a sample frequency of 96 kHz on 24 bits. The maximum allowed audio latency is imposed by the HDMI standard, which accepts a maximum of 251 ms [5]. The fulfilling of these requirements implies the real-time execution of an FFT, a vectored complex multiplication and iFFT on 32,768 audio samples on a stereo format.

FPGAs arise as a promising solution for large FFT convolution. We can see it in several works and application such as the implementation of low resource consuming FFT by diving the processing block by two [6]. Our work uses the same concept but requires higher processing resolution while having the same resource quantity; this leads to a slower - because less parallelized - implementation. Another work is the application of FFT convolution and overlap-add filtering on FPGA with 256 points FFT [7]; our project target is 32,768 points for audio quality requirements. We decided to focus on an FPGA implementation of the algorithm because of its high architectural flexibility that will permit to use pipelining and parallelization at different levels of our computing architecture. We have used Cyclone V devices from Altera [8], which are intended to be focused on low-cost and low-power systems. In other words, they are well suited for embedded systems.

In this paper we present thus a hardware architecture of a group delay distortion filter able to satisfy the constraints described before. The result is a compact and modular architecture that can be easily parameterized and evolved. The Sect. 2 of this paper introduces different problems related to streaming audio processing as well as the digital signal processing techniques that have been applied in our project in order to solve them. Section 3 presents the details of the hardware architecture which is based on a SoPC approach and makes use of Avalon memory-mapped and streaming interfaces in order to obtain an optimal dataflow execution. Section 4 presents some results about performance, system latency, and FPGA resource utilization. Finally, Sect. 5 concludes and gives some hints for further improvements.

2   Audio Signal Processing

As introduced in the previous section, the implementation of a group delay corrector for dealing with high quality audio requires a large filter. After a deep analysis of the required filter resolution we have found that our filter must take into account the last 32,768 samples. This is the minimal FFT input size required to obtain the desired filtering precision in the low frequencies. An analysis of the computational complexity of a FIR or IIR filter against an FFT convolution filter results in a clearly more efficient solution when filtering on the frequency domain given the size of the input vector [4]. Filtering on the frequency domain can be done by multiplying a frequency representation of the input signal with the vector of complex parameters characterizing the filter [4]. A fast Fourier transform (FFT) can be thus used for the initial transformation to the frequency domain, to be followed by a vectored complex multiplication, and finally transformed back to time domain with an inverse FFT (iFFT).

The FFT convolution filtering quality depends on multiple factors:

1. **The FFT size** (number of consecutive samples transformed) defines the filter resolution. Resolution is particularly important in the low audio frequencies where the human ear precision is higher due to its logarithmic response. When the length of the sample buffer is too short, low frequencies are only partially represented in frequency domain. Group delay filtering is mainly needed in low frequencies where distortion is more present. This is the reason why the need of 32 k sample, or larger, FFT size is justified.

2. **The processing resolution** needs to be as high as possible in order to reduce rounding errors during computation and keep sampling integrity. In this work, the 24-bit fixed point input audio samples are casted to a 32 bit floating point representation before starting the signal processing. Afterwards, the same representation is used during the FFT computation, the complex multiplication, and the iFFT. Finally, it is casted back to a 24 bits integer representation for audio reproduction. The floating point representation uses 23 bits for coding mantissa, 1 bit for sign and 8 bits for the exponent (IEEE 754).

3. **Truncation and overlapping:** The application of an FFT to a section of a data-stream like an audio-stream is similar to applying a rectangular windowing to the audio signal. This window induces a truncation effect, which generates distortions that are amplified by the filter. When the signal is transformed back in time domain these distortions appear at the edges of the resulting buffer. This distortion can be reduced by applying superposition to each consecutive iFFT output buffer with smooth transition. This implies overlapping with the previously processed samples and the use of a Hanning window function for the overlapping process. This window preserves constant output amplitude with a 50 % overlapping.

It is possible to configure an FFT IP core in an FPGA in order to directly deal with an input vector of size 32,768. However, the amount of logic resources required for doing so is beyond the amount of available resources in our FPGA. We have thus decomposed the FFT algorithm execution in order to allow it to fit in our Cyclone V FPGA. This results in a very important optimization in terms of the required resource utilization with a very low reduction on the execution performance. For doing so we used a single 16 K FFT for implementing a 32 K FFT. This reduction can be achieved by processing separately the even and odd points with a N/2 point core and use a last butterfly stage algebra to recombine them [4].

A radix 4 FFT core is used to accomplish the two 16,384 points FFTs which generate outputs the samples in digit-reverse order. The samples are naturally reordered when passed through inverse FFT. To save computation time, the filter,s transfer function is digit-reverse ordered and can be applied directly.

3   Architecture and Implementation

The system architecture is organized as a SoPC (System on Programmable Chip) based on a Nios II soft-processor and an Avalon bus. The main reason for using a SoPC organization is to permit to easily parameterize and configure the system, and to permit the addition of new interfaces in order to further provide new functionalities. The Nios II soft-processor is not used for computation purposes, it is only used for initializing configuration registers and to control the audio data stream through multiple hardware computation accelerators.

3.1   Overall Architecture

The overall system architecture, which is illustrated in Fig. 1, is composed of a CPU and a set of internal peripherals. These peripherals are controlled and configured through the Avalon bus with memory-mapped interfaces. The NIOS II CPU initiates every data processing task by passing descriptors to DMAs or streaming DMAs. It allows full control of the signal flow and filtering parameters with C programming. This architecture requires data transfers from the SDRAM external memory to the hardware accelerators and back to the memory for each filtering stage.

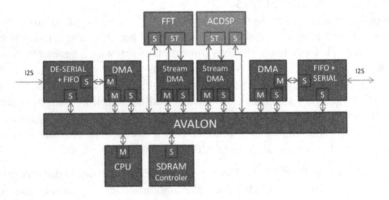

Fig. 1. Overall system architecture

An alternative architectural organization would be to implement a fully streamed dataflow pipe. Such approach should present a better performance than our architecture. However, one of our constraints is to keep a low hardware footprint while maintaining the imposed processing delay, we choose this method against a fully streaming architecture because it avoids redundancy of resource consuming blocks such as streaming DMA and floating point units. Moreover, the required memory space is also reduced by using the same buffering space for temporary data.

The SoPC contains a single hardware accelerator to process the FFT and iFFT and an accelerator for DSP computation (ACDSP) to compute filtering stages. The main FPGA resource consumer being the floating point streaming FFT core, the complete N points transform is processed with two passes through a single N/2 point core.

This requires an additional butterfly stage which is performed with the ACDSP. The same principle is applied to the iFFT computation by using the same hardware block. The filtering stage is a complex space multiplication between the N frequency domain points and the N points of the discrete filter transfer function. It is also done using the ACDSP. The whole process is realized in 32 bit floating point resolution.

3.2 Dataflow

A simplified view of the signal dataflow is illustrated in Fig. 2.

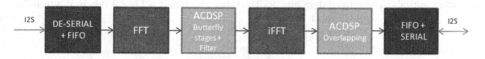

Fig. 2. Dataflow of the audio stream process

The first stage receives as input a stereo audio signal through an I2S serial interface; it is de-serialized and stocked in a FIFO internal to the I2S interface. Samples stored in the FIFO are transferred to an external SDRAM until a complete buffer of size N/2 is filled. We are now ready to start the signal processing.

In the second stage, samples for two consecutive buffers (even and odd samples buffer) are passed separately, one after the other, as a stream through the N/2 points FFT core.

Data is buffered in the external SDRAM after each processing block. This is mainly because it needs to be stored temporarily when the next processing stage requires other data that are not yet processed. This is the counterpart of using the same resources for different processing.

The third phase first recombines the two resulting vectors in a final butterfly stage with the ACDSP block in order to generate the complete frequency spectrum for N points. Afterwards, it computes the phase correction filtering, which is also executed by the ACDSP block. It is performed in the form of a streamed multiplication of two vectors of complex numbers: the frequency domain signal and the parameters of the filter.

In the fourth phase we split again the vector. This time it is the resulting spectrum of the filtering phase. It is split with an inverse butterfly stage and the samples are passed in two times through the FFT core (set in inverse mode).

The fifth stage uses again the ACDSP block for windowing and overlapping the two resulting time vectors. To reduce the throughput delay and improve the output signal quality, a 50 % overlapping with Hanning windowing is applied at the end of signal flow. This means the whole filter flow is applied every N/2 samples instead of N.

The last stage renders again an output audio signal in the form of an I2S streaming. For doing so we perform the opposite operation described in stage 1 by filing an output FIFO to be further serialized to I2S.

3.3 Data Management

Audio data is initially stored in the SDRAM by a DMA, which continuously reads I2S input FIFO. The left and right signals are interleaved in the same buffer.

For each processing stage, a complete input buffer is read in the SDRAM, passed in Avalon streaming format through the accelerator (FFT/ACDSP) and written in an output buffer. The modular Scatter-Gather DMA IP (mSGDMA) IP, illustrated in Fig. 3 makes this flow easy by allowing to synchronize a memory to stream master and a stream to memory master with a dispatcher. For our application, the input data bus width is set to 128 bits (read master) to allow the simultaneous streaming of two 32 bits floating point complex signals. The output data bus width (write master) is set to 64 bits to contain the single resulting complex signal.

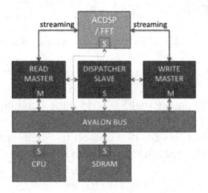

Fig. 3. Modular SGDMA architecture; the mSGDMA components are colored in red (Color figure online)

Depending on the stage type, output data can be interleaved with another signal by writing with address increments greater than one on the same buffer. The resulting interleaved buffers are used when two signals must be part of the same stream in the next process. This is used for all ACDSP processing. For example, interleaving frequency spectrum points with filter function points before they are streamed to ACDSP set in multiplication mode.

Thanks to this data management, every processing stage can be seen as a memory-to-memory transfer. By choosing the input and output buffer, the read and write address increases and the ACDSP or FFT mode, the user can control the complete dataflow from the Nios II processor as standard DMA transfers.

3.4 FFT IP Core

The main interest of using FPGAs to perform FFT processing is the possibility to parallelize the algorithm; therefore FPGA-based FFT accelerators can be very efficient. Altera proposes the FFT Megacore IP [9], which we configured for our design needs. We decided to use a 16,384 points FFT (used twice) instead of a single 32,768 points in order to spare resources.

The IP core proposes various settings and architectures. We used the variable streaming mode because it allows 32-bit floating point processing while providing an excellent throughput thanks to a radix-4 FFT architecture. The floating point resolution is required for signals with high dynamic range like intermediate values of FFT computation. The output is set digit-reversed order to avoid additional ordering logic. It is the samples ordering that is generated by the vector manipulation during the FFT computation. Since we perform a second pass in the core for the iFFT stage, the vector recovers its natural order with no other time consuming intervention.

We created a wrapper to interface the streaming IP with the design. Its architecture is shown on Fig. 4. The direction of the FFT (inverse or normal) is set with a control register, which is accessed through an Avalon memory-mapped interface by the Nios II processor. As the FFT is the first processing stage, the cast from 24-bit fixed point to 32 bit floating point is made inline (only in normal FFT direction).

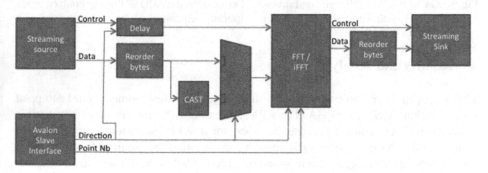

Fig. 4. FFT wrapper architecture

3.5 Accelerator for DSP Computation (ACDSP)

The ACDSP can be seen as an ALU for streamed data vectors. It is capable of four different operations on two floating point complex signals in streaming that can be seen as a simple memory transfer. Those operations are complex multiplication, complex addition/subtraction, copy and "addition + division + cast" in a single transfer. Its structure is shown in Fig. 5. In total, the audio stream goes through the ACDSP 22 times during filtering to process a complete stereo buffer.

The user sets the ACDSP mode by writing to a memory-mapped register. Depending on the mode, the streaming control signals are automatically delayed by the right number of clock cycles. The mode is changed before the data buffer is passed in streaming through the ACDSP. To operate on two complex signals, the input data bus is 128 bit wide and its output is 64 bit wide.

The basic operations are implemented using Altera floating point IP cores (multiplier, adder and cast). As an example, the complex multiplication block is illustrated in Fig. 5. The multiplication of two complex floating point samples takes 12 clock cycles at 100 MHz and is fully pipelined.

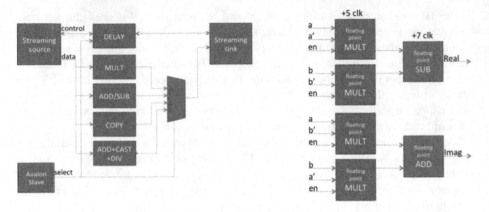

Fig. 5. On the left, ACDSP peripheral structure; On the right, the ACDSP floating point complex multiplication structure, respecting complex multiplication equation (a + ib) (a′ + ib′) = (aa′ − bb ′) + i(ab′ + ba′)

4 Results and Analysis

The system has been implemented and tested on a SoCKit development board equipped with a Cyclone V SX A6 FPGA. The ARM cortex-A9 HPS (hard processor system) is not used and even required because the processor is not intended to perform intensive computation, a Nios II processor is enough for executing the required functionalities, such as interrupt handling and memory-mapped peripherals access. This allows targeting FPGAs without HPS, which offer a better cost vs. resources ratio. The complete test setup depicted in Fig. 6 includes an I2S to S/PDIF I/O daughterboard for audio measurements and testing. The architecture supports a 32,768 points FFT resolution with 96 kHz 24-bit digital audio and induces a 169 ms pure delay.

Fig. 6. Test setup: On the left, SoCKit development platform coupled with the I2S to S/PDIF board; On the right, targeted Goldmund Apologue multiway loudspeaker system.

4.1 Performance Analysis

Every processing step duration is measured as shown in Table 1 in order to estimate the maximum resolution reachable with a 16,384 points core, for example when FFT is fractionated by 2, 3 or 4. The profiling realized using the Performance counter IP-core shows that for one stereo buffer and a resolution of 32,768 points, the computation time is 71 ms. The maximum allowed computation latency for a real-time execution of the application is 169 ms. This time is given by the audio input buffering time at a 96 kHz sampling rate and the resolution aimed, considering a 50 % overlapping. The calculation time margin (of 98 ms) allows further optimization to reduce design footprint and latency. The estimations show that, for instance, by fractioning by 3 (instead of 2 as the actual profile) we could obtain 120 ms calculation time and 49,152 points; by fractioning by 4, 224 ms for 65,536 points.

Table 1. Detailed stereo processing chain profiling for 32,768 points FFT convolution using a 16,384 points IP core

Process	Iterations	Duration (ms)	Total duration (ms)
FFT/iFFT	8	1.7	13.6
ACDSP	22	2.1	46.2
Copy	6	2	12
Overhead		0.09	0.09
Total			71.8
Available time (input buffering time)			169

4.2 Signal Quality and Filtering Efficiency

In order to validate the filter efficiency, a Phase vs. frequency measurement is performed using an AudioPrecision SYS-2722 signal analyzer interfaced with S/PDIF signals. Figure 7 illustrates the measured phase delay vs. frequency with and without the filter. The resulting system response corresponds to our expected phase variation. It can be observed that strong phase variations are occurring around 70, 400 and 7000 Hz. As group delay is the derivative of phase, these regions are those were the filter mostly applies the correction.

On the other hand, amplitude in function of frequency stays untouched and meets the requirement with less than ± 0.02 dBFS variation around the spectrum. With 32,768 points FFT, the frequency resolution of the implemented filter reaches 2.9 Hz which allows precise correction on the whole spectrum.

4.3 FPGA Resources Usage

One of our main goals is to fit our design into the smallest possible FPGA in order to minimize costs. For doing so we gathered the resource usage report generated by the

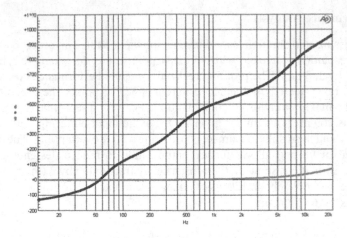

Fig. 7. Phase vs. frequency measurement. Unfiltered signal *(green trace)* and filtered signal *(blue trace)* (Color figure online)

Quartus synthesis and fitting report. The four main resources required are logic elements (LE), internal memory and internal DSP. External SDRAM memory is used for signal buffering and CPU memory. The first resource to lack when trying to choose the smallest FPGA target is the number of LE. The design reaches 80 % of its usage as shown in Table 2.

To go further, we examined the resource usage by entity of our design. As shown in Table 3, the highest consumer of LE is the FFT core, which uses 60 % of the design total. This clearly indicates that the first entity to be targeted for footprint optimization is the FFT core. The one currently used is the Altera Megacore FFT in variable streaming mode at 16,384 points. For a cost vs. performance analysis we show in Table 2 that the internal and external memory usage is proportional to the number of points, while other resources vary slightly.

Table 2. Resources used by the design for 8,192 and 32,768 points FFT using respectively 4,096 and 16,384 points cores.

Resource usage	Cyclone V SE A7 8'192 points	Cyclone V SE A7[a] 32'768 points	Cyclone V SX A5 32,768 points
Logic (ALM)	24'265 (76 %)	25'603 (80 %)[a]	27'691 (66 %)
Internal memory (kB)	101.5 (20 %)	347.75 (68 %)[a]	369.625 (52 %)
External memory (kB)	2,028 (3 %)	7'894 (8 %)[a]	7'894 (0.0008 %)
DSP	33 (38 %)	37 (43 %)[a]	37 (33 %)

[a]The 32,768 point system fits on the Cyclone V SE A7 but is not fully functional. This may be because the design fitting is not meeting all timing requirements due to resources over-use. FPGA resources cannot be used up to 100 % and routing issues can start appearing from 70 %. Efforts on fitting parameters such as speed vs. area or manual floorplan optimization could resolve timing issues.

Table 3. Resource usage by entity in % comparing to the full design usage for 32,767 point FFT using a 16,384 points core; *I-Con* is the Inter-Connection logic.

	FFT	I-Con	DDR3	ACDSP	NIOS II	3*SGDMA	2*DMA
Logic	66 %	8 %	8 %	7 %	3.5 %	2.4 %	1.2 %
Int. memory	92 %	0.3 %	4.8 %	<1 %	1 %	1.5 %	<1 %
DSP	28	0	0	4	2	3	0

5   Conclusions and Further Work

The work presented in this paper has been validated on an Apologue multiway loudspeaker system from Goldmund with a clear improvement on the perceived audio quality. This quality perception is completely subjective and it is therefore impossible to measure. However, the measured phase vs. frequency validates the desired filter response according to psychoacoustic models [2]. On the other hand the initially desired operation constraints in terms of performance, latency, and FPGA resource utilization have been fully fulfilled.

Nevertheless several optimizations are still possible in order to improve either the performance or reduce the system cost. Increasing the system performance can be interesting for pushing the processing audio vector size to 65 or 128 K samples resulting in a more accurate group delay correction at low frequencies. A smaller hardware footprint is also possible and in most of the cases the same architectural improvement that can drive us to increase performance while keeping the same amount of resources, can also be driven to reduce resource utilization without sacrificing performance.

As an alternative to Altera Megacore IP, we could use a slower FFT IP core to reduce the hardware footprint. This means increasing the throughput latency but our design is ready to support it. In slower IPs we find less hardware redundancy because some processing steps are realized in a sequential way instead of a parallel one. This kind of architecture is not available on Megacore IP and could help the design fitting in a smaller FPGA. Such iterative FFT IP cores can be generated online [10].

Another possible optimization is to augment the level of overlapping. Currently we are overlapping 50 % between every two consecutive time windows. More overlapping means performing signal chain more often and reducing overall latency. This is possible because the signal computation time is more than two time shorter than the audio signal input buffering time at 32,768 points. Higher overlapping will allow us to perform FFTs on more than 65,536 points while respecting the latency constraint of the HDMI standard.

We are currently using a 16 K FFT IP core for fragmenting a 32 k FFT execution in two. In order to reduce FPGA resource utilization, we can still use a smaller FFT IP core. In this case we would experience a reduction in performance since we will spend some more clock cycles merging again their partial results. This fragmentation permits us to tune the tradeoff performance vs cost for fitting the imposed constraints.

Acknowledgement. The research presented in this paper is initiated and supported by Goldmund Company, especially by Véronique Adam and Olivier Schmitt.

References

1. Fincham, L.R.: The subjective importance of uniform group delay at low frequencies. JAES **33**(6), 436–439 (1985)
2. Leonardo: group delay distortion and correction solutions, white paper. Goldmund company
3. Parks, T.W., Burrus, C.S.: Digital Filter Design. Wiley-Interscience, New York (1987)
4. Nussbaumer, H.J.: Fast Fourier Transform and Convolution Algorithms. Springer, Heidelberg (2012)
5. High-Definition Multimedia Interface Specification, Version 1.3a
6. Leclère, J., Botteron, C., Farine, P.A.: Implementing super-efficient FFTs in Altera FPGAs, EE Times Programmable Logic Designline (2015)
7. Ozdil, O., BILGEM, UEKAE/ILTAREN, TUBITAK, Gebze, Turkey: Implementation of a FPGA-based overlap-add filter. In: 2012 20th Signal Processing and Communications Applications Conference (SIU) (2012)
8. Altera Corp: Cyclone V Device Datasheet, June 2015
9. Altera Corp: FFT IP Core User Guide, October 2015
10. Nordin, G., Milder, P.A., Hoe, J.C., Püschel, M.: Automatic generation of customized discrete Fourier transform IPs. In: Design Automation Conference (2005)

Comparing Register-Transfer-, C-, and System-Level Implementations of an Image Enhancement Algorithm

Markus Weinhardt[✉]

Osnabrück University of Applied Sciences, Osnabrück, Germany
mweinhardt@computer.org

Abstract. This paper reports on a color image enhancement algorithm implemented on a reconfigurable SoC of the Xilinx Zynq family. The algorithm consists of histogram equalization followed by an unsharp masking filter. A pure software implementation running on the Zynq's ARM Core-A9 processor is compared to several hardware-accelerated versions with respect to the design effort and the quality-of-results. The accelerators are specified at register-transfer level, at high-level (C functions) and at system-level using the recently released Xilinx SDSoC tool. The latter approach is purely software-defined and generates all the interface code and circuitry automatically. Nevertheless, experience with high-level synthesis tools and a basic understanding of hardware coprocessor principles are also required in this approach to effectively use SDSoC.

The results show that the same, significant speedup as with manual implementation can be reached for our application, but the resulting circuit tends to be larger with the higher-level design tools.

Keywords: Image processing · Unsharp masking · Histogram equalization · FPGA · SoC · Vivado High-Level Synthesis · SDSoC · Zynq

1 Introduction

Xilinx's Zynq SoC has found widespread use in embedded applications. To increase acceptance in the software community, new design tools on higher abstraction levels have been released. We tested the latest of these tools with a color image enhancement algorithm implemented on a Digilent Zybo board [1] which features a Zynq XC7Z010 [2,3]. The algorithm consists of histogram equalization followed by an unsharp masking filter, cf. [4]. We compare a pure software implementation running on the Zynq's ARM Core-A9 processor to several hardware-accelerated versions, designed at (1) register-transfer level (RTL), (2) using the high-level synthesis (HLS) [5] tool Vivado HLS [6,7], and (3) using the recently released system-level tool SDSoC [8].

The remainder of this paper is organized as follows: First, related work is reviewed. Next, Sect. 3 presents the image enhancement application in software, and Sect. 4 elaborates on the various hardware implementations. Finally, Sect. 5 summarizes the implementation results and Sect. 6 concludes the paper.

© Springer International Publishing Switzerland 2016
V. Bonato et al. (Eds.): ARC 2016, LNCS 9625, pp. 245–257, 2016.
DOI: 10.1007/978-3-319-30481-6_20

2   Related Work

There are numerous studies of image processing implementations on FPGAs, e.g. [9][1], but only a few publications on HLS-based implementations: In [10], the implementation of a 3 × 3 Sobel filter using Vivado HLS is analyzed and optimized. Matai et al. [11] focus on code restructuring methods and the quality of the results. They also use the Sobel filter and Huffman Tree creation for testing Vivado HLS. In [12], a Canny edge detection algorithm is implemented by heavily using pre-optimized OpenCV functions. The 2D convolution filter implementations presented in these papers are comparable to our unsharp masking filter but are less flexible.

The author is not aware of any publication on using SDSoC for image processing besides an article in Xilinx's new Xcell Software Journal [13]. In contrast to our work, the authors of [13] use OpenCL libraries for imaging applications.

3   Image Enhancement Algorithm

As indicated in Fig. 1, the image enhancement algorithm performs histogram equalization and unsharp masking consecutively on a RGB color image (24 bpp). Figure 2 shows the result of applying this algorithm on a sample color picture.

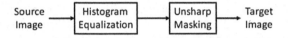

Fig. 1. Image enhancement overview.

Note that our current implementation reads and writes the images from and to files, respectively. Future extensions to this are discussed in Sect. 6.

3.1   Histogram Equalization

As the first stage of our algorithm, histogram equalization is applied to enhance the contrast in an image. For this operation, we chose the algorithm from [4, Sect. 5.5] and adapted it to RGB images as follows: First, the histogram $h(i)$ and the cumulative histogram $H(i)$ of the image's greyscale values as well as the equalization function $f_{eq}(i) = \lfloor 255 \times H(i)/(WIDTH \times HEIGHT) \rfloor$ (for image size $WIDTH \times HEIGHT$) are computed. Then, the equalization is applied separately to all color channels. Figure 3 shows the C function for the equalization of an RGB image.

---

[1] For more examples, consult the proceedings of the FPL (Field-Programmable Logic), ARC (Applied Reconfigurable Computing), FCCM (Field-Programmable Custom Computing Machines) or other conferences and workshops on FPGAs.

(a)   (b)

Fig. 2. Image enhancement. (a) original picture. (b) enhanced picture.

3.2   Unsharp Masking

The second stage of our algorithm sharpens edges in the equalized image. We
chose *Unsharp Masking* (USM), cf. [4, Sect. 7.6.2], which sharpens edges by
adding the source image to a weighted "mask" which is generated by subtracting
a blurred version of the image from the image. We use a 5×5 Gaussian filter
for blurring. The USM filter can be combined to one filter kernel as shown in
Fig. 4 which contains the software implementation of a linear filter which can
be applied to any convolution kernel of any size. Function `filter_frame` calls

```
1  void equalize_frame(unsigned *dest, unsigned *src) {
2      int i, grey;
3      uint32_t Hist[256] = { 0 };
4      uint8_t T[256];
5      uint32_t histcum;
6
7      // build histogram Hist of grey values
8      loop_hist: for (i=0; i< WIDTH*HEIGHT; i++) {
9          grey = (299 * (src[i]&0xff) + 587 * (src[i]>>8 & 0xff) +
10                  114 * (src[i]>>16 & 0xff)) / 1000;
11         Hist[grey]++;
12     }
13     // determine transfer function T
14     histcum = 0; // first cumulative histogram value
15     loop_histcum: for (i=0; i<256; i++) {
16         histcum = histcum + Hist[i]; // histogram accumulation
17         T[i] = 255 * histcum / (WIDTH*HEIGHT);  // transfer fct. values
18     }
19     // apply transfer function T independently on each color channel
20     loop_dest: for(i = 0; i < WIDTH*HEIGHT; i++) {
21         uint8_t r, g, b;
22         r = src[i] & 0xff;
23         g = (src[i] >> 8) & 0xff;
24         b = (src[i] >> 16) & 0xff;
25         // apply T on each color component individually:
26         dest[i] = T[r] | ((uint32_t)T[g]<<8) | ((uint32_t)T[b]<<16);
27     }
28 }
```

Fig. 3. Equalization function.

```
1   #define N 5 // kernel size
2   #define SCALE 118 // scaling factor for USM-kernel
3   static const int kernel[N][N] =    // USM: 2*I - Gauss(I)
4       {{0,-2,-3,-2,0},                // for weight factor 1,
5        {-2,-7,-11,-7,-2},             // to be scaled with 118
6        {-3,-11,218,-11,-3},
7        {-2,-7,-11,-7,-2},
8        {0,-2,-3,-2,0}};
9
10  // apply convolution kernel on window
11  unsigned compute_kernel(unsigned *src, int x, int y) {
12      int i, j, r=0, g=0, b=0;
13      loop_i: for (i = -N/2; i<=N/2; i++) { // filter loop vertical
14          loop_j: for (j = -N/2; j<=N/2; j++) { // filter loop horizontal
15              // compute result for each component:
16              r += ((src[(y+i)*WIDTH+x+j]>>16) & 0xff) * kernel[i+2][j+2];
17              b += ((src[(y+i)*WIDTH+x+j]>>8) & 0xff) * kernel[i+2][j+2];
18              g += ((src[(y+i)*WIDTH+x+j] & 0xff)) * kernel[i+2][j+2];
19          }
20      }
21      // clipping and saturation:
22      r = r/SCALE; if (r<0) r=0; else if (r>255) r=255;
23      g = g/SCALE; if (g<0) g=0; else if (g>255) g=255;
24      b = b/SCALE; if (b<0) b=0; else if (b>255) b=255;
25      return ((uint8_t)r)<<16 | ((uint8_t)b)<<8 | (uint8_t)g;
26  }
27
28  // apply filter to buffer src, resulting in dest
29  void filter_frame(unsigned *dest, unsigned *src) {
30      int x, y;
31      loop_y: for(y = 0; y < HEIGHT; y++) {
32          loop_x: for(x = 0; x < WIDTH; x++) {
33              if (y < 2 || y >= HEIGHT-2 || x < 2 || x >= WIDTH-2)
34                  dest[y*WIDTH+x] = 0xff0000; // blue border
35              else
36                  dest[y*WIDTH+x] = compute_kernel(src, x, y);
37          }
38      }
39  }
```

Fig. 4. Linear filter function.

compute_kernel for each image pixel or sets a constant border value. Function compute_kernel applies USM separately to each color channel and clips the values if required.

4   Hardware Implementation Details

The hardware component implementation is guided by block diagrams as designed by an experienced hardware engineer and implemented at RTL. However, maximal parallelism (by using multiple parallel components and wide memory interfaces) is not exploited.

Next, the C functions introduced in Sect. 3 are optimized such that the Vivado High-Level Synthesis (VHLS) tool generates structures similar to the manually designed ones. Though VHLS can be directly applied to any C functions as long as they are not recursive, do not use unrestricted pointers, and do not allocate memory, the result will most likely be disappointing. The main reason is that VHLS does not parallelize loops automatically. Since the FPGA fabric

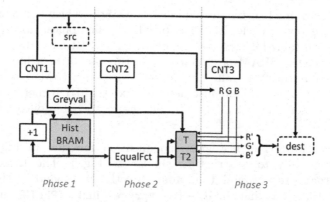

Fig. 5. Histogram equalization datapath.

is clocked at a fraction of the frequency of the ARM Cortex A9 processor (in our case 100 MHz vs. 650 MHz), a sequentially operating hardware component is slower than a software implementation. Hence, the hardware must be parallelized by *inlining inner functions* and by *unrolling or pipelining loops*. Memory accesses are another common obstacle to parallelization. Therefore accesses to global memory must be minimized. It is better to use small arrays since VHLS allocates them to Block RAMs (BRAMs) or registers which can be accessed independently. For even faster access, the arrays must be *partitioned* to several independent BRAMs. All these optimizations can be achieved buy adding *HLS directives* or by restructuring the entire function. VHLS produces reports with the estimated execution cycles and resource usage.

Finally, the integration of these components with the remaining software parts – either manually in the Vivado tool or automatically using SDSoC – is described in Sects. 4.3 and 4.4.

4.1   Histogram Equalization Component

Hardware Design. Figure 5 shows the datapath for histogram equalization. The controller is responsible for executing the three phases of the algorithm: (1) computation of the pixel's grey values and of the histogram values, stored within the FPGA fabric in BRAM Hist, (2) computation of the transfer function, stored in BRAMs T and T2, and (3) equalization of all pixels, separately for all color channels. All phases must be pipelined and are controlled by their respective counters CNTi.

Phase (1) cannot process a source image pixel every cycle since reading, incrementing and updating a Hist value in a BRAM takes at least two cycles on Xilinx FPGAs.[2] In contrast, phase (2) can be fully pipelined since the value

---

[2] Note that, in order to process one pixel every cycle, two BRAMs could be used alternately. Then, their values have to be added to compute the cumulative histogram. This further optimization is applicable to both the RTL and the HLS design.

histcum is stored in a register (inside block EqualFct) which can be read, modified and written every cycle. In order to fully pipeline phase (3) as well, three transfer function table lookups (for colors R, G, and B) have to be performed in parallel. Since the BRAMs are dual-ported, this cannot be achieved with one BRAM. Therefore the same values are stored twice (in BRAMs T and T2). Note that the buffer src has to be read twice from external DDR memory since it is too large to be stored in BRAMs, and buffer dest is written once.

HLS Description. The histogram equalization function in Fig. 3 can be mapped quite easily to a structure similar to Fig. 5. The three for-loops loop_hist, loop_histcum and loop_dest directly correspond to the counters in the datapath. By adding the directive #pragma HLS PIPELINE after the for loop headers (i.e. after lines 8, 15 and 20), VHLS attempts to pipeline these loops and reports the achieved initiation interval II, i.e. the number of cycles between loop iteration launches. While loop_histcum reaches the optimal value $II = 1$ right away, the other loops only achieve $II = 2$. For optimizing loop_dest, T is duplicated as in Fig. 5 by defining a second array T2 (in line 4 of Fig. 3), copying T2[i] = T[i]; (after line 17), and applying one of the table lookups in line 26 from T2.

4.2   Unsharp Masking Component

Hardware Design. An efficient hardware implementation for any 2D convolution filter like the unsharp masking filter consists of a datapath similar to Fig. 6 which exploits the following fact: Though a window of $N \times N$ neighboring source image pixels are used to compute a destination image pixel (cf. function compute_kernel in Fig. 4), only one *new* source image pixel has to be read per result pixel since the data window slides over the source image in one-pixel steps. All the other pixels in the $N \times N$ window have been read before. They have to be kept in BRAMs and registers so that they all can be accessed in parallel. In Fig. 6, the Line Buffers store $N - 1$ image lines for reuse in BRAMs, and the Data Window stores $N \times N$ pixels in registers assembled from the FPGA's D flipflops. The registers are combined to N shift registers, each containing N consecutive pixels of one image line. The pipelined Compute Kernel block can access all registers in parallel and therefore compute one result pixel every cycle. However, a delay occurs before the first result pixel is produced since the line buffers, shift registers and pipeline registers have to be filled first.

HLS Description. For an efficient mapping of the linear filter function in Fig. 4, function compute_kernel is inlined in function filter_frame, i.e. merged at the call site, by adding the directive #pragma HLS INLINE after line 11. Furthermore, loop_x in function filter_frame is pipelined by adding #pragma HLS PIPELINE after line 32. When attempting to pipeline a loop, VHLS tries to unroll all inner loops, i.e. replace the loops by individual instructions if the loop bounds are fixed. This is the case for loop_i and loop_j in Fig. 4. Unfortunately, this leads

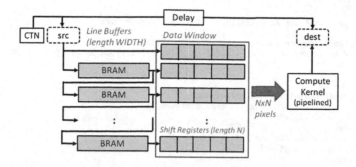

Fig. 6. Linear filter datapath.

to only $II = 21$ since 21 external memory accesses (to buffer `src`) are required for each result pixel. It is obvious that pipelining the outer loop `loop_y` does not make sense since the implied unrolling of `loop_x` would increase the hardware size and the number of memory accesses by a factor of `WIDTH`. Instead, we try to enforce the input reuse as outlined above in Fig. 6 in two steps. However, this requires some major code restructuring.[3]

The first optimization step introduces a data window with N shift registers. It reduces the number of external memory reads to N per result pixel, i.e. achieves $II = 5$ for the USM filter, cf. Sect. 5. The array `shift_reg_window[N][N]` is defined to hold $N \times N$ values and will be automatically implemented by registers. A new inlined function `shift_reg_in` (see Fig. 7) combines a line of the array to a shift register. It is called once for each shift register in `loop_x`.[4] Furthermore, the initialization of `loop_x` is changed to `x = -N/2;` in order to fill the shift registers. The conditions for setting the result pixel are also adjusted accordingly, and function `compute_kernel` is adapted to work on `shift_reg_window` instead of directly reading input pixels from external memory, cf. Fig. 7.

The second optimization step adds line buffers. Figure 7 shows the final result. The buffers are defined as the array `unsigned line_buffer[N][WIDTH];` in line 22. The directive in the following line instructs VHLS to implement the array as N separate BRAMs and split the array along the first dimension, i.e. into lines. The initialization of the outer loop `loop_y` is also changed to `y = -N/2;` in order to allow prefilling $N/2$ line buffers. Now only one external memory acess (line 29) is required per result pixel, thereby achieving $II = 1$. The line buffers are used in a rotating fashion modulo N, and the shift registers are now filled with the line buffer values (line 31). The conditions within `loop_x` are again adjusted accordingly. This C function results in a hardware structure similar to Fig. 6. However, note that VHLS synthesizes N rotating line buffers whereas the design in Fig. 6 uses $N - 1$ directly chained line buffers.

---

[3] Note that automatic data reuse as defined in [14] which restructures regular loops automatically is still not implemented in commercial HLS tools as Vivado HLS.

[4] Note that we do not use the line-buffer objects provided by VHLS for C++ programs.

```
1   ...
2   static const int kernel[N][N] = { ...} // as before
3
4   unsigned compute_kernel(unsigned window[N][N]) {
5     // as before, but uses window[i+N/2][N/2-j] instead of src[(y+i)*WIDTH+x+j]
6     ...
7   }
8
9   // shift register input processing
10  void shift_reg_in(unsigned* reg, unsigned in) {
11  #pragma HLS INLINE
12    int i;
13    unroll_loop: for(i = N-1; i > 0; i--)
14      reg[i] = reg[i-1];
15    reg[0] = in;
16  }
17
18  // apply filter to buffer src, resulting in dest
19  void filter_frame(unsigned  *dest, unsigned *src) {
20    int x, y, i; unsigned respix;
21    unsigned shift_reg_window[N][N]; // array for shift registers
22    unsigned line_buffer[N][WIDTH]; // array for line buffers
23  #pragma ARRAY_PARTITION variable=line_buffer block factor 5 dim = 1
24    loop_y: for(y = -N/2; y < HEIGHT; y++) {
25      loop_x: for(x = -N/2; x < WIDTH; x++) {
26        if (y >= HEIGHT-N/2 || x >= WIDTH-N/2)
27          respix = 0xff0000; // blue border
28        else {
29          line_buffer[(y+N/2)%N][x+N/2] = src_buffer[(y+N/2)*WIDTH+x+N/2];
30          loop_i: for (i = 0; i<N; i++)
31            shift_reg_in(shift_reg_window[i], line_buffer[(y+N/2-i)%N][x+N/2]);
32          if (x >= N/2 && y >= N/2)
33            respix = compute_kernel(shift_reg_window);
34          else
35            respix = 0xff0000; // blue border
36        }
37        if (x >= 0 && y >= 0)
38          dest[y*WIDTH+x] = respix;
39      }
40    }
41  }
```

Fig. 7. Linear filter function with data window and line buffers.

4.3   Hardware System Design with Vivado IP Integrator

Once the hardware components have been optimized in Vivado HLS, they need to be integrated in a Zynq design. For that, the external interface of the components must be defined by a HLS directive for the top-level function's parameters. For arrays in external memory as our image buffers, an AXI master interface which gives direct access to external DDR memory is most convenient. It can be selected with the directive #pragma HLS INTERFACE m_axi port=dest offset=slave. Then, the offset can be set by a software driver over a peripheral interface connected to the AXI-Lite bus.

Independent Components. A synthesized RTL component is exported and packaged into an XACT IP Catalog by Vivado HLS [6]. This IP Catalog – which also contains the drivers for accessing the IP – is then imported to a Vivado project and connected to the Zynq Processing System (PS) in a *Block Design*, using the *IP Integrator*. The automatic block connection adds AXI interconnect and reset blocks and configures them as required. Depending on which interfaces are activated for the Zynq PS, the IP's AXI master interfaces are connected to the cache-coherent ACP interface (Accelerator Coherency Port) or to AXI High-Performance ports. After a FPGA bitstream has been generated for the design (using Vivado logic synthesis), it is exported to the Xilinx Software Development Kit (SDK) [15]. The generated SDK project has access to the IP's drivers. In the application software, the calls to `equalize_frame` and `filter_frame` must then be replaced by calls to initialize the HLS-generated drivers, set the input parameters, start the coprocessor execution and wait until it has terminated.

Streaming Connection. When a hardware component directly uses the output of another component and the data can be transferred in a data stream (as the output of histogram equalization and the input of the optimized USM filter), the data should not be stored in memory. For this scenario, VHLS can be directed to generate AXI-Stream interfaces. The resulting stream ports then have to be connected manually in the IP Integrator, and the driver calls have to be adapted accordingly. The resulting design is much more efficient than the independent implementation since the storing and reloading of an entire image is removed. Furthermore, the two components now execute in parallel. Figure 8 shows the Block Diagram: The two components marked with the Vivado HLS logo in the middle have a stream connection between themselves and are connected to the Zynq PS (on the right-hand side) via AXI interconnect blocks (for AXI-Full and AXI-Lite, with the crossbar logos) and via a reset block (on the left-hand side).

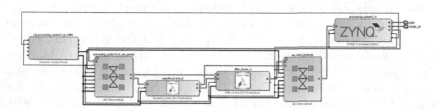

Fig. 8. Vivado Block Diagram with streaming connection between HLS components.

4.4 System-Level Codesign with SDSoC

The new "software-defined" SDSoC tool [8] performs all the steps described in Sect. 4.3 automatically. The SDSoC tool is similar to the standard SDK but allows to toggle functions between software and hardware implementation. If a hardware-software partitioning is chosen, clicking the *Build* icon calls all required tools "under the hood": It instruments the software with hardware calls, runs Vivado HLS for all selected components, and builds a Vivado project containing all the synthesized blocks. Finally, the generated bitstream can be downloaded to the FPGA and the application executed. The user does not have to worry if the interfaces he uses fit together. A *Data Motion Network report* tells him or her how the HLS components are connected, and HLS reports for all selected hardware functions give performance and area estimates. It is even possible to directly combine data streams between components. However, it should be checked in the reports whether this really worked since the functions have to be programmed as in the example code given, cf. [8].

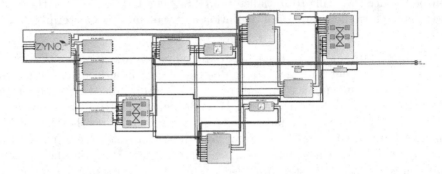

Fig. 9. Vivado Block Diagram automatically generated by SDSoC.

The resulting Vivado project can be opened and inspected, cf. e.g. Fig. 9. Since generic interface components are added to every HLS component, the resulting design tends to be larger then the manually implemented block. Nevertheless, complicated designs, which would require much experience if implemented manually, can be generated easily. It is e.g. possible to implement very efficient data streams directly to or from external DDR RAM. In this case, SDSoC implements and parameterizes complex scatter-gather DMA blocks.

The design productivity is increased considerably by using SDSoC, especially for beginners not familiar with Vivado. But all the HLS optimizations discussed in Sects. 4.1 and 4.2 need to be applied as well since SDSoC directly uses VHLS.

5   Results

All hardware components were implemented using the Vivado 2014.4 tools and reached 100 MHz, the chosen FPGA frequency.[5]

Histogram Equalization: Table 1(a) gives the *measured runtimes and speedups* of the equalization hardware variants for an image size of 320×240 over the software runtime of 5.9 ms (compiled with `gcc -O3` on one ARM core). The highest speedup achieved was 2.4. The table also shows the *estimated* resource

---

[5] The Zybo board also provides a 125 MHz clock for the FPGA fabric, but 125 MHz could not always be reached by VHLS.

usage reported by VHLS. For the last two hardware variants, the *reported post-P&R resource numbers for the entire design* are also given. Note that these values may be decreased by optimizations, but also include the interface components. The first version (IF1) was implemented with SDSoC and manually using Vivado IP Integrator. The runtime was the same, but the manually designed interconnect used fewer resources as expected. The second version (IF2) was only implemented with SDSoC. It uses an AXI stream interface which implies a large scatter-gather DMA block. However, for unclear reasons the speedup is not improved for this function.

Table 1. Performance and resource usage results.

	t_{exe} [ms]	Speedup	II_1	II_2	II_3	LUTs	FFs	BRAM	DSP
XC7Z010 resources						17,600	35,200	120	80
No optimization	9.3	0.6	-	-	-	1,072	981	2	12
Loops pipelined	3.1	1.9	2	1	2	1,108	986	2	12
2 BRAMs (T,T2), IF 1	**2.48**	**2.4**	2	1	1	1,113	982	3	12
entire design SDSoC:						3,008	3,851	7	10
entire design Vivado:						2,532	3,124	3	10
2 BRAMs (T,T2), IF 2	2.54	2.3	2	1	1	1,104	923	3	12
entire design SDSoC:						7,978	10,954	24	10

(a) Histogram equalization performance and resource usage. II_1 to II_3 refer to the function's three for-loops. Interface IF 1 connects both ports to AXI masters, whereas IF 2 connects the **dest** buffer to an AXI stream.

	t_{exe} [ms]	Speedup	II	LUTs	FFs	BRAM	DSP	LOC
No optimization	627.1	0.06	-	1,885	1,395	0	15	
loop_x pipelined	89.6	0.4	21	3,383	2,483	0	18	
With shift reg.s	23.1	1.5	5	2,449	2,446	0	18	
Full optimization, IF 1	6.0	5.8	1	4,148	4,149	5	18	
entire design SDSoC:				5,154	6,475	9	6	
entire design Vivado:				4,568	5,748	5	6	
Full optimization, IF 2	**0.97**	**36.1**	1	3,394	3415	5	18	117
RTL implement. (VHDL):				1,539	903	2	3	876
entire design SDSoC:				9,860	13,633	29	6	

(b) USM filter performance, resource usage, and lines of codes. Interface IF 1 connects both ports to AXI masters, whereas IF 2 connects both ports to AXI streams.

	t_{exe} [ms]	Speedup	LUTs	FFs	BRAM	DSP
Entire design SDSoC:	**2.5**	**16.6**	11,031	14,513	33	16
Entire design Vivado:	5.8	7.1	6,053	7,195	8	16

(c) Combined performance (speedup over $t_{SW} = 40.9$ ms) and resource usage.

Since AXI master interfaces are difficult to implement manually, we did not design this component in VHDL. However, we do not expect big differences since

VHLS reports a latency of 230,951 cycles (neglecting memory delays) which is close to the minimum for the given loop repetitions and II values and cannot be improved by a manual implementation. The same is true for the BRAM count. Only the other resource values could be smaller in an optimized RTL design.

USM Filter: Table 1(b) gives the same results for the USM filter hardware variants compared to the software runtime of 35.0 ms. The comparison between SDSoC and Vivado is similar to that for histogram equalization. Note that the highest speedup for this component is over 36 with IF2. It stems from the high parallelism in the filter processing and the very fast AXI stream access of both the src and dest buffers. However, the required DMA blocks imply a quite high resource usage.

Table 1(b) also contains resource values of a VHDL implementation using AXI streams (IF 2). It is obvious that the resource usage is considerably smaller compared to VHLS, but the implementation effort (indicated by the lines of code, including comments, options etc., in the last column) is very much higher. The development time was several months compared to days for the HLS version. An RTL simulation showed that the runtime (77,451 cycles, neglecting memory delays) is comparable to the latency of 77,947 cycles reported by VHLS.

Combined Implementation: Finally, Table 1(c) compares the combined, fully optimized components with a streaming interface. The manually integrated Vivado design is again slower and smaller since it does not use AXI-Stream interfaces with DMA. The SDSoC version achieves the highest overall speedup of 16.6 though it only accesses the src buffer via AXI-Stream. The SDSoC-generated system accessing both buffers via AXI-Stream did not fit in the Zynq XC7Z010 device. On larger chips, a higher speedup could be reached.

6   Conclusions and Future Work

The results of the previous section show that HLS- and SDSoC-based design can achieve the same performance as a manual implementation of the image enhancement application, but the resulting circuit tends to be larger with the higher-level design tools. VHLS increases the design productivity significantly over RTL design, and SDSoC automatically integrates hardware blocks in a Zynq system, thereby removing another tedious and error-prone process.

In future work we plan to read video frames directly from a camera and display the results on a screen. Then the histogram equalization component can be further pipelined: While the current frame is equalized and filtered, the histogram of the next frame is calculated in parallel. It is not clear whether SDSoC is applicable in such scenarios. While it is possible to integrate given IP as coprocessors, an entirely different setup with hardware blocks independent of the processor system and data streams flowing between them seems to be beyond SDSoC's capabilities.

References

1. ZYBO Reference Manual (2014). www.digilentinc.com
2. Crockett, L.H., Elliot, R.A., Enderwitz, M.A., Stewart, R.W. (eds.): The Zynq Book. Strathclyde Academic Media, Glasgow (2014). www.zynqbook.com
3. Zynq-7000 All Programmable SoC - Technical Reference Manual (UG 585) (2015). www.xilinx.com
4. Burger, W., Burge, M.J.: Digital Image Processing: An Algorithmic Introduction using Java. Springer, London (2008)
5. Gajski, D.D., Dutt, N.D., Wu, A.C.-H., Lin, S.Y.-L.: High-Level Synthesis, Introduction to Chip and System Design. Kluwer Academic Publishers, Norwell (1992)
6. Vivado Design Suite User Guide - High-Level Synthesis (UG 902) (2015). www.xilinx.com
7. Cong, J., Liu, B., Neuendorffer, S., Noguera, J., Vissers, K., Zhang, Z.: High-level synthesis for FPGAs: from prototyping to deployment. IEEE Trans. Comput.-Aided Des. Integr. Circ. Syst. **30**(4), 473–491 (2011)
8. SDSoC User Guide - Introduction to SDSoC (UG 1027) (2015). www.xilinx.com
9. Huang, M., Serres, O., El-Ghazawi, T., Newby, G.: Parameterized hardware design on reconfigurable computers: an image processing case study. Int. J. Reconf. Comput. **2010**, 1–11 (2010). Article No. 7
10. Monson, J., Wirthlin, M., Hutchings, B.L.: Optimization techniques for a high level synthesis implementation of the sobel filter. In: Proceedings of the International Conference on ReConFigurable Computing and FPGAs (ReConFig 2013). IEEE, December 2013
11. Matai, J., Richmond, D., Lee, D., Kastner, R.: Enabling FPGAs for the masses. In: Proceedings of the 1st International Workshop on FPGAs for Software Programmers (FSP), Munich, Germany (2014)
12. Abdelgawad, H.M., Safar, M., Wahba, A.M.: High level synthesis of canny edge detection algorithm on Zynq platform. Int. J. Comput. Electr. Autom. Control Inf. Eng. **9**(1), 148–152 (2015)
13. Neuendorffer, S., Li, T., Vallina, F.M.: Developing OpenCL imaging applications using C++ libraries. Xcell Softw. J., Issue **1**, 36–41 (2015)
14. Weinhardt, M., Luk, W.: Pipeline vectorization. IEEE Trans. Comput.-Aided Des. Integr. Circ. Syst. **20**(2), 234–248 (2001)
15. UltraFast Embedded Design Methodology Guide (UG 1046) (2015). www.xilinx.com

Multicore Systems

Evaluating Schedulers in a Reconfigurable Multicore Heterogeneous System

Jeckson Dellagostin Souza[1](✉), João Victor Gomes Cachola[1], Luigi Carro[1], Mateus Beck Rutzig[2], and Antonio Carlos Schneider Beck[1]

[1] Instituto de Informática, Universidade Federal do Rio Grande do Sul, Porto Alegre, Brazil
{jeckson.souza,jvgcachola,carro,caco}@inf.ufrgs.br
[2] Departamento de Eletrônica e Computação, Universidade Federal de Santa Maria, Santa Maria, Brazil
mateus@inf.ufsm.br

Abstract. The use of heterogeneous multicore processors is getting extremely common, and those that comprise reconfigurable logic are becoming an attractive alternative. However, to leverage them as much as possible to speed up applications, an effective scheduler, which can adequately distribute threads to cores with different processing capabilities, is required. Therefore, this work evaluates the implementation of three distinct scheduling approaches aiming at a reconfigurable heterogeneous architecture: a static algorithm that allocates the threads on the first free core, where they will run during the entire execution; an Instruction Count (IC) Driven scheduler, which reallocates threads during synchronization points accordingly to their instruction count; and an Oracle scheduler, which is capable of deciding the best thread allocation possible. The goal is to determine the necessity of scheduling algorithms and the potential of reconfigurable heterogeneous architectures. We show that a static scheduler might be used with minimal loss (0.01 %) in performance when applications have high load balancing between threads. For unbalanced applications, the static scheduler can reach only 40 % of the Oracle's performance. On the other hand, the dynamic scheduler varies from 97 % to 35 % of the Oracle's performance in similar conditions.

Keywords: Heterogeneity · Multicore · Scheduling · Reconfigurable architectures

1 Introduction

Most modern embedded processors have long abandoned the classic design approach, which aimed to execute programs with fixed homogeneous behavior. Today, these systems are required to execute many types of applications, which have heterogeneous characteristics (e.g.: internet access, audio and video decoding, graphic processing). Still, embedded processors must manage its resources efficiently, as most of them have to obey strict constrains of energy and area.

The aforementioned characteristics suggest that a different approach must be adopted for embedded processors. Heterogeneous organizations, such as the ARM's big.LITTLE [24],

© Springer International Publishing Switzerland 2016
V. Bonato et al. (Eds.): ARC 2016, LNCS 9625, pp. 261–272, 2016.
DOI: 10.1007/978-3-319-30481-6_21

are already being exploited by the industry. These multicore systems are composed of asymmetric cores that implement the same Instruction Set Architecture (ISA) with different organizations (i.e. microarchitectures). Their objective is to allocate light loaded jobs to smaller (and energy efficient) cores and heavy loaded tasks to larger (and high performance) ones. However, creating a scheduling algorithm for such systems is not a trivial task. The algorithm must be aware of many characteristics of the application, such as CPU utilization, frequency and the available level of instruction parallelism, as well as the resources available on each core [2, 3].

Reconfigurable systems are a promising alternative, with all the advantages that come along, such as performance improvements and energy savings, to compose such a heterogeneous environment. A significant example of a reconfigurable multicore system that follows the same idea as ARM's big.LITTLE (i.e.: it implements the same ISA with different organizations), is the heterogeneous CReAMS (Custom Reconfigurable Arrays for Multiprocessor Systems) [19, 21]. CReAMS comprises several processors coupled to a coarse-grained reconfigurable logic each; and each one of them uses a binary translation system to transform, at run-time, code sequences to a reconfigurable context. These contexts are stored within a cache memory, to be fetched in the future aiming and be executed in a combinational fashion, exploiting the Instruction Level Parallelism (ILP) in the reconfigurable datapath. Therefore, CReAMS can use its reconfigurability skill to create specific datapaths for code sequences, while maintaining binary compatibility. The heterogeneity of CReAMS comes from the coupling of different sizes of the reconfigurable datapath to each processor (further details on CReAMS are discussed later). However, this organization shares the same scheduling challenges of the conventional heterogeneous processors.

In this paper, we implement and evaluate three different scheduling policies, and analyze the tradeoffs in terms of performance (in time taken to execute the application) among them. The first one is the predictive scheduler (Oracle). The Oracle always chooses the best fitting core for a thread. It is able to do so by analyzing all the possible thread allocations, determining the combination that results in best performance through exhaustive search. With Oracle, it is possible to know the upper bound limit in performance that the heterogeneous configuration can provide and assert the potential of these systems. The second version is a static scheduler. It allocates each new thread to the first free core available, on which the thread is executed during its entire lifetime. The third version is the IC (Instruction Count)-driven algorithm, which reallocates tasks during synchronization points accordingly to the instruction count of the threads at each barrier.

Results show that the static scheduler reaches from 40 % to 90 % the Oracle's performance when considering applications with highly unbalanced threads. Thus, it may be worth to invest in more sophisticated scheduling algorithms when one considers these cases. On the other hand, when applications have good load balancing, the static scheduler reaches 99.9 % of the Oracle's performance. The simple IC-Driven algorithm have similar behavior to the static, but usually performs worst due to miss predictability of the scheduling policy.

This work is organized as follows: Sect. 2 presents the Related Work. Section 3 explains in details the organization of CReAMS. In Sect. 4, the proposed algorithms are presented. We expose and analyze the results in Sect. 5 and, finally, conclusions and future works are drawn in Sect. 6.

2   Related Work

2.1   Background

A reconfigurable system can adapt itself to provide hardware optimization for a particular application. It is achieved through an additional circuit that supplies reconfigurability, like a Field Programmable Gate Array (FPGA) or a reconfigurable array of functional units. These organizations provide performance gains and energy savings over General Purpose Processors (GPP), at the cost of extra area. The reconfigurable logic can be: (i) loosely connected to the processor as an I/O peripheral (communication is done through the main memory); (ii) attached as a coprocessor (coprocessor-like protocols do the communication); or (iii) tightly coupled as a functional unit (reconfigurable logic is inside the processor and share its resources, like its registers). Furthermore, the granularity of the reconfigurable logic determines its level of data manipulation. A fine-grained logic is implemented at bit level (like Look-Up Tables in FPGAs) while a coarse-grained logic implements word level circuits (like ALUs and multipliers) [8].

2.2   Multicore Reconfigurable Architectures

One can find different environments that apply some kind of adaptability to improve the performance of applications [4, 6, 8]. Considering only reconfigurable architectures built upon multicore systems, Watkins [23] presents a procedure for mapping functions in the ReMAPP system, which is composed of a pair of coarse-grained reconfigurable arrays that is shared among several cores. As an example of a system with homogeneous architecture and heterogeneous organization, one can find Thread Warping [15]. It extends the Warp Processing [16] system to support multiple threads executions. In this case, one processor is entirely dedicated to execute the operating system tasks needed to synchronize threads and to schedule their kernels in the accelerators. KAHRISMA [7] is another example of a totally heterogeneous architecture. It supports multiple instruction sets (RISC, 2-4- and 6-issue VLIW, and EPIC) and fine and coarse-grained reconfigurable arrays. Software compilation, ISA partitioning, custom instructions selection and thread scheduling are made by a design time tool that decides, for each part of the application code, which assembly code will be generated, considering its dominant type of parallelism and resources availability. A run-time system is responsible for code binding and for avoiding execution collisions in the available resources.

Heterogeneous CReAMS [21] is composed of cores with distinct reconfigurable datapaths in terms of amount of functional units. This strategy provides cores capable of exploiting different levels of instruction parallelism and energy consumption. CReAMS also keeps transparency to the programmer, as a binary translation system is responsible for automatically migrating code sequences from the general purpose processor to the reconfigurable datapath in each core. It eases the software development process since any well-known toolchain (i.e. gcc) can be used for any of its versions.

In contrast to ReMAPP and Thread Warping, CReAMS employs a coarse-grained reconfigurable fabric instead of a fine-grained one. Fine-grained architectures may provide higher acceleration levels, but their scope is narrowed to applications that have few kernels responsible for a large part of the execution time. On the other hand, coarse-grained reconfigurable architectures are capable of accelerating the entire application as they have reduced reconfiguration time.

2.3 Scheduling Algorithms for Heterogeneous Systems

When considering unaware schedulers (when no details of the cores are necessary), Becchi et al. [2] and Kumar et al. [14] works are two of the most well-known in the literature. Both rely on online performance checks to determine the best thread allocation on a dual core ("fast" and "slow" cores) system. Becchi uses an IPC (Instruction Per Cycle)-driven algorithm to sample threads' instructions per cycle (IPC) on the two types of cores. Threads with high IPC ratio have priority to be assigned to the fast core, as they can achieve higher speedups on it. Kumar's work creates an oracle heuristic to optimize energy efficiency and energy-delay product in superscalar cores. Then, it compares the optimal results with a similar approach to Becchi's. Differently from Becchi's, Kumar's work makes many performance samples of groups of threads in different core types. This allows for finding globally optimal allocations instead of making local decisions on thread swapping.

On the other hand, many other works for aware heterogeneous scheduling have also been proposed [1, 18, 22]. Shelepov proposes HASS [20], a heterogeneous aware algorithm that creates architectural signatures of applications. The scheduler must know in advance the cache sizes and frequencies from the distinct cores. By profiling the application before execution, HASS identifies its memory-boundedness and use it to predict the best core to allocate the threads, considering expected cache misses and clock frequency. However, none of the above proposals have been applied in heterogeneous systems with reconfigurable logic.

2.4 Contribution

While none of the aforementioned works in heterogeneous reconfigurable systems uses a dynamic scheduler for the threads, no scheduling algorithms were ever applied to reconfigurable organizations as well. Therefore, we aim to bridge this gap by implementing and evaluating different threads algorithms, using CReAMS as case study. The goal is to determine whether a more sophisticated scheduling algorithm, which considers specific application characteristics, is necessary or not according to the application at hand; and to evaluate the maximum potential of heterogeneous multicore systems.

3   CReAMS Organization

A general overview of CReAMS is given in Fig. 1(a). The thread-level parallelism is exploited by replicating the number of Dynamic Adaptive Processors (DAPs) [3, 5] (in the example of the Fig. 1(a), by four DAPs). Each DAP is a transparent single-threaded reconfigurable architecture coupled to the processor. The communication among DAPs is done through a 2D-mesh Network on Chip using an XY routing strategy. CReAMS also includes an on-chip unified 512 KB 8-way set associative L2 shared memory, illustrated as SM in the Fig. 1(a). We divided the DAP in four blocks to better explain it, as illustrated in Fig. 1(b).

Block 1 in Fig. 1(b) shows the structure of the reconfigurable datapath. It is composed of registers for input and output context and a matrix of functional units. The matrix is a combinational block with ALUs (Arithmetic and Logic Units), Multipliers and Memory access ports and is composed of levels that run in parallel with the General Propose Processor (GPP) (block 2). Each level has columns and rows. The rows have units that can run in parallel, executing instructions that do not have data dependency. As the multiplier stands as the critical path of the level, it is possible to align three ALUs in each row and keep the base operating frequency of the processor unchanged. Thus, each ALU row has three columns and can execute three data dependent ALU instructions in the same level. During the reconfiguration process, a basic block is mapped to the matrix, in order to execute the whole block in a combinational fashion.

Block 2 shows the processor coupled with the matrix. In this work, we use a SPARCV8 architecture running at 600 MHz. The processor is five-stage pipelined, which reflects a traditional RISC design (instruction fetch, decode, execution, memory access and write back). In block 3, the necessary storage components are illustrated. Apart from the usual L1 caches, two other memories are used. The address cache holds the address for each basic block decoded by the dynamic detection hardware (block 4) and is used as an index (and to check existence) for the datapath configurations. The reconfiguration memory holds the bits necessary to reconfigure the datapath into a basic block indexed by the address cache.

The Dynamic Detection Hardware (DDH), represented in block 4, does the binary translation and data dependency check of the instructions in a basic block. DDH is four-stage pipelined circuit and runs in parallel to the GPP being out of the critical path of the entire system. Instruction Decode (ID) stage is responsible for decoding the operands in the base processor instruction to datapath code, while Dependence Verification (DV) checks if these operands have any dependency with the instructions already stored in the configuration being built. Resource Allocation (RA) stage uses the DV analysis to determine the best functional unit for the operation inside the array. Finally, Update Tables (UT) stage saves the new allocation in the reconfiguration memory for future use. Every time a jump or an incompatible instruction is detected, a new configuration is started by the DDH and a new entry is created in the address cache.

During the Instruction Fetch (IF) stage of the base processor, the Program Counter (PC) is compared to the values in the address cache. A hit on this cache means that the following sequence of instructions were already translated to a configuration. In this case, the processor's pipeline is stalled and the configuration is executed in the reconfigurable datapath, greatly exploiting the ILP of the application.

In [19] CReAMS was introduced as a homogeneous system. Some CReAMS characteristics: homogeneous in architecture; keeps binary compatibility; and it is coarse-grained (with small reconfigurable contexts/reconfiguration time), facilitates thread migration among cores, and because of these it was chosen to be used as case study. This paper, on the other hand, exploits a heterogeneous version of CReAMS, which is a configuration where each DAP has a different reconfigurable datapath. This allows for some cores to be bigger than others by having more resources (i.e. functional units, input and output context registers). In other words, they are more efficient to execute threads that can exploit higher levels of instruction level parallelism. Similarly, smaller DAPs would be allocated to run threads with low ILP. Figure 1(a) shows a heterogeneous CReAMS of four cores where two of them are small, one is medium and the last is large.

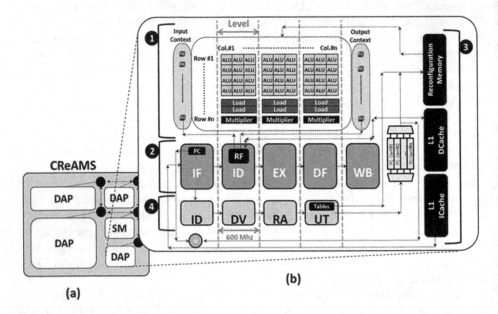

Fig. 1. (a) CReAMS: a multiprocessor system composed of DAPs (b) DAP blocks: A core processor coupled with a reconfigurable datapath

4   Scheduling Algorithms

As previously mentioned, the main advantage of a heterogeneous system is to execute tasks accordingly to their needs. For this, a scheduler is necessary. In this work, we present three schedulers for CReAMS: The Oracle, which can always choose the best fitting core for performance; a static scheduler, which allocates a thread to a core and never changes it; and an IC (Instruction Count)-driven algorithm that can swap threads accordingly to their instruction count. We present further details on each algorithm in the following subsections.

4.1   The Oracle

The Oracle is a predictive scheduler implemented in C language, whose objective is to analyze which core – among all – best fits a thread. In this regard, the Oracle uses results generated by pre-executed simulations of all threads in all possible core sizes. Firstly, one needs to define the number of cores of the heterogeneous system and their sizes. The algorithm assumes that the number of executed threads is equal to the number of cores, exploiting the maximum possible TLP. Thereafter, the Oracle evaluates each synchronization point (i.e. a point where all threads must meet, such as a join or a barrier) of the program, generating every possible combination of thread-core scheduling. The implementation is based on an exhaustive search through these combinations, ultimately selecting the one that outputs the fewer number of cycles. However, this kind of search does not scale to a solvable number of combinations as the number of cores grows. To resolve the allocation problem for this work's target number of cores (up to 16), we designed an algorithm capable of discarding repeated combinations. Figure 2 illustrates the Oracle in three steps.

Step 1 in Fig. 2 shows how the threads are initially arranged in the cores. A disjunctive set of threads is associated with a core size. The allocation process is done in a sequential and pre-defined way. In the example, a set is allocated to large cores, followed by medium cores and finally by small cores. This configuration defines the first combination, which will be analyzed by the Oracle, and it will be, mandatorily, the one with the fewest number of cycles at that moment.

Step 2 in Fig. 2 shows how partial changes of sets occur in order to analyze a set of combinations. Two of the three disjunctive sets are reconfigured and allocated to distinct sizes of cores, generating a new combination. In the example, medium and small cores have their threads deallocated, while threads that are in large cores remain unchanged. Next, a new set of threads (which had not yet been analyzed) is generated and allocated to medium cores, while the remainder is allocated to small cores. This new combination is analyzed and then compared with the combination that has generated the fewest number of cycles at this point. This continues until all formed combinations of disjunctive sets of threads are generated and analyzed.

Step 3, in Fig. 2, shows how changes in the remaining set of threads occur in order to analyze all possible combinations. The remaining disjunctive set is kept unchanged until the moment that all possible combinations of this set with the other two sets are analyzed. When this condition is met, all allocated threads in the system will be deallocated, and a new set is configured for the core size where past unaltered threads were allocated. In the example, after generating all possible combinations in medium and small cores, all threads were deallocated, including those present in large cores. Afterwards, a new combination is generated for large cores, and then step 2 repeats. This continues until all possible combinations in large cores are generated. The whole process is then repeated for the next synchronization point.

The criterion that defines the dynamics of disjunctive sets in each different core size relates with the number of combinations generated by each of them. In this case, the performance gain is associated with the generation of the minimum number of combinations to result in the fewest number of cycles. This is possible because the algorithm needs to generate all combinations only for two core sizes. The third size will be automatically resolved, as it will take the remaining threads.

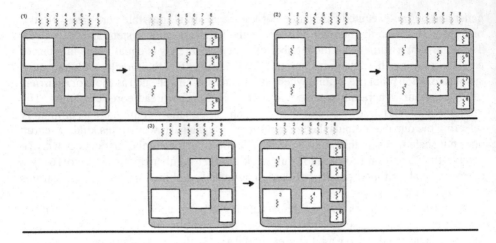

Fig. 2. Steps for the Oracle allocation algorithm

4.2 Static Scheduler

In this solution, when a new thread is created, it is allocated to the next free core, blind to any consistency between what the thread needs and the core resources. After allocation, the thread executes on the same core until completion. The static scheduler adds no complexity to the hardware or operating system nor extra overhead due to swapping threads between cores. Furthermore, most applications have a master thread, which composes the most sequential parts of the application. Another property of the static scheduler is that the master thread is always allocated to a large core in the heterogeneous CReAMS.

4.3 IC-Driven Scheduler

This algorithm inserts a simple instruction counter for each thread. When a synchronization point is reached, the scheduler is activated. The threads with the highest instruction count are swapped to the larger cores, while threads with fewer instructions are allocated to medium and small cores. Figure 3 shows a simplified pseudo-code for the IC-Driven scheduler. The proposal of this algorithm is not to reach near

```
While notEmpty ThreadList
    Thread    Remove(Max(ThreadList))
    If notEmpty LargeCoreList
        Allocate(Thread, Unqueue(LargeCoreQueue))
    Else If notEmpty MediumCoreList
        Allocate(Thread, Unqueue(MediumCoreQueue))
    Else If notEmpty SmallCoreList
        Allocate(Thread, Unqueue(SmallCoreQueue))
```

Fig. 3. Pseudo-code for the IC-Driven scheduler

Oracle performance results, but rather to evaluate the impact of having a simple real-time dynamic scheduler on the system. This implementation is the instinctive way to exploit ILP from cores with different resources.

5 Results

We have created a heterogeneous version of CReAMS and simulated it using the three different schedulers proposed in Sect. 4. The reconfigurable datapath resources of this version are presented in Table 1. This heterogeneous processor is composed of 50 % large cores, 25 % medium cores and 25 % small cores. For example, a 4-core processor would have two large, one medium, and one small core, while an 8-core configuration would have four large, two medium and two small cores, and so on.

Table 1. Heterogeneous configuration

Cores	Lines	Multiplier	Load/Store	ALU	Reconfiguration cache	Input context
Small	9	1	2	3	32 Configurations	8
Medium	15	2	2	4	64 Configurations	14
Large	24	2	2	4	128 Configurations	20

This work uses the Simics simulator [17] to generate the instruction trace from a set of applications. Instructions from the application's trace are sorted according to their threads and each of these threads is allocated to an instance of a DAP simulator, accordingly to the scheduling algorithm. Benchmarks of different suites were chosen to cover a wide range of applications in terms of available parallelism (i.e. TLP and ILP). We have selected benchmarks from the suites OpenMP [10], MiBench suite [11] and SPEC OMPM2001 [9]. The latter is originally composed of single-threaded applications that we have ported to take advantage of multi-threaded environments.

The benchmarks *susan_c*, *susan_s*, *fft*, and *swaptions* have good load balancing between their threads, making them fine examples for TLP exploitation. Additionally, *lu*, *susan_e*, *susan_c*, and *susan_s* have big mean basic block sizes (i.e.: more instructions between control ones), which make them potential candidates to take advantage of ILP. Finally, *equake* has neither good load balancing nor big basic blocks, so it should be less sensitive to both kinds of parallelism.

Figure 4 shows the results of the simulations. The baseline for comparison is the Oracle algorithm that reflects the ideal scheduling, thus its results are fixed in 1. The benchmarks are TLP sorted, i.e., *lu* is has the lowest TLP from the list, while *swaptions* has the most TLP. Each barrier in the Fig. 4 shows the results for a benchmark and, for each benchmark, there are results for simulations with four, eight and sixteen cores. First, we analyze the impact of the schedulers considering the low TLP applications (left most), followed by the benchmarks with high TLP (right most).

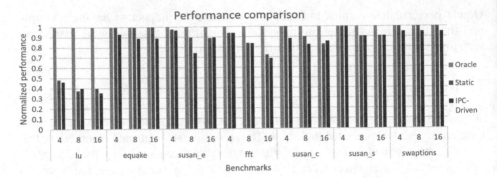

Fig. 4. Performance comparison between scheduling algorithms. Data is split between benchmarks and number of cores and is normalized with the Oracle performance

As shown in Fig. 4, the IC-Driven algorithm follows the same behavior as the static algorithm, but performing lightly worse than the latter. The IC-Driven allocator uses the instruction count of the currently finished barrier to decide whether the next barrier will execute on a different core or not. This decision may be misleading, as the next barrier might have lower (or higher) workload, which can result in performance losses. The application *lu*, which has high mixed loads between threads, is where the Oracle performs better, in general, against the other algorithms. In this benchmark, the Oracle is 2.5× faster than the other schedulers are. Another interesting result comes from the *equake* application, which has neither good load balancing nor big basic blocks. This application does not take advantage of the extra cores as it does not exploit TLP and it barely uses the reconfigurable datapath as it does not exploit ILP. Thus, the static scheduler has almost the same performance as the Oracle, as most of the work is done on the master thread (which, in this scheduler, is always allocated on a large core).

For applications with perfect TLP, such as *swaptions* and *susan_s*, the static scheduler has almost the same performance as the Oracle (99.9 %). These applications are so well balanced that changing allocation will have no effect, as the smaller cores will always hold back the faster ones. In the remaining benchmarks with high TLP (such as *susan_e* and *fft*), the schedulers have also near Oracle performance. However, as the number of cores increases, the performance of the schedulers decreases due to unbalance in the threads workload. In other words, as the heterogeneity of the threads increases, the impact of being able to perfectly allocate the tasks also increases. When considering all benchmarks, statically scheduling the threads provide an average loss of only 15 % when compared to the Oracle's best case, while the IC-Driven scheduler loses 20 % in performance.

6   Conclusions

In this work, we have evaluated three scheduling algorithms and their performance when applied to a heterogeneous reconfigurable organization. Implementing the Oracle in real hardware would be a herculean task considering real world constraints.

However, it stands as a tool to assess the potential of heterogeneity and to compare with other realistic algorithms. The IC-Driven algorithm follows the same behavior as the costless static scheduler, however with worse performance. Results suggest that the proposed dynamic scheduler needs to consider other details of the reconfigurable datapath during allocation. Finally, the schedulers show good overall performance when compared to the Oracle. In fact, they can reach almost the same results as the Oracle when applications have high TLP. A static scheduler has very low cost to implement and might be a good option for less complex systems. As future work, we intend to add an analysis of energy and energy-delay to the heterogeneous system and consider them as scheduling parameters.

References

1. Balakrishnan, S., et al.: The impact of performance asymmetry in emerging multicore architectures. In: Proceedings of International Symposium on Computer Architecture, pp. 506–517 (2005)
2. Becchi, M., Crowley, P.: Dynamic thread assignment on heterogeneous multiprocessor architectures. In: Proceedings of 3rd Conference Computing Frontiers, CF 2006, 29 April 2006, vol. 10 (2006)
3. Beck, A.C.S., et al.: A transparent and adaptive reconfigurable system. Microprocess. Microsyst. **38**(5), 509–524 (2014)
4. Beck, A.C.S., et al.: Adaptable Embedded Systems. Springer, New York (2013)
5. Beck, A.C.S., et al.: Transparent reconfigurable acceleration for heterogeneous embedded applications. In: Proceedings of Design, Automation and Test in Europe, DATE, pp. 1208–1213 (2008)
6. Beck, A.C.S., Carro, L.: Dynamic Reconfigurable Architectures and Transparent Optimization Techniques. Springer, Heidelberg (2010)
7. Bingfeng, M., et al.: Architecture exploration for a reconfigurable architecture template. IEEE Des. Test Comput. **22**(2), 90–101 (2005)
8. Compton, K., Hauck, S.: Reconfigurable computing: a survey of systems and software. ACM Comput. Surv. **34**(2), 171–210 (2002)
9. Dixit, K.M.: The SPEC benchmarks. In: Computer Benchmarks, pp. 149–163. Elsevier (1993)
10. Dorta, A.J., et al.: The OpenMP source code repository. In: 13th Euromicro Conference on Parallel, Distributed and Network-Based Processing, pp. 244–250. IEEE (2005)
11. Guthaus, M.R., et al.: MiBench: a free, commercially representative embedded benchmark suite. In: Proceedings of the Workload Characterization, pp. 3–14. The University of Michigan Electrical Engineering and Computer Science (2001)
12. Jeff, B.: big.LITTLE Technology Moves Towards Fully Heterogeneous Global Task Scheduling, pp. 1–13 (2013)
13. Kim, M., et al.: Utilization-aware load balancing for the energy efficient operation of the big.LITTLE processor, pp. 3–6 (2014)
14. Kumar, R., et al.: Single-ISA heterogeneous multi-core architectures: the potential for processor power reduction. In: Proceedings of the 36th Annual IEEE/ACM International Symposium on Microarchitecture 2003, MICRO-36 (2003)
15. Lee, J., et al.: Thread tailor. ACM SIGARCH Comput. Archit. News **38**(3), 270–279 (2010)
16. Lysecky, R., et al.: Warp processors. ACM Trans. Des. Autom. Electron. Syst. **11**(3), 659–681 (2006)

17. Magnusson, P.S., et al.: Simics: a full system simulation platform. Computer **35**(2), 50–58 (2002). (Long. Beach. Calif)
18. Mogul, J.C., et al.: Using asymmetric single-ISA CMPs to save energy on operating systems. IEEE Micro **28**(3), 26–41 (2008)
19. Rutzig, M.B., et al.: A transparent and energy aware reconfigurable multiprocessor platform for simultaneous ILP and TLP exploitation. In: Proceedings of Design, Automation and Test in Europe Conference and Exhibition (DATE 2013) (2013)
20. Shelepov, D., Alcaide, J.S.: HASS: a scheduler for heterogeneous multicore systems. Oper. Syst. **43**(2), 66–75 (2009)
21. Souza, J.D., et al.: Towards a dynamic and reconfigurable multicore heterogeneous system. In: 2014 Brazilian Symposium on Computing Systems Engineering, pp. 73–78 (2014)
22. Teodorescu, R., Torrellas, J.: Variation-aware application scheduling and power management for chip multiprocessors. In: Proceedings of International Symposium on Computer Architecture, pp. 363–374 (2008)
23. Watkins, M.A., Albonesi, D.H.: Enabling parallelization via a reconfigurable chip multiprocessor. In: Workshop on Parallel Execution of Sequential Programs on Multi-core Architecture, vol. 2, pp. 59–68 (2010)
24. big.LITTLE Technology. http://www.arm.com/products/processors/technologies/big LITTLEprocessing.php

Programmable Logic as Device Virtualization Layer in Heterogeneous Multicore Architectures

Falco K. Bapp[✉], Oliver Sander, Timo Sandmann, Hannes Stoll, and Jürgen Becker

Karlsruhe Institute of Technology (KIT), Karlsruhe, Germany
falco.bapp@kit.edu

Abstract. In latest heterogeneous multicore architectures, the number of cores competing for a shared resource is further increasing. Such shared resources range from simple I/O interfaces to memory controllers. The performance of the complete System-On-Chip (SoC) is directly correlated to the sharing of resources. Especially the hardly predictable blocking of resources for a certain time, forces the system to slow down in a way that is not intended. Hence new concepts for the sharing of resources need to be developed. The use of virtualization provides possibilities to handle the sharing of resources but always introduces an overhead in software in form of a hypervisor and also needs support on hardware level. In this contribution we explore the idea of using the FPGA fabric as intermediate hardware virtualization layer between the cores and existing peripherals in a heterogeneous multicore SoC. This paper applies the idea exemplarily to Controller Area Network (CAN) virtualization, including concept and evaluation. We show the transparency of a virtualization layer and its introduction with low overhead of area and latency, which might serve as efficient add-on in a virtualized environment.

1 Introduction

Modern embedded systems tend to hold more and more functionality in one single device. Especially applications where Size Weight and Power (SWaP) are limited and costs are crucial show a trend for consolidation of electronic components. Large scale software integration for example is one of the terms in automotive industry, referring to this trend. Key technology for this proceeding are (heterogeneous) multicores that have enough performance for high integration [12].

However, embedded multicore also means sharing resources like memory and peripherals. Systems with safety-critical functionality, such as in automotive or avionics, require segregation in space and time, which become a severe challenge, especially when talking about mixed-criticality. Embedded virtualization is seen as one of the promising solutions here, but also introduces overhead that might be unacceptable in embedded systems. Hardware support for virtualization helps to solve this problem.

© Springer International Publishing Switzerland 2016
V. Bonato et al. (Eds.): ARC 2016, LNCS 9625, pp. 273–286, 2016.
DOI: 10.1007/978-3-319-30481-6_22

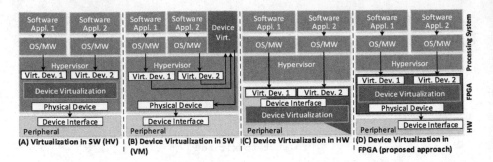

Fig. 1. Overview of device virtualization methods (Color figure online)

Within this context, we focus on the unique abilities of modern Xilinx Zynq FPGAs that provide a very tight coupling between a quite powerful ARM Cortex A9 Dual Core Processing System (PS) and a Programmable Logic (PL). We describe a novel approach that adds a hardware virtualization layer on top of existing hard coded peripherals (e.g. CAN controller) in a Zynq SoC. This way a very low virtualization overhead with a small amount of needed resources can be achieved. To the best of our knowledge this is the first work on device virtualization on the heterogeneous Zynq architecture, putting a reconfigurable hardware virtualization layer in between the hard coded peripheral and software running within the processing system.

The paper is structured as follows: In Sect. 2 we provide a brief summary on embedded virtualization and brief a short overview on work performed based on reconfigurable architectures. Section 3 explains the concept and is followed by a description of the implementation in Sect. 4. Experiments and results are presented in Sect. 5 and discussed in Sect. 6. The paper closes with the conclusion in Sect. 7.

2   State of the Art

2.1   Virtualization Technology

Virtualization technology helps to share resources like CPU, I/O components, memory or coprocessors between different isolated partitions, referred to as virtual machines. It can be more or less transparent for applications and drivers running inside the virtual machine. Although virtualization had its main focus in datacenter environments, the usage becomes more and more attractive also for the embedded domain [1,3]. As system integrators drive the consolidation of diverse functions, often with different requirements regarding performance, response time, and reliability, existing mechanisms for system-level virtualization within the server room are being adapted for use in mixed-critical embedded applications. A virtualization layer, which can be implemented purely in software or with the help of hardware support, does arbitration control and employs suitable scheduling with access policies to maintain the illusion of explicit hardware access to the virtual machines. Hereby the focus in traditional virtualization solutions lies on average-case performance and throughput while also enforcing access control and thus spatial separation of memory regions to improve the overall system stability. It therefore is a prerequisite for many virtualized systems in safety-related domains. Different approaches of peripheral virtualization are graphically shown in Fig. 1 and will be discussed in the following.

2.2 Related Work

Maximizing throughput and minimizing latency of peripheral virtualization are the key aspects for the performance of virtualized systems. Using device driver emulation is one technique for peripheral accesses as described in [14]. Device drivers inside the VMs can be left unmodified. Privileged instructions executed by these drivers are trapped by the hypervisor. The main disadvantage here is the cost of trapping and emulating as well as for the necessary context switches. Figure 1(A) illustrates this approach for device virtualization. The actual sharing of the accesses to the device is done inside the hypervisor, which can be an issue in terms of safety because of its increased code complexity.

To overcome the performance issue of device emulation, paravirtualization for devices was introduced, where a back-end driver resides inside the hypervisor (as shown in Fig. 1(A)) or a dedicated VM (Fig. 1(B)) and a modified front-end driver is used inside the VMs [10]. Therefore no traps are needed, so the virtualization overhead can be reduced. Because of the need for data copy and context switches, the overhead still runs up to 20 % assuming driver VM and application VM are executing on different cores as shown in [8]. For sharing CAN controllers in Integrated Modular Avionics by the use of paravirtualization, Kim et al. [7] showed an added latency of about 200 μs compared to a non-virtualized system. Using a dedicated VM for implementing device sharing, the hypervisor code can be slimmed down. An improved implementation of using a dedicated driver/proxy virtual machine for sharing GPU devices between virtual machines for automotive HMI applications is presented by Gansel et al. [2]. The approach focuses on safety requirements from the automotive domain and integrates efficient compositing strategies especially for automotive HMI systems.

To further reduce the virtualization overhead, self-virtualized devices were presented by Raj et al. [11]. By moving the virtualization layer in hardware close to the actual device, the achieved throughput could be doubled. This alternative is depicted in Fig. 1(C). With the help of direct device assignment, device accesses can be done without a hypervisor activation. This scenario is possible with peripherals implemented in hardware (illustrated as gray boxes in Fig. 1) or alternatively in an FPGA (green boxes).

In [4] a comparison of two different approaches for sharing a CAN controller between different virtual machines is presented. The first approach described in [13] uses paravirtualization similar to Fig. 1(B) on an AURIX multicore running at 200 MHz and introduces an overhead of about 35 μs for the virtualized CAN setup. The second approach presented in [5,6] is based on a self-virtualized CAN controller using SR-IOV for interfacing via PCI express to an Intel Core i7 host system running at 2.5 GHz and introduces an overhead of about 7 μs for the device virtualization. CAN controller and device virtualization are completely implemented in an FPGA as indicated in Fig. 1(C) by the green box style.

In [9] Pham et al. present an approach with a hypervisor for a hybrid ARM-FPGA architecture, supporting reconfigurable functions in hardware, another approach for FPGAs is presented in [15]. But both still introduce an overhead in software. A pure hardware virtualization on Zynq is practically not existing in literature. Especially none of the known approaches mixes hard coded components with FPGA-based virtualization support. Peripheral virtualization techniques in literature either use a pure software approach or add the hardware sharing support directly to the peripheral (implemented in FPGA or silicon).

3   Concept

The Zynq from Xilinx combines significant CPU computing power based on a dual core ARM Cortex A9 with several peripherals and a modern FPGA fabric in one single chip [16]. Unique for such architectures is the very tight coupling of a powerful Processing System (PS) and the Programmable Logic (PL), thus enabling a close interaction between both parts. While the Zynq does not provide hardware support for peripheral sharing, it allows for a very special approach of virtualization, which has to the very best of our knowledge, never been evaluated before. The fundamental idea is given in comparison to the other virtualization approaches (see Fig. 1(D)). We propose to use the hard coded SoC peripheral and add the virtualization support in the programmable logic (incl. handling of device sharing and virtual interfaces). This corresponds directly to shifting device sharing from software or hardware into some kind of intermediate layer implemented in the FPGA. This approach combines the flexibility of software virtualization (number of interfaces) with the performance of hardware virtualization.

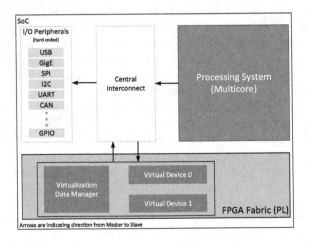

Fig. 2. Overview of the concept

An abstract mapping of this approach to the Zynq architecture is shown in Fig. 2. PS and hard coded peripherals of the SoC are used as follows. Any outgoing communication from the PS to the peripheral goes to the virtual device within the PL. The outgoing data packets are then scheduled according to a predefined priority of the corresponding virtual device and finally forwarded to the real peripheral by a virtual data manager (VDM). Incoming communication is fetched by the VDM, handled and put in the receive buffers of the virtual devices. Then the interrupt is assigned to the affected virtual machine. Finally, the data is handed to the virtual machine. As the virtual interfaces are similar to the real interface in their behavior as well as their structure, no modifications in the drivers of the virtualized system are needed, thus providing a full virtualization with transparency for the programmer.

However several drawbacks of this approach could arise. The rerouting of all communication to the PL corresponds to an address change in software but leads to additional communication on the internal infrastructure as well as handling time in the FPGA. Resource consumption in the programmable logic might also become an issue. These effects are investigated in detail in this paper.

4 Implementation

For the evaluation of the concept, a CAN controller is used for device virtualization because of its importance for many embedded applications as well as the ability to compare to related work. The CAN controller (compatible to the ISO11898-1, CAN 2.0A and CAN2.0B) is a Xilinx hard coded IP (marked in yellow in Fig. 3), which is internally connected to an advanced peripheral bus (APB). Different modes of operation are settable: amongst others, normal mode and loopback mode are available. In loopback mode, the *CAN Rx* and *CAN Tx* lines of the controller are connected, so that the sent messages are received directly. In order to transmit a message, the data has to be written into the TxFIFO of the controller. The hard coded controller itself takes care about sending the message without software interaction (comp. Xilinx Zynq Reference Manual [16]).

4.1 Basic Setup

The Virtual Devices and Virtual Data Manager are the basis of the implementation. The interconnection of the blocks is depicted in Fig. 3. First of all, the virtual interfaces, actually the AXI slave ports for communication with the processing system (PS), are connected to a master interface of the PS. Innately the PS, respective the central interconnect, provides two AXI master interfaces for slaves in the PL. The second connection of the virtual device (AXI slave to interface the VDM) is connected to the respective *virt* port according to the index of the interface at the VDM block as well as the VDM control interface. Additionally the interrupt signal of the CAN controller is connected to the virtual interface.

4.2   Virtual Device

The virtual device is the interface to the VM in the PS (compare Fig. 4(a)). This device is built up as AXI-slave to be accessible from the processing system. Addresses needed for registers and data are mapped into the address space of the SoC. Since many communication interfaces are equipped with FIFOs to receive and send messages, also the virtual interface must provide them. The AXI slave interface is the only visible interface of the virtual devices to the PS and hence the only one, which is addressed. Furthermore, the virtual interface is connected via another AXI-slave to the virtualization data manager. Via this connection, descriptors and data for the transfer are transmitted between the two blocks.

FIFOs: In order to achieve the virtualization of the CAN controller, only some parts of it have to be replicated. The CAN controller within the SoC uses FIFOs to send and receive messages. Especially the receive FIFO (RxFIFO) is replicated in the virtual device. This is necessary to buffer the received messages until they are collected by software. In the presented implementation the FIFO width, depth, and amount are configurable to achieve a better flexibility and adaptability for other interfaces than CAN. Messages that are received in the physical device are read from the physical RxFIFO and broadcast to the RxFIFOs of the virtual devices. Transmit FIFOs (TxFIFOs) are not replicated but buffered.

Buffer: In the case where the processing system intends to send a CAN message via the virtual device, it writes to its TxFIFOs. This buffer stores the CAN message and requests a data transfer from the buffer to the TxFIFOs of the physical interface. Hence, the data is transmitted to the physical CAN controller.

Interrupt Handling Logic: At arrival of a new message in the physical CAN controller, the new message interrupt is asserted. This interrupt is routed to the *AXI slave interface - VDM* in the PL. The *AXI slave interface - VDM* checks for running transmissions. When no transmission is active, the interrupt status register of the physical device is fetched and evaluated. In case of arrival of a new message the broadcast of the RxFIFO as described above is triggered. After a successful broadcast of the RxFIFO, the interrupt is cleared in the physical CAN controller. This is followed by the assertion of the interrupt in the virtual interface (in *AXI slave interface - PS*) to signal a new message to the PS.

Data Control Logic: This logic, generates the descriptors for the VDM, which are needed to provide the source, destination address and the amount of data. Furthermore, it is responsible for the assertion of a data transfer request.

Virtualization Data Manager: The Virtualization Data Manager (VDM) is depicted in Fig. 4(b). Integrated are a DMA controller, a bidirectional multiplexer and the amount of needed AXI burst interfaces. This modular design of the VDM allows for an easy and fast adaption of interfaces and virtual interface instances. The virtualization data manager provides several interfaces for communication with the rest of the SoC. It provides 2 AXI master interfaces for the source and destination bus of transfers and furthermore n AXI master

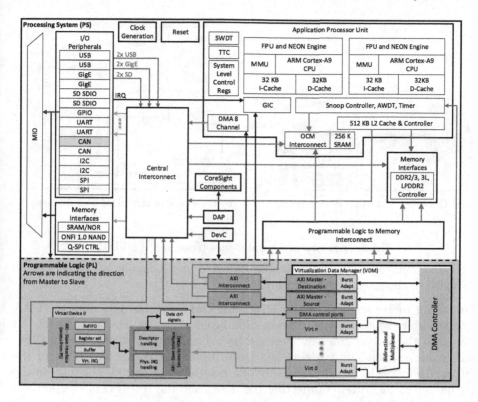

Fig. 3. Overview of the implementation (upper part comp. [16])

interfaces for the virtual devices, with n being the number of virtual devices. Furthermore, there are ports for the control of the VDM. To increase its performance, the DMA controller supports bursts and pipelining for memory accesses and addressing. In the presented implementation the DMA controller is responsible for the transfer of data from/to the physical device to/from the virtual interface.

4.3   Data Flow

Writing to the Physical Device via the Virtual Device: In the case of a write access to the virtual device, which means that data is written into the memory space of the virtual device, the data also has to be provided to the physical interface. This is done, using a simple DMA mechanism.

Reading from a Physical Device via the Virtual Device: In case of a register read, the register contents of the physical device are fetched via VDM and held in the register set of the virtual device. When trying to read the RxFIFOs from a virtualized device, the actual access is to the FIFOs within the virtual device. The replication of the read FIFOs is needed in order to isolate virtual devices from each other. Depending on the requirements and use case of the

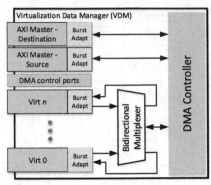

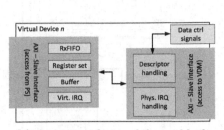

(a) Overview of virtual device block

(b) Overview of the VDM and its components

Fig. 4. Overview of virtual device block and the VDM

virtualization, the FIFO depth can be adjusted and incoming messages can be provided in the intended FIFOs only.

Handling of Interrupts of the Physical Device: Interrupts from the CAN Controller are routed to the virtualization layer. When an interrupt occurs and signalizes the arrival of a new message (new message flag is set), the RxFIFO has to be read and its contents has to be broadcast to the RxFIFOs of the virtual devices. The broadcast is only one possibility to provide the data in the virtual interfaces. After transferring the data from the RxFIFO of the physical device to the RxFIFOs of the virtual devices, the interrupt clear register has to be written, in order to regain the state of the physical interface. On the other hand, the new message flag of the virtual devices has to be asserted. Especially the interrupt handling must be done by only one instance of the virtual devices to avoid conflicts. This instance is declared as master instance at design time.

5   Evaluation

5.1   Measurement Setup

For the evaluation a bare metal software application is used to keep it simple and comprehensible. The use of an operating system would not lead to other results of the HW implementation. The dual core ARM Cortex A9 on the SoC is clocked at $ARM_{clk} = 666$ MHz. It has a private 32 Bit timer integrated within the core, which is fast accessible ($\sim$6 processor clock cycles, measured separately beyond this paper) and is running at $ARM_{clk}/2 = 333$ MHz. This timer is exclusively used for the measurements from software. The measured values are validated using the global timer of the SoC, which is not generally used due to its longer access times. The involved interconnects to access an AXI slave in the programmable logic, are beginning from the processing core via the snoop control unit (SCU) through the L-2 cache controller, both clocked at ARM_{clk}, to the slave interconnect that provides the AXI master interfaces, clocked at

$CPU_{2x} = 266\,\text{MHz}$. The programmable logic of the Zynq Z-7020 is clocked in our implementation at $FPGA_{clk} = 100\,\text{MHz}$. The used CAN controller is configured to a baudrate of 500 kBaud. The physical CAN controller (Can0) is compared with the virtualized controller (Virt0), which is the virtualized Can0, for the evaluation. Each measurement is executed 1000 times. The experiments are performed based on the code in Listing 1.1.

Listing 1.1. CAN message transmit-receive-loop sourcecode

```
//Check TxFIFO is full #1
 while (( Xil_In32(BaseAddr + 0x1C) & 0x400) != 0x0);
//Write TxFIFO #2
 Xil_Out32(BaseAddr + 0x30, TxFrame[0]);
 Xil_Out32(BaseAddr + 0x34, TxFrame[1]);
 Xil_Out32(BaseAddr + 0x38, TxFrame[2]);
 Xil_Out32(BaseAddr + 0x3C, TxFrame[3]);
//Check if RxFIFO is empty #3
 while (( Xil_In32(BaseAddr + 0x1C) & 0x80) == FALSE);
//Read RxFIFO #4
 RxFrame[0] = Xil_In32(BaseAddr + 0x50);
 RxFrame[1] = Xil_In32(BaseAddr + 0x54);
 RxFrame[2] = Xil_In32(BaseAddr + 0x58);
 RxFrame[3] = Xil_In32(BaseAddr + 0x5C);
//Clear pending interrupts #5
 Xil_Out32(BaseAddr + 0x24, ( Xil_In32(BaseAddr + 0x1C) & 0x80));
```

5.2   Measurement Scenarios

A complete transmit-receive-loop, which is built up of several software function calls, and the hardware realization are evaluated.

Register Read: A register read builds the basis of most of the following measurements, hence its duration is measured at first. For the physical as well as for the virtual device (ISR in PL) the interrupt status register (ISR) is read to achieve comparability. The access times for the physical device are in average at 49 cycles @ 333 MHz, compared to 64 cycles @ 333 MHz for the virtual device. The variation of the measured results are in both cases +/- 2 cycles.

TxFIFO Check (Listing 1.1: #1): As first step for the transmission of a CAN message the filling level of the TxFIFO of the CAN controller is read. Hence, a register read of the CAN controller's status registers is performed. The register access is implemented bare metal, to avoid overhead due to an operating system. In Fig. 5 the duration of the TxFIFO level readout of the hard coded controller (Can0) and via the virtual device (Virt0) is depicted. The mean value of this measurement for the physical device is 67 cycles @ 333 MHz and for the virtual device 83 cycles @ 333 MHz, resulting in an overhead of approx. 23 %.

Write Data to TxFIFO (Listing 1.1: #2): After checking the level of the TxFIFO, the second step to transmit a CAN message is to write the CAN frame into the TxFIFO. The frame is written by four 32 Bit write accesses to the

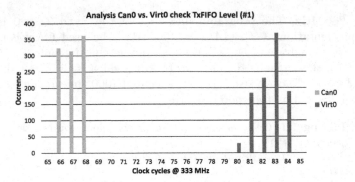

Fig. 5. TxFIFO full check

address of the CAN controller FIFO. These four accesses are blocked together as one measurement. The mean value to write the TxFIFO of the physical device is 405 cycles @ 333 MHz; the filling takes 501 cycles @ 333 MHz in case of the virtual device. The distribution of the measurement is shown in Fig. 6. The maximum deviation for the physical as well as for the virtual device is 63 cycles @ 333 MHz. The overhead for the virtual device is approx. 23 %.

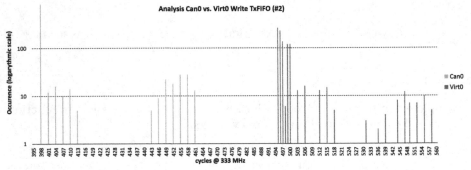

Fig. 6. Write TxFIFO

Wait for New Message in RxFIFO (Listing 1.1: #3): In the presented implementation the reception of new CAN messages is implemented using polling the new message flag in the interrupt status register. While the flag is not set, the processor stays in a while-loop. The time in which the processor stays in this loop is for the physical device 42911 cycles @ 333 MHz. On the other side, the overhead is 1 %, meaning that the wait time of the virtual device is 43378 cycles @ 333 MHz. This value differs depending on the CAN baud rate, because the message is transmitted on the CAN bus. The maximum deviation is 342 cycles for the physical device, respective 354 cycles for the virtual device.

Read Data from RxFIFO (Listing 1.1: #4): After the new message flag of the CAN controller is recognized, the data from the RxFIFO has to be fetched. The read of the message is handled in the same way as the transmission, meaning that four 32 Bit values are fetched from the RxFIFO. The results are depicted

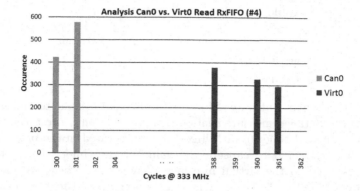

Fig. 7. Read RxFIFO

in Fig. 7. The maximum deviation of the measurement of the physical device is 1 cycle @ 333 MHz while the deviation of the virtual device is 3 cycles @ 333 MHz. The overhead for the RxFIFO readout is at 20 %.

Clear New Message Flag in ISR Register (Listing 1.1: #5): After fetching the message from the RxFIFO of the CAN controller, the new message flag in the ISR has to be cleared. This is done by setting a Bit in the ISR. To estimate the overhead for clearing the ISR also this time is measured. The result is depicted in Fig. 7. The overhead of the hardware solution is at 33 %, the variation in case of the physical device is at 0 cycles, in the virtualized case 5 cycles @ 333 MHz.

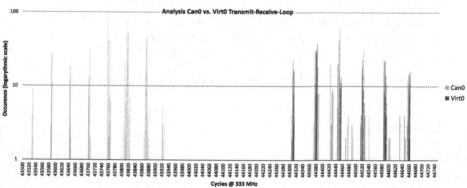

Fig. 8. CAN message transmit-receive-loop

CAN Message Receive-Transmit-Loop: To validate the partial measurements, the complete loop is also measured. The results show that the difference to the calculated value is less than 1 %. The results are shown in Fig. 8. The variation in the non-virtualized and the virtualized case show only a difference of 2 cycles @ 333 MHz, the absolute value is 410 cycles. For the complete loop the overhead of the virtualized solution is only 1.64 %.

Table 1. Evaluation of hardware latency

	Cycles@100 MHz	μs	Variation
Transmit msg	30	0,30	0
Receive msg	125	1,25	1

Detailed Hardware Latency Measurement: Additional to the measurements from PS, detailed measurements of hardware latency are taken. For this measurement an AXI-timer from Xilinx [17] is integrated in the programmable logic, which is triggered to capture the value of the timer when a transmit request is asserted to the virtual interface. When the message is sent to the physical device's TxFIFO, the timer is stopped. The AXI-timer is clocked with $AXI_{clk} = 100$ MHz. For the reception of a message, the timer captures the value, when the new message interrupt of the physical device is signaled. The timer is stopped, when the virtual device signals an interrupt to the PS. The results of the transmit and receive latency are shown in Table 1. There, the amount of cycles @ 100 MHz, the time in μs and the variation are presented for either way.

Resource Utilization: The needed logic in the PL per component is presented in Table 2. Depending on the number of virtual devices, the appropriate hardware utilization of the virtual device has to be multiplied, whilst the VDM (incl. DMA, 10 AXI Burst Interfaces, MUX) stays constant up to 8 virtual devices.

Table 2. Logic resource utilization per component

Resource type	LUT	FLOP-LATCH	DMEM
Zynq7020 available	53200 (100 %)	106400 (100 %)	17400 (100 %)
VDM (incl. DMA)	12516 (~23 %)	4279 (~4 %)	–
DMA	3912 (~7 %)	1953 (<1 %)	–
Virtual device	1893 (~%)	1493 (<1 %)	192 (~1 %)

6 Discussion

The results demonstrate a low overhead for the introduced virtualization solution on a heterogeneous SoC. The latency, which is introduced due to the additional layer is low, meaning that the timing overhead compared to the physical device for a complete transmit-receive-loop of a CAN message is only 1.64 %. When taking the results of [5, 6, 13] as references, the presented approach reduces the latency by far. To rate the results in a correct manner, the clock frequencies, processor architectures, and evaluation setups have to be respected, but even compared to the high performance setup, used in [6], the latency is further improved on a slower and less performing processor architecture. Furthermore the presented approach is fully transparent for software, hence already existing code can be reused. For transmission and reception of a CAN message, the additionally introduced latency of 0.34 μs respective 0.30 μs are by far within a tolerable range for a CAN controller. Regarding the pure hardware latency, the approach is not limited to CAN. Depending on the needed data throughput for other peripherals, further evaluations need to be done, but the concept is re-usable.

7   Conclusion

The work presented in this paper targets the hardware support for virtualization in heterogeneous multicore architectures that include an FPGA. We show the feasibility of using the FPGA fabric as intermediate hardware virtualization layer between cores and existing peripherals in the Zynq from Xilinx. The innovation in the concept relies on the implementation of a hardware virtualization layer in a programmable fabric. Existing peripherals in the SoC can be virtualized without introducing a software overhead. The concept is implemented and evaluated exemplary for a CAN controller. The results show an improvement in terms of latency, compared to other approaches in literature. Here we focus on a detailed evaluation on the hardware overhead. The detailed inspection of the software based virtualization solutions (e.g. from Sysgo and OpenSynergy) and a detailed comparison will be the next step in our research.

Acknowledgment. This work was funded within the project ARAMiS by the German Federal Ministry for Education and Research with the funding IDs 01IS11035. The responsibility for the content remains with the authors.

References

1. Aguiar, A., Hessel, F.: Embedded systems' virtualization: the next challenge? In: 21st IEEE International Symposium on Rapid System Prototyping, pp. 1–7, June 2010
2. Gansel, S., Schnitzer, S., Dürr, F., Rothermel, K., Maihöfer, C.: Towards virtualization concepts for novel automotive HMI systems. In: Schirner, G., Götz, M., Rettberg, A., Zanella, M.C., Rammig, F.J. (eds.) IESS 2013. IFIP AICT, vol. 403, pp. 193–204. Springer, Heidelberg (2013)
3. Heiser, G.: The role of virtualization in embedded systems. In: Proceedings of 1st Workshop on Isolation and Integration in Embedded Systems. ACM (2008)
4. Herber, C., Reinhardt, D., Richter, A., Herkersdorf, A.: HW/SW trade-offs in I/O virtualization for controller area network
5. Herber, C., Richter, A., Rauchfuss, H., Herkersdorf, A.: Self-virtualized CAN controller for multi-core processors in real-time applications. In: Kubátová, H., Hochberger, C., Daněk, M., Sick, B. (eds.) ARCS 2013. LNCS, vol. 7767, pp. 244–255. Springer, Heidelberg (2013)
6. Herber, C., Richter, A., Rauchfuss, H., Herkersdorf, A.: Spatial and temporal isolation of virtual can controllers. SIGBED Rev. 11(2), 19–26 (2014)
7. Kim, J., Lee, S., Jin, H.: Fieldbus virtualization for integrated modular avionics. In: IEEE 16th Conference on Emerging Technologies & Factory Automation (ETFA) (2011)

8. Menon, A., Santos, J.R., Turner, Y., Janakiraman, G.J., Zwaenepoel, W.: Diagnosing performance overheads in the xen virtual machine environment. In: Proceedings of the 1st ACM/USENIX International Conference on Virtual Execution Environments (2005)

9. Pham, K.D., Jain, A., Cui, J., Fahmy, S., Maskell, D.: Microkernel hypervisor for a hybrid arm-FPGA platform. In: Application-Specific Systems, Architectures and Processors (ASAP) (2013)

10. Pratt, I., Fraser, K., Hand, S., Limpach, C., Warfield, A., Magenheimer, D., Nakajima, J., Mallick, A.: Xen 3.0 and the art of virtualization. In: Proceedings of the 2005 Ottawa Linux Symposium, July 2005

11. Raj, H., Schwan, K.: High performance and scalable I/O virtualization via self-virtualized devices. In: Proceedings of the 16th International Symposium on High Performance Distributed Computing, HPDC 2007, New York, NY, USA (2007)

12. Reinhardt, D., Adam, D., Luebbers, E., Amarnath, R., Schneider, R., Gansel, S., Schnitzer, S., Herber, C., Sandmann, T., Michel, H.U., Kaule, D., Olkun, D., Rehm, M., Harnisch, J., Richter, A., Baehr, S., Sander, O., Becker, J., Baumgarten, U., Theiling, H.: Embedded virtualization approaches for ensuring safety and security within e/e automotive systems. In: Embedded World Conference (2015)

13. Reinhardt, D., Güntner, M., Obermeir, S.: Virtualized communication controllers in safety-related automotive embedded systems. In: Pinho, L.M.P., Karl, W., Cohen, A., Brinkschulte, U. (eds.) ARCS 2015. LNCS, vol. 9017, pp. 173–185. Springer, Heidelberg (2015)

14. Sugerman, J., Venkitachalam, G., Lim, B.H.: Virtualizing I/O devices on vmware workstation's hosted virtual machine monitor. In: Proceedings of the General Track: USENIX Annual Technical Conference (2001)

15. Vuletic, M., Righetti, L., Pozzi, L., Ienne, P.: Operating system support for interface virtualisation of reconfigurable coprocessors. In: Proceedings of the Design, Automation and Test in Europe Conference and Exhibition (2004)

16. Xilinx: Zynq-7000 All Programmable SoC, technical Reference Manual (2013)

17. Xilinx: LogiCORE IP AXI Timer v2.0, product Guide (2014)

Zynq Cluster for CFD Parametric Survey

Naru Sugimoto[1]([✉]), Takaaki Miyajima[2], Ryotaro Sakai[1], Yasunori Osana[3],
Naoyuki Fujita[2], and Hideharu Amano[1]

[1] Keio University, Yokohama 223-8522, Japan
cfd@am.ics.keio.ac.jp
[2] Japan Aerospace Exploration Agency, Tokyo 182-8522, Japan
[3] University of the Ryukyus, Okinawa 903-0213, Japan

Abstract. Fast Aerodynamics Routines (FaSTAR) is a state of the art
Computational Fluid Dynamics (CFD) software package to enable high
precise analysis. Due to its complicated data structure from unstructured grid, the acceleration with GPU or massively parallel machines is
not efficient. Although a hardware accelerator on an FPGA is a hopeful
candidate, the complicated FaSTAR program is difficult to pick up time
consuming cores and implement them on an FPGA. In practical aircraft
design, a parametric survey, which executes FaSTAR jobs in parallel with
different conditions is commonly used. Here, we propose a Zynq cluster
as a cost and power efficient solution of FaSTAR parametric survey. By
introducing high-level synthesis and partial reconfiguration, the FaSTAR
job with a specific condition runs on a simple node with a Zynq-7000 AP
SoC. Now a part of FaSTAR job can be executed on FPGA of Zynq board
about 1.3 times faster than Intel's Xeon E5-2667 2.9 GHz software.

1 Introduction

Computational Fluid Dynamics (CFD) has been developed for designing wings
or body of airplanes without frequent wind tunnel experiments. Fast Aerodynamics Routines (FaSTAR) is a CFD software package developed by JAXA [1].
Unstructured mesh is used for highly accurate analysis of complicated target
structures. Several solvers can be selected by the requirements of the designer.
Since its unstructured data structure and complicated control flow are not suitable for General Purpose computing on Graphics Processing Units (GPGPU),
hardware acceleration with FPGAs has been investigated [2,3]. Although they
were successful to improve the performance of a certain part of the software, the
data communication and control of the accelerator on the FPGA have not been
well designed. Considering the cost and performance overhead for connecting an
FPGA accelerator into a powerful host PC, advantages as a cost-power efficient
solution would be degraded.

Recently, a cost efficient board which provides an embedded CPU, a middle-
scale FPGA and DDR SDRAM is available. Zynq-7000 All Programmable System on Chip (Zynq) is a representative example. Unlike the system in which a
powerful FPGA board is connected to the host PC with PCIe, the embedded

© Springer International Publishing Switzerland 2016
V. Bonato et al. (Eds.): ARC 2016, LNCS 9625, pp. 287–299, 2016.
DOI: 10.1007/978-3-319-30481-6_23

CPU and the FPGA are tightly connected and efficient off-loading is done with SW/HW co-synthesis design. From the practical viewpoint, a parametric survey which run a large number of simulation with different parameters or solvers is commonly used in the early stage of the analysis. If a FaSTAR program can work on a such platform in the stand-alone manner, we can build a cost-power efficient cluster by using a large number of platforms as nodes of the cluster. Even if the performance of each node is not so high, cost-power efficient supercomputing environment can be built by increasing the number of nodes. Only solvers used in the specific analysis are quickly selected by using the partial reconfiguration.

The main contribution of this paper is as follows: (1) The trial to work a practical scientific software package on Zynq board with a combination of an embedded CPU and an FPGA is reported. Although Zynq board has been used various kinds of application, it has been believed not to be suitable for a practical scientific software. This research shows the possibility for parametric survey of the CFD application. (2) The total architecture for off-loading a part of large software package on Zynq board with partial reconfiguration is proposed. The efficient use of DDR SDRAMs and internal buses are keys of the design. (3) The experimental results of the wing analysis on Zynq board is reported from the viewpoint of performance, resource usage and power consumption.

2   Zynq Cluster

2.1   Zynq Cluster for Parametric Survey

Although Zynq board has been used for various applications, it has not been used for practical scientific computation because of the performance gap. A combination of a high performance CPU and powerful FPGA or GPU can achieve much more floating point computation performance than that of Zynq board with an embedded CPU and a middle-scale FPGA. However, the combination of CPU and powerful FPGA board with PCIe is not often an efficient solution because of the overhead for data communication and poor programming environment. This is the main reason why FPGA board is not popularly used compared to GPU as an accelerator. An FPGA accelerator can only survive in scientific application when the target application has a complicated data structure and control flow which cannot be treated efficiently by the SIMD manner. For such a target, Zynq board can be more advantageous than the combination of a powerful FPGA board connected to a powerful host PC, from the following reasons: (1) Since the FPGA is tightly connected to an embedded CPU, the communication overhead between them can be easily hidden or optimized. (2) Compared to sharing the host PC memory through PCIe, on-board DDR SDRAM modules which can be shared by the CPU and the acceleration logic can be efficiently used in off-loading. (3) A programming environment provided for Zynq is more convenient than that for the FPGA connected to the host PC, and the operating system on the embedded processor can control acceleration logic much more easily. In order to make the use of these advantages, we focus on a parametric survey of the practical software package FaSTAR.

In a Zynq cluster proposed here, each node is consisting of a Zynq board or simpler node with ARM Cortex CPU, an FPGA, DDR SDRAM modules, SD card and a simple Ether network. For parametric survey, various combinations of solvers and parameters are used. For quickly configuring off-loading part, partial reconfiguration is used. For example, when a job uses solver A and B in different part of the process, they are implemented on independent partial reconfiguration domain. Other nodes can use different combinations, so various combination can be implemented on each node. Linux operating system is working on the ARM CPU, and the grid data to be computed and parameter file are downloaded through Ethernet and stored into SD card under the control of the OS. The job starts after configuration data are loaded into FPGA, and the results are also transferred to the host. Since all nodes can work in the stand-alone mode, a board can take the role of the host processor and job scheduling for parametric survey.

In the current art of the technology, the performance of the board is much lower than that of the high-performance PC. However, the cost and power consumption can be potentially much better when simpler boards than Zynq are used in future.

2.2 Related Work

Accelerators with FPGAs have been researched for CFD applications. The implementation by Andres et al. [4] and the systolic architecture approach by Sano [5] achieved better performance compared to powerful multi-core CPUs. However, their implementations are not for practical software packages. Sofian and his colleagues tried to implement a part of FaSTAR but his acceleration has not integrated into the total FaSTAR processing. Our previous trial [2] only focuses on the out of order execution required in unstructured mesh. Zedwulf [6] also aims cost/power efficient cluster, but their target is graph analysis and not for the scientific computation.

3 FaSTAR and Our Off-Load Plan

FaSTAR is a CFD software package developed by JAXA to simulate compressible flow using unstructured grids [1]. Its source code is written in Fortran 90 with module structure considering the maintenance and extension. By choosing certain solvers, users can select various solutions supported by the application and run simulation in parallel with their systems without specific software tuning. Users are just requested to prepare a parameter file and a grid data file before the simulation.

3.1 FaSTAR Overall

FaSTAR uses Navier-Stokes's equation as fundamental equations, which is represented as follows:

$$\frac{\partial}{\partial t} \int_V \mathbf{Q} \cdot dv + \int_S [\mathbf{F}(\mathbf{Q}) - \frac{1}{Re}\mathbf{F_v}(\mathbf{Q})] \cdot \mathbf{ds} = 0 \qquad (1)$$

where $\mathbf{Q}$ is a conserved quantity vector, $\mathbf{F}$ is inviscid vector. $\mathbf{F_v}$ is a viscosity vector, Re is Reynolds number and $\mathbf{ds}$ is an outside vertical vector whose absolute value corresponds to the area. The steps to solve the equation is presented in Fig. 1.

It adopts the cell center of the finite volume method for the space discretization method represented as the following expression:

$$\int_S \mathbf{F}(\mathbf{Q}) \cdot \mathbf{ds} = \sum_{kmax} [\mathbf{F}_k(\mathbf{Q}) \cdot \mathbf{ds}_k] \qquad (2)$$

Here, it is represented as the sum of flow rate of vertical direction in each surface by its area. k shows the number of surface in a cell.

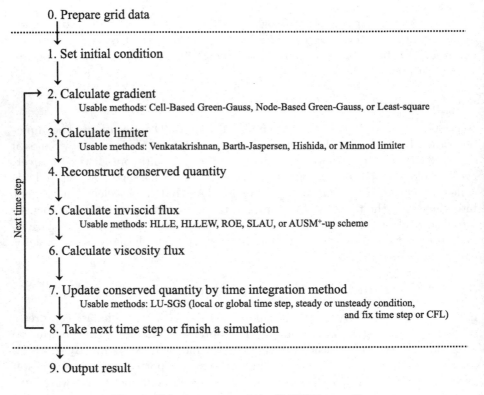

Fig. 1. Calculate steps of the FaSTAR overall.

3.2   Target Subroutine "Advection Term"

Here, as the first step of acceleration, Advection term is adopted as a target of off-loading. Advection term is a subroutine for reconstructing conserved quantity

Q and computing inviscid flow rate **F** in the Eq. 1. It occupies about 25 % of the total execution time of FaSTAR. This part is corresponding to step 4 and 5 in Fig. 1. There are several algorithms to compute **F** and the system can use only required one by using the partial reconfiguration.

3.3 Steps of Advection Term

Advection term is consisting of Pre-Advection, Flux-Calculation and Post-Advection. (1) Pre-Advection fetches data used in the following steps and reconstructs conserved quantity, and (2) Flux-Calculation computes inviscid flow rate at cell boundaries. In FaSTAR, five solvers HLLE, HLLEW, ROE, SLAU, and AUSM+-up can be selected [7]. It is specified in the parameter file before execution. (3) Post-Advection computes surface integration represented in Expression 2. Here, a frequent Read After Write (RAW) hazard is caused in the pipeline because of the irregular memory access.

Considering these features, here, Pre-Advection and Flux-Calculation are implemented by Vivado HLS as hardware modules. Since Post-Advection suffers frequent RAW hazard, it is executed with the software in Zynq CPU. That is, the fluid rate in the cell surface is computed in FPGA and the surface integration is executed with the Zynq CPU software. Five solvers are implemented with the partial reconfiguration as shown later.

Sofian and his colleagues tried to off-load three solvers of Advection term by using the partial reconfiguration in an FPGA [3]. However, his implementation is only for hardware design of each solver without input/output mechanisms nor communication of the host processor. The implemented functions have not been embedded into total execution of FaSTAR software. In this paper, five solvers are fully implemented and work cooperated with the software as a part of the whole FaSTAR execution.

4 Implementation

4.1 System Overview

The overview of the proposed cluster is shown as Fig. 2. It is an Ethernet connected simple cluster whose node is consisting of Zynq. Since it executes different jobs with different parameters and solvers, no data communication are needed between nodes. Grid data and parameter files are distributed before computation and stored in the SD card attached to a node. Linux running on the CPU in Zynq controls the distribution of grid data and parameter files, starts jobs and returns the results to the host.

4.2 Hardware of Each Node

As a node of the cluster, Xilinx ZC706 board is adopted. As shown in Fig. 3, the node structure is consisting of Processing System (PS), Programmable Logic (PL), two 1 GB-DDR SDRAM modules, and an SD card.

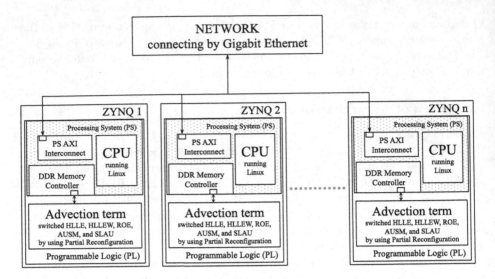

Fig. 2. Cluster overview.

In the PS, APU using ARM Cortex-A9 on which Linux is operating, executes the processing which is not off-loaded to the PL. Data transfer to the PL, and controls partial reconfiguration for processing of Advection term are also managed with APU. Also, through GbE, it receives/sends the parameter file, grid data and result file between host node.

In order to off-load a core of scientific computation, tightly connection between the hardwired logic, DDR SDRAM which stores the data and APU is needed. In the cluster node, they are connected standard bus and interface supported by Xilinx.

The PL is consisting of the off-load logic, AXI Central Direct Memory Access (CDMA), DATA stream-in controller, DATA stream-out controller, AXI Interconnects and the Memory Interface Generator (MIG) core. Here, Advection term is implemented as the off-load logic. All of modules are generated with IP core generator and Vivado HLS, and adopted 64 bit AXI/AXI stream Interface. Although some cores are connected with the PS through the AXI Lite Interface for control, they are omitted in Fig. 3.

AXI CDMA is an IP core supported by Xilinx for controlling data transfer between DDR SDRAMs. The data transfer control is done from the APU through the AXI Lite Interface. Data stream-in controller and Data stream-out controller manage the data input and output to/from Advection term core. MIG core, a DDR SDRAM controller is wrapped with AXI interface and data access with the AIX protocol is done.

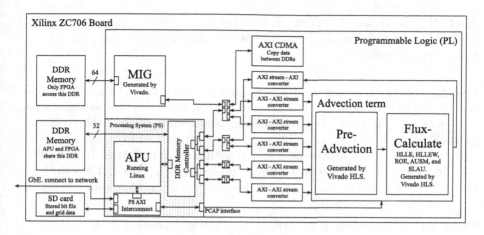

Fig. 3. Structure of each node.

4.3 Advection Term Core

As described in Sect. 3.3, we implemented Pre-Advection and Flux-Calculation by the hardware. Figure 3 also shows the structure of Advection term core. Flux-Calculation core switches five circuits: HLLE, HLLEW, ROE, SLAU and AUSM+-up, and the configuration data for reconfiguration are transferred through PCAP from the PS.

Implementation with Vivado HLS. Pre-Advection and Flux-Calculation including five solvers are designed with Vivado HLS. All of them are implemented as follows: (1) Fortran source code was manually translated into C, since Vivado HLS never accepts Fortran. (2) Parameters for each analysis, for example ratio of specific heat γ must be given from the CPU. They are implemented as arguments of the top level function. This re-structuring of the program was also done manually. (3) Input data depending on the boundary surface are inserted with AXI stream protocol. The input array must be also an argument of the top level function. After using the array data from the index 0 in order, then the array of indexes is specified to AXI stream protocol by using Pragma in Vivado. (4) The calculation results are outputted with AXI stream protocol also by using indexes of the array. (5) Finally, pipeline structure is specified for high speed execution.

4.4 Software Control

Data Transfer. A large data transfer between PS-PL is done with the PS side DDR SDRAM. 512 MB of the PS side DDR SDRAM is under the management of Linux, while remaining 512 MB is the area where the PL can access freely. By using "mmap" system call, the PL side memory area is mapped into the Linux virtual memory address which can be accessed by the PS. The problem is that

FaSTAR is described in Fortran and cannot use "mmap" system call directly. Thus, only the part including "mmap" is described in C language and called by the Fortran program.

Overlap Data Transfer and Calculation. Since the memory access pattern in FaSTAR is complicated, data must be aligned when they are transferred into the advection term module as a form of stream data. In order to efficient off-loading, the data copy from Linux memory region to FPGA memory region with data alignment must be overlapped with the computation. In this implementation, the time for the data copy is hidden by using parallel description of OpenMP for parallel execution of data copy and computation with two cores.

Partial Reconfiguration Control. The partial reconfiguration is controlled by the software using Linux xdevcfg device driver supported by Xilinx. The implementation was done according to the application note XAPP1159 [8]. The pseudo code of the software is shown as follows.

List 1.1. Software code for partial reconfiguration.

```
1  fd = open("/sys/.../is_partial_bitstream");
2  fd_devcfg = open("/dev/xdevcfg");
3  write(fd, "1", 2);
4  if (scheme == hlle)
5      fd_pr = open("/mnt/hlle_partial.bin");
6  fstat(fd_pr, &fs);
7  pr_bit = (char*)mmap(fs.st_size, fd_pr);
8  write(fd_devcfg, pr_bit, fs.st_size);
```

Partial reconfiguration is executed by setting is_partial_bitstream to '1' in /sys, then, sending the bitstream into /dev/xdevcfg. "mmap" system call is used again for mapping the bitstream on Linux virtual memory address. The function described in C is also called by Fortran for this purpose.

5   Experimental Result

The specification of the system introduced in Sect. 4 is summarized in Table 1.

5.1   Utilization Result

The resource usage of each solver: HLLE, HLLEW, ROE, SLAU and AUSM+-up, PBLOCK reserved for the partial reconfiguration, and the total utilization of our design are shown in Table 2. ROE requires the largest resources, and uses about 20 % of Slices and DSPs of ZC706. It is corresponding to 65 % of total resource in PBLOCK. Although five target circuits never use the Block RAM, PBLOCK must include Block RAM for keeping continuous area of the chip. It wastes about 30 % of block RAM in ZC706.

Table 1. Evaluation environment.

Zynq device	Board	Xilinx ZC706 (xc7z045ffg900-2)
	FPGA	Kintex7 150 MHz
	CPU	ARM CortexA9 800 MHz
	OS	Linaro Linux 12.09
	Compiler	GNU Fortran 4.6.3 added -O3 and -fopenmp option
Comparison	CPU	Intel Xeon E5-2667 2.9 GHz
	Memory	128 GB DDR3 1600 MHz
	OS	CentOS 6.5
	Compiler	GNU Fortran 4.8.2 added -O3 option

Table 2. Resource utilization of flux calculation part and overall.

	Slice LUTs ratio for		Slice registers ratio for		36 kb block RAM ratio for		DSPs ratio for	
	PBLOCK	ZC706	PBLOCK	ZC706	PBLOCK	ZC706	PBLOCK	ZC706
HLLE	33.9 %	10.0 %	23.2 %	6.9 %	0.0 %	0.0 %	36.8 %	11.4 %
HLLEW	44.4 %	13.2 %	28.1 %	8.3 %	0.0 %	0.0 %	47.9 %	14.9 %
ROE	50.2 %	14.9 %	33.2 %	9.8 %	0.0 %	0.0 %	63.6 %	19.8 %
SLAU	33.7 %	10.0 %	24.0 %	7.1 %	0.0 %	0.0 %	37.9 %	11.8 %
AUSM+-up	40.3 %	12.0 %	26.4 %	7.8 %	0.0 %	0.0 %	45.7 %	14.2 %
PBLOCK	100.0 %	29.6 %	100.0 %	29.6 %	100.0 %	25.7 %	100.0 %	31.1 %
TOTAL	-	40.6 %	-	55.9 %	-	37.6 %	-	40.1 %
ZC706(xc7z045)	-	100.0 %	-	100.0 %	-	100.0 %	-	100.0 %

In summary, about 45 % slice registers are unused and more resources are remained in other modules. Thus, the remaining area for off-loading other solvers than Advection term is enough.

Figure 4 shows the resources with and without the partial reconfiguration. This table shows that all resources are reduced by using the partial reconfiguration. Especially, the usage of DSP is reduced to less than 50 %.

5.2   About Execution Time

Here the analysis time of "NACA0012" was evaluated. "NACA0012" is a type of wing defined by National Advisory Committee for Aeronautics (NACA). The grid data used is 11,564 cells providing 22,882 boundary surfaces between cells and 23,620 boundary surfaces.

Estimate Advection Term Computation Time. The total clock cycles to compute inviscid flux of all neighboring surfaces and boundary surfaces are calculated by the following expressions.

$$\text{Clock Cycle} = L_{\text{Pre−Advection}} + L_{\text{Flux−Calculation}} + I \times (N_{\text{face}} + N_{\text{bd−face}}) \quad (3)$$

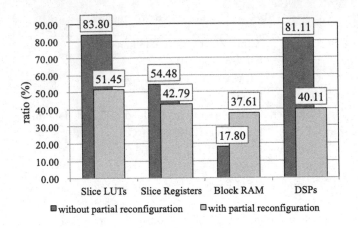

Fig. 4. Resources usage with and without partial reconfiguration.

Table 3. Latency and interval of Vivado HLS circuits.

	Latency	Interval
Pre-Advection	147-cycle	15-cycle
HLLE	478-cycle	15-cycle
HLLEW	645-cycle	15-cycle
ROE	542-cycle	15-cycle
SLAU	373-cycle	15-cycle
AUSM+-up	660-cycle	15-cycle

where $L_{\mathrm{Pre-Advection}}$ is Latency of Pre-Advection, $L_{\mathrm{Flux-Calculation}}$ is Flux-Calculation Latency. I represents Interval. N_{face} is the number of neighboring surfaces and $N_{\mathrm{bd-face}}$ shows boundary surfaces. Table 3 shows the interval and latency of the implemented computing circuits. In the case of HLLEW, $147 + 645 + 15 \times (22,882 + 23,620) = 698,322$ cycles are required. Since the operational frequency is 150 MHz, the computation requires about 4.7 ms.

Execution Time of Advection Term Computation. Figure 5 shows the measurement results of computation time for Advection term. For HLLEW, it was about 1.3 times faster than that by Intel Xeon E5-2667 software. Although it was faster than the software execution, the different was not so large as expected. It was caused by the bandwidth limitation of the PS side DDR SDRAM. The maximum bandwidth of the PS side DDR SDRAM is 4 byte $\times$ 533 MHz $\times$ 2 = 4,264 MB/s. On the other hand, Pre-Advection requires 8 byte $\times$ 150 MHz $\times$ 4 = 4,800 MB/s data reading ratio. The results of Flux-Calculation are required to be stored simultaneously, and the requirement for the PS side DDR SRAM is further increased. The bi-directional access of the PS side DDR SDRAM also degrades the performance.

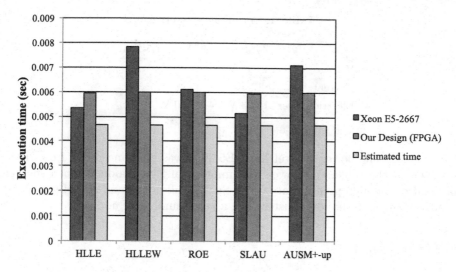

Fig. 5. Computation time of Advection term.

Total Execution Time. When HLLEW is selected as a solver of Flux-Calculation, the ARM core on Zynq node executes the total analysis with 369.50 s. By off-loading Advection term part onto the hardwired logic in the partial reconfiguration domain, it was improved to 325.57 s. It shows that the current off-loading works efficiently. By off-loading other parts of FaSTAR, further performance improvement can be expected. However, compared to a high performance CPU node, the performance is not enough; Xeon E5-2667 executed it in 29.67 s. Since our challenge is building a cost-and-power efficient cluster node for scientific computation with an embedded CPU and an FPGA, the performance of a single node performance would be difficult to overcome that of the high-performance CPU node. Nevertheless, the current difference must be reduced by further off-loading.

Time for Partial Reconfiguration. The size of bitstream for reconfigurable module is depending on the size of PBLOCK. Here, the bitstream for the total system is 106 Mb and bitstream for the partial reconfiguration is 30 Mb. Since the bandwidth of Zynq PCAP interface was 400 MB/s, the time for partial reconfiguration becomes: $30\,\mathrm{Mb} \div 8 \div 400\,\mathrm{MB/s} \approx 9.4\,\mathrm{ms}$. Usually, it does not influence the total execution time.

5.3   Consuming Power

We measured the power of Zynq node in operation and compared with Intel Xeon E5-2667. The result of measurement is shown in Table 4. The current and supply voltage were measured with multi-meter KEYSIGHT 34410A and MASTECH MAS-344. The supply voltage was measured at the power connection point of

Table 4. Consuming power.

	Zynq cluster	Xeon E5-2667
Voltage	11.45 V	-
Current	1.042 A	-
Electric power	11.93 W	130 W

ZC706 board. The power of Intel Xeon E5-2667 was announced one from Intel. As shown in the table, the power consumption of Zynq node is much smaller than that of the high performance CPU. Such small power and size of the board are advantageous to build a cluster with a large number of nodes.

6   Conclusion

A cost/power efficient scientific cluster for parametric survey for aerodynamics analysis is presented. A node is consisting of an embedded CPU/FPGA, DDR SDRAM and Ethernet. Although a middle scale FPGA is used, required solvers are off-loaded by using the partial reconfiguration. Here, Zynq is used as a node, and stand-alone execution mechanism with standard buses and DDR SDRAM modules is built. Linux running on each CPU can manage the setting for the parametric survey. Implementation for FaSTAR, a software package for aerodynamics simulation appears that the off-loaded part of Advection term runs 1.3 times faster than that of Intel Xeon E5-2667 with about 1/11 of power consumption.

However, in the current implementation, the total execution time of FaSTAR is more than 10 times. Since we focused on building the framework to off-load various functions using partial reconfiguration and Vivado programming environment, only Advection term was implemented. Other parts of FaSTAR will be off-loaded by using the established framework.

References

1. Hashimoto, A., Murakami, K., Aoyama, T., Hishida, M., Paulus R.L., Sakashita, M., Sato, Y.: Development of fast flow solver FaSTAR. In: Proceedings of 42nd Fluid Dynamics Conference/Aerospace Numerical Simulation Symposium (2010)
2. Akamine, T., Inakagata, K., Osana, Y., Fujita, N., Amano, H.: Reconfigurable out-of-order mechanism generator for unstructured grid computation in computational fluid dynamics. In: 22nd International Conference on Field Programmable Logic and Applications (FPL 2012), pp. 136–142, August 2012
3. Talip, M., Akamine, T., Hatto, M., Osana, Y., Fujita, N., Amano, H.: Partially reconfigurable flux calculation scheme in advection term computation. In: International Conference on Field-Programmable Technology, ICFPT 2013, pp. 382–385, December 2013

4. Andres, E., Molina, M., Botella, G., del Barrio, A., Mendias, J.: Aerodynamics analysis acceleration through reconfigurable hardware. In: 4th Southern Conference on Programmable Logic, 2008, pp. 105–110, March 2008
5. Sano, K., Iizuka, T., Yamamoto, S.: Systolic architecture for computational fluid dynamics on FPGAs. In: 15th Annual IEEE Symposium on Field-Programmable Custom Computing Machines, FCCM 2007, pp. 107–116, April 2007
6. Moorthy, P., Kapre, N.: Zedwulf: power-performance tradeoffs of a 32-node zynq soc cluster. In: IEEE 23rd Annual International Symposium on Field-Programmable Custom Computing Machines (FCCM 2015), pp. 68–75, May 2015
7. Einfeldt, B.: On Godunov-type methods for gas dynamics. SIAM J. Numer. Anal. **25**(2), 294–318 (1988)
8. Kohn, C.: Partial reconfiguration of a hardware accelerator on zynq-7000 all programmable soc devices. http://www.xilinx.com/support/documentation/ application_notes/xapp1159-partial-reconfig-hw-accelerator-zynq-7000.pdf

Invited Paper on Funded RD Running and Completed Projects Posters

Fast and Resource Aware Image Processing Operators Utilizing Highly Configurable IP Blocks

Konrad Häublein[✉], Christian Hartmann, Marc Reichenbach,
and Dietmar Fey

Department Computer Science, Chair of Computer Architecture,
Friedrich-Alexander-University Erlangen-Nürnberg, Erlangen, Germany
{konrad.haeublein,christian.hartmann,marc.reichenbach,dietmar.fey}@fau.de

Abstract. Due to raising system complexity and higher "time to market" demands in industry, hardware development for fast image processing applications is becoming more and more important. In order to ease and accelerate the design flow, special frameworks aim to hide the HDL code from the developer. On the one hand, many frameworks generate HDL code from a programming language like C++ to synthesize hardware from a higher abstraction level. On the other hand, HDL libraries, which instantiate predefined hardware components, are utilized. In contrast to high level synthesis, hardware designs, resulting from such a library, will lead to resource utilizations close to hand written implementations. Therefore, we propose a library of highly configurable IP blocks and demonstrate how they can be used on different Altera and Xilinx FPGAs. Our blocks are designed in a generic way, which makes the design very flexible in several functional parameters. At the current stage of our block library, it is possible to synthesize hardware for common local operations like Sobel, Laplacian or Median filter, but also complex operations like stereo matching and Canny edge detector. Moreover, we designed an XML based language interface, that gives users, who have only low specific hardware knowledge, access to predefined filter operations. With these features a rapid implementation of image processing operators for FPGA designs becomes possible.

Keywords: Architectures for image processing · IP block library · HDL design frameworks · Generic architectures

1 Introduction

Implementing image processing filters or operators on FPGAs is a challenging and time consuming task. While *Point Operators* in image processing, like color conversion or gamma correction, can be mapped through a simple pipeline, *Local Operators* require more sophisticates memory structures for neighborhood accesses. Consequently, the design flow demands specific hardware knowledge

© Springer International Publishing Switzerland 2016
V. Bonato et al. (Eds.): ARC 2016, LNCS 9625, pp. 303–311, 2016.
DOI: 10.1007/978-3-319-30481-6_24

from the developer and an investment of tremendous effort in testing or debugging the HDL code. The leading FPGA manufacturer *Xilinx* and *Altera* have perceived this issue and provide solutions to simplify the design process, e.g. by hiding the hardware layer from the developer. Thereby one of two basic approaches is applied. In the first approach, the designer has access to an IP core library of predefined operations. But the provided libraries from the FPGA manufactures only holds basic operations and consist of limited components for image processing. In recent years a second approach has obtained even more attention. High level synthesis, by generating HDL code from a high level language like Xilinx does with *Vivado HLS* [11] or Altera with OpenCL, as demonstrated in [1], becomes possible. However, an efficient code generation with acceptable resource usage can not be guaranteed, especially in more complex designs.

Thus, we followed the first approach and propose a set of IP blocks for basic and complex operations in image processing. Since many operators in image processing are based on local operations, we concentrated on utilizing special memory structures for these kind of operations. The blocks are written in plain VHDL without specific macro instances in order to be platform independent. All blocks are designed in a generic manner, meaning they can be reused for arbitrary parameters like image or filter size. Enabling hardware unexperienced users to work with our IP blocks is another import aspect of our work. As an interface we chose the domain specific design language IPOL, as described in [5]. This meta language is specifically designed to describe complex image processing applications in an abstract way and is based on XML.

The paper is structured as followed: In Sect. 2 a selection of existing design frameworks and architectures for image processing operations on FPGAs will be briefly discussed. The context between structures of local filters and the IP block library is explained in Sect. 3, while Sect. 4 outlines the implementation of our operators. How our IP blocks can be configured by the domain specific language IPOL, will be outlined in Sect. 5. In Sect. 6 the results from the hardware synthesis for chosen local operators will be analyzed and compared with state of the art design frameworks and vendor specific IP core libraries. The paper finishes with a conclusion and outlook.

2   Related Work

As mentioned in Sect. 1, IP Core libraries from Xilinx and Altera provide basic arithmetic operations and memory structures, among other components. Concerning local operations, the Xilinx *LogiCore IP* library [10] contains only an image enhancement block, which basically is a 2D FIR filter construct. By setting the filter behavior, either fixed mask pattern values for edge enhancement or noise canceling are applied. The 2D FIR filter from the Altera *Video and Image Processing Suite* [2] goes one step further. Setting the mask filter values in a predefined GUI, applies an arbitrary convolution operation, but mask size is limited to 3×3, 5×5 and 7×7.

One possible solution to map more complex operations to FPGAs is to utilize high level synthesis. This approach off course has the advantage, that the designer does not need to describe the operator in complex HDL code, instead a high level language like C or C++ can be used. On the downside, the synthesis needs to include a more complex optimization process, which results in a more time consuming synthesis and very often in higher resource utilization. Xilinx promotes the tool Vivado HLS for this use case. The OpenCV library [12] consists of several software C functions for many common image processing operations and can employ Vivado HLS. In [7] a similar approach has been demonstrated. With *Hipacc* it is possible to generate code for parallel architectures like FPGAs and GPUs through a domain specific language based on C++. Hipacc also utilizes the high level synthesis tool Vivado HLS as FPGA back end. Hence, the generated code is limited to selected FGPAs from the Xilinx family.

3   IP Block Design

By utilizing a proper buffering technique for local operators, the use of a frame buffer in form of external memory can be avoided. Since the information can be refained inside the FPGA, image data is processed right away, with lower latency. Such a structure must be described in a scalable way, which makes it flexible for various operations and image sizes. How a buffering structure for local operators can be described with such generic constructs, has been published in [9]. The presented *Template* is based on the *Full Buffering* scheme and has been approved for fast image processing on reconfigurable hardware, since it allows to process a pixel within a single clock cycle. Besides parameters like image size, filter size, and pixel width, the template supports further parallelization techniques. With our paper we want to exploit the template structure and integrate it in our set of IP blocks in order to provide a database for designing generic image processing filters or operations on FPGAs.

Our component types are ordered in a hierarchical way. The left side of Fig. 1 illustrates the hierarchy. A *Template* is defined as highest level in filter stage. Within a template one full buffer and a *Kernel* gets instantiated. The kernel deals as an interface and has parallel access to the mask values. In order to form a filter the developer connects either existing or new defined *Building Blocks* within the kernel. Thus, he or she has only access to the kernel and does not has to take care of the memory structure. Setting a standard interface for the building blocks, simplifies their concatenation. A building block performs an arithmetic or logical function on single input data or a vector, e.g. the entire window.

4   Kernel Descriptions

A local operation in image processing can occur either as basic operation or complex operation. We define a *Basic Operation* as one operator, which can be described through one kernel definition and hence require only one full buffer structure. *Complex Operations* on the other hand either are a concatenation of several basic operations or require a more complex buffering structure. Basic

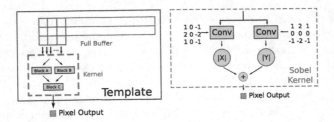

Fig. 1. Left: Component types of the library. Within the template a full buffer and a kernel is instantiated. Right: Kernel description of a Sobel filter. The building block convolution is instantiated twice and can perform calculations in X- and Y-direction in parallel.

Operations are split into linear and nonlinear filters. Linear filter operations are based on a convolution operation (multiply and accumulate: MAC) of the given filter coefficients and the pixel values in the local neighborhood of the applied input image. Depending on the filter coefficients the filter operation results either in image enhancement or image restoration. Very common filter examples of both types are the Gaussian blur and the Sobel edge detector. The working schemes of a Sobel filter is displayed in Fig. 1. The scalable multiplication process of vectorized inputs can be described quite simple by utilizing the *For Generate* construct. Accumulating the multiplication results is not that simple. The process needs to be pipelined in order to achieve appropriate clock frequencies, which can be realized by forming a binary adder tree. Nonlinear filters very often require a sort operation of all neighboring cells, like the Median filter, a dilatation or erosion operator. How a sorting operation in hardware can be implemented in a pipeline is further described in [3]. We extended this description for a full generic input vector.

Many algorithms in image processing are defined by a concatenation of various basic operations in a pipeline structure, which are considered as a complex operation. Hence, kernel definitions can be reused for forming a more complex structure as shown in Fig. 2. One example of such an operator is the Canny edge detector from [4]. In *Kernel_0* a Gaussian operator gets instantiated, while in the second stage (*Kernel_1*) a Sobel operator extracts edges and calculates gradient directions. Finally, a normalized cross correlation combined with a hysteresis is performed in *Kernel_2*. This operation leads to a binary output image with closed edges of only one pixel width.

Some operators require a modified buffering structure, since more than one input image needs to be processed or compared with each other. A representative example of this type is the stereo matching technique and has already been implemented as generic architecture in [6]. Also, a detailed description of the technique is explained in this work. In Fig. 2 a block diagram of the technique is depicted and illustrates how the hardware structure can be defined as new template for stereo matching.

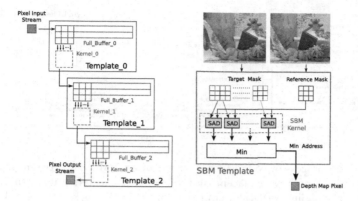

Fig. 2. Left: Forming a complex operator by concatenating several templates. Parameters like window size, can be set in each stage individually. Right: Block diagram of a modified buffering structure for stereo matching applications.

5   Code Generation and IPOL Interface

Utilization of HDL libraries usually requires hardware knowledge. Users, who want to utilize predefined filters or operations of the library, should not need to study HDL languages. In most cases, the operation should be adaptable to functional parameters like image size or local window size. Since our filters are designed in a scalable manner, these parameters can be set in a single configuration or package file. Hence, an interface, which sets the parameters in the package file and generates the correct VHDL source files, must be defined.

As input data structure we chose the Image Processing Operator Language (IPOL), which is based on XML [5]. This meta language is designed for describing image processing applications in a very abstract way and can be used to distribute complex operations to a heterogeneous hardware platform. In order to read the parameters from the XML file and set the arbitrary parameters, parsing the XML file and code generation must be performed by a separated tool. For parameterizing predefined filters, text replacement in combination with XML parsing has been utilized in a shell script. The processing scheme is illustrated in Fig. 3.

6   Implementation Results

In this Section we will demonstrate the flexibility of our IP blocks by presenting synthesis results for several use cases with alternating functional parameters and various FPGAs from Altera and Xilinx. Additionally, in order to prove the resource awareness by utilizing our IP blocks, we show resource utilization and clock speed compared to the IP core library from Altera. In a second comparison we are taking our synthesis result in contrast to the high level synthesis tool Vivado HLS employed by OpenCV and Hipacc. Our Implementations have been

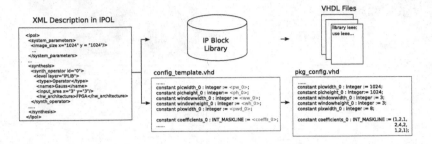

Fig. 3. Abstract process of code generation out of an XML file, written in IPOL. A separated parsing and text replacement tool takes parameters out of an XML file, selects the corresponding VHDL files out of a library of IP blocks, and sets the correct parameters to generate a *pkg_config.vhd* file.

executed with the tool *Synopsis Synplify Pro* in combination with either *Xilinx Vivado 2015.2* or *Altera Quartus II 15.0*.

In Table 1 our post synthesis results of a 2D median filter are compared with the synthesis outcome from the Altera Mega Core Function Suite [2]. The Implementation has been performed with a 3 × 3 window on 2 common Altera FPGAs. The image resolution has been set to 1280 × 720. Our design clearly outperforms the solution from the Altera IP Core library regarding LUT and memory usage and operation speed. Numbers in brackets indicate the required amount of block RAM macro cells (M9K blocks for Cyclone 4 and M20K blocks for Stratix 5).

Table 1. Comparison results of a 2D Median filter applied on a 3 × 3 window.

FPGA device	Our IP block design				Altera IP core library			
	LUT	FF	Memory bits	F[MHz]	LUT	FF	Memory bits	F[MHz]
Cyclone 4	301	553	20480(6)	263.92	1567	1724	25600(6)	245.64
Stratix 5	241	553	20480(2)	541.52	1011	1200	25602(2)	353.61

Considering solutions designed with an HLS tool we made a second comparison. In the work of [7] a Laplacian edge detector has been synthesized with the OpenCV library and framework Hipacc. The operator was altered in its mask coefficients and mask size. The LPHV regards horizontal and vertical edges, while LPD additionally is sensitive to horizontal edges. Both masks are defined by sized 3 × 3. In the LP version the window size has been set to 5 × 5. All implementations have been executed for a Xilinx Zynq 7045 platform on a 1024 × 1024 input image. Analyzing Table 2 reveals that Hipacc is able to synthesize designs with much lower logic utilization and lower flip flop usage in most cases. This might result from the domain specific constructs for image processing operations, employed by Hipacc. However, our IP blocks outperforms the Hipacc results by utilizing at least 50 % less logic and memory resources. Especially larger designs like the 5 × 5 Laplace operator seem to corrupt the optimization of HLS. Additionally, our designs do not require DSPs since the convolution with a constant coefficient of the Laplacian operator can be mapped to LUTs, which is recognized during the optimization process. Compared to the HLS approaches our resulting clock frequencies remain constant on a high level with 395 MHz.

Table 2. Comparison results of Laplacian Operator.

	Our IP block design			HIPACC			OpenCV		
	LPHV	LPD	LP 5 × 5	LPHV	LPD	LP 5 × 5	LPHV	LPD	LP 5 × 5
LUT	143	172	290	288	398	4521	3515	3470	5316
FF	212	257	507	521	1034	23795	8772	8768	9076
BRAM	1	1	1	2	2	4	12	12	10
DSP	0	0	0	0	0	200	75	75	103
F[MHz]	395	395	395	349.9	341.1	220.1	258.3	247.2	201.7

Canny Edge Detector: The Canny edge detector has been implemented as described in Sect. 4. Implementation results are listed in Table 3 for the image resolution of 640 × 480 and 1920 × 1080. The window size of the Gaussian blur filter has been set to 5 × 5 and for Sobel and non-maximum suppression to 3 × 3.

Table 3. Synthesis results for Canny edge detector on Zynq 7020.

$m × n$	LUT	FF	BRAM	DSP	F[MHz]
640 × 480	1030 (1 %)	831 (1 %)	3 (2 %)	31 (15 %)	183
1920 × 1080	1044 (1 %)	837 (1 %)	6 (4 %)	31 (15 %)	180

Stereo Block Matching: For testing the functionality of the block matching technique we used image pairs from the authors of [8], which are widely used for benchmarking stereo matching algorithms. The resolution has been set to 450 × 375. For a proper death map results 60 SAD blocks have been instantiated in parallel. The synthesis for several window sizes are listed in Table 4. Our results show, that this operator requires 25 % LUT usage of the Zynq 7020 for the 3 × 3 window and up to 69 % LUTs for the 5 × 5 window. Hence, for larger window sizes the Zynq 7100 must be used. This complexity also leads to much lower maximum clock frequencies as presented in the table.

Table 4. Synthesis results for stereo block matching template with SAD kernel.

	$p \times q$	LUT	FF	BRAM	F[MHz]
Zynq 7020	3×3	13402 (25 %)	11057 (10 %)	7 (4 %)	157
	5×5	36993 (69 %)	29121 (27 %)	13 (9 %)	138
Zynq 7100	9×9	120250 (43 %)	93509 (16 %)	25 (4 %)	157
	11×11	179133 (64 %)	137338 (24 %)	31 (4 %)	124

7   Conclusion

In this work we presented a new IP block approach for mapping image processing applications on FPGAs. We utilized a specialized memory structure in form of a generic template and showed how full buffering can be exploit to build more complex operators in a streaming fashion. With an interface to the domain specific language IPOL it is possible to generate synthesizable VHDL code of a well known filter out of an XML file and therefore, reduces the required expertise necessary for utilizing our IP blocks. We demonstrated how our operators can be mapped to several FPGA devices of different manufactures. Regarding FPGA resources and maximum clock frequencies our IP Block implementations outperforms HLS solutions and even Alteras IP Core library. In future projects we aim to extend the code generation in order to describe more complex filter structures from an IPOL description.

Acknowledgment. This work was financially supported by the Research Training Group 1773 "Heterogeneous Image Systems", funded by the German Research Foundation (DFG).

References

1. Altera: Implementing FPGA Design with the OpenCL Standard - White Paper, November 2013. https://www.altera.com/en_US/pdfs/literature/wp/wp-01173-opencl.pdf
2. Altera: Video and Image Processing Suite, February 2014. www.altera.co.jp/ja_JP/pdfs/literature/ug/ug_vip.pdf
3. Bailey, D.G.: Design for Embedded Image Processing on FPGAs. Wiley-IEEE Press, Singapore (2011)
4. Canny, J.: A Computational approach to edge detection. In: Pattern Analysis and Machine Intelligence, pp. 679–698, November 1986
5. Hartman, C., Reichenbach, M., Fey, D.: Ipol - a Domain specific language for image processing applications. In: Proceedings of the International Symposium on International Conference on Systems (ICONS), pp. 40–43, March 2015
6. Häublein, K., Reichenbach, M., Fey, D.: Fast and generic hardware architecture for stereo block matching applications on embedded systems. In: Proceedings of the International Conference on Reconfigurable Computing and FPGAs (ReConFig), pp. 1–6, December 2014

7. Reiche, O., Schmidt, M., Hannig, F., Membarth, R., Teich, J.: Code generation from a domain-specific language for C-based HLS of hardware accelerators. In: Proceedings of the 2014 International Conference on Hardware/Software Codesign and System Synthesis, pp. 1–10, October 2014

8. Scharstein, D., Szeliski, R.: High-accuracy stereo depth maps using structured light. In: IEEE Computer Society Conference on Computer Vision and Pattern Recognition (CVpPR 2003), pp. 195–202, June 2003

9. Schmidt, M., Reichenbach, M., Fey, D.: A generic VHDL template for 2D stencil code applications on FPGAs. In: 15th International Symposium on Object/Component/Service-Oriented Real-Time Distributed Computing Workshops, pp. 180–187, April 2012

10. Xilinx: Image Enhancement v8.0: LogiCORE IP Product Guide, October 2014. http://www.xilinx.com/support/documentation/ip_documentation/v_enhance/v8_0/pg003_v_enhance.pdf

11. Xilinx: Vivado Design Suite User Guide: High-Level Synthesis, October 2014. http://www.xilinx.com/support/documentation/sw_manuals/xilinx2014_3/ug902-vivado-high-level-synthesis.pdf

12. Xilinx: Accelerating OpenCV Applications with Zynq-7000 All Programmable SoC using Vivado HLS Video Libraries, June 2015. http://www.xilinx.com/support/documentation/application_notes/xapp1167.pdf

Performance Evaluation of Feed-Forward Backpropagation Neural Network for Classification on a Reconfigurable Hardware Architecture

Mahnaz Mohammadi[1]([✉]), Rohit Ronge[1], Sanjay S. Singapuram[2], and S. K. Nandy[1]

[1] Indian Institute of Science, Bangalore, India
{mahnaz,rohit}@cadl.iisc.ernet.in, nandy@serc.iisc.in
[2] Birla Institute of Technology and Science, Pilani, Hyderabad, India
sssv96@gmail.com

Abstract. Performance of classification using Feed-Forward Backpropagation Neural Network (FFBPNN) on a reconfigurable hardware architecture is evaluated in this paper. The hardware architecture used for implementation of FFBPNN in this paper is a set of interconnected HyperCells which serve as reconfigurable data paths for the network. The architecture is easily scalable and able to implement networks with no limitation on their number of input and output dimensions. The performance of FFBPNN implemented on network of HCs using Xilinx Virtex 7 XC7V2000T as target FPGA is compared with software implementation and GPU implementation of FFBPNN. Results show speed up of 1.02X-3.49X over equivalent software implementation on Intel Core 2 Quad and 1.07X-6X over GPU (NVIDIA GTX650).

Keywords: Reconfigurable architecture · Hardware accelerator · Backpropagation · Pattern recognition · Classification

1 Introduction

In the field of data classification, neural network methods have been found to be useful alternatives to statistical techniques such as those which involve regression analysis or probability density estimation. The execution speed provided by a software simulation of neural networks running on a sequential, general purpose computer will not be sufficient for many applications of neural networks as the size of the network increases. Therefore, efforts have been made to speed up neural network execution by implementing them on massively parallel machines with thousands of processors (Multicore machines), Graphic Processing Units (GPUs) or on special purpose hardwares. Application Specific Integrated Circuits (ASICs) and Field Programmable Gate Arrays (FPGAs) are hardware technologies that have been used widely for speeding up execution of neural networks such as Feed-Forward neural Networks with Backpropagation Algorithm

© Springer International Publishing Switzerland 2016
V. Bonato et al. (Eds.): ARC 2016, LNCS 9625, pp. 312–319, 2016.
DOI: 10.1007/978-3-319-30481-6_25

(FFBPNN) [2,8,10]. High degree of parallelism of neural networks make them an ideal choice to be implemented on ASIC or FPGA. Some of these hardware implementation make use of fixed point arithmetics in the learning algorithm to decrease the amount of hardware required [9]. There are methods which try to decrease the area by limiting the resolution of the computations [1] or by replacing higher resolution operations with those of lower resolution [5]. Reconfigurable architectures are another option for implementing neural networks [3]. HyperCell is a reconfigurable data path composed of an array of Compute Units (CUs) laid over a switch network [4]. In this paper FFBPNN is implemented on limited number of interconnected HCs without restriction on the size of the network.

Rest of this paper is organised as follows: Sect. 2, describes the learning phase and classification phases of FFBPNN and also the Data Flow Graphic(DFG) of FFBPNN. Section 3 provides the proposed hardware design for FFBPNN. Section 4 presents the performance of FFBPNN on CPU, GPU and on proposed reconfigurable architecture. In Sect. 5 our contribution to this paper is concluded.

2   FFBPNN

The operation of FFBPNN can be divided into learning and classification phases.

2.1   The Learning Phase

In the learning process, to reduce the inaccuracy of network, the backpropagation algorithm employs gradient descent algorithm. In machine learning, the delta rule is a gradient descent learning rule for updating the weights of the inputs to artificial neurons in a single-layer neural network. The delta rule is derived by attempting to minimize the error in the output of the neural network through gradient descent. For a neuron j, with activation function $g(x)$ the delta rule for the weight between hidden neuron j and input neuron i, w_{ji} is given by:

$$\Delta w_{ji} = \alpha(t_j - y_i)g'(h_j)x_i$$

where :

α : is a small constant called learning rate $g(x)$: is the neuron's activation function
h_j : is the weighted sum of the inputs t_j : is the target output
y_i : is the actual output x_i : is the ith input

In each iteration of training in backpropagation a particular case of training data is fed through the network in a forward direction, producing results at the output layer. For a given input vector, the output vector is compared with the correct answer. If the difference is zero, no learning takes place; otherwise, the weights are adjusted to reduce this difference. The effects of error in the output node(s) are propagated backward through the network after each training case. It should be noted, however, that most implementations of this algorithm employ an additional class of weights known as biases. Biases are values that are added to the sums calculated at each node (except input nodes) during the Feed-Forward phase. A bias value shifts the activation function to the left or right, which can be critical for successful learning.

2.2 The Classification Phase

In the classification phase, the weights of the network are fixed. A pattern, presented at the inputs, will be transformed from layer to layer until it reaches the output layer. The nodes in output layer correspond to different classes in the neural network.

2.3 Data Flow Graph of FFBPNN

Network parameters (number of hidden neurons, weights, biases) are defined during training of the network which is done offline for this paper. After fixing the structure of the network new patterns can be classified using the trained network in the following method:

- Each Input will be multiplied by its respective weight.
- Biases will be added to the weighted sum of the input.
- Logistic function will be calculated at each hidden node.
- The output of hidden neurons will be multiplied by their respective weights between hidden layer and output layer.
- Bias will be added to each previous result and finally output will be generated at each output node. The maximum value at output neurons will define the class label of the pattern.

Data Flow Graph (DFG) of FFBPNN for classification of newly introduced patterns to the constructed network is shown in Figs. 1, 2 and 3. The DFG of FFBPNN is partitioned to three parts. Calculation of weighted sum of input patterns with added bias to it (**Base Structure**) is shown in Fig. 1. The base structure operations are just additions and multiplications. The output of base structure will be fed as input to the second partition (**Kernel**). Sigmoid function is used as the kernel at hidden neurons. Figure 2 represents the operations needed to calculate sigmoid kernel. Figure 3 shows the DFG for the third partition which involves calculation output at each output neuron. The output of each kernel is received as input to this partition (**Accumulator**). Each input will be multiplied by its respective weights and finally bias is added to it. To be able to implement FFBPNN on HC the operations in DFG of FFBPNN should be mapped optimally on the HC fabric. Because of limitations in the number of input and output ports of HC and also to avoid switch traversal while mapping and maximize utilization of CUs on HC mapping should be done optimally. Mapping strategy and the conditions that has to be considered to have an optimal mapping on HC is mentioned in [7].

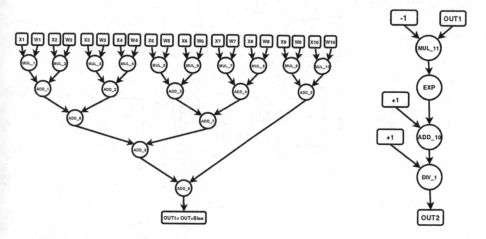

Fig. 1. Data flow graph of base structure of FFBPNN

Fig. 2. Data flow graph of sigmoid kernel of FFBPNN

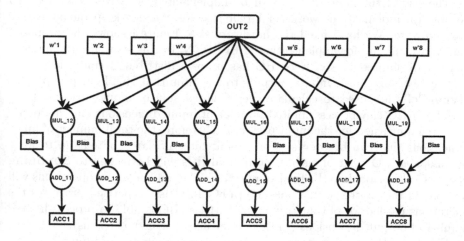

Fig. 3. Data flow graph of accumulator part of FFBPNN

3   Proposed Reconfigurable Hardware Architecture for Implemeting FFBPNN

The architecture of FFBPNN is an interconnection of HCs as reported in [6]. HC [4] compromises an array of compute units (CUs) interconnected through configurable circuit switch network. Number of operations that can be processes on each HC is equal to the number of CUs on the HC (i.e. size of the HC). Each CU is able to perform double precision floating point arithmetic operations needed to compute the output of the FFBPNN with higher accuracy. More details on the architecture of HC is mentioned in [4].

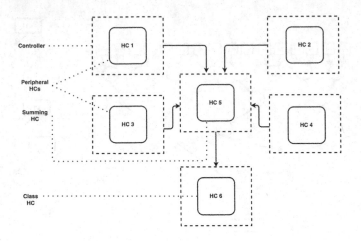

Fig. 4. Hardware structure for implementing FFBPNN

The size of the network that can be implemented on a HC is limited. To be able to implement networks of larger size we can not keep on increasing the hardware. We have fixed the hardware size. Figure 4 shows the proposed hardware structure for implementing of FFBPNN. In this structure the number of HCs are limited to six. Each HC has its own distributed controller which takes care of scheduling inputs/outputs to and from that HC. Four **peripheral HyperCells** are used to calculate the weighted sum of input patterns. Each peripheral HC can process limited number of input dimensions (in this paper up to ten dimension for the input pattern). Therefore, the total number of input dimensions that can be processes on this architecture are limited (up to forty in this paper). Output of each of peripheral HCs will be passed to **Summing HyperCell** to calculate the final summation. The hidden kernel operations will be done in the controller of **Class HyperCell**. Class HyperCell processes the operations needed for output computation. Class HC is able to process limited number of output dimensions (in this paper up to eight dimensions).

Fixed size of hardware imposes limitation on the number of inputs and outputs that can be processed. A folding strategy which can provide scalability to implement networks with no limitations on the size of the network is needed. The folding strategy used here is the third folding strategy mentioned in [6].

4   Results

Standard data sets from UCI Machine Learning Repository were used for classification using FeedForward Neural Network with Backpropagation learning algorithm. Table 1 shows the data sets used in this experiment with their number of neurons in the input, hidden and output layers. This table also shows total number of neurons in the network for each of data sets. Comparison of hardware implementation of FFBPNN over software implementation which is shown in

Table 2. This table shows the speed up of our design for implementing FFBPNN over implementing it on a general purpose computer. The BLAS (Basic Linear Algebra Subprograms) routines that provide standard building blocks for performing basic vector and matrix operations and the NVIDIA CUDA Basic Linear Algebra Subroutines (cuBLAS) library which is a GPU-accelerated version of the complete standard BLAS library are used for software and GPU implementation of RBFNN in this paper. Table 3 shows performance comparison of implementing FFBPNN on GPU and on HC. The operating frequency of FFBPNN on HCs running on Xilinx Virtex 7 XC7V2000T is 100 MHz. GPU and CPU operating frequencies are 1058 MHz and 2.83 GHz respectively. To measure the efficiency of the hardware solution for FFBPNN, all numbers in this table are normalized. Normalization is done by dividing the execution time by the number of the cores available on GPU and HCs, and also by the number of folds necessary for each data set. For NVIDIA GTX650 the number of cores are 384 and the total number of cores with HCs is 150 (i.e. 25 cores per HC). Folding is done for data set with dimension larger than the dimension that can be processed at a time on either GPU and HC. GPU shows its true performance when one can take advantage of high parallelism and thus provides a large enough data set for it to work on (i.e. GPUs are optimized for throughput rather than latency). Results in this table show that GPU fare worse for smaller data sets compared to larger data sets. Moreover, this table reveals that in spite of high processing speed of GPUs, our proposed design found to be more efficient for implementation of FFBPNN. Resource utilization of our design on Xilinx Virtex 7 XC7V2000T is reported in Table 4.

Table 1. Data sets used with their Input, Hidden, Output and Total number of neurons

Data set	No of input neurons	No of hidden neurons	No of output neurons	Total number of neurons
Iris	4	8	3	15
Wine	13	26	3	42
SPECTF	22	44	2	68
Breast Cancer	30	60	2	92
SPECTF Heart	44	88	2	134
Libras Movement	90	90	15	195
Semeion	256	512	10	778
LSVT Voice Rehabilitation	310	40	2	352
Madelon	500	1000	2	1502
Isolet	617	390	26	1033

Table 2. Time performance of FFBPNN on CPU and HyperCell

Data set	CPU (µs)	HC (µs)
Iris	8	2.57
Wine	8	2.97
SPECTF	9	3.62
Breast Cancer	9	4.18
SPECTF Heart	11	5.59
Libras Movement	16	15.59
LSVT Voice Rehabilitation	96	27.46
Semeion	69	42.81
Madelon	209	62.06
Isolet	295	171.46

Table 3. Time performance of FFBPNN on GPU and HyperCell

Data set	CPU (µs)	HC (µs)
Iris	0.067	0.017
Wine	0.067	0.019
SPECTF	0.065	0.024
Breast Cancer	0.065	0.027
SPECTF Heart	0.067	0.037
Libras Movement	0.070	0.034
LSVT Voice Rehabilitation	0.072	0.022
Semeion	0.072	0.012
Madelon	0.075	0.031
Isolet	0.076	0.071

Table 4. Resource utilization for Xilinx Virtex 7 XC7V2000T

	Used	Available	Utilization (%)
LUTs	867406	1221600	71.00
Registers	706872	2443200	28.93
Block RAMs	26	1292	2.00
Bonded IOB	663	850	77.99

5   Conclusion

Performance of Feed-Forward Backpropagation Neural Network for classification on a reconfigurable hardware architecture has been evaluated in this paper. The proposed reconfigurable architecture is a network of interconnected HyperCells that can process networks with no restrictions on their number of input and output dimension. This has been possible by a folding strategy that has been applied to the proposed design. The performance of FFBPNN implemented on network of HyperCells using Xilinx Virtex 7 XC7V2000T as target FPGA was compared with software implementation and GPU implementation of FFBPNN. Results show speed up of 1.02X-3.49X over equivalent software implementation on Intel Core 2 Quad and 1.07X-6X over GPU (NVIDIA GTX650). We have shown that our hardware design is scalable in terms of both input dimensions (features) and output dimensions (classes). Our results also show that our design is more efficient in terms of processing speed, compared to software implementation and GPU implementation of FFBPNN.

References

1. Cloutier, J., Simard, P.Y.: Hardware implementation of the backpropagation without multiplication. In: Proceedings of the Fourth International Conference on Microelectronics for Neural Networks and Fuzzy Systems, pp. 46–55. IEEE (1994)

2. Domingos, P.O., Silva, F.M., Neto, H.C.: An efficient and scalable architecture for neural networks with backpropagation learning. In: International Conference on Field Programmable Logic and Applications, pp. 89–94. IEEE (2005)
3. Eldredge, J.G., Hutchings, B.L.: Rrann: a hardware implementation of the backpropagation algorithm using reconfigurable fpgas. In: IEEE International Conference on Neural Networks, IEEE World Congress on Computational Intelligence, vol. 4, pp. 2097–2102 (1994)
4. Madhu, K.T., Das, S., Madhava Krishna, C., Nalesh, S., Nandy, S.K., Narayan, R.: Synthesis of instruction extensions on hypercell, a reconfigurable datapath. In: International Conference on Embedded Computer Systems: Architectures, Modeling, and Simulation (SAMOS XIV), pp. 215–224. IEEE (2014)
5. Mahoney, V., Elhanany, I.: A backpropagation neural network design using adder-only arithmetic. In: 51st Midwest Symposium on Circuits and Systems, MWSCAS, pp. 894–897. IEEE (2008)
6. Mohammadi, M., et al.: An accelerator for classification using radial basis function neural network. In: 28th IEEE International System-On-Chip Conference (SOCC) (2015)
7. Mohammadi, M., et al.: A flexible scalable hardware architecture for radial basis function neural networks. In: 28th International Conference on VLSI Design, pp. 505–510. IEEE (2015)
8. Ortega-Zamorano, F., et al.: Efficient implementation of the backpropagation algorithm in fpgas and microcontrollers. IEEE Trans. Neural Netw. Learn. Syst. (2015)
9. Kimball Presley, R., Haggard, R.L.: A fixed point implementation of the backpropagation learning algorithm. In: Southeastcon 1994. Creative Technology Transfer-A Global Affair, Proceedings of the IEEE, pp. 136–138 (1994)
10. Rajeswaran, N., Madhu, T., Suryakalavathi, M.: Vhdl synthesizable hardware architecture design of back propagation neural networks. In: IEEE Conference on Information and Communication Technologies (ICT), pp. 445–450 (2013)

FPGA-Based Acceleration of Pattern Matching in YARA

Shreyas G. Singapura[1]([✉]), Yi-Hua E. Yang[2], Anand Panangadan[3],
Tamas Nemeth[4], Peter Ng[4], and Viktor K. Prasanna[1]

[1] Ming-Hsieh Department of Electrical Engineering,
University of Southern California, Los Angeles, USA
{singapur,prasanna}@usc.edu
[2] Google Inc., Mountain View, CA, USA
yeyang@google.com
[3] California State University, Fullerton, USA
apanangadan@fullerton.edu
[4] Chevron, San Ramon, USA
{Tamas.Nemeth,PeterN}@chevron.com

Abstract. String and regular expression pattern matching is an integral
part of intrusion detection systems to detect potential threats. YARA is
a pattern matching framework to identify malicious content by defining
complex patterns and signatures. Software implementations of YARA
on CPU do not meet the throughput requirements of core networks.
We present a FPGA based hardware accelerator to boost the performance of pattern matching in YARA framework. The proposed architecture consists of pattern matching engines organized as two-dimensional
stages and pipelines. We implemented rulesets of sizes varying from 8 to
200 rules with total number of patterns ranging from 128 to 6000. Post
place-and-route results demonstrate that the proposed design achieves
throughput ranging from 12.85 Gbps to 21.8 Gbps. This is an improvement of 8.8× to 14.5× in comparison with the throughput of 1.45 Gbps
for a software implementation on a state of the art multi-core platform.

1 Introduction

Intrusion detection systems [1,2] in applications such as network security, content
filtering and data mining use pattern matching as a key kernel. The number of
malware patterns and their complexity is increasing due to the large number
and diversity of devices. YARA [3] has emerged as a widely used tool [1,2]
which helps users to create signatures and patterns specific to malware patterns
and perform traffic analysis to detect these patterns. It is also used in research
tools such as Cuckoo [3] and VirusTotal [4]. With regards to the implementation
of YARA, the focus has been on its software implementation on general purpose
processors (CPU). CPU-based implementations are however not able to meet the

V.K. Prasanna—This work is supported by Chevron U.S.A. at the University of
Southern California.

© Springer International Publishing Switzerland 2016
V. Bonato et al. (Eds.): ARC 2016, LNCS 9625, pp. 320–327, 2016.
DOI: 10.1007/978-3-319-30481-6_26

demands of the internet for higher throughput and lower latency. In the future, the complexity of pattern matching activities such as deep packet inspection will further increase and CPU-based solutions may be unable to keep up with the requirements of the next generation network processing systems [5].

In recent years, interest in hardware accelerators such as GPUs and FPGAs for real time network processing systems has increased [6]. This is due to their ability to perform application specific computations faster than software-based implementations on CPU. In this paper, we focus on FPGA as the hardware accelerator. State of the art FPGA devices [7] provide large amount of parallel logic to create deep pipelines and large amount of high bandwidth on-chip memory. FPGAs are also programmable and can be optimized to match the application requirements.

Our work focuses on implementation of pattern matching algorithms on FPGA in order to accelerate the YARA tool. We extend the work of [8] and modify the architecture to perform pattern matching in YARA. To the best of our knowledge, this is the first work to accelerate the pattern matching in YARA framework using an FPGA platform. Main contributions of this paper are:

- *Modular implementation of YARA on FPGA*: We develop a mapping of every multi-pattern rule to a stage in a 2-D pipeline on FPGA.
- Our architecture achieves a throughput in the range of 12.8 Gbps - 21.8 Gbps for rulesets consisting of 6000 and 1600 patterns respectively. In comparison with the implementation on CPU, we demonstrate 8.8× to 14.5× improvement in performance.

The rest of the paper is organized as follows: Sect. 2 provides background information about the YARA tool and pattern matching techniques while Sect. 3 describes prior work. Section 4 discusses the pattern matching architecture in detail. In Sect. 5, various patterns and metrics used in performance evaluation are explained. The experimental results and our analysis is provided in Sect. 6. Section 7 concludes the paper with directions for future work.

2   Background

2.1   YARA Framework

In the YARA framework, input data is analyzed for a set of rules and match or no match is output as the result for each rule in the ruleset. A representative format of YARA rules is shown in Definition 1.

Definition 1. *rule yara_example*
{
    meta: description = "This is an example of YARA rule"
    strings:
        $a = "ZINGAWI2"
        $b = {6A 40 68 00 30 00 00 6A 14 8D 91}
        $c = /md5: [0-9a-zA-Z]32/

condition:
    $a or $b and $c
}

Each YARA rule contains pattern(s) to be matched and a condition which is used to determine the final result. A YARA rule consists of the keyword "rule" followed by the rule name and 3 components:

Meta: This section of the rule is used to store the metadata such as description, date of creation, references etc. *Strings:* The pattern(s) to be matched is defined in this part of the rule. 3 types of strings can be defined: Text, Hexadecimal, Regular expression. *Condition:* This part of the rule determines the logic to combine the results of pattern matching of individual strings.

YARA framework can also be used to perform pattern matching. While using YARA as a pattern matching tool, it accepts two files as input: one file containing data to be processed and another file containing rules to be matched. The tool outputs the name of matching rules present in the data file.

2.2 Pattern Matching Techniques

There are two classes of pattern matching techniques: string matching (SM) and regular expression matching (REM). SM is used to match a set of strings against a stream of incoming characters and REM refers to regular expression matching which are regular languages constructed using character classes over a fixed alphabet. Since strings are a special case of regular expressions, we apply the REM approach to perform pattern matching of both strings and regular expressions in this paper. A pattern matching engine can be implemented as a finite state machine for each individual pattern. In this study, we focus on the design of Nondeterministic Finite Automata (NFA) based pattern matching engines wherein each pattern is converted to a NFA and is processed in parallel independent of each other.

3   Related Work

Many research works have used YARA as a malware analysis framework. In [9], the authors use YARA as one of the detection methods to develop an analysis engine for malware identification. The authors in [10] develop methodology to protect against script based cyber attacks and YARA is used as a pattern matching tool in the process. To the best of our knowledge, performance of YARA has not been studied and the focus has been on using an implementation of YARA framework on general purpose processor to perform malware detection.

Pattern matching has been a topic of interest in the academia for many years. Large scale string matching on FPGA was designed in [11]. Although the authors utilize FPGA for implementation, the experiments is limited to small problem size (200 patterns). A memory efficient and modular architecture on FPGA is proposed in [12] for large scale string matching.

Regular expression matching architectures on FPGA have been studied before. NFA based regular expression matching on hardware was studied by Floyd and Ullman [13]. They used $O(n)$ circuit area to implement an n-state NFA. Sidhu and Prasanna [14] proposed an algorithm to translate a regular expression onto FPGA which is used by several other implementations [15]. Shift register lookup tables for single character repetitions was implemented in [15]. Hardware accelerators for pattern matching in YARA framework have not been studied before and to the best of our knowledge, this is the first work to provide an FPGA implementation of pattern matching in the YARA framework.

4   Pattern Matching Architecture on FPGA

In this paper, we extend the previous work of [8] and modify the architecture in the context of pattern matching in YARA framework. Here, we present a brief overview of the architecture developed in [8] and the modification required for implementing YARA rules.

NFA Construction and Pattern Matching Engine: The patterns are transformed into a token list data structure which is a mutli-level linked list and multiple token lists are chained together to generate the NFA. Each pattern is mapped to a pattern matching engine constructed based on the NFA of the pattern. A matching engine accepts data to be analyzed and the result of character classification as inputs and outputs a match or no match result.

Stage: Each pattern in a YARA rule requires a matching engine and all the patterns in the same rule require additional logic to implement the condition aspect of the rule. In our architecture, we group all the pattern matching engines belonging to the same rule and the logic to implement the condition to form a *stage*. A stage consisting of 4 matching engines is shown in Fig. 1. The condition logic can be either "all of them", "any of them" or expressions such as "2 of them", "3 of them". When mapped onto a FPGA, all these conditions are implemented using LUTs by the EDA software. Therefore, all these conditions will have the same effect on the clock frequency and resource usage irrespective of which condition is employed in a rule. The matching results are combined as per the condition of the rule to obtain the final matching output.

Pipeline: Each pipeline has a group of stages sharing a centralized BRAM which is used for character classification. In a given clock cycle, the incoming character is passed as input to all the matching engines in the first stage of the first pipeline (S1 in P1) along with the results of character classification. In the next clock cycle, the buffered signals are passed as inputs to the second stage in the first pipeline (S2 in P1) and the first stage of second pipeline (S1 in P2) as well. Meanwhile, the first stage of the first pipeline (S1 in P1) accepts the second set of input characters. An architecture using 2 pipelines made of 4 stages is illustrated in Fig. 2.

Mapping YARA Ruleset to Our Architecture: We map each rule in a given YARA ruleset to a stage in our architecture. Each stage consists of matching

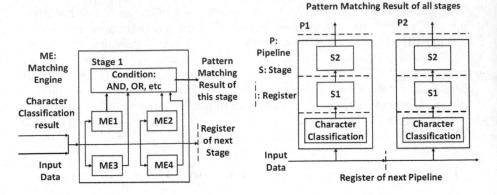

Fig. 1. Architecture of a stage   **Fig. 2.** Overall architecture

engines equal in number to the number of patterns in the rule and a LUT to implement condition aspect of the rule. Each stage produces a single bit output corresponding to match/no match for that particular rule. Our architecture consists of multiple pipelines with multiple stages in each pipeline and the output of all the stages across all the pipelines cumulatively form the result of pattern matching of the input for the ruleset.

5   Performance Evaluation

5.1   Rulesets

We use two types of rulesets for our performance evaluation: publicly available real-world YARA rules [16], plus a larger number of synthetic rules.

Real World Rules: The public repository of real-world YARA rules [16] contains about 6000 patterns distributed among 1500 rules. Most of the patterns in the public YARA rules were strings ($\geq$ **95** %); regexes accounted for fewer than 250 ($\leq$ **4** %) patterns.

Synthetic Rules: To increase the number and diversity of rules, two types of synthetic rules are constructed: *string-based rulesets* contain rules that match strings only and *regex-based rulesets* contain rules that match regexes.

For the string-based rulesets, each string is a sequence of random alphanumeric characters. For the regex-based rulesets, we borrowed the PCRE (Perl-Compatible Regex Expression) patterns from a Snortrules [2] repository. Figure 3 describes the characteristics of different rulesets.

Although in principle, a YARA rule can have complex conditions such as backreferences and iteration over string occurrences; in the public repository [16] of 1500 rules, "all of them", "any of them" and conditions such as "2 of them", "3 of them" constitute 900 rules, i.e., 60 % of the total number of rules. Therefore, for both string-based and regex-based rulesets, we use similar conditions in the rules.

5.2   System Configurations

The proposed YARA acceleration architecture (YARA-FPGA) is evaluated against an official YARA software (YARA-CPU) as the baseline. With YARA-CPU, experiments were conducted through the Python interface in YARA software [3] and Python's "cProfile" library. The experiments were performed on a platform with an AMD Opteron 6278 processor and 64 GB DDR3 memory. The processor consists of 16 cores, running at 2.4 GHz with 16 KB L1 data 2 MB L2 and 8 MB L3 cache memories. Only 1 core is utilized by the YARA software as we are comparing the per-stream throughput, rather than the aggregated throughput.

With YARA-FPGA, the acceleration engine was implemented on a Xilinx Virtex-7 FPGA device (xc7v2000tfhg1761-2). The design was written in VHDL and configured to match 8 input characters per clock cycle. A character is assumed to have 8 bits. The performance was estimated from post place and route (PAR) resource and timing results reported by Xilinx Vivado 2014.2.

5.3   Evaluation Metrics

We use throughput as the primary metric for performance evaluation. *Through-put* is defined as the amount of input data processed (matched) by the YARA implementation per unit time. It is measured in Gigabits per second (Gbps).

With YARA-CPU, throughput is calculated as the *input file* size divided by the run time of the pattern matching routine *over* that file (as reported by cProfile). With YARA-FPGA, throughput is estimated as the input bus width (8 input characters per cycle) divided by the post place-and-route clock period.

6   Experimental Results

We evaluate the implementation of YARA on FPGA and compare its performance with that of software implementation on CPU for various values of number of rules (R), number of patterns (P) and number of characters per pattern (C).

6.1   String-Based Rulesets

The performance comparison of YARA-CPU and YARA-FPGA is illustrated in Fig. 4(a). The parameters R, P and C do not appear to affect the string matching performance of YARA-CPU significantly. Performance of the software implementation remains stable at approximately 1.45 Gbps. On the other hand, performance of YARA-FPGA implementation shows performance degradation due to decreasing clock frequency with increasing R, P and C. With higher amount of resources consumed by the design, lower amount of resources are available for routing and this causes long interconnects due to reduced flexibility. Increasing R, P and C all have the net effect of increasing the circuit size, which increases both logic depth and interconnect length.

Parameter	Range of Values
No. of Rules	8 - 192
Strings per Rule	16, 64
Characters per String	50, 100
Condition	"all" / "any" / "some"

(a) String based Rulesets

Parameter	Range of Values
No. of Rules	16 - 125
Regexes per Rule	16, 32
States	>100,000
Condition	"all" / "any" / "some"

(b) Regex based Rulesets

Fig. 3. Characteristics of rulesets

6.2 Regex-Based Rulesets

We grouped the 240 regular expressions obtained from Real World Rules (Sect. 5.1) into 15 rules of 16 patterns per rule. The condition "all of them" is used in the rules. The peak performance of the implementation on CPU is 0.160 Gbps. The degradation in performance is attributed to the fact that regular expression matching is more complex in comparison to exact string matching. YARA-FPGA achieves a throughput of 18.5 Gbps, an improvement of over 115×, therefore, we do not perform experiments for regex-based rulesets with Snort rules on YARA-CPU and focus on the FPGA implementation in this section.

The performance comparison for rulesets containing regular expressions as patterns is illustrated in Fig. 4(b). The performance of regex-based rulesets depends on the structure and operators in the regular expressions. Operations such as Kleene closure (∗) and Union (|) operators result in large number of state transitions and longer wires.

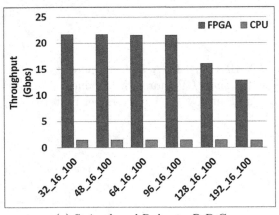

(a) String-based Rulesets: R_P_C

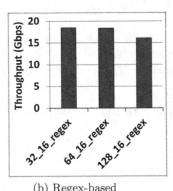

(b) Regex-based
Rulesets: R_P_regex

Fig. 4. Throughput comparison of FPGA and CPU based Pattern Matching

7   Conclusion and Future Work

In this paper, we presented a high performance modular architecture on FPGA to accelerate pattern matching in the YARA framework. We compared the performance of FPGA implementation with the software implementation on CPU. Our FPGA architecture achieves a throughput of up to 21.8 Gbps with 14.5× improvement in performance in comparison with the throughput of 1.47 Gbps for the implementation on CPU. In the future, we plan to implement the YARA framework using a heterogeneous architecture consisting of CPU and FPGA for complex conditions such as backreferences and iteration over string occurrences.

References

1. Bro, Intrusion Dectection System. http://bro-ids.org
2. Snort, Intrusion Dectection System. http://www.snort.org/
3. YARA, Patter Matching Tool. http://plusvic.github.io/yara/
4. VirusTotal. https://www.virustotal.com/
5. Weaver, N., Paxson, V., Gonzalez, J.M.: The shunt: an FPGA-based accelerator for network intrusion prevention. In: Proceedings of the ACM/SIGDA 15th International Symposium on Field Programmable Gate Arrays, 2007, pp. 199–206. ACM (2007)
6. Nikitakis, A., Papaefstathiou, L.: A memory-efficient FPGA-based classification engine. In: 16th International Symposium on Field-Programmable Custom Computing Machines, FCCM 2008, pp. 53–62. IEEE (2008)
7. Xilinx. Virtex 7 FPGA. http://www.xilinx.com/support/documentation/data_sheets/ds183_Virtex_7_Data_Sheet.pdf
8. Yang, Y.-H.E., Prasanna, V.K.: High-performance and compact architecture for regular expression matching on FPGA. IEEE Trans. Comput. **61**(7), 1013–1025 (2012)
9. Mansoori, M., Welch, I., Fu, Q.: YALIH, yet another low interaction honeyclient. In: Proceedings of the Twelfth Australasian Information Security Conference, vol. 149, pp. 7–15. Australian Computer Society Inc. (2014)
10. Jung, J.-H., Kim, H.-K., Choo, H.-L., ByungUk, L.: The protection technology of script-based cyber attack. J. Commun. Comput. **12**, 91–99 (2015)
11. Sourdis, I., Pnevmatikatos, D.: Fast, large-scale string match for a 10Gbps FPGA-based network intrusion detection system. In: Cheung, P.Y.K., Constantinides, G.A. (eds.) FPL 2003. LNCS, vol. 2778, pp. 880–889. Springer, Heidelberg (2003)
12. Le, H., Prasanna, V.K.: A memory-efficient and modular lpproach for large-scale string pattern matching. IEEE Trans. Comput. **62**(5), 844–857 (2013)
13. Floyd, R.W., Ullman, J.D.: The compilation of regular xpressions into integrated circuits. J. ACM (JACM) **29**(3), 603–622 (1982)
14. Sidhu, R., Prasanna, V.K.: Fast regular expression matching using FPGAs. In: The 9th Annual IEEE Symposium on Field-Programmable Custom Computing Machines, FCCM 2001, pp. 227–238. IEEE (2001)
15. Bispo, J., Sourdis, I., Cardoso, J.M., Vassiliadis, S.: Regular expression matching for reconfigurable packet inspection. In: IEEE International Conference on Field Programmable Technology, FPT 2006, pp. 119–126. IEEE (2006)
16. Public Repository of YARA Rules. https://github.com/Yara-Rules/rules

Efficient Camera Input System and Memory Partition for a Vision Soft-Processor

Jones Yudi Mori[1,2]([✉]), Frederik Kautz[1], and Michael Hübner[1]

[1] ESIT - Embedded Systems for Information Technology,
Ruhr-University Bochum, Bochum, Germany
{Jones.MoriAlvesDaSilva,Frederik.Kautz,Michael.Huebner}@rub.de
[2] Department of Mechanical Engineering, University of Brasilia, Brasília, Brazil

Abstract. One key issue in the design of Real-Time Image Processing and Computer Vision (IP/CV) systems is the massive volume of data to process. Not only the number of arithmetic and logic operations over the data but also the access to these data represents an important issue. An Application-Specific Instruction Set Processor (ASIP) focused on Real-Time IP/CV algorithms was developed in this work. Starting from a standard 32-bit Reduced Instruction Set Computer (RISC) as a benchmark, we analyzed the different issues and optimized the processor incrementally. We derived an economical image memory partition and also a new data path concept to speed up the processing. RTL models were synthesized for an FPGA, enabling an analysis of power consumption, area, and processing speed, to show the corresponding overheads in comparison with the original processor architecture.

Keywords: ASIP · Image processing · Processor architecture · Real-time

1 Introduction

The efficient design of Embedded Real-time IP/CV (Image Processing and Computer Vision) processing platforms must focus on fast memory access, parallelism exploration and power efficiency [4]. A common IP/CV application is composed by a sequence of steps, as shown in Fig. 1 [5].

Depending on the application's complexity - more complexity implies more steps in the processing chain - the memory consumption can be large enough to surpass the available memory. To optimize the memory utilization, we developed a memory partition model specifically for IP/CV chains. Also, an input-to-datapath scheme was used to speed up pixel access and processing, by connecting pixel buffers directly to the executing stage of processor's pipeline.

A common IP/CV application, the Sobel algorithm, is depicted in Fig. 2. This algorithm's execution needs to store four images (1 original + 3 intermediary). This application is used throughout the paper as an example for analysis.

Section 2 presents a bibliographical review of ASIP design methodologies and real-time IP/CV hardware/software platforms, discussing their advantages,

© Springer International Publishing Switzerland 2016
V. Bonato et al. (Eds.): ARC 2016, LNCS 9625, pp. 328–333, 2016.
DOI: 10.1007/978-3-319-30481-6_27

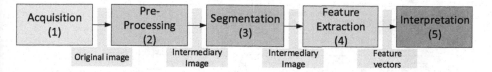

Fig. 1. Typical processing chain for an image processing application.

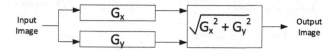

Fig. 2. Processing chain of the Sobel edge enhancement algorithm.

disadvantages, and how we could extend these approaches in our work. Section 3 shows the incremental design process of the new architecture. In Sect. 4, we present a trade-off analysis of the solutions proposed, and a comparison against some state-of-the-art solution from the literature. Section 5 shows the conclusions of this work and the future directions envisioned.

2 Related Work

There are several works in the literature regarding ASIP design methodologies and embedded real-time IP/CV processing platforms. In [8], a methodology for the development of ASIPs based on LISA is described in details. [2] uses profiling methods to the design of efficient computer vision algorithms for robotics applications in space.

In [7], DSP-based implementation and comparison of several different algorithms for edge detection are performed. Several different optimization techniques were used, as Cache Optimization, Compiler Intrinsics, and Software Pipelining. In [6], the authors show similar FPGA-based designs, not only for convolution but other neighborhood operations, such as rank-order filters and binary morphology.

The current work was developed based on the standard architecture shown in [6]. By taking advantage of the literature, it was possible to design an efficient hardware/software structure, turning the standard RISC processor into an efficient ASIP.

3 ASIP Design

The Synopsys Processor Designer tool was used to describe the hardware models (in LISA language), customize the compiler, simulate, debug and generate RTL. The PD-RISC processor is a standard RISC architecture, shipped with the Synopsys Processor Designer tool to be a starting point for new architecture designs.

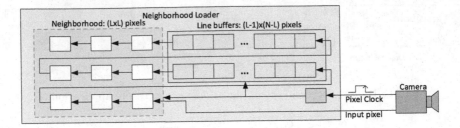

Fig. 3. Neighborhood Loader architecture.

It is a 32-bit load-store architecture, with a 6-stage fully-bypassed pipeline and separated ALU and Multiplication units.

PD-RISC is similar to some conventional processors (such as DLX, MIPS, OR1K), so the analysis performed over it is general enough to be applied to other similar processor architectures. We use the original PD-RISC as a benchmark to compare the new proposed architectures with the standard one.

3.1 Memory Partition

In common processing chains, an image is needed only in the subsequent step, and then can be discarded. To improve the memory efficiency, we divided the processor's memory space into two separated parts: one for pixels and the other one for any other variable in the program. The Neighborhood Loader (NL) architecture, found in the literature, displays a new neighborhood at each pixel_clock cycle.

A new entire neighborhood is loaded every cycle after the initial delay, and the already processed pixels are taken away, saving memory and reducing the total amount of instructions needed by the application. The NL architecture is a long shift register that works as a peripheral, receiving and storing the pixels automatically from the input pins, without using the processor's datapath.

To have access to the available neighborhood from the program, we created a new instruction (*getnl*). This instruction was then added to the PD-RISC's ISA, generating a new processor hence called NL-RISC. The *getnl* instruction maps a value from a specified NL location to a program variable.

3.2 Input-to-Datapath

A new instruction, *GETMAC* was designed to, in a single cycle, get the pixel value from the NL and compute a *MAC* operation. Its CKF is called with three input parameters: an accumulator; filter coefficient; position in the NL. This architecture is hence called PWA (Process-While-Acquiring), Fig. 4.

4 Results

The charts on Fig. 5 show that the two main goals of this work were achieved: efficient memory partition and fast input-to-datapath. The PWA architecture

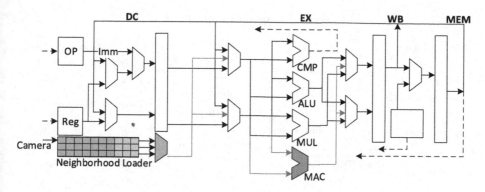

Fig. 4. PWA architecture: Extended PD-RISC's microarchitecture.

provides an enhanced throughput (4× cycles/pixel), higher frame rate (ca. 4× speed-up), less memory utilization (25 % reduction) and less energy consumption per pixel (2.8× reduction) than the original PD-RISC. However, it has a drawback: the overhead in the area (ca. 25 %).

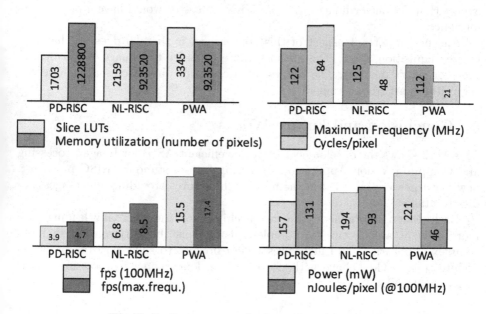

Fig. 5. Performance results for each architecture.

Table 1 shows a comparison of the architectures presented in the current work and similar ones found in recent literature. The custom architecture from [1] presents the highest throughput, however it is not programmable. The area occupied by our final processor (PWA) is half of the area of the Microblaze, the standard Xilinx softprocessor.

Table 1. System's comparison

Work	Arch	Device	Area Slices	Frequency (MHz)	Throughput (Cycles/pixel)	Power (mW)
Current	PD-RISC	Xilinx xc7k325t	1703	122	84	157
Current	NL-RISC	"	2159	125	48	194
Current	PWA	"	3345	112	21	221
[1]	custom	Xilinx xc6vlx75T	409	420	*10	n/a
[3]	Microblaze	Xilinx xc6vlx240T	7376	150	488	n/a
[3]	VLIW rho-VEX	"	7506	75	183	n/a

Regarding the frequency, the PWA processor achieved a frequency higher than the rho-VEX processor. However, the rho-VEX is a VLIW, which offers a smaller Cycles/Instruction factor. The throughput obtained by the PWA processor (Cycles/pixel) is higher than the rho-VEX and the Microblaze processors. However, in [3], can be seen that for higher resolution images, the VLIW processor surpasses the Microblaze processor by a factor of more than 3×. Considering that the PWA processor is an RISC architecture - like the Microblaze - we can expect that for bigger images, the rho-VEX processor would have a better performance.

Another important aspect of this comparison is that [3] does not have an image acquisition stage. The authors there consider the image pre-loaded in the processor's memory. The results we present for our processors include the acquisition part from a camera.

5   Conclusion and Future Works

This work shows the development of power efficient ASIP for Image Processing and Computer Vision Applications. Starting from a standard RISC processor, new features were included in the microarchitecture, providing advantages and disadvantages.

Each design step generated a new architecture, incrementally leading to a more efficient architecture. A complete study must be performed with more complex applications and higher resolution images, to show how the proposed architecture would behave with, for example, longer image processing chains and/or more NLs.

Acknowledgment. CAPES Foundation/Brazilian Ministry of Education (Science without Borders Program, Grant Process Nr. 9054-13-8) and the University of Brasilia.

References

1. Brost, V., Meunier, C., Saptono, D., Yang, F.: Flexible vliw processor based on fpga for real-time image processing. In: 2011 Conference on Design and Architectures for Signal and Image Processing (DASIP), pp. 1–8, November 2011

2. Diamantopoulos, D., Siozios, K., Lentaris, G., Soudris, D., Rodrigalvarez, M.: Spartan project: on profiling computer vision algorithms for rover navigation. In: 2012 NASA/ESA Conference on Adaptive Hardware and Systems (AHS), pp. 174–181, June 2012
3. Hoozemans, J., Wong, S., Al-Ars, Z.: Using vliw softcore processors for image processing applications. In: Proceedings of the 15th International Conference on Systems, Architectures, Modeling and Simulation (SAMOS) (2015)
4. Kehtarnavaz, N., Gamadia, M.: Real-time image and video processing: from research to reality. Synth. Lect. Image Video Multimedia Process. $2(1)$, 1–108 (2006)
5. Mori, J., Huebner, M.: A high-level analysis of a multi-core vision processor using systemc and tlm2.0. In: 2014 International Conference on ReConFigurable Computing and FPGAs (ReConFig), pp. 1–6, December 2014
6. Mori, J., Sanchez-Ferreira, C., Llanos, C.: Real-time image processing based on neighborhood operations using fpga. In: Proceedings of the XVIII International IBERCHIP Workshop, February 2012
7. Musoromy, Z., Bensaali, F., Ramalingam, S., Pissanidis, G.: Comparison of real-time dsp-based edge detection techniques for license plate detection. In: 2010 Sixth International Conference on Information Assurance and Security (IAS), pp. 323–328, August 2010
8. Schliebusch, O., Meyr, H., Leupers, R.: Optimized ASIP Synthesis from Architecture Description Language Models. Springer, The Netherlands (2007)

A *Lost Cycles* Analysis for Performance Prediction using High-Level Synthesis

Bruno da Silva[✉], Jan Lemeire, An Braeken, and Abdellah Touhafi

INDI and ETRO Department,
Vrije Universiteit Brussel (VUB), Brussels, Belgium
{bruno.da.silva,jan.lemeire,an.braeken,abdellah.touhafi}@vub.ac.be

Abstract. Today's High-Level Synthesis (HLS) tools significantly reduce the development time and offer a fast design-space exploration of compute intensive applications. The difficulty, however, to properly select the HLS optimizations leading to a high-performance design implementation drastically increases with the complexity of the application. In this paper we propose as extension for HLS tools a performance prediction for compute intensive applications consisting of multiple loops. We affirm that accurate performance predictions can be obtained by identifying and estimating all overheads instead of directly modelling the overall execution time. Such performance prediction is based on a cycle analysis and modelling of the overheads using the current HLS tools' features. As proof of concept, our analysis uses Vivado HLS to predict the performance of a single-floating point matrix multiplication. The accuracy of the results demonstrates the potential of such kind of analysis.

Keywords: High-Level Synthesis · Lost cycles · FPGA · Performance prediction · Overhead analysis

1 Introduction

High-Level Synthesis (HLS) tools allow FPGA designers to develop their implementations in high level languages such as C or C++. Despite the high-level representation of the algorithms accelerates the Design-Space Exploration (DSE), the multiple implementation choices, thanks to the large set of available optimizations, make the DSE a non-trivial task. Since this kind of tools provide detailed information about the latency, frequency and an estimation of the resource consumption of each implementation, we believe that current HLS tools manage enough information to provide an accurate performance prediction. Such performance prediction would lead to a much faster DSE of compute intensive applications.

To address this challenge, we propose a cycle-based analysis for performance prediction as extension for HLS tools. The principles of such analysis are originally presented in [1,2], where the overheads of parallel programs are identified and modelled in order to predict performance. The performance of any implementation reflects not only the quality of the implementation but also the impact

© Springer International Publishing Switzerland 2016
V. Bonato et al. (Eds.): ARC 2016, LNCS 9625, pp. 334–342, 2016.
DOI: 10.1007/978-3-319-30481-6_28

of its overheads. We propose an in-depth performance analysis based on those inefficiencies. The identification, the classification, and the modelling of those overheads would lead to an accurate performance prediction. The analysis of the inefficiencies, referred as overheads from now on, drives to a model which can be used to guide and to reduce the DSE. Consequently, the most appropriated HLS optimization can be used to reduce a particular overhead, increasing the overall performance. Our purpose is to demonstrate that a *lost cycles* analysis of compute intensive kernels leads to an accurate performance prediction using HLS tools.

This paper is organized as follows. Section 2 presents related work. The definition of *lost cycles* and their classification is introduced in Sect. 3. A methodology using the proposed analysis is detailed in Sect. 4. In Sect. 5 our *lost cycles* analysis is applied to a well-known algorithm. Finally, the conclusions are drawn in Sect. 6.

2 Related Work

During the last years, researchers have proposed many techniques to reduce the DSE. We focus on some of those models which predict and model performance based on the exploration of the available HLS' optimizations. Several papers such as [3] incorporate certain overhead predictions in their performance models. Their overhead model, however, only targets loop unrolling and do not consider the use of HLS tools. The authors in [4] reduce the DSE by first modelling the performance and the area before evaluating their prediction using Vivado HLS. However, their approach only target nested loops and loop unrolling while we consider different loop hierarchies and multiple optimizations. In [5] a *divide and conquer* algorithm to accelerate the DSE using HLS tools is presented. They propose a partition of the algorithm for their individual and exhaustive design exploration by invoking the HLS tool, which leads to a long simulation and synthesis runtime. Our approach only requires a short DSE using an HLS tool to elaborate accurate performance predictions. Finally, the authors in [6] use several HLS tools for their performance prediction. However, this approach does not predict the performance of a single design neither the potential impact of the optimizations, which can be obtained thanks to the *lost cycles* analysis.

Most of the strategies elaborate their performance models based on the performance analysis of multiple configurations. Our approach targets the modelling of the overheads in order to generate a more accurate and less time-consuming DSE. As far as we know, this is the first time a *lost cycles* analysis is applied for FPGAs, specially considering HLS tools.

3 Definition of *Lost Cycles*

A clock cycle can be considered as the minimum unit of time that one operation needs to be executed. The clock cycle is defined by the operational frequency of the design. Thus, despite the number of cycles to execute an operation changes based on the target frequency, the time for one operation remains constant. Our cycle-based analysis considers the frequency, which defines the accuracy of the use of clock cycles as time unit, when calculating the performance.

Let the useful operations be the main operations characterizing the algorithm to be implemented. The *lost cycles* (L_o) of a design are all those clock cycles which are not dedicated to compute useful operations. The remaining clock cycles are the useful cycles, also called *compute cycles* (L_c), which are the cycles dedicated to compute useful operations. The overall number of clock cycles (L_{imp}) that an algorithm composed by n loops $\{L_1, L_2, ...L_n\}$ needs can be expressed as Eq. 1.

$$L_{imp} = [(((L_{c_1} + L_{o_1}) \cdot I_{L_1} + (L_{c_2} + L_{o_2})) \cdot I_{L_2} + ... + L_{c_n} + L_{o_n}] \cdot I_{L_n} \quad (1)$$

Equation 1 reflects the loop hierarchy by grouping those cycles associated to each loop. L_{c_i} and L_{o_i} are the useful and lost cycles associated to loop i respectively, while I_{L_i} is the number of iterations of loop i. This equation can be rearranged to group all the useful and lost cycles as shown in Eq. 2.

$$L_{imp} = [(L_{c_1} \cdot I_{L_1} + L_{c_2}) \cdot I_{L_2} + ... + L_{c_n}] \cdot I_{L_n}$$
$$+ [(L_{o_1} \cdot I_{L_1} + L_{o_2}) \cdot I_{L_2} + ... + L_{o_n}] \cdot I_{L_n}$$
$$= L_c + L_o \quad (2)$$

The use of the standalone latency reported by the HLS tool as metric of the design performance could lead to wrong conclusions. In order to avoid any incoherence, we use the latency reported at certain frequency (F_{imp}) and the assumption that L_c is the minimum number of clock cycles to compute at such clock rate (Clk_{imp}). Let OP_{imp} be the number of operations executed in L_{imp}, the execution time of a design (t_{imp}) can be expressed as $t_{imp} = Clk_{imp} \cdot L_{imp}$. Hence, Eq. 3 defines the design performance (P_{imp}) and, based on Eq. 2, reflects how the overheads affect.

$$P_{imp} = \frac{OP_{imp}}{t_{imp}} = \frac{OP_{imp}}{Clk_{imp} \cdot (L_c + L_o)} \quad (3)$$

3.1   Assumptions

Before development of our overhead analysis, we make a few more assumptions. Firstly, we assume that each operation is exclusively composed by dedicated amount of resources. Therefore, the consumed resources are not reused to execute different operations. Secondly, despite different types of operations (integer, floating point, ...) must be considered, we only consider single floating-point operations (FP) to introduce our methodology. Thirdly, to facilitate the explanation of our definitions, only DSPs are considered despite FP operations can also be implemented using logic resources. This assumption, for instance, simplifies the equation to obtain L_c. Nevertheless, L_c can be obtained for other type of operations, such as fixed-point integer operations, thanks to the reports of current HLS tools. For the sake of simplicity, our analysis targets application kernels consisting of multiple loops and compute intensive operations.

3.2   Identifying the Useful Cycles

The number of useful cycles is directly related to the number of operations implemented on the FPGA. Therefore, it is possible to obtain L_c from the resource
consumption of a particular implementation. Let be OP_p the number of operations which can be executed in parallel and L_{DSP} the minimum latency of a
FP operation implemented exclusively using DSPs. Equation 4 relates L_c with
the consumed area and shows how L_c decreases when the number of operations
executed in parallel increases.

$$L_c = \frac{L_{DSP} \cdot OP_{imp}}{OP_p} \tag{4}$$

3.3   The *Lost Cycles* Classification

The proper selection of *lost cycles* categories is needed for our approach. We
propose the following categories:

Initialization Overhead (O_{Init}). The initialization overhead models those
overheads related to the filling of the stages of a pipelined operation with streaming data.

Non-overlapping Memory Accesses (O_{Mem}). The non-overlapping memory
accesses are all those memory accesses which are not overlapped in time with
any useful computation or with another latency overhead.

Logic Control (O_{Ctrl}). The latency related to the loop control or to the synchronization of the operations belong to the logic control category of overhead.

$$L_o = O_{Init} + O_{Mem} + O_{Ctrl} \tag{5}$$

Those categories are similar, but not the same as the latency overheads identified in [3]. It may occurs that, due to pipeline operations, two overheads are
overlapped. Those overlapped *lost cycles*, however, must be considered only once
and included in one of the categories.

4   Proposed Methodology Overview

The proposed methodology consists in a *lost cycle* analysis using the HLS tool
while exploring the target optimizations. During an initial exploration phase the
impact of each optimization on the HLS design is profiled in order to fetch our
lost cycle analysis. Figure 1 shows how this initial DSE helps to identify, classify
and quantify each *lost cycle* in order to generate a model for each overhead.
The analysis of L_o is only possible when L_c is obtained since L_{imp} is already
reported by the HLS tool. The parameters in Eq. 4 used to calculate L_c can be
extracted from the reports of the HLS tool, from the hardware specifications or
from empirical study.

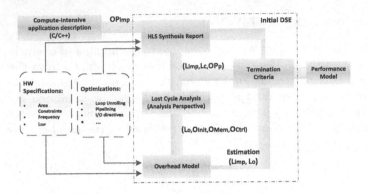

Fig. 1. Main Steps of the proposed methodology.

- OP_{imp} represents the total number of operations which must be executed and is usually known.
- L_{DSP} is specified by the hardware and is usually available in technical documents [7]. For instance, the reported latency for FP additions with our target FPGA is 1, meaning that one FP operation can be computed per clock cycle.
- OP_p determines the level of concurrency and is extracted from the resource consumption. OP_p can be easily obtained using current HLS tools, where the resource consumption is reported for each particular design.

Once L_c, and consequently L_o are obtained for a particular design, the overhead analysis can continue exploring the latency impact of the application size, the compiler optimizations or source code modifications. When each overhead is properly modelled, L_o can be estimated following Eq. 5. The performance prediction of a configuration (optimizations, hardware specifications,...) is obtained from the L_o estimation, which leads to L_{imp}, since L_c remains constant while none of the parameters of Eq. 4 changes.

Our methodology is designed to exploit the Vivado HLS features. Vivado HLS not only generates a synthesis report for every design solution but also provides a useful *analysis perspective* which details the intermediate operations. Both, the information reported by the compiler and the information extracted from the *analysis perspective* are used to fetch our analysis. For instance, Fig. 2

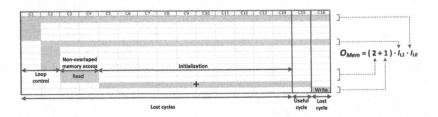

Fig. 2. Example of how the overheads of a FP matrix addition can be modelled.

Table 1. Example of a short DSE to profile the optimizations and to generate a model of each overhead.

Matrix size	FLOPs (OP_{imp})	Optimizations	Latency (L_{imp})	O_{Init}	O_{Mem}	O_{Ctrl}
4 × 4	128	None	1066	768	128	106
		PLU x2 L0	1064	768	128	104
		PLU x2 L1	1058	768	128	98
		PLU x2 L2	858	608	96	90
		Pipeline L0	97	27	3	3
		Pipeline L1	103	33	3	3
		Pipeline L2	706	528	32	3
32 × 32	65536	None	526402	393216	65536	34882
		PLU x2 L0	526386	393216	65536	34866
		PLU x2 L1	525890	393216	65536	34370
		PLU x2 L2	412738	311296	49152	19522
		Pipeline L0	32786	12	3	3
		Pipeline L1	33010	229	3	10
		Pipeline L2	274434	234496	2048	5122

exemplifies what information can be extracted from *Analysis perspective* for a FP matrix addition.

HLS Synthesis Report. Vivado HLS generates at every compilation a detailed report with useful information about latency and resource consumption. It's possible to derive from Eq. 4 that L_c equals Op_{imp} since each FP addition is implemented exclusively with DSPs, and both OP_p and L_{DSP} are one [7]. The iteration time together with the number of iterations determines the number of clock cycles needed by the implementation.

Lost Cycle Analysis. The execution trace depicted in Fig. 2 shows how the *Analysis perspective* allows to identify and quantify the different overheads in great detail. For instance, one FP addition requires 11 clock cycles to be completed but only 1 clock cycle can be considered useful. Extra cycles like O_{Init} are consumed by the inner operations needed to compute any FP operation. O_{Mem} includes two clock cycles to load the input values and one extra cycle to write the output. Finally, O_{Ctrl} is needed to initiate the iteration of the loop and to check the exit condition.

Overhead Model and Performance Estimation. Once O_{Init}, O_{Mem} and O_{Ctrl} have been measured they can be modelled based on the selected configuration of the design. Their modelling is possible by analysing the variation of the parameters of the target configuration. The impact of the optimizations, the source code modifications or the application scaling on L_o differs.

Performance Estimation. Once the *lost cycles* are properly modelled, the performance prediction for one implementation can be easily calculated (Eq. 3).

The main target is the elaboration of a table such as Table 2, where the overheads are modelled based on the explored optimizations.

Table 2. Summary of the overhead models based on the optimizations explored.

Opt.	Loop	O_{Init}	O_{Mem}	O_{Ctrl}
None	–	$(7+5) \cdot I_{L0} \cdot I_{L1} \cdot I_{L2}$	$2 \cdot I_{L0} \cdot I_{L1} \cdot I_{L2}$	$(I_{L1} \cdot (I_{L2}+2)+2) \cdot I_{L0}+2$
PLU	L0	$\frac{I_{L0}}{U_0} \cdot I_{L1} \cdot I_{L2} \cdot (U_0 \cdot (7+5))$	$2 \cdot U_0 \cdot \frac{I_{L0}}{U_0} \cdot I_{L1} \cdot I_{L2}$	$\frac{I_{L0}}{U_0} \cdot (U_0 \cdot I_{L1} \cdot (I_{L2} + 2) + U_0 + 1) + 2$
	L1	$I_{L0} \cdot \frac{I_{L1}}{U_1} \cdot I_{L2} \cdot (U_1 \cdot (7+5))$	$2 \cdot U_1 \cdot I_{L0} \cdot \frac{I_{L1}}{U_1} \cdot I_{L2}$	$I_{L0} \cdot (\frac{I_{L1}}{U_1} \cdot (U_1 \cdot I_{L2} + U_1 + 1) + 2) + 2$
	L2	$I_{L0} \cdot I_{L1} \cdot \frac{I_{L2}}{U_2} \cdot (U_2 \cdot 7 + 5)$	$3 \cdot I_{L0} \cdot I_{L1} \cdot \frac{I_{L2}}{U_2}$	$I_{L0} \cdot (I_{L1} \cdot (\frac{I_{L2}}{U_2}+3)+2)+2$
Pipeline	L0	$7 + 5$	3	3
	L1	$(7 \cdot I_{L0}) + 5$	3	$3 + \frac{I_{L0}}{4}$
	L2	$(7+5) + 7 \cdot I_{L0} \cdot I_{L1} \cdot (I_{L2} - 1)$	$3 \cdot I_{L0} \cdot I_{L1}$	$2 + 2 \cdot (2 \cdot I_{L0}) \cdot I_{L1}$

5   Experimental Results

Despite we consider that our methodology can be potentially automated, many steps still need to be manually elaborated. The main purpose of this case study is to exemplify how our overhead analysis metric is elaborated using the information provided by an HLS tool in a reasonable time. Our DSE is done using Vivado HLS 2014.2 targeting an Xilinx Virtex6 lx240t FPGA at 250 MHz.

The implemented FP matrix multiplication consists of an outer-most loop (L0), a the middle loop (L1) and an inner-most loop (L2). No register is used in L2 to store intermediate accumulated values. Table 1 summarizes the Vivado HLS reports when different optimizations are applied. Vivado HLS reports the total number of clock cycles required to execute all the computations (L_{imp}). OP_p is extracted from the number of instances reported in the resource estimation. By default, Vivado HLS instantiates two dedicated cores to execute the addition and the multiplication. Op_{imp} represents the number of additions that must be computed, which is simply $2 \cdot I_{L0} \cdot I_{L1} \cdot I_{L2}$. Consequently, L_c is obtained from Eq. 4 and equals $I_{L0} \cdot I_{L1} \cdot I_{L2}$, which is the minimum number of clock cycles that a matrix multiplication needs when only 2 dedicated operations are executed in parallel. The addition and the multiplication require 7 and 5 clock cycles respectively to be initialized (O_{Init}). O_{Mem} only demands 2 clock cycles because the cycles dedicated to write the generated output back ($I_{L0} \cdot I_{L1}$) are overlapped with O_{Ctrl}. The modelling of each overhead is summarized in Table 2.

The left figure in Fig. 3 depicts the evolution of the *lost cycles* of a matrix with 64×64 elements when loop L2 is unrolled. A higher impact is obtained for

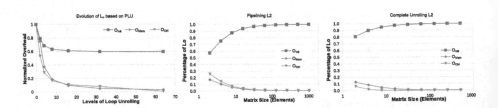

Fig. 3. Modelling the impact of L_o when using different optimizations.

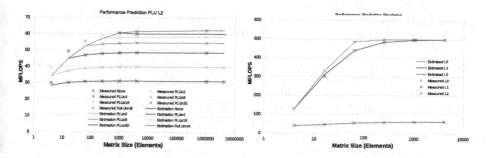

Fig. 4. Comparison of our performance predictions versus HLS reports.

low levels of unrolling. Further levels of unrolling evidence that O_{Init} dominates L_o and can not be reduced beyond a certain limit. The middle and the right figures in Fig. 3 show the evolution of the overheads while increasing the matrix size. In both cases, L_o is dominated by O_{Init}. This result is expected since O_{Init} is determined by the latency of the FP operations.

Figure 4 compares our performance predictions and the HLS reported performance. The left figure shows the impact of unrolling loop L2. Notice how our performance prediction is slightly pessimist when the loop is completely unrolled. The equations in Table 2 consider additional control, which increases O_{Ctrl} but that is removed when the loops are completely unrolled. Nevertheless, our predictions are extremely accurate for any level of unrolling or matrix size. The right figure shows the same comparison when pipelining loops, where our performance prediction achieves a high accurate estimation. Both figures depict how our technique performs an accurate prediction, which leads to a fast DSE.

6 Conclusion

The modelling of the overheads, a concept originally designed to analyse performance of parallel software, has been successfully adapted to the domain of FPGAs. Our proposed methodology shows an accurate performance prediction and enough flexibility to be applied for complex designs. Despite this approach is still manually elaborated, we believe that current HLS tools can be extended to offer such kind of performance prediction for the designer. Nevertheless, the automation of our methodology is our main priority as future work.

References

1. Crovella, M.E., et al.: The search for lost cycles: a new approach to parallel program performance evaluation. Rochester University NY Department of Computer Science (1993)
2. Crovella, M. E., et al.: Parallel performance prediction using lost cycles analysis. In: Proceedings of the ACM/IEEE Conference on Supercomputing, pp. 600–609. IEEE Computer Society Press (1994)

3. Park, J., et al.: Performance and area modeling of complete FPGA designs in the presence of loop transformations. IEEE Trans. Comput. **53**(11), 1420–1435 (2004)
4. Zhong G., et al.: Design space exploration of multiple loops on FPGAs using high level synthesis. In: 32nd IEEE International Conference on Computer Design (ICCD), pp. 456–463. IEEE (2014)
5. Schafer, B.C., et al.: Divide and conquer high-level synthesis design space exploration. ACM Trans. Design Autom. Electron. Syst. (TODAES) **17**(3), 29 (2012)
6. da Silva, B., et al.: Performance modeling for FPGAs: extending the roofline model with high-level synthesis tools. Int. J. Reconfigurable Comput. **7** (2013)
7. Xilinx. Xilinx logicore IP floating-point operator v6.1 product specification. Technical report, Xilinx (2012)

A Dynamic Cache Architecture for Efficient Memory Resource Allocation in Many-Core Systems

Carsten Tradowsky[✉], Enrique Cordero, Christoph Orsinger,
Malte Vesper, and Jürgen Becker

Institute for Information Processing Technologies,
Karlsruhe Institute of Technology, Karlsruhe, Germany
{tradowsky,becker}@kit.edu,
{enrique.cordero,christoph.orsinger,malte.vesper}@student.kit.edu

Abstract. Today's computing systems still mostly consist of homogeneous multi-core processing systems with statically allocated computing resources. Looking into the future, these computing systems will evolve to heterogeneous processing systems with more diverse processing units and new requirements. With multiple applications running concurrently on these many-core platforms, these applications compete for computational resources and thus processing power. However, not all applications are able to efficiently make use of all available resources at all times, which leads to the challenge to efficiently allocate tasks to computational resources during run-time. This issue is especially crucial when looking at cache resources, where the bandwidth and the available resources strongly bound computation times. For example, streaming based algorithms will run concurrently with block-based computations, which leads to an inefficient allocation of cache resources.

In this paper, we propose a dynamic cache architecture that enables the parameterization and the resource allocation of cache memory resources between cores during run-time. The reallocation is done with only little overhead such that each algorithm class can be more efficiently executed on the many-core platform. We contribute with a cache architecture that is for the first time prototyped on programmable hardware to demonstrate the feasibility of the proposed approach. At last we evaluate the overhead introduced by the increased flexibility of the hardware architecture.

1 Introduction

Performance gains by increasing frequency have hit the power-wall and the field has turned towards parallelization [9]. Today's systems exploit many heterogeneous resources that are allocated dynamically during run-time to different tasks. The number of resources available on a chip can easily be varied during the design phase with such architectures.

Reducing abstraction and giving the programmer control over hardware parameters can have multiple benefits. For example, this kind of control allows the

© Springer International Publishing Switzerland 2016
V. Bonato et al. (Eds.): ARC 2016, LNCS 9625, pp. 343–351, 2016.
DOI: 10.1007/978-3-319-30481-6_29

programmer to adapt the hardware to the application's needs. This work examines this approach particularly for dynamic reallocatable caches.

Relevant papers show that cache design is a trade-off between power and performance, for which there is no general optimal solution [1,2,4–6,8]. However, there are optimal solutions for specific programs, in terms of power, performance, or performance per watt. The solution, relieving the chip designer of this burden and allowing the application developer to unleash higher performance, is to let the application choose the optimal cache configuration. The choice has to be made either by the compiler or the developer. This choice will be put beyond the silicon implementation stage to exploit performance gains that are higher than the cost arising from added complexity. While this strips an abstraction layer, which makes the cache truly transparent, it is a necessary step in uncovering additional performance. Not too long ago, caches were seen as something for which cache oblivious algorithms could be written [7].

This work is prototyped on programmable hardware. However, it is possible to utilize this approach in an ASIC implementation as well, since we don't use FPGA-specific functions such as dynamic or partial reconfiguration. We strictly restrict us to exploit the architecture's adaptivity features to efficiently reallocate the cache.

The paper is structured as follows: Sect. 2 presents the state of the art and underlines the difference to our work. Section 3 describes the conceptional idea behind the dynamic cache reallocation from system (application, software) and hardware view. Section 4 details the realization in hardware, which could target both FPGAs and ASICs. However, we focus in the realization using the FPGA's Block RAM resources. In Sect. 5, we present the potential resulting from the dynamic cache reallocation. Finally, in Sect. 6, we conclude the paper and provide an outlook for future work.

2   State of the Art

The performance of a multi-core processor system is highly dependent on the performance of the cache memory system. For this purpose, we present the dynamic cache reallocation.

Albonesi presents Selective Cache Ways [1], in which he provides the ability to disable a subset of cache ways in a set associative cache during periods of modest cache activities. He focuses on application-specific tailoring within the cache of one processor core. Instead, we want to make cache ways from one cache available as additional ways for other caches that are located on the same processing tile.

Tao et al. present an interesting approach for run-time adaptive caches. Their cache infrastructure is studied in a self-developed cache simulator [10]. After showing first performance benefits, Nowak et al. implement their design using a PowerPC FPGA processor macro [6]. They connect their cache architecture over a comparably slow peripheral bus. Instead, our deep knowledge of the microarchitecture enable us to realize a run-time adaptive cache architecture that allows partitioning of cache resources between different processor cores within a compute tile. This enables a more efficient and yet predictable resource utilization that will enable the same objectives that are presented for single core scenarios.

The performance of a given cache architecture is largely determined by the behavior of the application using that cache. It is crucial that the application developers have knowledge about the processor architecture to achieve the different objectives (e. g. , performance per watt) of the application scenarios. The approach presented in [3,5] tunes the cache for inner loops before the start of each run. This enables us to make more efficient use of the available cache resources and thus increase the benefits of the adaptations. At first glance, it seems obvious that the highest associativity (fully associative cache) would yield best performance since the cache misses can be minimized. However, the gain diminishes vastly after an associativity of four or eight while the hardware expenditure keeps rising [11]. We will make use of this performance-per-watt knowledge in our proposed dynamic intra-tile cache reallocation to be able to exploit the available cache resources in a more predictable way according to the requests of the application.

3   Design of Dynamic Cache Reallocation

The main goal of this work is to enable the dynamic cache reallocation. To achieve this, we need additional functionality within the cache. This section details the requirements and design trade-offs of the dynamic cache architecture.

3.1   Requirements

The dynamic cache architecture is designed to fit very well on programmable hardware. However, the additional features of programmable hardware should not constrain the dynamic cache design. Thus, dynamic reconfiguration is not applied to the design. This makes it possible to port the concept to an ASIC design with little effort while keeping the cache reallocation features intact. Another requirement is the single cycle latency of the cache architecture. In contrast to literature, the design is directly connected to the CPU and is used as L1 cache. Consequently, the performance is the main focus of the dynamic cache design. It will be realized with little additional overhead as presented in Sect. 4 and evaluated in Sect. 5.

3.2   Necessary Modules

The ultimate goal is the dynamic reallocation of cache memory between processors in a multi-core scenario. The necessary modules are shown in Fig. 1. To achieve this functionality, first the cache memory should be partitioned to be allocatable in smaller tiles between the processors. These cache memory tiles are connected to the cache controller

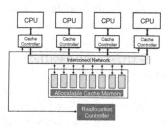

Fig. 1. Dynamic cache architecture.

through the interconnect network. It will be crucial to realize the interconnect network with no latency and as little overhead as possible not to impact the overall efficiency of the architecture. An individual cache controller is necessary per CPU that is able to cope with different parameters like line length, associativity, strategies or policy. The last piece is one global reallocation controller that is responsible for the management and the assignment of the individual cache memory tiles.

Cache Memory. The cache must consist of individual memory tiles to be able to allocate the cache memory to different processors. Another important feature is the ability to fully disable individual tiles if they are not connected to a processor, for example for energy saving reasons. As each tile only provides data in case of a hit, it is possible to connect them to a single bus, which reduces the complexity of the interconnect network. Because of the integrated functionality a single tile can be considered a one small direct mapped cache. One n-way cache is regarded as n parallel direct mapped caches. This makes it possible to link the cache size and the associativity to achieve an optimal degree of utilization within each tile. Consequently by linking tiles, it is possible to achieve higher associativity and larger cache size.

Interconnect Network. The interconnect network is an important part of the dynamic cache architecture. It has to cope with the added flexibility and introduced complexity explained above and must be able to connect every processor with each cache memory tile. On the one hand the performance is very important. As we are targeting L1 cache, it is not acceptable to introduce additional latency or decrease the throughput. On the other hand the newly added flexibility should be managed with as little overhead as possible. Consequently, it is not acceptable to degrade the performance in comparison to dedicated connections between each processor and its cache. It has to fulfill the requirements to (i) always have single cycle read access from processor to the cache and (ii) not degrade CPU cycle time.

4   Realization of Dynamic Cache Reallocation

The following section explains the realization of the concept developed for the dynamic cache reallocation, which consists of two main parts: the tile controller and the cache controller. At last the adaption sequence and the related control software are presented.

The I-Cache and the D-Cache each have their individual cache controller. The I-Cache controller is more light-weight than the D-Cache controller since it only has to support read operations. Therefore, we will focus on the more complex D-Cache controller functionality in this section, while keeping in mind that this is reused for the I-Cache controller as well. This enables us to reallocate the I-Cache and the D-Cache independently from each other, which has significant advantages in application scenarios. For instance in streaming applications the I-Cache memory could be reallocated to enlarge the D-Cache memory.

4.1 Reallocation

The reallocation sequence requires multiple communication stages between the cache controller and the tile controller. To maximize the achieved performance during the reallocation sequence, the cache is not stopped for reallocation until the tile controller has successfully provided the new configuration. Depending on the desired parameterization, certain rules must be followed in order to avoid undefined states.

Possible reallocation sequences consist on changing the size of the cache lines and changing the amount of tiles per CPU. Changing the cache line size can lead to necessary data invalidation in the line.

5 Evaluation of Dynamic Cache Reallocation

The advantages of a dynamic cache reallocation need to be evaluated by analyzing the introduced overhead compared to a static design. As described in the previous section, we prototype the system on a Xilinx Virtex-5 XUPV5 evaluation board. The following section presents an evaluation of the hardware implementation and the necessary resources contained in the reallocation logic, the memory tiles and the tile controller. Further, it compares the obtained results to an unmodified LEON3 design to determine the advantages and disadvantages of this approach.

The hardware utilization of the design is evaluated using three specific cases in a dual-core design: a 2-way D-Cache with 2 tiles per CPU, a 4-way D-Cache with 4 tiles per CPU and an 8-way D-Cache with 8 tiles per CPU. By varying the amounts of bytes per tile the impact of the cache size on the hardware utilization can be evaluated.

5.1 Overall Programmable Hardware Utilization

First we analyze the overall programmable hardware utilization of the complete dual-core LEON3 design by looking at the slices, BRAMs and DSP blocks used after implementation. The tile size of the adaptive design is varied between

Table 1. Overall programmable hardware utilization with four tiles with different tile sizes in comparison to the LEON3 reference design on XUPV5.

	Reference 2 Cores 2 W	2 W 1 KB 4 T 256 B/T	2 W 2 KB 4 T 512 B/T	2 W 4 KB 4 T 1024 B/T
Slices	7932	7413	7612	7576
BRAM	21	27	27	27
DSP48Es	8	8	8	8

256, 512 and 1024 bytes per tile and we compare it to a standard dual-core LEON3 design with the same associativity and a cache size of 1 KB per set.

The same comparison is performed for a 2-way and a 4-way associative cache. Tables 1 and 2 show the overall results respectively.

The results show a fairly constant utilization of the resources regardless of the selected tile size. Further, the adaptive design shows a slightly lower utilization of slices but a higher BRAM utilization for comparable cache size. There is a small overhead introduced by the adaptability that will be further investigated in the following sections.

An overall look at the results of the adaptive design shows that despite the varying cache sizes and amount of tiles, the programmable hardware resources being used experience no significant variation. The amount of BRAMs and DSPs stays constant across the different tile sizes and the amount of slices only varies slightly. This shows that the cache tiles are being implemented in BRAMs as intended, and that the overhead in the tile controller and reallocation logic is not causing a significant hardware overhead when varying the cache size from 1 KB to 8 KB.

Table 2. Overall programmable hardware utilization with eight tiles with different tile sizes in comparison to the LEON3 reference design on XUPV5.

	Reference 2 Cores 4 W	4 W 2 KB 8 T 256 B/T	4 W 4 KB 8 T 512 B/T	4 W 8 KB 8 T 1024 B/T
Slices	8084	7676	7772	7806
BRAM	29	39	38	39
DSP48Es	8	8	8	8

5.2 Programmable Hardware Utilization by Hierarchy

Second, we analyze the programmable hardware utilization by hierarchy of the design in order to determine the resource distribution and utilization of the tile controller and the multiple tiles in the design. Figure 2 presents an overview of these results. As expected from the previous analysis, we see that for each of the 2-way, 4-way and 8-way the utilization corresponding to the tile controller is constant despite the change in the cache size. For the 2-way cache, for instance, we see an almost equal utilization of slices when the tile size is 256 Bytes and when it is doubled to 512 Bytes. The same

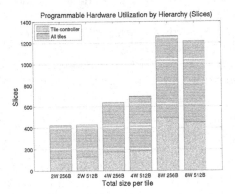

Fig. 2. XUPV5 slice utilization by hierarchy with two, four and eight ways.

behavior can be seen for the 4-way and 8-way scenario. We can draw the conclusion that the higher the associativity of the cache, the larger the tile controller will be. This makes sense since a higher associativity means that more ways (tiles) need to be checked in parallel. Further, we see that the utilization overhead introduced by the tile controller is rather small compared to the utilization of all tiles.

5.3   Programmable Hardware Utilization by Increasing the Tile Size

At last, we explore the behavior of the slice and BRAM utilization by increasing the tile size in powers of two. In the previous analysis, we saw that the slice utilization appeared to remain constant for a specific associativity scenario regardless of the tile size. To further investigate this we choose the same dual-core design with 2-way cache and 4 tiles per cache and we increase the tile size from 256 Bytes to 65 KB.

Figure 3 shows the behavior of the slice utilization when changing the tile size. Only relatively small variations in the slice utilization can be seen for the tiles and for the tile controller. This means that the slice utilization overhead is fairly constant once the associativity of the cache is chosen. However, as mentioned before, this was expected since the actual memory for the cache is mapped into BRAMs.

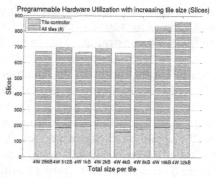

Fig. 3. XUPV5 BRAM utilization with increased tile size.

As a next step we analyze the BRAM utilization for each of these scenarios. Figure 4 shows an overview of the BRAM utilization. We can see a constant total BRAM utilization of 24 BRAMs up to a tile size of 4 KB. For larger tile sizes the cache memory is mapped using more BRAMs. Even though the Virtex-5 XUPV5 contains BRAMs with sizes of 18 KB and 36 KB the tiles get spread into more BRAMs after a size of 4 KB in the case of a 4-way associative cache. This can be explained with the high degree of parallel operations that need to be performed in an adaptive cache architecture. Since the BRAM blocks available are dual-port memory blocks, mapping an entire cache into the same BRAM would cause only an availability of two parallel access points into the memory. In the cache, however, many more access points are needed in order to check in parallel all the tags depending on the associativity of the cache. This leads to an implementation of the cache in many more BRAMs to allow parallel access even if the BRAM blocks are not used to full capacity.

This shows that there is a range of cache sizes, which is still under the full memory utilization of a XUPV5 BRAM block, which can be used to maximize cache memory availability with the same resource utilization. This is a large advantage because the overhead introduced by hardware resources is constant in specific memory ranges within the programmable hardware specific BRAM size boundaries. This introduces a degree of

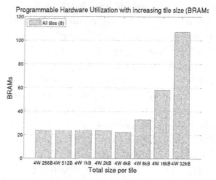

Fig. 4. Utilization by hierarchy (BRAMs)

freedom in the design that can be used to increase the efficiency of the utilized hardware.

6   Conclusion and Future Work

We present a dynamic cache architecture that enables the reallocation of cache memory between CPUs in a many-core system during run-time. The design is carefully weighted and a method with as little overhead as possible is chosen without degrading the performance of the cache architecture to be applicable under L1 cache constraints. This is to the best of our knowledge the first time that a successfully implemented hardware realization is presented. Our L1 cache design is integrated into the CPU microarchitecture and is evaluated on programmable hardware. However, it is possible to transfer this concept to an ASIC realization with little effort as we do not use FPGA-specific features such as dynamic reconfiguration. The evaluation show that a slight hardware overhead below 10 % enables the dynamic run-time cache architecture. Consequently, we show that it is possible to achieve optimally utilized cache memory tile according to the used on-chip memory target architecture.

For further work, we will look into more concurrent application scenario that are enabled by an enlarged many-core platform including a scalable network on chip. Furthermore, we want to introduce internal monitoring to enable efficient background defragmentation, self-adaptive efficiency curves, and dark silicon-specific energy management during run-time.

Acknowledgment. This research work is supported by the German Research Foundation (DFG) within the Transregio SFB *Invasive Computing* (DFG SFB/TRR89).

References

1. Albonesi, D.: Selective cache ways: on-demand cache resource allocation. In: Proceedings of the 32nd Annual ACM/IEEE International Symposium on Microarchitecture (1999)
2. Gordon-Ross, A., Lau, J., Calder, B.: Phase-based cache reconfiguration for a highly-configurable two-level cache hierarchy. In: Proceedings of the 18th ACM Great Lakes symposium on VLSI (2008)
3. Ji, X., Nicolaescu, D., Veidenbaum, A., Nicolau, A., Gupta, R.: Compiler Directed Cache Assist Adaptivity. Technical report, University of California Irvine (2000)
4. Malik, A., Moyer, B., Cermak, D.: A low power unified cache architecture providing power and performance flexibility (poster session). In: Proceedings of the International Symposium on Low Power Electronics and Design (2000)
5. Nicolaescu, D., Ji, X., Veidenbaum, A.V., Nicolau, A., Gupta, R.: Compiler-directed cache line size adaptivity. In: Chong, F.T., Kozyrakis, C., Oskin, M. (eds.) IMS 2000. LNCS, vol. 2107, pp. 183–187. Springer, Heidelberg (2001)
6. Nowak, F., Buchty, R., Karl, W.: A run-time reconfigurable cache architecture. In: Advances in Parallel Computing (2008)
7. Prokop, H.: Cache-oblivious algorithms. Master's thesis, MIT (1999)

8. Ranganathan, P., Adve, S., Jouppi, N.P.: Reconfigurable caches and their application to media processing. In: Proceedings of the 27th Annual International Symposium on Computer Architecture - ISCA 2000 (2000)
9. Sutter, H.: The free lunch is over: a fundamental turn toward concurrency in software. Dr. Dobb's Journal (2005)
10. Tao, J., Kunze, M., Nowak, F., Buchty, R., Karl, W.: Performance advantage of reconfigurable cache design on multicore processor systems. Int. J. Parallel Program. **36**, 347–360 (2008)
11. Zhang, C., Vahid, F., Najjar, W.: A highly configurable cache architecture for embedded systems. In: 30th Annual International Symposium on Computer Architecture (2003)

Adaptive Bandwidth Router for 3D Network-on-Chips

Stephanie Friederich$^{(\boxtimes)}$, Niclas Lehmann, and Jürgen Becker

Karlsruhe Institute of Technology (KIT), Karlsruhe, Germany
stephanie.friederich@kit.edu

Abstract. As system on a chip (SoC) designs continue to head in the direction of miniaturization, with an ever increasing size of components, three-dimensional (3D) integration technologies are used to satisfy performance enhancements. With increasing number of cores, bus based SoC designs do not scale well, hence network on chip (NoC) architectures are introduced to avoid communication bottlenecks. Since two-dimensional NoC designs are not easy to partition across 3D chip layers, we introduce an adaptive 3D NoC architecture. The bandwidth and frequency of inter layer connections can be chosen independently from the router links within a layer. To prevent thermal hot spots in the middle of the chip, memory layers are placed in between compute layers. Supplemental this solves the high demand of our distributed memory architecture.

1 Introduction

Due to continuously growing system on a chip (SoC) architectures, communication becomes one of the bottlenecks in large mutli-core designs. *Network on chip (NoC)* structures offer a scalable solution for this problem, where a network adapter connects existing muti-core bus based systems with network routers. Accordingly the routers are connected with each other to build up a network topology. The most common topologies are mesh or torus based networks. While the last years many 2D networks have been proposed, e.g. the TILE64 multi-core processor manufactured by Tilera [2]. *NoCs* offer good scalability, but with an increasing size of the networks, communication latency increases dramatically due to long interconnects.

Since the packing density of single layer chips can not be further increased, three-dimensional integrated circuits (3D ICs), which are build of multiple layers of chips are introduced to further increase the chip density and performance [7,9]. Multiple layers of silicon are stacked together with short vertical separation. The layers are vertically connected using short through-silicon-vias (TSV). Short vertical connections can significantly reduce the latency, but since these connections are physically restricted, partitioning a design across multiple layers poses a challenge.

The combination of multi-layer chips and 3D networks on chips (NoCs) opens up new opportunities and have not been fully explored yet. The partitioning of the design across the chip layers is optimally done at the router borders.

© Springer International Publishing Switzerland 2016
V. Bonato et al. (Eds.): ARC 2016, LNCS 9625, pp. 352–360, 2016.
DOI: 10.1007/978-3-319-30481-6_30

We present an implementation of a 3D network, where the data width and frequency of each link between two routers can be chosen independently. As a result we are able to define the bandwidth of TSV connections independently of other router links on a chip layer.

The rest of this paper is organized as follows. Section 2 surveys state-of-the-art 2D networks and technology and existing implementation of 3D NoCs. Section 3 presents characteristics of mesh networks. In Sect. 4, the implementation of adaptive bandwidth routers is introduced. The following Sect. 5 presents performance evaluation results. Finally, Sect. 6 concludes this paper.

2 Related Work

Since bus based multi-core designs are not scaling well, network based designs have been introduced in large SoCs. Thereby either single cores are directly connected with a network router or cluster nodes are connected via routers. Several implementations of two-dimensional NoC are already established on the market, e.g. Intel SCC [10] or Tilera TILE64 [2]. Both architectures are mesh based network structures where single processing engines are connected with a five port router. Moreover Pavlidis et al. [8] investigates three-dimensional network topologies.

There are different methods to construct 3D ICs [7]. The first one is chip stacking, where multiple fully processed and tested stand-alone components are stacked to one system-in-package. Second transistor stacking, where multiple layers of transistors are stacked on a single substrate. And last wafer-level stacking where entire wafers are stacked. While our proposed concept of a 3D NoC works with all construction methods, the chip stacking is not recommended due to long interconnects. According to the 2011 International Technology Roadmap for Semiconductors (ITRS) interconnect edition [3], the maximum number of connections between two layers can be calculated for each interconnection method.

Dividing a simple planar design into different layers and then connect the layers among themselves with short vertical interconnects has been described in [1]. The connection of multiple layers could be achieved without any other design changes. Also there have been first investigations on how to cope with the restricted amount of vertical interconnects in 3D NoC designs. Liu et al. [6] describe a scheme for sharing vertical interconnects among neighboring routers in a time division multiplex mode. Xu et al. [11] investigates the impact of TSV placement to 3D NoC designs, while restricting the number of TSV to a minimum.

3 Basic Network Topologies

In supercomputer network structures, mesh and torus networks have proved themselves over the years as the best topologies to achieve high communication performance. Figure 1 shows three basic mesh and torus based network implementations.

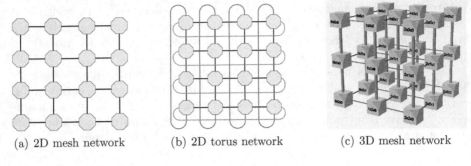

(a) 2D mesh network   (b) 2D torus network   (c) 3D mesh network

Fig. 1. Two and three dimensional network topologies

To meet statements about communication latencies, networks are characterized by their average distance between nodes. Networks are either described by their dimensions (dim_i) or by the amount of network nodes N. Another important indicator for communication latency is the average distance between nodes which relies on the traffic pattern. In this work only XY and XYZ routing is considered. Accordingly the average distance between nodes in 2D mesh networks is given as $\Delta_{2D} = \frac{2}{3}\sqrt{N}$ and for a 3D mesh it is $\Delta_{3D} = \sqrt[3]{N}$.

To reduce the network diameter in mesh networks, the network is extended by a third dimension. Following a 3D mesh network implementation will be introduced. Reducing the network diameter results in shorter average latencies and thereby considerably improves the overall performance. The partitioning of the network across the chip layers is one of the biggest design challenges. Especially due to limited interconnections between the layers.

The invasive NoC forms the basis for this work. Figure 2(a) shows an example implementation of this architecture. Each router is connected to its direct neighbors and in addition has a connection to a cluster based tile via a network adapter (i-NA). Due to the distributed memory structure, each tile comprises its own tile local memory (TLM). A detailed overview of the communication infrastructure is given in [5].

The original router was designed for 2D networks and in scope of this work the router has been extended to work as well in higher dimensional networks. The basic router design was described in [4]. For a network extension in a third dimension the routers were modified by adding two additional ports in vertical direction. In addition, this comprised an adaption of the crossbar and routing algorithm. Figure 2(b) shows a block diagram of the router design. Since we are using a virtual channel (VC) based wormhole switching network, each port holds as many input buffer as the number of VC. Increasing the number of ports results in major increasing resource consumption, since the largest part of router resources is spend on the buffers.

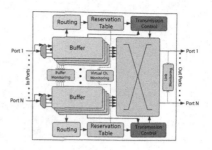

(a) Invasive 2D cluster based NoC   (b) Router block diagram

Fig. 2. Invasive many core architecture and detailed router block diagram

4 Concept

Thermal issues are increasing if we stack multiple layers of electronic components on top of each other. The compound rise in temperature can cause massive damage in the chip. For this reason inter layer cooling becomes mandatory when multiple chip layers are stacked. Putting one layer of SRAM memory in between two layers of routers and clusters, two problems can be fixed at once. First a placement of the memory as a separate layer, leads to meet the required size for the distributed memory structure of our design. Second the heat production of memory is much less than the heat production of computational layers. Hence the memory layer will prevent thermal hotspots due to chip stacking.

The number of vertical connections between layers is restricted and hence a partitioning of a design across the layers is a big issue. The 3D mesh or torus based network architecture gives the opportunity to partition the design across the chip layers in the same degree as the network layers. Hence the wires between the chip layers are only representing router links. Due to physical restrictions the achievable communication bandwidth between different layers is much smaller compared to an inner layer connection. Identical bandwidth requirements on all router ports would result in a low overall network performance. Our router design enables a heterogeneous bandwidth, where the data width and frequency of each link can be chosen independently during design time. Thus the designer gets the possibility to adapt the cross layer bandwidth according to the requested TSV technology and the size of the network (Fig. 5).

4.1 Through-Silicon-Vias

Stacked chips are connected vertically through short interconnects, called TSV. The number of TSV depend on the chip dimension and the technology. The pitch size of TSV are in the micro meter range [3], while the pitch size of on chip connections is one dimension smaller [7]. Hence the amount of TSV in a given chip region is limited and often the bottleneck of 3D chip designs.

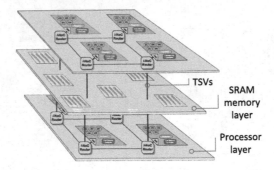

Fig. 3. Multi layer network with memory layer in-between two layers containing the routers and processing elements.

One possible solution to cope with limited inter layer connections, only a portion of routers are connected across the chip layers. However this would require a more complex routing algorithm than XY-routing and result in longer distances between nodes and hence a larger average package latency. The routing mechanism within a router takes more time than transmitting data over links with lower bandwidth. Therefore we are reducing the data link width of vertical connections.

Figure 4 shows the basic physical interface between two routers. The bit width of the links depends on the link configuration. Each router has one input and one output link per port. The number of connections per link is defined as: $N_{link} = ld[ceil(N_{VC})] + n + d + 2$.

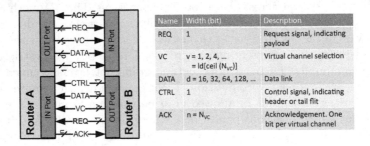

Name	Width (bit)	Description
REQ	1	Request signal, indicating payload
VC	v = 1, 2, 4, ... = ld[ceil (N_{VC})]	Virtual channel selection
DATA	d = 16, 32, 64, 128, ...	Data link
CTRL	1	Control signal, indicating header or tail flit
ACK	n = N_{VC}	Acknowledgement. One bit per virtual channel

Fig. 4. Physical router interface, including the link width of the router ports

The number of connections between two neighboring layers hence is made up of the product of number of routers and the double of the link width. Taking the mesh based design discussed in Sect. 5 as an example, with 4×4 routers per layer, we need a total of 4,352 links between two layers, if we take a design where each router has four VC per port and a data link width of 128 bit.

4.2 Heterogeneous Bandwidth Router

In order to avoid a reduction of the router bandwidth in the complete network, due to limitations given by the vertical connections, a router with optional low bandwidth ports has been developed. In addition, these ports uses their own clock domain to smooth clock synchronization problems due to a partitioned design across different chip layers. Figure 5 shows a simplified design with only two routers connected with each other. The multiplexer firstly handle the clock domain crossing and secondly they are connected to the input buffers for flow control reasons. This connection between the multiplexer and input buffers is necessary to assure that new data is not transmitted, as long as the multiplexer is busy with the serial transfer of the data. Henceforth there are no additional registers mandatory for flow control at the low bandwidth ports. Flits which shall be transmitted through the low bandwidth link, are split in the multiplexer and transmitted sequentially. At the neighbor router input port, the flit fragments are reassembled before the complete flit is stored in the input FIFO. The designer can specify the bandwidth of usual and through-silicon router links during design time. Also the clock frequency can be chosen by the designer depending on physical parameters of inter layer connections. But since these connections are shorter than router links on one chip layer, it is possible to use a higher frequency for the TSV. Accordingly it is possible to reduce the delay which originates from serial data transfer.

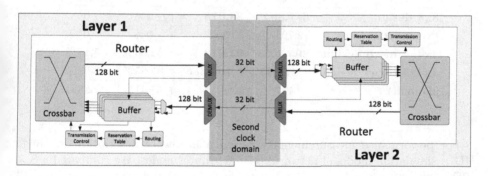

Fig. 5. Structure of inter layer connection between two routers, connected through multiplexer running in a different clock domain

5 Experimental Results

In order to prove the design and investigate the systems functionality including extensive software benchmarks, we implemented an field programmable gate array (FPGA) based prototype of our 3D network. But since the technology of FPGAs differ tremendously from 3D ASIC implementations, it could only be used as a prototype of the design. To realize a design with millions of gates, multiple FPGA devices are necessary. We are using a platform with six Virtex5

LX330 FPGAs. Each FPGA represents one layer of the final chip design. The different FPGAs are connected via cables with each other. While the memory builds a separate layer in the target chip, the memory on the prototyping system is realized as extension boards.

Table 1 shows the resource consumption of different network implementations. Routers which are placed at the border of the network do not need to have input buffers for each port. Only those ports which are connected with another router hold input buffers. Hence the resource consumption of one router within the network varies for mesh based networks. The additional ports per router result in a 32.06 % higher look up table (LUT) consumption for a 3D mesh network, compared to an equivalent 2D implementation with the same number of nodes. In torus networks, all ports of the border routers are connected and following from that, all router in the network consume the same resources. This results in a even higher resource consumption than 3D mesh networks. A 3D torus network consumes 87.85 % more LUT than an equivalent 2D mesh implementation.

Table 1. Resource consumption of a 2D and 3D router design

Component	Resources			
	Absolute		Relative	
	[LUTs]	[Register]	[LUTs]	[Register]
8x8 design	**677,894**	**88,073**	+/- 0 %	+/- 0 %
Primary 2D router	12,793	1,534	+/- 0 %	+/- 0 %
4x4x4 mesh design	**895,203**	**92,613**	+ 32.06 %	+ 5.15 %
4x4x4 torus design	**1,273,452**	**1,164,485**	+ 87.85 %	+ 32.26 %
3D router	20,137	1,885	+ 57.41 %	+ 22.88 %

For performance measurements we used a hardware description language (HDL) simulation model of networks with 64 router nodes. We compared a 8 × 8 2D mesh network, a 4 × 4 × 4 3D mesh, and a 4 × 4 × 4 3D torus network, all with constant router links of 128 bits and four VC. The results of the throughput are shown in Fig. 6. Since higher dimensional networks have a lower average distance between nodes, the average latency of packages is lower in the 3D mesh network implementation, see Fig. 6(b). The latency is even further reduced if we take a three-dimensional torus network. In equal measure, the throughput is increased for torus networks and the saturation point is at an injection rate of 0.6 instead of 0.4 for two-dimensional mesh networks, see Fig. 6(a).

However, since the torus network consumes a much higher resource overhead than the mesh network and the throughput gain is negligible higher, the best trade-off to minimize the resource consumption while maximizing the throughput is to take a 3D mesh network.

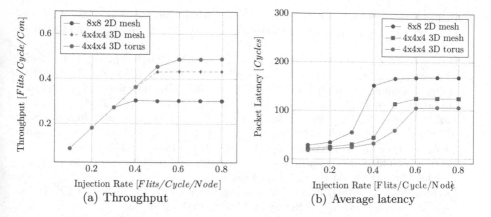

Fig. 6. Network performance of two dimensional mesh and three dimensional mesh and torus networks, each with 64 nodes and homogenous bandwidth of 128 bit.

6   Conclusion

In this paper we presented a temperature aware 3D NoC architecture with adaptive inter layer bandwidth. Though the extension to a third dimension costs about one-third more resources for mesh networks and more than 85 % for torus networks. But due to shorter average distances between the nodes, the latency could be decreased and hence communication performance rises. The router possesses two different kinds of ports. The bandwidth and frequency of these ports can be chosen independently. Hence it is possible to compensate the restricted number of inter layer connections without performance degradation in the other network segments. Further there is no need of additional clock synchronization between the chip layers because it is handled by the routers as well.

Acknowledgment. This work was supported by the German Research Foundation (DFG) as part of the Transregional Collaborative Research Center "Invasive Computing" (SFB/TR89).

References

1. Banerjee, K., Souri, S.J., Kapur, P., Saraswat, K.C.: 3-D ICs: A novel chip design for improving deep-submicrometer interconnect performance and systems-on-chip integration. Proc. IEEE **89**(5), 602–633 (2001)
2. Bell, S., Edwards, B., Amann, J., Conlin, R., Joyce, K., Leung, V., MacKay, J., Reif, M., Bao, L., Brown, J., et al.: TILE64-processor: a 64-core SoC with mesh interconnect. In: IEEE International Solid-State Circuits Conference on Digest of Technical Papers, 2008, ISSCC 2008, pp. 88–598. IEEE (2008)
3. Committee, I.R., et al.: International technology roadmap for semiconductors, 2011 edn. Semiconductor Industry Association (2011). http://www.itrs.net/ITRS

4. Heißwolf, J.: A Scalable and Adaptive Network on Chip for Many-Core Architectures. Ph.D. thesis, Karlsruhe, Karlsruher Institut für Technologie (KIT), Diss., 2014 (2014)
5. Heisswolf, J., Zaib, A., Weichslgartner, A., Karle, M., Singh, M., Wild, T., Teich, J., Herkersdorf, A., Becker, J.: The invasive network on chip - a multi-objective many-core communication infrastructure. In: 2014 27th International Conference on Architecture of Computing Systems (ARCS), pp. 1–8. VDE (2014)
6. Liu, C., Zhang, L., Han, Y., Li, X.: Vertical interconnects squeezing in symmetric 3D mesh network-on-chip. In: Proceedings of the 16th Asia and South Pacific Design Automation Conference, pp. 357–362. IEEE Press (2011)
7. Patti, R.S.: Three-dimensional integrated circuits and the future of system-on-chip designs. Proc. IEEE **94**(6), 1214–1224 (2006)
8. Pavlidis, V.F., Friedma, E.G.: 3-D topologies for networks-on-chip. IEEE Trans. Very Large Scale Integr. (VLSI) Syst. **15**(10), 1081–1090 (2007)
9. Topol, A.W., La Tulipe, D., Shi, L., Frank, D.J., Bernstein, K., Steen, S.E., Kumar, A., Singco, G.U., Young, A.M., Guarini, K.W., et al.: Three-dimensional integrated circuits. IBM J. Res. Dev. **50**(4.5), 491–506 (2006)
10. Van der Wijngaart, R.F., Mattson, T.G., Haas, W.: Light-weight communications on intel's single-chip cloud computer processor. ACM SIGOPS Operating Syst. Rev. **45**(1), 73–83 (2011)
11. Xu, T.C., Liljeberg, P., Tenhunen, H.: Optimal number and placement of through silicon vias in 3D network-on-chip. In: 2011 IEEE 14th International Symposium on Design and Diagnostics of Electronic Circuits & Systems (DDECS), pp. 105–110. IEEE (2011)

Reduced-precision Algorithm-based Fault Tolerance for FPGA-implemented Accelerators

James J. Davis$^{(\boxtimes)}$ and Peter Y.K. Cheung

Imperial College London, London SW7 2AZ, UK
{james.davis06,p.cheung}@imperial.ac.uk

Abstract. As the threat of fault susceptibility caused by mechanisms including variation and degradation increases, engineers must give growing consideration to error detection and correction. While the use of common fault tolerance strategies frequently causes the incursion of significant overheads in area, performance and/or power consumption, options exist that buck these trends. In particular, algorithm-based fault tolerance embodies a proven family of low-overhead error mitigation techniques able to be built upon to create self-verifying circuitry.

In this paper, we present our research into the application of algorithm-based fault tolerance (ABFT) in FPGA-implemented accelerators at reduced levels of precision. This allows for the introduction of a previously unexplored tradeoff: sacrificing the observability of faults associated with low-magnitude errors for gains in area, performance and efficiency by reducing the bit-widths of logic used for error detection. We describe the implementation of a novel checksum truncation technique, analysing its effects upon overheads and allowed error. Our findings include that bit-width reduction of ABFT circuitry within a fault-tolerant accelerator used for multiplying pairs of 32×32 matrices resulted in the reduction of incurred area overhead by 16.7% and recovery of 8.27% of timing model f_{max}. These came at the cost of introducing average and maximum absolute output errors of 0.430% and 0.927%, respectively, of the maximum absolute output value under transient fault injection.

1 Introduction

ABFT relies upon the augmentation of data with additional information—checksums formed from that data—to provide post-operation verification of results with low overheads compared to alternatives including modular redundancy. While previous fixed-point ABFT-related work has assumed all data and checksums to be n-bit integer (i.e. modulo-2^n), it is possible to break this relationship and consider data and checksum precision independently. By making informed decisions regarding exactly which information to discard when forming and manipulating checksums, the incurred overheads can be reduced at the cost of accepting some data error tolerance. The methods introduced in this work lend themselves to FPGAs thanks to their efficient simultaneous implementation of multiple arbitrary-precision datapaths. Here, as a case study for the

© Springer International Publishing Switzerland 2016
V. Bonato et al. (Eds.): ARC 2016, LNCS 9625, pp. 361–368, 2016.
DOI: 10.1007/978-3-319-30481-6_31

investigation into reduced-precision ABFT, we use hardware-accelerated matrix multiplication: a benchmark for which the ABFT operation is straightforward yet that is representative of commonly hardware-accelerated operations.

The novel contributions of this work are: (1) the first consideration of distinct data and checksum bit-widths within ABFT-protected operations, which we call *reduced-precision* or *RP*-ABFT, (2) an implementation of circuitry incorporating RP-ABFT for resilience against hardware faults, (3) analysis of the costs and benefits of applying RP-ABFT at various levels of precision and (4) insight into the fault tolerability of RP-ABFT.

2   Application-level Fault Tolerance

Tailoring fault tolerance to particular applications can facilitate drastic overhead reduction versus general-purpose methods. ABFT represents a methodology for achieving such reduction while maintaining high fault detectability. A subclass of linear algebra operations exists that can be protected by ABFT; amongst these are matrix operations (multiplication, addition, LU decomposition, etc.) [4] and Fourier transformations [7]. Linear filtering operations can be protected when considered in state-space form [4]. These operations are also highly suited to hardware acceleration thanks to their inherent parallelism. Beyond low area overhead, ABFT has two further key advantages: (1) its application requires no fundamental changes to the datapaths used for performing mathematical operations and (2) output and error-indicating data are produced simultaneously.

While ABFT has traditionally been used to protect fixed-point operations, the methods are compatible with floating-point arithmetic as well. Of particular relevance to this work are the errors introduced by floating-point operations, which necessitate error bounding to distinguish them from those caused by other mechanisms [6]. Recent work [1] sought to lower the required bounds in a GPU-accelerated floating-point benchmark by analysing input data a priori.

ABFT-protected accelerators implemented in FPGAs have been the focus of several recent publications. Jacobs et al. implemented algorithmic protection of several matrix multiplication architectures [5]. ABFT was called upon for error detection of the same operator in more recent work, with resource reallocation performed using additional logic [2] and dynamic partial reconfiguration [3] in order to avoid faulty components at runtime. Area overheads for accelerators capable of multiplying pairs of 32×32 matrices were found to be 17.3% and 10.1%, respectively, therein. While error correction is not the focus of this work, previously published fault avoidance strategies [2,3] are directly compatible.

3   Principles of ABFT

The mechanics of ABFT checksumming are described here [4]. Any $m \times n$ *data* matrix D can be supplemented with an additional row of column-wise checksums to produce an $(m + 1) \times n$ *column checksum-encoded* matrix D_c. The transformation, achieved with *generation* matrix G_c, is $D_c = G_c D = \begin{pmatrix} I_{m \times m} \\ 1_{1 \times m} \end{pmatrix} D$.

Note that I is the identity matrix and 1 a vector of ones. Similarly, row-wise checksums can be added within an additional column to form an $m \times (n+1)$ *row checksum-encoded* matrix D_r with generation matrix G_r by performing $D_r = DG_r = D\begin{pmatrix} I_{n \times n} & 1_{n \times 1} \end{pmatrix}$. An $(m+1) \times (n+1)$ *full checksum-encoded* matrix D_f can be produced by performing $D_f = G_c DG_r$.

Following storage, transmission or computation that preserves the form of checksum-encoded matrices, data integrity can be verified by producing a *discrepancy* vector δ. Column- and row-wise discrepancy vectors can be produced, using *verification* vectors v_c and v_r, by performing $\delta_c = v_c D_c = \begin{pmatrix} 1_{1 \times m} & -1 \end{pmatrix} D_c$ and $\delta_r = D_r v_r = D_r \begin{pmatrix} 1_{n \times 1} \\ -1 \end{pmatrix}$. Non-zero elements indicate the presence, locations and magnitudes of errors within checksum-encoded matrices. A full checksum-encoded matrix D_f can be verified by independently producing both δ_c and δ_r.

Consider $A = \begin{pmatrix} 1 & 2 \\ 3 & 4 \end{pmatrix}$ and $B = \begin{pmatrix} 5 & 6 \\ 7 & 8 \end{pmatrix}$. For simplicity and clarity, we assume the data matrices used to always be square with dimensions $s \times s$, although this is not a requirement. Since matrix multiplication is a *checksum-preserving* operation, $C = AB$ can be protected by forming A_c and B_r as explained in Sect. 3 and then performing $C_f = A_c B_r$. The transformations and subsequent computation are shown in (1), with column- and row-wise checksums shown in red and blue, respectively. The result's corner element is shown in magenta to indicate that it is both column- *and* row-wise checksum. Note that the data present in (1)'s unprotected result is preserved in its protected result. The protected result can be verified by calculating discrepancy vectors δ_c and δ_r, as shown in (2).

$$\begin{pmatrix} 1 & 2 \\ 3 & 4 \end{pmatrix} \begin{pmatrix} 5 & 6 \\ 7 & 8 \end{pmatrix} = \begin{pmatrix} 19 & 22 \\ 43 & 50 \end{pmatrix} \rightarrow \begin{pmatrix} 1 & 2 \\ 3 & 4 \\ 4 & 6 \end{pmatrix} \begin{pmatrix} 5 & 6 & 11 \\ 7 & 8 & 15 \end{pmatrix} = \begin{pmatrix} 19 & 22 & 41 \\ 43 & 50 & 93 \\ 62 & 72 & 134 \end{pmatrix}. \tag{1}$$

$$\begin{pmatrix} 1 & 1 & -1 \end{pmatrix} \begin{pmatrix} 19 & 22 & 41 \\ 43 & 50 & 93 \\ 62 & 72 & 134 \end{pmatrix} = \begin{pmatrix} 0 & 0 & 0 \end{pmatrix}, \quad \begin{pmatrix} 19 & 22 & 41 \\ 43 & 50 & 93 \\ 62 & 72 & 134 \end{pmatrix} \begin{pmatrix} 1 \\ 1 \\ -1 \end{pmatrix} = \begin{pmatrix} 0 \\ 0 \\ 0 \end{pmatrix}. \tag{2}$$

4 Principles of RP-ABFT

To reduce overheads while maintaining sensitivity to faults that cause high-magnitude errors, truncation can be performed from the least significant bits (LSBs) of data elements 'upwards' when forming and manipulating checksums. In this paper, all input data elements are n-bit signed integers and we call the number of bits of precision removed from each during checksum generation the *truncation width*, represented by r. Output data elements are always $2n$-bit. We label input and output data elements within ABFT-protected matrix multiplication as d_{in} and d_{out}, respectively. cs_{in} and cs_{out} are input and output checksums, while *corner* checksum $cs_{out, c}$ is special, being formed exclusively from cs_{in} elements. We use $\vee(.)$ to represent *maximum absolute value*, while $\epsilon(.)$ is the *maximum absolute error* introduced by truncation.

$\vee(d_{in})$ is 2^{n-1}. The r-bit truncation of a d_{in} element, performed with bitwise shifts as $(d_{in} \gg r) \ll r$, is represented as $\lfloor d_{in} \rfloor_r$ since rounding, for both positive and negative values, is towards negative infinity. Note that $\vee(\lfloor d_{\mathrm{in}}\rfloor_r) = \vee(d_{\mathrm{in}})$; the maximum negative value, for which truncation by any $0 \leq r < n$ will have no effect, also represents the maximum absolute value. $\epsilon(\lfloor d_{\mathrm{in}}\rfloor_r) = 2^r - 1$. Each input checksum element, cs_{in}, is formed from s independently truncated d_{in} elements. $\vee(cs_{\mathrm{in}})$ and $\epsilon(cs_{\mathrm{in}})$ are therefore simply $s2^{n-1}$ and $s(2^r - 1)$, respectively.

Output checksum elements, cs_{out}, are comprised of s multiplied pairs of d_{in} and cs_{in}. Since the d_{in} element used within each multiplication is not truncated, it does not introduce error: this comes purely from each cs_{in}, so $\epsilon(cs_{\mathrm{out}}) = s\vee(d_{\mathrm{in}})\epsilon(cs_{\mathrm{in}}) = s^2(2^r - 1)2^{n-1}$. The corner output checksum element, $cs_{out, c}$, is formed of s multiplied pairs of cs_{in} elements. Unlike for each cs_{out} element, therefore, error can be introduced by both of the multiplicands within each product. Consequently, $\epsilon(cs_{out, c}) = s\big(\vee(cs_{\mathrm{in}})\epsilon(cs_{\mathrm{in}}) + \epsilon(cs_{\mathrm{in}})\vee(cs_{\mathrm{in}}) + \epsilon(cs_{\mathrm{in}})^2\big) = s^3(2^r - 1)(2^n + 2^r - 1)$.

5   Implementation

The datapath of the fault-tolerant matrix multiplication accelerator used in this work is shown in Fig. 1. At its core lie $s + 1$ identical multiply-accumulators (MACs), each responsible for calculating the values of elements between exactly one column of output matrix $\boldsymbol{C}_{\mathrm{f}}$. All data is signed fixed-point, with n-bit input elements and $2n$-bit outputs. Wide—ns-bit input and $2n(s + 1)$-bit output— RAMs prevent starvation, allowing complete matrix rows to be accessed on a cycle-by-cycle basis. When $r = 0$, the paths for $\boldsymbol{A}_{\mathrm{c}}$ and $\boldsymbol{B}_{\mathrm{r}}$ are $n + \log_2 s$ bits per element: this prevents overflow within the input checksums, allowing output checksums to be valid up to the required $2n$ bits.

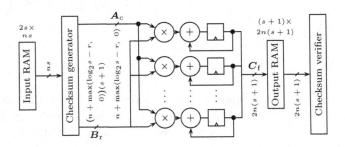

Fig. 1. Datapath

Checksum generation and verification logic, shown in Fig. 2, serves to perform the ABFT procedures described in Sect. 3. Rows of $\boldsymbol{B}$ are first fetched in turn such that the checksums in $\boldsymbol{B}_{\mathrm{r}}$ can be calculated. The adder, narrow register and cs_r RAM are used for this purpose. Multiplication proceeds thereafter: $\boldsymbol{A}$'s first row is stored in the wide register, then the rows of $\boldsymbol{B}_{\mathrm{r}}$ are presented in turn to the MACs for computation. $\boldsymbol{A}_{\mathrm{c}}$, calculated using the adder and cs_c RAM as an accumulator, occurs on-the-fly as its columns are consumed. These steps are repeated until all rows of A have been accessed. On the output side, complete rows of C_f are verified immediately after being stored in a similar manner to generation; results are fed into shift registers for later analysis. Note that, when $r = 0$, the right-shifters do not exist and, since no output error is tolerated, the comparison logic shown in the dashed rectangle reduces to just two comparators.

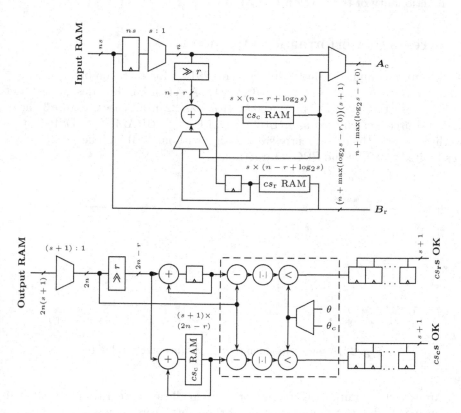

Fig. 2. Checksum generation and verification logic

When $r > 0$, output checksum error must be tolerated up to the levels theorised in Sect. 4. Clearly, there is no reason to actually perform the left-shifting shown in the explanation of the truncation procedure; for this reason, error thresholds θ and θ_c for cs_{out} and $cs_{out,\,c}$ elements, respectively, need to be based upon, not equal to, $\epsilon(cs_{out})$ and $\epsilon(cs_{out,\,c})$. cs_{out} elements have their widths reduced by r bits due to the right-shifter in Fig. 2's checksum generation logic; as a result, $\theta = \frac{\epsilon(cs_{out})}{2^r} = \frac{s^2(2^r-1)2^{n-1}}{2^r} \approx s^2 2^{n-1}$. $cs_{out,\,c}$ elements, however, are subject to magnitude reduction by *both* right-shifters, so $\theta_c = \frac{\epsilon(cs_{out,\,c})}{2^{2r}} = \frac{s^3(2^r-1)(2^n+2^r-1)}{2^{2r}} \approx s^3 2^{n-r}$. Note that the per-element paths for A_c and B_r are each $n + \max(\log_2 s - r,\ 0)$-bit to optimally fit the single largest element.

All hardware shown in Figs. 1 and 2 was implemented in the programmable logic portion of a Xilinx Zynq-7000 XC7Z020 system-on-chip. Supporting hardware, formed of Xilinx IP cores, included BRAM and direct memory access controllers for facilitating data transfer between BRAM and off-chip dynamic RAM. One of the XC7Z020's two hard ARM CPU cores was used as a controller to trigger memory transfers and accelerator runs. The CPU is not integral to the functionality of the developed hardware.

6   Area and Performance Overheads

Designs were compiled using Xilinx Vivado 2014.4 for each combination of $s \in \{2, 4, 8, 16, 32\}$ and $r \in \{0, 4, 8, 12, 16, 20, 24\}$. A set of baseline designs without ABFT protection was also produced, and n was 32 in all cases. Figure 3 shows the total area—calculated as $\mu(\text{LUT } (\%), \text{ FF } (\%), \text{ BRAM } (\%), \text{ DSP } (\%))$—overhead versus the equivalently sized design without ABFT. The matrix size s was limited to 32 by the FPGA targetted.

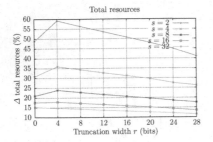 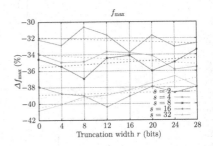

Fig. 3. Resource usage and $f_{\max}$ vs unprotected design

Area overhead initially increased for $r > 0$ in all cases other than $s = 32$. This was primarily due to the introduction of the subtractors shown in Fig. 2. Gains were realised in the $s = 16$ case for $r \geq 8$, $r \geq 16$ in the $s = 8$ case and $r \geq 20$ in the remaining two. The maximum area gain, again for $s = 32$ and $r = 28$, was 23.8%. It should be noted that BRAM and DSP usage are independent of r since truncation affects only the checksum generation and verification logic, which is devoid of multipliers and contain only small, distributed memories.

The reported timing model $f_{\max}$ of each design was also recorded. Changes versus the equivalently sized unprotected designs are captured in Fig. 3. To overcome the effects of CAD noise, linear regressions are included for each plot, shown as dashed lines. Note that the value of r chosen does not affect the (clock cycle) latency of a design versus its standard ABFT equivalent, allowing $f_{\max}$ to be used for performance comparison directly. $f_{\max}$ reductions begin significantly: for $s = 32$ and $r = 0$, $f_{\max}$ dropped by 40.8%. Designs with $r > 0$ exhibited relatively small performance improvements: for $s = 32$, a drop in frequency impact

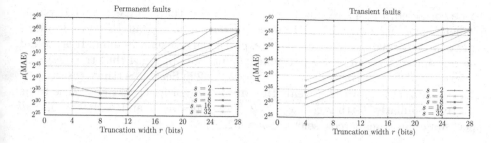

Fig. 4. Means of maximum absolute errors encountered within false negative results

of 7.23% was found. Although trends for smaller s are actually negative, those for larger s are positive. This is a result of the lack of severe output truncation and the introduction of additional logic. Nevertheless, frequency gains were realised for larger designs, with $s = 32$ showing increasing gains for $r \neq 28$.

7   Fault Observability

Functional simulations were performed to assess the fault observability of the proposed designs across the range of implementation variables used in Sect. 6 under the presence of both permanent and transient faults. The fault model applied was that of individually targetted stuck-at-one accumulator bits. Such faults were chosen since they are representative of a range of phenomena under different conditions, e.g. worn transistors or bridged interconnects in the case of permanent faults and register or memory upsets in the case of transients. Accumulator outputs were manipulated since these components lie at the ends of the datapaths of interest, reducing the probability of logical masking and representing somewhat of a worst-case operating scenario. For each combination of implementation variables, the following steps were repeated 1,024,000 times:

1. Generate two $s \times s$ matrices, $\boldsymbol{A}$ and $\boldsymbol{B}$, and populate their elements with n-bit signed integer data selected randomly from a uniform distribution.
2. Add checksumming to $\boldsymbol{A}$ and $\boldsymbol{B}$ to form $\boldsymbol{A}_c$ and $\boldsymbol{B}_r$ as explained in Sect. 3.
3. Perform $\boldsymbol{C}_f = \boldsymbol{A}_c \boldsymbol{B}_r$, element-wise modulo-$2^{2n}$.
4. Perform $\boldsymbol{C}'_f = \boldsymbol{A}_c \boldsymbol{B}_r$, element-wise modulo-$2^{2n}$, with fault emulation:
   - For a permanent fault, select a (column, bit) combination from a uniform distribution. During all accumulation steps, force this bit high.
   - For a transient fault, select a (row, column, step, bit) combination from a uniform distribution. Force this bit high during computation.
5. If comparison of data and checksums within $\boldsymbol{C}_f$ and $\boldsymbol{C}'_f$ reveals that the fault was missed, record the maximum absolute error of $\boldsymbol{C}'_f$'s data elements.

Figure 4 shows the means of errors encountered within results flagged as false negative; those that were missed. Assuming that unmissed errors are able to be corrected, Fig. 4's results therefore represent the average expected worst-element errors introduced by RP-ABFT. They indicate that RP-ABFT allows only relatively small errors to propagate, particularly when r is small. It is around the first inflection seen in the permanent fault plots in Fig. 4 that the detection logic starts to become ineffective. Consider $s = 32$ in Sect. 4. Setting $\epsilon(cs_{out,\ c}) = 2^{63}$, i.e. $\vee(d_{out})$ for $n = 32$, reveals that at $r \approx 16$ corner checksums cease to be effective. Similarly, setting $\epsilon(cs_{out}) = 2^{63}$ for the same s and n shows that *all* checksumming is rendered useless at $r \approx 22$.

8   Conclusion

In this paper, we introduced reduced-precision algorithm-based fault tolerance, or RP-ABFT. RP-ABFT with LSB-first checksum truncation was theorised and implemented in hardware using matrix multiplication as a case study. Our results showed that meaningful overhead reduction can be achieved by sacrificing some fault observability. Our future work on RP-ABFT will explore the false positive-to-false negative tradeoffs achievable through the manipulation of output error threshold values. We will also explore enhancements to the checksumming logic, particularly for performance, as well as output-only truncation to introduce additional tradeoff data points.

The authors acknowledge the support of the EPSRC-funded PRiME project (http://www.prime-project.org); grant number EP/K034448/1.

References

1. Braun, C., et al.: A-ABFT: Autonomous Algorithm-based Fault Tolerance for Matrix Multiplications on Graphics Processing Units. In: International Conference on Dependable Systems and Networks (DSN) (2014)
2. Davis, J.J., et al.: Datapath Fault Tolerance for Parallel Accelerators. In: International Conference on Field-Programmable Technology (FPT) (2013)
3. Davis, J.J., et al.: Achieving Low-overhead Fault Tolerance for Parallel Accelerators with Dynamic Partial Reconfiguration. In: International Conference on Field-programmable Logic and Applications (FPL) (2014)
4. Huang, K.H., et al.: Algorithm-based Fault Tolerance for Matrix Operations. IEEE Trans. Comput. **C–33**(6), 518–528 (1984)
5. Jacobs, A., et al.: Overhead and Reliability Analysis of Algorithm-based Fault Tolerance in FPGA systems. In: International Conference on Field Programmable Logic and Applications (FPL) (2012)
6. Rexford, J., et al.: Algorithm-based Fault Tolerance for Floating-point Operations in Massively Parallel Systems. In: International Symposium on Circuits and Systems (ISCAS), vol. 2 (1992)
7. Wang, S.J., et al.: Algorithm-based Fault Tolerance for FFT Networks. IEEE Trans. Comput. **43**(7), 849–854 (1994)

Author Index

Printed in the United States
By Bookmasters